ORIGINS

ORIGINS

*On the Genesis of
Psychic Reality*

JON MILLS

McGill-Queen's University Press
Montreal & Kingston · London · Ithaca

© McGill-Queen's University Press 2010
ISBN 978-0-7735-3680-7

Legal deposit second quarter 2010
Bibliothèque nationale du Québec

Printed in Canada on acid-free paper that is 100% ancient forest free (100% post-consumer recycled), processed chlorine free

This book has been published with the help of a grant from the Canadian Federation for the Humanities and Social Sciences, through the Aid to Scholarly Publications Programme, using funds provided by the Social Sciences and Humanities Research Council of Canada.

McGill-Queen's University Press acknowledges the support of the Canada Council for the Arts for our publishing program. We also acknowledge the financial support of the Government of Canada through the Book Publishing Industry Development Program (BPIDP) for our publishing activities.

LIBRARY AND ARCHIVES CANADA CATALOGUING IN PUBLICATION

Mills, Jon, 1964–
Origins : on the genesis of psychic reality / Jon Mills.

Includes bibliographical references and indexes.
ISBN 978-0-7735-3680-7

1. Subconsciousness. 2. Psychoanalysis – Philosophy.
3. Mind and reality. I. Title.

BF315.M54 2010   154.2   C2009-906797-8

Set in 10.5/13.5 Minion Pro
Book design & typesetting by Garet Markvoort, zijn digital

For my daughter Ivy
—honor virtutis praemium

CONTENTS

About the Texts
ix

Introduction: Rethinking Mind in the Age of the Brain
3

Axioms
23

Prolegomena to a System
33

1
Spacings of the Abyss
61

2
Deciphering the "Genesis Problem":
On the Origins of Psychic Reality
89

3
Mind as Projective Identification
145

4
Unconscious Semiotics
171

5
Ego and the Abyss
207

Acknowledgments
259

Notes
261

Bibliography
277

Subject Index
297

Author Index
302

ABOUT THE TEXTS

From the *Encyclopaedia of the Philosophical Sciences*, M.J. Petry, ed., outlines Hegel's *Philosophy of Spirit* in *Hegel's Philosophy of Subjective Spirit*, vol. 1: *Introductions*; vol. 2: *Anthropology*; and vol. 3: *Phenomenology and Psychology* (Dordrecht, Holland: D. Reidel Publishing Company, 1978). Petry's edition provides a photographic reproduction of Hegel's original text published in the 1830 revision, along with the *Zusätze*, or *Additions*, supplied by Boumann when the material was republished in 1845. Petry's edition also indicates variations between the 1827 and 1830 editions of the *Encyclopaedia*. His edition has several decisive advantages over A.V. Miller's edition of the *Philosophie des Geistes*, which was translated as the *Philosophy of Mind*. In addition to having the original German text and his notations of the variations between the 1827 and 1830 editions, Petry also provides notes from the *Griesheim* and *Kehler* manuscripts. Further, he accurately translates the word *bewußtlos* as "unconscious," whereas Miller translates it as "subconscious." For these reasons, Petry's edition is a superior text to the Miller translation. For comparison, I have also examined Hegel's 1827–28 lectures on the Philosophy of Spirit: *Vorlesungen über die Philosophie des Geistes* (Hamburg: Felix Meiner, 1994). I have mainly relied on Petry's translation but provide my own in places that warrant changes. Hereafter, references to the *Philosophy of Spirit* (*Die Philosophie des Geistes*), which is the third part of Hegel's *Enzyklopädia*, will customarily be referred to as EG followed by the section number. References to the *Zusätze* are identified as such.

All references to Freud's texts refer to the original German monographs compiled in his *Gesammelte Werke, Chronologisch Geordnet*, 18 vols., ed. Anna Freud, Edward Bibring, Willi Hoffer, Ernst Kris, and Otto Isakower, in collaboration with Marie Bonaparte (London: Imago Publishing Co., Ltd., 1968 [1940–52]). Most translations are mine. Because most English-speaking psychoanalysts neither own nor readily have access to these original texts, I have cited *The Standard Edition of the Complete Psychological Works of Sigmund Freud*, 24 vols. (1886–1940), trans. and gen. ed. James Strachey, in collaboration with Anna Freud, assisted by Alix Strachey and Alan Tyson (London: Hogarth Press, 1966–95 [1886–1940]). References to quotations are designated by SE followed by the appropriate volume and page numbers.

I have made little effort to engage the secondary source literature in this book. I have always found it an illegitimate precedent, set forth in psychological writings, to assume that an author should address and cite the secondary literature on a particular topic when many published monographs often tend to gloss over or entirely omit a close reading of the original texts under inquiry. Here I do not engage other psychoanalysts who summarize previous knowledge, especially when they do not meticulously examine original sources. For this reason, I primarily focus on the texts of Freud and Hegel and a few notable analysts while deliberately ignoring the conventional imposition to cite other authors who have written on these topics beforehand. In this way, I approach the text with a fresh perspective, from my own reading and interpretation, without the need to offer the reader a banal literature review. This is a scholarly standard I wish to emphasize in order to obviate criticism from analysts who may object to my lack of observed convention.

Attempts have been made to use gender-neutral referents. Most references cited in the text refer to the following abbreviations followed by their volume, section, and/or page numbers. For complete details, see the Bibliography:

BN	*Being and Nothingness*
BT	*Being and Time*
CP	*Collected Papers of Charles Sanders Peirce*, 6 vols.
CPR	*Critique of Pure Reason*
E	*Écrits: A Selection*
EG	*Philosophie des Geistes*, trans. *The Philosophy of Spirit*, part 3 of the *Encyclopaedia of the Philosophical Sciences*
EL	*Encyclopaedia Logic*, vol. 1 of the *Encyclopaedia of the Philosophical Sciences*
FC	*The Four Fundamental Concepts of Psycho-Analysis*

GW	*Gesammelte Werke, Chronologisch Geordnet*, 18 vols.
PN	*Philosophy of Nature*, vol. 2 of the *Encyclopaedia of the Philosophical Sciences*
PR	*Process and Reality*
PS	*Phenomenology of Spirit*
RH	*Reason in History*, the Introduction to the *Lectures on the Philosophy of History*
SE	*Standard Edition of the Complete Psychological Works of Sigmund Freud*, 24 vols.
SL	*Science of Logic*
STI	*System of Transcendental Idealism*
W	*Wissenschaftslehre*, trans. *The Science of Knowledge*

בראשית

ORIGINS

INTRODUCTION

Rethinking Mind in the Age of the Brain

This book is a treatise on the unconscious mind. It attempts to reclaim and clarify many key elements from classical psychoanalytic doctrine through a Hegelian revisionist perspective I have called *dialectical psychoanalysis*, or *process psychology*. Although process psychology has potential applications for theoretical, clinical, and applied psychoanalysis, here I am mainly concerned with explicating its conceptual explanatory power. It is my hope that this work will be received as a fresh paragon for the advancement of psychoanalytic inquiry grounded in a solid philosophical foundation. If it finds verification among the social and behavioural sciences it stands a chance of enjoying greater receptivity across disciplines; but this work ultimately rests on philosophical justification alone. Thus, my approach is founded in a theory-based practice that further informs methodological considerations. Here I am concerned with first principles, namely, the ontological configurations of mind and the logical precepts that lend cohesion and intelligibility to human experience.

Because I am preoccupied with articulating the basic constituents of psychic reality derived from process thought, some readers may find this work to be tedious and/or irrelevant to therapeutic practice. It is my intention, however, to introduce a conceptual shift in addressing the axiomatic principles that inform our presuppositions of mental functioning on the most fundamental level, a subject matter that has been uniformly neglected within the psychoanalytic literature since Freud and Lacan. It is largely for this reason that I attempt to show how psychoanalysis is ultimately a metaphysical enterprise.

Since Freud's (1933) denunciation of psychoanalysis as a *Weltanschauung*, psychoanalysis has largely remained sceptical towards philosophic speculation while favouring a scientific attitude. But with increasing attention paid to philosophical paradigms within contemporary psychoanalysis, new vistas emerge for mutual dialogue and theoretical advance. Throughout this project, I attempt to offer the first systematic account of a psychoanalytic metaphysics grounded in process philosophy largely derived from Hegel's dialectical logic. After rectifying many misconceptions about Hegel's dialectic, I endeavour to provide a process account of the coming into being of unconscious agency that conditions the subsequent emergence and organization of all other forms of psychic realty. This naturally includes the nature and structure of the ego, consciousness, object relations and intrapsychic defence, semiotics, intersubjective dynamics, and the higher tiers of psychical life that belong to the cultivated mind. Of course, mind cannot exist independently of social life, which informs and to some degree defines our cultural ontology, so the reader should not be misled into thinking that the intrapsychic and the intersubjective are mutually exclusive categories. Rather, they are dialectically, hence ontologically, wed; yet, they are capable, in theory, of being phenomenologically analyzed as distinct objects of study from various contingent, intervening perspectives. The main point is that – whether we speak of subject or object, inner or outer – perspective, phenomenon, and reality are ontologically conjoined within a complex process holism that permeates all forms of mentation, both individually and collectively realized. Here it is my hope that process psychology will stimulate new directions in psychoanalytic inquiry.

In *The Unconscious Abyss: Hegel's Anticipation of Psychoanalysis* (2002), I provide the first systematic application of Hegel's philosophy of mind to psychoanalytic thought.[1] This is where I comprehensively point towards a process account of psychoanalysis grounded in dialectical logic and show how it has the potential to advance the discipline itself. While many psychoanalysts, psychologists, behavioural scientists, and clinicians of all kinds may find this approach to be highly abstruse and esoteric, I nevertheless believe that psychoanalysis stands everything to gain from philosophical fortification.

It should be noted that this project is principally directed towards the psychoanalytic community, but I hope academic philosophers will find if of interest. Hegel scholars in particular may find it appealing for its applied value. I realize that a book of this kind is bound to be very strange to psychoanalytic audiences, especially psychoanalytic practitioners who pride themselves on clinical work rather than on theory. I must apologize for not satisfying their expectations. Psychoanalysts who merely critique ideas based on clinical applications will be sorely disappointed – if not lost – in wading through such complex theory. But appealing to the practitioner is not the intention of this book. I follow a structural format that is attentive to the philosophical parameters of clinical theory rather than centring on clinical material itself. Here I am concerned with speculative metaphysics, a subject matter that cannot elude the behavioural sciences, humanities, or even the natural sciences (such as quantum physics). What I optimistically hope for is that the clinician will learn to see and appreciate value in theoretical sophistication and accept it for its own intrinsic benefit, if for no other reason for the sake of advancing our critical science. If practitioners can apply philopsychoanalytic theory in the consulting room, then all the better.

Because psychoanalysis conceptually addresses all aspects of the human condition, including the nature and structure of mind, society, and culture, it is by definition a philosophical enterprise. Although perhaps unintended by Freud and his followers, or seen as a corollary to the psychological observations advanced by psychoanalysis as a behavioural science, psychoanalysis as a discipline is a mode of philosophical inquiry by virtue of the fact that it critically examines and speculates on the ontological, epistemological, and phenomenological aspects of human existence through the puissance of reason,[2] or what Freud (1927b, 1930, 1933a) refers to as *Logos* – the scientific intellect. The criterion of reason, however, does not preclude the study, role, or value of the emotions, the passions, moral sentiment, and irrationality; rather, it only insists that we must respect the need for intelligibility governing our conception and comprehension of these polarities and divergent processes that animate human existence.

These three aspects of philosophical inquiry, namely, ontology, epistemology, and phenomenology, cannot be divorced from the broader rubric of metaphysics, for all propositions are ultimately claims about what is real: it is for descriptive purposes that I briefly highlight their distinctions here. Psychoanalysis makes fundamental assumptions concerning each of these philosophical domains, including (1) the ontological – the nature of psychic reality; (2) the epistemological – how we justify our knowledge claims and clinical practices; and (3) the phenomenological – the disclosure, appearance, and quality of lived experience.

While psychoanalytic process psychology has implications for all of these philosophical traditions, I mainly focus on its conceptual application for understanding the ontology of the unconscious. Like Plato, Freud saw psychoanalysis as the science of the life of the soul (*Seelenleben*). Through philosophical inquiry into the nature and operations of the psyche, psychoanalysis is first and foremost an inquest into the quandaries of the unconscious mind. Dialectical psychoanalysis is therefore concerned with expatiating the ontological conditions that make knowledge and experience possible, and this has its root and etiology in the dialectic of process.

I must inform the reader that dialectical psychoanalysis, or process psychology, is differentiated from the tradition of process philosophy based upon the influential work of Alfred North Whitehead and the contemporaneous ideas of Charles Hartshorne and Samuel Alexander.[3] It also diverges from Jung's dialectic of opposites and, more contemporarily, Arnold Mindell's process-oriented psychology. Despite similarities and shared affinities with these respective philosophies, dialectical psychoanalysis is primarily derived from Hegel's dialectical ontology. For Hegel, mind is an active process of becoming forged through negation and conflict. His metaphysical system is a grand and dauntless attempt to derive unity from disunity, order from disorder, and purpose from pattern by highlighting particularity and contextuality within a dynamic self-elucidated and complex universality. Process psychology amends certain facets of Hegel's system, as I expatiate in my prolegomena, but without abandoning the primacy and structural organization of the dialectic. Of course any metaphysical system is bound to be inadequate from the standpoint of phenomenology. I hope that phenomenologists will at least appreciate the effort to begin to question – let alone articulate – how experience is even made possible.

Our dialectical system is teleological, but it has no proper beginning or end. That is, there is a purposeful, persistent, and meaningful order that is not predetermined or predesigned, nor is it superimposed; rather, it is determinate and procreative as it progressively unfolds through various maturational contingencies that are derived from its own interior constitution. The system is unifying, not unified: it is always maintained in a state of flux and process, which can never be complete or static, yet everything is intertwined. One can enter the system at any given point and still remain ontologically bound to the whole despite highlighting a particular piece of activity, perspective, or experience of mind and, by extension, collective social life. The structure of the system is non-linear, hence privileging a unifying matrix of intercessions that assume a web-like development and presupposes the whole system at the very start. This may appear rather contradictory given that we are to be preoccupied with the origins of psychic life (hence beginnings) and particularly with what I call the "genesis problem" (hence the ground of becoming), namely, the coming into being of psychic existence. But this contradiction soon dissolves when you realize that everything is interconnected. Although the system is holistically encompassing and coherently circular, thus presupposing multiple complexities and processes at once that stand in ontic relation to one another,[4] in order to minimize opacity for the reader, I attempt to present this book in linear and progressive terms by providing a successive treatment of the subject matter.

Joseph Newirth (2003) recently reminds us that the unconscious is generative, a thesis that was originally promulgated by the German idealist F.W.J. von Schelling (1800), a contemporary of Hegel.[5] What I am interested in exploring throughout this project is not only how the unconscious is generative but also how it generates being, that is, how psychic reality is constituted. Reality is constituted by mind as agentic process that emerges, grows, and matures from its basal primitive form to more robust configurations of conscious life, self-reflection, and social order. Psychic reality begins as unconscious experience constituted through presubjective events that collectively organize into an unconscious sense of agency. The coming into being of this agentic function signals the coming into being of subjectivity, which becomes the fountainhead for future forms of psychic life to materialize and thrive. What this means is that, before we can speak of the infant, before we can speak of the mother or the attachment system, before we can speak of culture or language, we have to account for the internally derived activity that makes consciousness, attachment, and social relations possible.

Process psychology shows how internally mediated relations become the ground and prototype for all external relations as well as how the structures of unconscious subjectivity allow for intersubjective dynamics to unfold and transpire. Put laconically, what *Origins* endeavours to explicate is the domain, scope, and limits to unconscious mentation prior to the birth of the human subject, culture, and language. Of course this assumes that psychic life is endogenously organized from the start (*endon*, within) and prepares the organism to experience and acquire information from any mode of information-emitting sources, including exogenous channels – but mind is not solipsistic. Even in the womb, the foetus finds itself socially embedded in a matrix of embodied form that receives many types of communication. These communications are multifaceted and spring from diverse sources – biologic, perinatal, environmental, anaclitic, etc. – but they are also prefigured by an objective cultural society that predates the birth of the human subject and, hence, commands an ontological facticity that cannot be annulled or ignored.

In order to avoid a hopelessly infinite regress, I forgo the temptation to insist on the ontological primacy of the object over that of the subject, or vice versa. The question of whether a social ontology exists prior to the birth of the human subject is not as important as the question of *how* the unborn and incipient mind, uninitiated in the experiential world of consciousness, becomes internally organized and receptive to events it processes from all modes of information emittance. Therefore, we must centre our inquiry from the speculative standpoint of an unconscious phenomenology, phenomena we cannot directly observe or measure, despite the fact that what we are positing is based in ontological discourse. This makes our inquiry a metaphysical enterprise and not an empirical one; for how can one measure that which cannot be observed? Instead, we are forced to rely on logic and on logic alone. Here we must summon the principle of sufficient reason: Is there a ground to every mental event, a ground from which all else emerges, even if that ground is amorphous, unrefined, incomplete, unobservable, ungrounded?

"I," or, more appropriately, the "sense of I," is not a declarative we make from the start, unlike Fichte's (1794) notion of the absolute I (*Ich*) that posits itself into existence and declares its being ex nihilio.[6] The I develops naturally and organically proceeds as an epigenetic architectonic, self-organizing achievement. It must emerge from the organic contingencies in which it finds itself, and this process logically must be prepared from a priori structures the field of psychoanalysis has customarily called the unconscious. What would it be like for mind to know itself upon birth, to know it is an entity that is sentient, that feels, that thinks, and that is self-conscious of itself as a knowing self-reflective being? Would this not be fantastic, merely a fantasy, merely a creative stretch of imagination? But what if there were some small modicum of thought, of self-certainty, of self-awareness – abandoned to the naked facticity in which mind originally finds itself?

The unconscious, properly understood, is not an archaeological find; rather, it is a *series of spacings*. Although the archaeology metaphor may have a certain legitimacy when we consider the purpose of psychoanalytic method, there is never truly a pristine uncovering of an artefact as the pure deposit of psychic occurrence or event, as if it were some buried relic of the discovered past. Rather, whatever psychic events that are roused, dislodged, or realized are necessarily subject to translation and transmogrification by virtue of the fact that consciousness mediates, and therefore a fortiori transforms unconscious process. Because all psychic events are processes, they never remain static or unaltered. Any conscious recollection or awareness of the past will undergo alteration to various degrees by the mere fact that we posit them, hence bringing the past into a new mediated dynamic. When we envision psychoanalysis as an archaeological endeavour, our subject matter becomes history – the past – accompanied by an interpretive, often speculative, explanation about what preceded the present and went on originally (hence, in the *arkhē*). What becomes important to reemphasize is our quest for understanding the most rudimentary structures of mind as a return to the most original or, more appropriately, aboriginal (*ab-*, from + *origine*, beginning) motifs that govern unconscious life. Just as the term ἄβυσσος refers to the being (ου) of the unfathomable, boundless abyss – the infinite void of the underworld – so does ἀρχή (origin) refer to a first principle, element, or source of action. This first element as pure activity is unconscious genesis.

The unconscious is real although it is not an entity. It is more appropriately understood as a spacing or presencing of certain facets of psychic realty having loci, shape, and force in the indefinite ways in which they manifest as both the interiorization and external expression of agentic events. Here we are mainly concerned with the reality of the unseen and the ontological invisibility of the abyss. Process psychology displaces the primacy of language over the primacy and ubiquity of unconscious mentation, instead radicalizing an unconscious agency that modifies and differentiates itself, and disperses its essence throughout its dialectical activities. Here we must begin with prebeginnings, with addressing the philosophical notion of how agency first emerges from the psyche's unconditional embodiment. This requires us to address the mind/body question from the inception of unconscious life before the ego of consciousness is aware that it is embodied. Here it is necessary to explore the notion of *Trieb* as a pulsional bodily organization.[7] The specific question of how agency emerges from drive and, even more specifically, how self-directed teleological processes emerge from teleonomic pressures inherent to the bodily pulsions,[8] is closely examined.

Following a naturally organic and developmental process of dialectical unfoldings, the unconscious soul erupts from its corporeality to find itself as a sentient affective life that is desirous and driven by lack – a lacking or absence it wishes to satiate. But, unlike a wish or a drive, desire cannot be sated. It is an endless striving that seeks fulfilment through many circuitous routes and endless forms of content-specific appetition. In the initiation and wake of desire lies the causal force behind the dialectic, namely, the engine of appetitive motivational longing within which mind finds itself immersed. Here lies the gestation of a certain form of pre-reflective self-consciousness we may call *unconscious apperception*. Unconscious mind becomes pre-reflectively aware of its self-certainty as a desirous apperceptive being that wants, that craves, that becomes. This dialectical progression traces the coming into being of the unconscious ego that emerges from its desirous rupture to experience and transcend its confinement to its mere corporeal nature while remaining an embodied experiential subject. This dialectical and architectonic process potentially explains the initial origins of psychic reality.

In this age of the brain, the notion of mind has largely become relegated to a reductive category subsumed under some form of materialism spearheaded by cognitive neuroscience and philosophies of mind. Indeed, some developments in cognitive science and neurobiology are content with displacing a dynamic unconscious altogether, instead substituting the language of dissociation, attachment processes, and the implicit forms of memory that are, in turn, shaped by corresponding brain asymmetry (see Siegel 1999). With the focus on neuroimaging technologies, as they observe the functions of the brain, many researchers are enticed by the lure of material reduction and commit the fallacy of misplaced concreteness or simple location.[9] Here they illegitimately conclude that unconscious processes are *caused* by brain events and are reducible to brain activity rather than that they are merely *correlated*. In other words, scientists often mistake observable, measurable phenomena for their simple location and make inconclusive causal claims. This fallacy is committed when observable physical locality, such as functional magnetic resonance imaging (fMRI) or positron emission tomography (PET) scans, are equated with the mental functions and representational content we ontologically *infer* to be causal rather than correspondent and, therefore, hastily conclude that mind equals brain.

I am sympathetic to advances in the neurosciences and value consilience, complementarity, and symmetry between theoretical and empirical work. In fact, process psychology needs to account for empirical science if it is to have any theoretical currency. On the face of things, this is not hard to support: in the hard and soft sciences, including anthropology, sociology, and the humanities, mind and culture are mainly conceived as a plurality and series of interactive systemic processes. Some of these processes are cohesive and harmonious, while some are chaotic and destructive and, hence, governed by unpredictable possibilities. Each process, however, has its own psychophysical correlates and social order. In other words, we can never abolish the fact that we are embodied in space and time within a biological, cultural, and linguistic milieu that informs our being in the world. And to a large degree this is observable, measurable, and quantified. But let us not fool ourselves into thinking that empiricism holds a privileged touchstone to truth or is of superior value when, by its very nature, it is limited in scope and in what it can control and measure. By definition and design, empiricism observes Occam's razor and follows the law of parsimony. As a corollary, it is unable to control for, manipulate, and observe all phenomena it sets out to study. Therefore, it must artificially contrive a "laboratory," or a "controlled" set of experimental "variables," that discards other variables and dislocates its operations from the original phenomena being "observed." Any conclusions and generalizations made cannot ignore the parameters within which empiricism limits it activity and, hence, at best can only offer limited inferences based on its circumscribed method and object of study. In other words, unlike metaphysical inquiry, empiricism certainly cannot address questions outside its realm of experimentation, measurement, data manipulation, and statistical analysis.

Certain conclusions made by contemporary theoreticians and researchers – such as that there is no dynamic unconscious or that nonconscious encoded events implicit in memory structure displace our previous understanding of unconscious activity (see Iannuzzi 2006) – do not hold up to logical scrutiny when they fall under a category mistake or are guilty of the fallacy of simple location. Furthermore, this line of thinking, namely, that the brain is the cause of mind and all mental activity, is what, in neuroscience, Bennett and Hacker (2003) refer to as the "merelogical fallacy." This is a fundamental attribution error where one ascribes the acts or characteristics of a whole to its parts. This argument is derived from Aristotle's notion of formal causality: one cannot reduce the complexity of a whole system or design (e.g., selfhood, personality) to its material substance (e.g., brain). But this is precisely what neuroscience attempts to accomplish: the human being, personhood, or mind devolves into material-efficient reductive forces. From this paradigm, mind is nothing but brain. So, contra John Searle (1992), who insists on consciousness as a property of the brain, or Daniel Dennett (1991), who ascribes psychological processes to parts of the brain, these explananda are mereological errors because they do not take into account the psychical acts that constitute the person as a whole; rather, they reduce the human being to a subsystem of parts that fracture the supraordinate nature of a complex system.

What we can legitimately say is that mental processes (particularly neural states that are inductively well correlated) correspond to brain events, but we cannot epistemologically ascertain that they are unequivocally causal or that they are identical in composition. Furthermore, there are qualitative variations in what we experience, believe, and feel from what we observe and know. Psychoanalysts who advocate for a sufficient conceptualization of the unconscious from the standpoint of neuroscience displace the allegorical, metaphorical, aesthetic, and spiritual expressions of human subjectivity and the qualia of lived experience that cannot be adequately captured by biologistic language. Although neurobiology is a necessary condition of our embodiment, it is not a sufficient condition to explain the complexifications of lived experiential reality. For these reasons, the mind/body conundrum needs to be bracketed from the materialist enterprise and engaged from the standpoint of ontology that is compatible with the language of embodiment and the interstices of human experience without evoking a causally reductive argument under the banner of science and at the expense of philosophical sophistication.

We are accustomed to think of mind and self as being largely defined by conscious experience (such as the impact of early childhood attachment and interactional patterns with others, culture, and the linguistic forces operative within our social ontology) as well as being biologic organisms that encounter these environmental influences. In psychoanalysis, little attention is paid to the philosophic notion of how embodied organizations derive and modify from their material nature as desirous-ideational units of agentic order within social and linguistic parameters without devolving into biological and/or linguistic determinism. Mind remains embodied but it supersedes material reduction by virtue of the fact that it becomes uniquely ideational, emotive, and valuational. It is from its embodied thrownness and sentient impingements that it emerges as a self-articulated, self-defining developmental agency. Modified from its original pulsional constellations, mind is oriented towards instituting action, processing events, and experiencing itself as being-in-becoming. When I speak of mind, I do not mean some panpsychism or invisible spiritual-immaterial force that inhabits and animates the universe; rather, I am speaking of the universal aspects of mental functioning that all people to some degree possess regardless of gender, race, or historicity. Contra postmodern psychoanalytic theories that displace metaphysics, process psychology attempts to situate phenomena, contingency, and contextual complexity within a subjective universality that accounts for individual variance and plurality within an encompassing holistic governing totality, despite the concession that this totality is never complete, united, or unified. Conflict, negation, and strife are its very essence, the engines propelling development, the positive significance of the negative.

Just as our recognition of the unconscious as an entity is an antiquated notion, so the postmodern collapse of the subject and subjectivity for the reification of language is a misguided project. Because psychic reality is process oriented, and initially derived from its own internal constitution, the linguistic turn only partially accounts for unconscious dynamics. That is, before the breach into consciousness, the dialectical unfolding of the psyche originally constitutes itself as the coming into being of the unconscious ego, which acquires agency as a teleologic determinate being-for-self. In its generative activity of self-enactment, unconscious agency institutes its own network of semiotics as the original mode of signification and meaning relata. Desire as being-in-relation-to-lack interjects its own semiotic markers within its unconscious interior, which structurally prepares a priori the capacity for linguistic receptivity and production encountered in the field of consciousness. Rather than adopt the postmodern turn, process psychology attempts to articulate the functional structures of semiotic meaning relations that unfold prior to the conscious birth of the ego. What this means is that unconscious signification precedes linguistic signification. In other words, language is conditioned on unconscious precipitants.

Unconscious semiotics initially materialize and unfold as agentically assigned and often segregated units of embodied affective sentience that disperse yet simultaneously coalesce as a plurality of unconscious schemata under the rubric of the unconscious ego. Unconscious schemata take their incipient forms as somatic and emotional organizations that may be partially autonomous from one another and comprise nonconceptual pre-reflective representations of internal experience that further execute and convey their own meaning relations through a combinatory of signifiers within its embodied affective resonance states. Schemas start off as primitive process systems derived from immediate bodily impulses and sensations, such as those belonging to the psychophysicality of teleonomic-somatic and affective reverberations, and later become more organized through perception and the higher-order conceptual capacities afforded through linguistic cognition, which lend cohesion, clarity, and vitality to inarticulate unconscious experience.

Schemata comprise the building blocks of psychic reality. They may be viewed as microcosmic units or self-states that have various characteristics or properties peculiar to their own internally derived constitutions, such as specific contours, impressions, affect, or desirous-riddled content that compose the microdynamic processes relative to a particular schema. These microcosmic units can communicate with other individual schemata that exist within the plurality of unconscious process and may form interrelationships between other schematic entities. Schemata may take on more zest in organization and structure and can form elaborate phantasy systems fuelled by unconscious intent, restraints, and pressures.[10] These process systems infiltrate unconscious life and can hold a certain dominion over the underworld. Furthermore, groups that are aligned in terms of their internal structures may form communities of schemata that can further colonize other schemata that are more susceptible to being annexed or overthrown. In other words, lesser organized or weaker schemata can be incorporated within more dominate and vibrant communal structures. Despite the capacity for the subexistence of competing mental units within the abyss, the plurality of schemata that populate mental life fall within the overarching supraordinate, governing totality of the dialectic. Therefore the dialectic is the macrocosmic unifying suprastructure that provides organization, order, and direction to the infinite flux of events that comprise psychic reality.

Schemata are information-emitting and information processing *microagents*, or self-states, that form communication channels and linkages through their semiotic relations. They may facilitate or oppose linkages by ingressing into – hence incorporating – one another or by negating one another through defensive fortifications, of course depending upon which movement of the dialectic is operative at any given moment within each schema's internal structure. Phantasy systems are forged or aborted through the way in which semiotic relata are formed and reinforced. This ensures that, potentially, there will always be quasi-autonomous activity performed by each schema that conform to or resist the greater pressures of the dialectic. Not only does this independent functionality of schematic action account for variation in different and distinct modes of expression, but it also accounts for agentic choice and the bid for freedom each schema intrinsically possesses. In more common language, drives, affect, and phantasies may take on their own unique autonomous existence within the abyss despite the fact that other phantasy systems – what we commonly call defences – negate or subsume them within their internal constitutions.

Unconscious schemata are infinite by virtue of the fact that psychic reality multiplies and produces an innumerable deferral of signifiers within its interiority. Of course, infinity is always operative within the constants of finitude (i.e., when organic nature dies or expires). Until then, all schemata are subject to the overarching governance and sublating movements of the dialectic, but they are also capable of resisting sublation and may even regress or stay ossified in unconscious points of fixation or stagnation. This is why at times somatic and affective schemata express themselves as bodily symptoms and emotional dysregulation (e.g., as compromise formations) that are recalcitrant to conceptual mediation or understanding. In effect, conflicted affects, traumas, and phantasies are confined to earlier forms of embodiment that characterize unconscious schematic structure and resist articulation through linguistic media. Instead, they remain embedded within their original modes of signification and appear as symptoms with overdetermined attributes, properties, and expressive value. For example, what the fields of psychoanalysis, psychiatry, and psychology call mental disorders (i.e., hysteria) are fuelled by disordered states of unconscious schemata. The autonomous nature of schematic structure and designation point towards how symptom formation is under the influence of earlier forms of unconscious representation. The fate of each schema is contingent upon the dominate processes at work in the mind and the supraordinate directionality and mediatory operations of the dialectic. Some schemata will flourish while others will perish; however, all schematic activity is subject to the synthetic functions of the dialectic. Here psychopathology would largely result from autonomous self-states resisting integration or warring schemata that subvert the synthetic and sublating features of mind.

The underworld of unconscious semiotics ontologically prepares the psyche for the acquisition and production of language, which is filtered through, mediated, assimilated, and amalgamated within the psychic register. This, of course, is initiated at actual birth when the infantile ego encounters the external world. The unconscious emergence and breach of the ego into consciousness signals a second awakening of the ego, which now has as its task the role of mediating objects of conscious cognition and all its new-found experiences. Ego development now becomes a flourishing and robust process in the ontogenesis of the self because it is no longer constricted to unconscious embodiment and non-linguistic schematic representation. Here the nature of maternal attachment, nurturance, affective attunement, and empathic responsiveness from the relational milieu within the broader parameters of the subject's social ontology provide the contents, patterns, and forms of experience that condition the contours of the ego's burgeoning personality and characterological habits of defence. As conscious cognition expands ego boundaries and functional operations inherent to perceptual consciousness and self-experience, schematic representation and signification naturally progress to acquire higher-order organizations such as perception, imagination, and conceptual thought.

Reality is constituted by mind by virtue of the fact that we can only have commerce with reality as we conceive it to be. This ensures that ego and reality will always be informed by the abyss. The ego of consciousness now must encounter the manifold of sense experience and form meaning relations that help define its adaptation, functionality, and self-identity within the plurality of competing objects it encounters. The dialectic of internal modification that characterizes the developmental epigenesis of the unconscious ego is now extended to the mediatory modifications it must perform in its external relations to objects. Here the ego must set itself over against its objects of experience in its quest for achieving being-for-self as a fully self-articulated individuated agent within the intersubjective contexts that define its being in the world. This is facilitated through the mediation of the m/other as both the original attachment figure and as the symbolic cultural signifier.

In its labour for self-definition, the ego must execute another series of dialectical movements in which it distinguishes and separates off various portions of the external world from its own immediate unity. That is, the ego is originally not aware of itself as a subject, which it has the developmental task of becoming. Because it takes its immediate sense experience to be all-encompassing and totalizing, this basic simple unity with reality must undergo inner division, separation, differentiation, and restructuring. Here the infantile ego must differentiate out the various elements of its experience, which it takes for its totality as an immediate universality, and, through dialectical operations peculiar to its contingent thought processes, it interjects difference, categorization, and discreteness into concrete elements of particularity that comprise the plurality and flux of the competing phenomena it encounters. One task the emergent conscious ego must execute involves differentiating out self from others, and this specifically includes familial attachment figures. This includes differentiating out language as a distinct medium of communicative relations from the maternal environment, which the ego at first takes to be merged in its symbiotic union with the mother. This is where a sense of I, or personal identity, is rudimentarily formed in relation to difference. More precisely, the ego differentiates out a sense of self from the mother through her affective attunement and responsiveness, which facilitates the emergence of an autonomous sense of self while remaining in relation to the reciprocal dyadic system.

The institution of pre-reflective judgments (such as division, negation, universalizing, determining similarity and difference, etc.) allow the ego's experience of reality to proliferate in magnitude and qualitative depth. Over its developmental maturation, mediated by its intersubjective relations with psychosocial life, the ego forges various fluid boundaries between inner and outer, particularity and universality, self and other, being and the world. This dialectical process unfolds within the larger movements of progression from unconscious apperception to consciousness and then to self-consciousness as capacities in self-reflectivity allow for cultivation of the ego. The generic movement of the self that splits and divides itself, projects or externalizes parts of its interior onto the external world, which it then gathers and reincorporates back into its interiority, constitutes the antediluvian cycle we have come to call projective identification. Here mind is conceived as a trajectory of dynamic pattern that unfolds as projective identification, which is none other than the sublating animating force of the dialectic that vanquishes new shapes in its quest for self-consciousness and wholeness. The multiple, overdetermined dialectical processes that are operative in generating higher forms and shapes of mind and social structures through this generic sublating dynamic point towards the logical universal laws of generative process that govern the evolution of mind and society. In its pilgrimage towards self-actualization, fulfilment, and betterment, the general thrust of the human intellect instantiated in subjective personality and cultural conscience seeks to fulfil and become its possibilities.

Mind, or, more generally, the human spirit (*anima*), can never fully complete itself, whether this be reflective of the individual or collective society as a whole. To imagine such a state would necessarily entail the death of the dialectic: mind would no longer strive to surpass itself, to better itself, to create and achieve higher tiers of unification, satisfaction, and experiential complexity. It simply would no longer desire. The human psyche is inherently restless and seeks to cultivate and advance itself in novel ways governed by the idiosyncratic aims of freedom and choice that each individual or collective group executes for itself. This is an orienting principle for the dialectic that naturally strives towards ascendance within the face of decent, fruition within decay, and harmony within chaos that saturates our concrete lives and communal world. This orienting principle exemplifies the self-articulated complex holism that we may more properly observe in civilization as the concrete universals that define a collectively shared social value system based upon the identification with and fulfilment of objective human ideals.

The crusade for holism is a struggle through metaphysical labour and existential suffering that is both individually and collectively borne. Although individual people and societies will only partially attain such exalted ideals, it is the striving that signifies the value of human desire. This quest belongs to the higher faculties of self-consciousness that are embedded in our social valuation practices and that govern our educational systems; economic, social, and political structures; policing and law; religious institutions; cultural centres; and works of artistic expression. The pursuit of an intellectual contemplative life will naturally lead one to engage the question and meaning of the ethical, of religion, and of aesthetic taste and judgment. These human ideals and values are connected to the greater whole, where reason, emotion, aesthetics, and justice participate in spiritual communion with nature and the universe as being in the world with self and others. While the masses are mainly preoccupied with the pragmatics of daily life, self-preservation and survival, and the pursuit of enjoyment, gratification, and pleasure, the higher shapes of self-consciousness are only attained by few. However, they are nonetheless embodied in our communal cultural practices, which define modern society and, hence, speak to the upward acclivity of the dialectic. Of course, any progressive achievement of civilization occurs within the context of death, trauma, and despair, which fall short of attaining such ideals. Here the dialectic stagnates, regresses, or resists sublating itself. Multiple complexities and pluralities of experience and social array exist within a systemic unifying network that governs process dialectics. Of course negativity and chaos saturate progression, even when a discernable pattern or purpose emerges as we look back at the process of its own becoming. Among so much death and decay, which saturates our daily world preoccupations, here we may enjoy some optimism that all this suffering is a necessary and meaningful dimension of the dialectic, which is part and parcel of the positive significance of the negative that brings about a better world. Without conflict there can be neither growth nor betterment. To reappropriate Leibniz, this is the best of all reasonable worlds.

But what do we make of this striving of the ego to sublate itself? What is its motivation? What is its object? There is a deep structural impetus that is ontologically constituted within the rotary motion of the dialectic in order to satisfy its longings, its *telos*. Is there an overarching teleology towards which the ego strives? Perhaps this question is only legitimate within the nature of contingent choice each subject encounters. But contingency is never devoid of universality, which structures the dialectic. What I fundamentally believe the human psyche strives for in all its unadulterated instantiations is the wish for unity and peace, free of trauma and violence – whether externally imposed or self-implosive. What resonates within us all is a wish to be free of negativity, of our suf fering, or *pathos* (πάθος), which is none other than a dialectical renunciation of, yet paradoxical call for, death – for termination, the desire to end the lack. This fundamental desire to expurgate the lack, this gap in being, the lacuna that informs the abyss, is simultaneously the wish to recapture the symbiotic reunion with our original natural sentient slumber from which unconscious subjectivity first awakens. Here lies the conundrum of how the desire for holism is simultaneously a desire to recapitulate its original totality, to repossess its original undifferentiated unity through reintegrated unification, at once a return and a sublation, where being and nothing are the same.

And so begins our sojourn into the abyss.

In the beginning (Ἐν ἀρχή) ... darkness covered the abyss (ἄβυσσος).
—Genesis 1:1

origin (ôr´ə-jĭn) *n.* **1. a.** A point of origination. **b.** Source. **c.** First cause. **2. a.** Ancestry. **b.** derivation. **3.** A coming into being. **4.** Beginning, *arkhē.* **5. a.** Ground. **b.** Foundation. **6. a.** An abyss. **b.** under-ground. **c.** fathomless. [ME *origine*, ancestry < Lat. *origo* < *oriri*, to rise; Gk. ἀρχή, opening]

AXIOMS

Ab Initio

THE PRIMACY OF PROCESS

I.1 Mind is constituted as process.
I.1a Process is the essence of all psychic reality and the indispensable ontological foundation of all forms of mental life. Every mental derivative – from unconscious to conscious, intra psychic to relational, individual to collective – is necessarily predicated on process.
I.2 Process underlies all experience as an activity of becoming.
I.2a As becoming, process is pure event, unrest, transmogrification, and experiential flow.
I.3 Essence is process.
I.3a Essence is neither fixed nor static, neither inert nor predetermined; rather, it is a spontaneous motional flux and trajectory of dynamic pattern lending increasing order, organization, and zeal to psychic development.
I.3b As process, essence must appear in order for any psychic event to be made actual.
I.4 Process is teleonomically constituted and teleologically driven.
I.4a Process as teleonomy is the orienting regulatory, lawful (causal), self-organizing capacities directing psychic governance, which are formal in essence and impersonal in nature.
I.4b Process as teleology is the agentically designed self-determinate action underlying mental structure.
I.4.c Psychic structure is not immutable, idle, rigid, or immobile but, rather, transforming, malleable, mediating activity that

           provides functional capacities and vivacity to mind within its
           teleologically self-generative, purposeful process of becoming.
I.4d   Mind is teleological insofar as it constitutes a purposeful,
           dynamic, goal-directed activity of becoming mediated by subjective unconscious and conscious processes among extrinsic
           interactions encountered in relation to its archaic past, its
           present immediacy, and its future (projective) trajectory.
I.4e   Teleology is interactional self-determinate freedom within the
           context of mediated contingency, not predetermined causal
           design.
I.5   There is an equiprimordiality to the subject-object contrast
           allowing for multiple teleological processes within both subjective intrapsychic organizations and the relational-intersubjective matrices that mutually inform the phenomenological structure of experience within our cultural
           ontology.
I.5a   The subject-object contrast may be properly appreciated as an
           intrinsic dynamic totality whereby each event and its internal
           relation is emphasized as a particular moment in the process
           of becoming. From the mutual standpoint of shared-difference, each individual subject stands in relation to the
           multiply contoured intersubjective matrix that is generated when particular subjectivities collide and interact. This
           ensures that process multiplies exponentially ad infinitum
           and acquires more complexifications within social life.
I.5b   Process is both individual and collective, personal and
           impersonal, thus allowing for exclusive particularity in content as well as inclusive (shared) universality in form.
I.5c   Although subjective experience is radically individualized and
           idiosyncratic, subjectivity further unfolds within universal
           dialectical patterns – as subjective universality (not as predetermined, reductive mechanisms but, rather, as purposeful
           contextual operations) – that lend actuality, structure, and
           coherence to lived reality.

           ## THE ONTOLOGY OF THE DIALECTIC

II.1   Process is dialectically governed by competing and opposing
           forces that are interrelated and mutually implicative; hence,

	all forms of psychic reality are dialectically mediated, interdependent, and spatiotemporally occupied.
II.1a	Opposition is ubiquitous to psychic reality and operative within all subjective and intersubjective experience.
II.2	There is an equiprimordality to all dichotomous relations: that which *is* is always defined and experienced in relation to what it is *not* through mutual relata. Thus, affirmation and negation are ontologically conjoined.
II.2a	All polarity is mutually related and inseparable; hence, one pole may only be differentiated from the other in formal logical thought, within epistemic contextuality, or by phenomenological perspective.
II.2b	Polarities of similarity and difference, identity and otherness, are experiential encounters in time within their own spacings, each highlighted by its respective positionality towards the other, even though their mutual relation to opposition co-constitutes their existence.
II.2c	Identity and difference, universality and particularity, multiplicity and unity are thus formed in mutual relation to opposition, negation, and conflict: each is ontologically interdependent and dynamically composed of fluid processes that evoke, construct, and sustain psychic organization and structure.
II.3	Psychic reality *is* the dialectic, experientially realized or not.
II.3a	Dialectic is understood as a simultaneous threefold progressive evolutionary process that at once enters into opposition, annuls such opposition as it elevates itself over its previous moment, and, at the same time, preserves such opposition within its internal structure.
II.3b	Three primary movements constitute the dialectic: at once they cancel or annul, transcend or surpass, retain or preserve. All of these are aspects of every transmogrification.
II.3c	This threefold activity constitutes the process of sublation.
II.4	There is a selective retention to the dialectic: it selects, holds onto, digests, and memorializes certain aspects of its experience, while it negates, ignores, regurgitates, contests, opposes, dissociates, and/or forgets others.
II.4a	The preservative element of the dialectic is therefore variable, idiosyncratic, and discerning.

II.4b   Selection highlights the microdynamic telic freedom of determinate choice in the moment, which has many possible mutative influences on how the dialectic unfolds in immediacy and in future encounters when stimuli are activated or constrained in relation to certain contingencies.

II.5   The dialectic is both architectonic and epigenetic: it builds upon its previous experiences and progressively redefines its interior constitution, thus fashioning and fortifying its structural organization in its evolutionary drive towards self-generative development.

II.5a   All particularities of conscious and unconscious experience (whether individually or collectively instantiated) are ontologically informed by the universal, motional principles that fuel the dialectic.

II.5b   Each movement, each shape of the dialectic, is merely one moment within its holistic teleology, differentiated only by immediate form.

II.5c   As each valence or unit of experience is highlighted in its immediacy or lived-phenomenal quality, it is merely one appearance among many appearances in the overall process of its own becoming.

THE SCHEMATIC STRUCTURE OF MIND

III.1   Mind is composed of a multitude of schemata, which are the building blocks of psychic reality. They originate from an unconscious nucleus of desire ensconced in negativity as Being-in-relation-to-lack, the ontological precondition, ground, and symbiotic unity from which the unconscious ego emerges.

III.1a   A schema is a desirous-apperceptive-ideational unit of self-experience that teleologically participates in the universal laws that govern the dialectic.

III.1b   Schemata are microagents and operate as self-states that possess semi-autonomous powers of telic expression. They create spacings within the unconscious abyss, each with its own intrinsic pressures, valences, intensities, intentional and defensive strategies, and unconscious qualia.

III.1c	The microdynamics of schematic expression can be highly individualistic in their bid for creativity, complexity, freedom, and agentic intent, yet they remain ontologically interconnected to the whole dialectical system we equate with mind.
III.1d	The self-constitution of a schema may take on many different forms, including somatic, sensuous, affective, perceptual, and conceptual (symbolic) order, depending upon the level of developmental sophistication and complexity each schema achieves. Hence, schematic form and expression is highly contingent and contextual.
III.2	Schemata exist as a multiplicity of process systems in the mind that commune, interact, and participate in a community of events that influence the unique constitution of each schematic structure.
III.2a	Schemata may develop relations with other schemata and communicate through their shared co-existence, or, as semi-independent quasi-agents, they can actively resist, defend, compartmentalize, or segregate themselves from external encroachments. Schemata may therefore vigorously absorb or incorporate elements from other schemata into their internal organizations, or they can block, censor, dissociate, combat, and even vitiate aspects of opposing schemata.
III.2b	Schematic activity entails a tertiary, or three-way, relation between the mediated dynamics of inner experience, the outer registrations of external vectors or stimuli making their presence felt and known to schematic apperception, and the content or specific datum that is mediated by the intercepting processes of agency that propel dialectical relations.
III.3	The multitudinous complex microsystems or communities of schemata evolve from an interceptive source we may properly attribute to an unconscious ego as the locus and executor of subjective agency. While schemata may persist and sustain their existence within the abyss of psychic reality, the unconscious ego is the synthetic unifying agency of mind. It is, in fact, the unconscious ego that further assigns agency to schemata, which allow for their autonomous actions. Schemas are therefore emergent properties of the unconscious ego that retain certain attributes of its original form while developing

their own subjectively derived internal organizations. In this way, the multiplicity of schematic structure participates in the same essence that define their ontological origin.

III.3a Communities of schemata form elaborate phantasy systems that become the principle activities of psychic reality under the execution of the unconscious ego. Here there is a vast underworld composed of groupings, precincts, factions, and colonies of schemata that cluster around various internal resonance states, sensuous experience, affective ties, ideation, and semiotic organizations that are peculiar to unconscious life.

III.3b Unconscious semiotics transpire in the abyss of interrelatedness in which all schemata engage when they ontically commune. Because all plurality participates in an overarching universality that properly defines the dialectical system of mind, any element of schematic individuality or assertion is ontologically interconnected to the whole.

III.3c Regardless of the diversity of internal spacings within the abyss, all unconscious experience is potentially linked together by an extended chain of signification with an infinite deferral of associations forming and occluding semiotic connections.

III.3d Within the combinatory of signifiers that populates the psychic web of signification, it is here that phantasy, which is initiated and sustained by the unconscious ego, becomes the mediating liaison and central nexus for apprehending, manipulating, unifying, and thwarting semiotic expressions.

PSYCHIC HOLISM

IV.1 Psychic reality is experienced, defined, and situated within the formal parameters that define the dialectic executed though a process of projective identification.

IV.1a Mind seeks to express itself and cultivate greater developmental complexities through externalizing its interiority, only to re-gather, re-introject, and re-incorporate itself back into its internal structure as a sublating dynamic.

IV.1b   Mind becomes a dynamically informed, self-articulated complex totality that seeks synthetic integration aimed at psychic holism.

IV.1c   Psychic holism celebrates the self-determinate, liberating freedom of mind that only its teleological, dialectical progression affords.

IV.1d   The upward drive of the dialectic is oriented towards wholeness, actualization, and contentment achieved through higher shapes of self-conscious realization.

IV.1e   Mind is neither conceived as the product and aggregation of predetermined causal design nor as material reduction or cultural determinism. Rather, agency and choice are instituted and realized in each moment of becoming as self-generative elevating-procreative succession, thus lending structure, meaning, and coherence to psychic development.

IV.1f   Only by looking back at the process of epigenesis can a discernable purpose emerge as a series of dynamic patterns of mediated immediacy forging the upward progression towards sublation.

THE INHERENT NEGATIVITY OF SUBLATION

V.1   The nature of psychic process is derived from an active organizing principle that is replete with conflict and destruction, hence providing thrust, progression, and ascendance within a dynamically informed ontogenetic system.

V.1a   This is the positive significance of the negative as conflict and negation forge the progressive path towards sublation.

V.1b   Under certain contingencies, once it has sublated itself, mind may revert or regress back to more archaic, dysfunctional, or primitive shapes of mental life. Or, if certain sublating propensities are truncated or retarded, it may remain ossified in stagnation. This is the inherent *pathos* of the dialectic.

V.2   The orienting principle of mind has dual, bicameral modes of expression.

V.2a   The dialectic of desire seeks quiescence, to fill the lack – the hole in being – and it may do so in one of two primary ways:

	through transcendence as sublation or through inversion and withdrawal.
V.2b	Mind seeks wholeness, yet fights within itself the regressive pull of the dialectic, which calls for a return to prior shapes of mental life – shapes that were once experienced as familiar, as less threatening or austere, and/or as comforting.
V.2c	Desire wants to advance, to go beyond its immediacy, to complete itself, yet it also wishes to return to the symbiotic unity it once felt as undisturbed, secure, and/or serene.
V.3	The competing, contradictory dual orientation of desire is radically governed by unconscious forces and subjective proclivities belonging to the unique psychic configurations and conflicts of each individual.
V.3a	This double orientation may also manifest itself within the communal or social life of a group or culture.
V.3b	When intrapsychic deficits, vulnerabilities, and oppressive external factors impinge on psychic reality, mind is seduced into returning to earlier phases of its development.
V.3c	These regressive currents are exacerbated when pathogenic markers are activated and subsequently tax or eclipse the transcending self-strivings towards sublation and wholeness.
V.3d	All subjects struggle with this fundamental tension between progression and regression, even if regression is only temporarily mobilized.
V.4	Although the doubling function, or aim, of the two orientations is the same – to end the lack – the experiential forms are antithetically instantiated: one wants to surpass absence by acquiring presence, while the other wants to end absence by recovering lost presence.
V.4a	But desire always confronts limits: impasse, deprivation, and discontent are inevitable aspects of psychic development and are replete with the contextual contingencies that the dialectic must encounter and attempt to synthetically resolve.
V.4b	Desire ultimately realizes that it cannot go beyond itself, thus surpass itself, for if it were to complete itself, it would no longer desire: the dialectic would vanish entirely, hence it would no longer be.

V.4c This is why death becomes the foundation of life: we are condemned to experience lack, an eternal affliction.

V.4d In their competing drives towards elevation and destruction, progression and regression, ascendance and decay, being and nothing – life and death – are the same.

PROLEGOMENA TO A SYSTEM

There has always been a tension between psychoanalysis and philosophy, primarily because each discipline privileges its own discourse and agenda over that of the other. While psychoanalysis largely heralds itself as a behavioural science, philosophy sees science as being only one species within its vast metaphysical genus. This tension was present from the start, for it was Freud (1916–17) who envisioned psychoanalysis as a scientific discipline superior to philosophic speculation (SE 15:20), not to mention the fact that he loathed metaphysics. Within the past two decades, however, psychoanalysis has grown more friendly towards philosophy and, in some contemporary circles, has embraced a variety of phenomenological, hermeneutic, and postmodern sensibilities towards theory and practice. We may observe this trend among many poststructuralist, feminist, constructivist, and narrative perspectives as well as among contemporary relational and intersubjective paradigms. But without exception, psychoanalysis has not endeavoured to offer its own formal metaphysics.

It is my intention throughout this book to show the value of philosophy for psychoanalytic investigation through theoretical enrichment and, more specifically, to advocate for a revisionist Hegelian approach to understanding and broadening psychoanalytic theory grounded in a rigorous logical methodology. Although Freud says much to align psychoanalysis with science, this does not in itself negate the value and practical utility of subjecting psychoanalysis to philosophical standards. In seeing that it has much to gain by broadening its domain of inquiry, psychoanalysis advances its descriptive power and explanatory breadth. Perhaps, more auspiciously, process psychology may offer contributions that help reorient the domain of theoretical, clinical, and applied psychoanalysis.

In our quest to understand the origins, ground, and essence of psychic reality – from the inception of unconscious life to the fundamental principles of mental functioning – dialectical psychoanalysis is concerned with expatiating the ontological conditions that make human experience possible, and this has its root and etiology in the dialectic of process. It becomes increasingly important to emphasize and meticulously show how process is ontologically constituted, is predicated on a logic of the dialectic, and underlies all domains of psychoanalytic investigation. Here it becomes necessary to offer a prolegomena to our revisionist system, thus orienting us towards the broader task that lies ahead. Psychoanalytic audiences are generally quite unfamiliar with Hegel's philosophical system, so it is necessary to provide a preliminary overview of his process metaphysics. After advocating for the value of process thought through Hegel's logic, I then provide detailed amendments to Hegel's dialectic and argue for a process account of reality and psychoanalytic epistemology that emphasizes a striving for the holistic interpretation of the psychodynamics of mind. In this way, I hope to show that process dialectics is a promising means for advancing psychoanalysis.

PROCESS DIALECTICS

The notion of process, activity, event, or change has an inextricable relation to the nature and meaning of dialectic. In ancient philosophy, *dialektikē* (διαλεχτχή), derived from the Greek *dialegein*, meaning to "converse," "argue," or "discourse," involved a conversational method of argumentative exchange. By Plato's time, the term acquired a technical sense in the form of question and answer similar to a debate, and it is now generally equated with Socrates' pedagogical style, which is primarily represented in Plato's dialogues. In this sense, dialectic is both the art of refutation and the quintessential method for ascertaining knowledge. Notice here that dialectic has a double or inverted implication – at once a negation in the service of affirmation.

Aristotle attributes Zeno of Elea with inventing the notion of dialectic thanks to his paradoxical arguments against motion and multiplicity, which rest on premises yielding contradictory consequences (Smith 1999). Aristotle is one of the first philosophers to organize formal procedures for dialectical debates, and he did so in the *Topics*, which reappeared centuries later in the formalized disputations practised in European universities throughout the Middle Ages. Responding to the ancient's alleged "illusory" logic, Kant (1781) introduced the notion of the "transcendental dialectic" in his first *Critique* as a means of analyzing antinomies, or contradictions, in reasoning, while Fichte (1794) attempted to bridge opposition by showing how thought seeks a natural synthesis. Hegel (1807, 1817) extended his dialectic of spirit (*Geist*) to a metaphysical enterprise that attempts to account for logic, nature, mind, and human history, while Marx, in turn, reduced spirit to matter. Whitehead (1929), on the other hand, reanimated nature as mind in his cosmology and established the last great metaphysical system in the history of philosophy to emphasize the primacy of process.

The pre-Socratic philosopher Heraclitus was the first to emphasize unity in the process of change, which necessarily evolves out of contraries that compose the world. Interpreted from the few fragments and epigrams he left behind, Heraclitus posited that there is a hidden harmony in the universe that sustains reality despite the conflict of opposites that we experience. Although there is some scholarly dispute (Kirk, Raven, and Schofield 1957), for Heraclitus, process *is* reality and the underlying source of the unity of phenomena. Following the law of process and opposition, Heraclitus affirms both the unity of contradictory appearances and the reality of process (Graham 1999). All things come to pass over into their opposite form, which is the edict of change and its expression. While the emphasis on locomotion and flux is often attributed to Heraclitus, the kernel of his philosophy is probably most clearly represented in his thesis on unity in diversity and difference in unity, which shows that the tension of opposites is essential to the notion of the one (Copleston 1946).

Over two thousand years later, the German Idealist, Georg Wilhelm Friedrich Hegel (1812, 1817), established a comprehensive science of the dialectic based on the logic of process. Drawing on Heraclitus' ideas on change, the strife and tension of opposition, and the many within the one, Hegel's dialectical logic is a monistic metaphysical system that attempts to account for all aspects of reality. Hegel viewed logic as a movement rather than as a pure analysis of how form could be applied to content or content fit into form. Form and content, particulars and universals, are indivisibly united in a process that describes not only human cognition and patterns of rational thought but also the process of nature and experience itself. What Heraclitus inferred in his fragments, Hegel systematized through rigorous logical methodology.

For Hegel, logic is the natural starting point for philosophy because it is the only discipline that thinks about itself and its operations. Hegel (1812) painstakingly shows how, unlike other reflective disciplines (which presuppose something given in nature or presume that thinking is self-evident), thought dialectically progresses from the most elemental to the most convoluted and profound modes of self-organization and dynamic expression. In fact, he delves so deeply into the very essence and contours of thought, making such subtle moves and inferences, that most people would never even become aware of them (Burbidge 1993). In this sense, Hegel is a true pioneer with regard to uncovering the unconscious operations of mind. Because there are so few scholars who are prepared to work out in full detail the logical processes and transitions through which we actually think and reason, it is not surprising that Hegel's dialectical logic challenges traditional analytic philosophy (see Hylton 1993).

Although it was Hegel who first argued systematically that reality is a process of becoming, it is Alfred North Whitehead (1925, 1929) who is most commonly referred to as the founder of process philosophy. A mathematician, logician, philosopher of science, and metaphysician, Whitehead argued that the fundamental activity that comprises and underlies the cosmos is the eternal process of experience constituted through a dynamic flux of microcosmic orderly events, many of which are non-conscious organizations defined as "drops of experience, complex and interdependent" (PR 18). For Whitehead, process reality comprises a motion of energy continuous throughout nature and is the fundamental building block of the universe. Whitehead's system emphasizes the creative and novel advance of nature as a continuously transforming and progressive series of events that are purposeful, directional, and unifying. Like Heraclitus and Hegel before him, Whitehead stresses the dialectical exchange of oppositions that advance the process of becoming.

Whether we accept Heraclitus' dictum: "Everything flows" (*panta hrei*), Hegel's dialectic of spirit, or Whitehead's process philosophy, the notion of transformation, evolution, and change is the one constant that underlies all reality. This is especially applicable to psychic structure, interpersonal relations, and the psychosocial contexts that constitute our cultural and sociopolitical conditions. Although the notion of the self-as-process has been discussed among some contemporary psychoanalytic thinkers (see Joseph 1989; Kristeva 1986), the significance of a psychoanalytic process psychology has been virtually ignored. In what follows throughout this book, I hope to stimulate a conceptual shift in our understanding of several key psychoanalytic tenets – from classical metapsychology to contemporary intersubjectivity theory – by systematically introducing process dialectical thought.

Dialectical psychoanalysis relies largely on Hegel's general logic of the dialectic and its reappropriation for psychoanalytic investigation without, however, inheriting the onerous baggage associated with Hegel's entire philosophical system. We need not adopt Hegel's overall system, much of which is non-relevant and/or incomprehensible to psychoanalytic sensibility, in order to appreciate his science of the dialectic and the logical operations in which it unfolds. The adoption of his dialectical method may complement or augment existing theoretical innovations that enrich our understanding of mind and human nature. Juxtaposed to current paradigms that lack systematization or cohesiveness, a revisionist reappropriation of Hegel's dialectic may fill this gap in psychoanalytic inquiry.

With increasing tolerance for philosophical exploration, process psychology could open up new directions in psychoanalysis. Process psychology is an essentialist position – not as fixed or stagnant attributes and properties that inhere in the structure of a substance, object, or thing – rather like a dynamic flux of transmuting and self-generative, creative processes having their form and content within the dialectic of becoming.[1] Process is the essence of mental life insofar as, if it were removed, psychic reality would perish. As I intend to show, the appropriation of process psychology within psychoanalysis rests upon a proper appreciation of the dialectic. Understanding the dynamics and nuances of Hegel's dialectical method can lead to advances in theory, practice, and applied technique. Not only does the dialectic apply to the nature of intrapsychic development, interpersonal relations, and social and institutional reform but it also has direct implications for the consulting room. The dialectic informs the very nature of intersubjectivity, the therapist-patient dyad, group dynamics, organizational development, and the historical progression of culture. This issue is of particular importance when examining the dialectical polarities, forces, and operations of the mind outlined by various psychoanalytic theories and how the field itself may be shown to participate in this dialectical process. From this vantage point, Hegel's dialectic is especially helpful in understanding the historical development of psychoanalysis (see Mills 2002a, 196–200). Psychoanalysis, like Hegel's conception of *Geist*, is a process of becoming.

HEGEL'S DIALECTICAL METHOD

Geist is customarily translated as "spirit" or "mind," both of which have entirely different meanings in English. There is no appropriate German equivalent for the word "mind," which, in English, is often associated with brain dependence and its emergent mental processes, the field of cognitive neuroscience, and consciousness studies, while "spirit" often evokes religious sentiments, theology, mysticism, or supernatural ideology. Neither is the case in German; therefore, making any translational meaning of *Geist* is difficult at best. In general, psychoanalysis would possibly contend that the dialectical modes of *Geist* are themselves differentiated and modified forms of the mind as part-objects or self-states maintained by unconscious motivations or through ego manoeuvres of intentionality, dissociation, or defence,[2] yet this does not fully capture Hegel's project. *Geist* intimates a complex integration of an individual's personality as a whole, including one's intellect, character, ethical or moral sensibilities, and personal maturity as well as the refinement of one's more basic desires or passions. Therefore, *Geist* assumes a developmental ascendance and transcendental quality that embodies an ideal value, human striving, or pursuit. To refer to a person's *Geist* is to import a measure of respect for its superiority because it implies a cultivated degree of self-awareness through laborious developmental achievement. *Geist* is also a term used for God – *der heilige Geist* (the holy ghost) – thus it commands a degree of exaltation. Of course, this process is not the same for all people. While all human beings are primarily equal with regards to their soul (*Seele*), in German a term devoid of any religious connotations whatsoever, people are vastly different when it comes to their *Geist*. This is why, when we refer to spirit, we signify the coming into being of a privileged form of subjective transcendent awareness, hence the coming to presence of pure self-consciousness. Hegel wants to extend this notion of the individual mind to the collective element of humankind realized through our historical cultural practices, which define the process and progress of civilization. Therefore, spirit is the unification of nature within mind, hence body and spirit instantiated throughout history and objective social life as the sublimation of human subjectivity. In psychoanalytic language, *Geist* is the amalgamation of Freud's tripartite division of the psyche within the process of actualizing its rational, aesthetic, and ethical potential, hence a triumph of the human spirit.[3]

Although Hegel is one of the most prodigious and influential thinkers in the history of philosophy, his dialectical method remains one of his least well understood philosophical contributions. While philosophers have made scores of commentaries and interpretations of Hegel's dialectic (Beiser 1993; Burbidge 1981; Hibben 1984; McTaggart 1964), some interpreters have gone so far as to deny Hegel's method (see Solomon 1983) or to render it opaque, simplistic, and imprecise (Forster 1993). Hegel's dialectical method governs all three dimensions of his overall philosophical system, namely, the *Logic*, the *Philosophy of Spirit*, the *Phenomenology*, and the *Philosophy of Nature*. The dialectic serves as the quintessential method not only for explicating the fundamental operations of mind but also for expounding the nature of reality.

Hegel's philosophy of mind or spirit rests on a proper understanding of the ontology of the dialectic. Hegel refers to the unrest of *Aufhebung* – customarily translated as "sublation" – a continuous dialectical process entering into opposition within its own determinations and thus raising this opposition to a higher unity, which remains at once annulled, preserved, and transmuted. Hegel's use of *Aufhebung*, a term he borrowed from Schiller but also an ordinary German word, is to be distinguished from its purely negative function, whereby there is a complete cancelling or drowning of the lower relation in the higher, to also encompass a preservative aspect. Therefore, the term *aufheben* has a threefold meaning: (1) to suspend or cancel, (2) to surpass or transcend, and (3) to preserve. In the *Encyclopaedia Logic*, Hegel makes this clear: "On the one hand, we understand it to mean 'clear away' or 'cancel,' and in that sense we say that a law or regulation is canceled (*aufgehoben*). But the word also means 'to preserve'" (EL § 96, *Zusatz*).

Hegel's dialectical logic has been grossly misunderstood by the humanities and social sciences largely due to historical misinterpretations dating back to Heinrich Moritz Chalybäus, an earlier Hegel expositor, and unfortunately perpetuated by current mythology surrounding Hegel's system. As a result, Hegel's dialectic is inaccurately conceived of as a three-step movement involving the generation of a proposition, or "thesis," followed by an "antithesis," then resulting in a "synthesis" of the prior movements, thus giving rise to the popularized and bastardized phrase: thesis-antithesis-synthesis. This is not Hegel's dialectic; rather, it is Fichte's (1794) depiction of the transcendental acts of consciousness, which he describes as the fundamental principles (*Grundsätzen*) of thought and judgment.[4] Yet this phrase is a crude and mechanical rendition of Fichte's logic and does not properly convey even his project. Unlike the meaning that Fichte assigns to the verb *aufheben*, which he defines as to eliminate, annihilate, abolish, or destroy, Hegel's meaning signifies a threefold activity by which mental operations at once cancel or annul opposition, preserve or retain it, and surpass or elevate its previous shape to a higher structure.

Fichte's dialectic is a response to Kant's (1781) *Critique of Pure Reason*, in which Kant outlines the nature of consciousness and addresses irreconcilable contradictions that are generated in the mind due to inconsistencies in reasoning.[5] For both Kant and Fichte, their respective dialectics have firm boundaries that may not be bridged. Hegel, on the other hand, shows how contradiction and opposition are annulled but preserved, unified, and elevated within a progressive evolutionary process. This process of the dialectic underlies all operations of mind and is seen as the thrust behind world history and culture. It may be said that the dialectic is the *essence* of psychic life for if it were to be removed, consciousness and unconscious structure would evaporate.

Aufhebung is itself a contradiction: the word contradicts itself. Thought as a contradiction is constituted in and through bifurcation, a rigid opposition as antithesis. Thus, as a process, reason cancels the rigid opposition, surpasses it by transcending or moving beyond it in a higher unity, and simultaneously preserves it in the higher unity rather than simply dissolving it. The preservation is a validating function under which opposition is subsumed within a new shape of development. Reason does not merely set up over and against these antitheses, it does not merely set up a higher unity; rather, it also reasons a unity precisely through these opposites. Thus, the dialectic has a negative side and a positive side. This is echoed in Hegel's (1812) *Science of Logic*:

> "*To sublate*" has a twofold meaning in the language: on the one hand it means to preserve, to maintain, and equally it also means to cause to cease, to put an end to. Even "to preserve" includes

a negative element, namely, that something is removed from its immediacy and so from an existence which is open to external influences, in order to preserve it. Thus what is sublated is at the same time preserved; it has only lost its immediacy but is not on that account annihilated. (SL 107)

In order to dispense with this erroneous yet well conditioned assumption about Hegel's dialectic, which is uncritically accepted as fact, I wish to reiterate myself. When psychoanalysis refers to dialectics, it often uses Fichte's threefold movement of thought in the form of thetic, analytic or antithetic, and synthetic judgments, giving rise to the crassly misleading phrase: thesis-antithesis-synthesis – a process normally and inaccurately attributed to Hegel;[6] or it describes unresolvable contradictions or mutual oppositions that are analogous to Kant's antinomies or paralogisms of the self. It is important to reemphasize that Hegel's dialectic is *not* the same as Kant's, who takes contradiction and conflict as signs of the breakdown of reason, nor is it the same as Fichte's, who does not explicate the preservative function of the lower relation's remaining embedded in the higher. Furthermore, when psychoanalysts and social scientists apply something like the Fichtean dialectic to their respective disciplines, the details of this process are omitted. The presumptive conclusion is that a synthesis cancels the previous moments and initiates a new moment that is once again opposed and reorganized. But the synthesis does not mean that all previous elements are preserved or that psychic structure is elevated. In fact, this form of dialectic may lead to an infinite repetition of contradictions and conflict that meets with no resolve.

Thomas Ogden and Irwin Hoffman are two of the most frequently noted analysts who regularly employ the term "dialectic" in their writings, but they have yet to explain with any precision what they mean by this term. Take, for example, Hoffman's (1998) use of the term "dialectical constructivism." Is he merely invoking the interplay of opposition? Does this imply difference only or also similarity? How about the role of symmetry, continuity, measure, force, unity, and/or synthesis? Is there a certain function to the dialectic, a movement, a process, or an emergence? If so, how does it transpire? Does it follow formal causal laws or logical operations or is it merely acausal, amorphous, accidental, invariant, undecidable, spontaneous? Is it universal or merely contingent? Is it a necessary and/or sufficient condition of interaction or perhaps just superfluous? Is his approach Socratic? Does he engage the impact of Kant, Fichte, Schelling, Hegel, or Marx on his view of the dialectic? He does not say. Hoffman emphasizes "ambiguity and construction of meaning." While I do not dispute this aspect to the dialectic, I am left pining for more explanation. Is there a teleology to the dialectic, or is everything "unspecified and indeterminate" (xvii), what he tends to emphasize in a move from "symbolically" well defined experience to "underdeveloped, ambiguous" features of mental activity or the lived encounter, to "totally untapped potentials" (22)? Here Hoffman seems to be equating dialectics with construction qua construction. We might ask: Constructed from what? Cursory definitions are given, such as the implication of "an interactive dynamic between opposites" (200n2), but he ultimately defers to Odgen (1986, 208): "A dialectic is a process in which each of two opposing concepts creates, informs, preserves, and negates the other, each standing in a dynamic (ever changing) relationship with the other." This definition emphasizes dichotomy, polarity, and change but does not articulate how opposition brings about change, let alone what kind (e.g., progressive or regressive [given that change annuls the concept of stasis]) or whether this process is subject to any formal laws, pressures, trajectories, or developmental hierarchies. Nor does it explain how opposition emerges to begin with. The question of whether there is an elevating, ascending aspect to psychic development is also left unanswered. Is the dialectic presumed to be the force behind all construction? And, if so, why? Furthermore, the dialectic is reduced to "two opposing *concepts*" rather than being acknowledged as an ontological valence in the mind that underlies being or the process of presencing.

While Hegel's *Science of Logic* has attracted both philosophical admiration and contempt, we need not be committed to the fine distinctions of his Logic, which is confined to the study of consciousness. What is important for process psychology, however, is understanding the essential structure of the dialectic as sublation denoted by these three simultaneous movements: at once they cancel or annul, transcend or surpass, retain or preserve. These are aspects of every transmogrification. The dialectic as process is pure activity and unrest, which acquires more robust organization through its capacities to negate, oppose, and destroy otherness; yet, in its negation of opposition, it surpasses difference through a transmutational process of enveloping otherness within its own internal structure and, hence, elevates itself to a higher plane. Not only does the psyche destroy opposition but it also subsumes and preserves it within its interior. Death is incorporated, remembered, and felt as it breathes new life in the mind's ascendance towards higher shapes of psychic development: it retains the old as it transmogrifies the present, aimed towards a future existence it actively (not pre-determinately) forges along the way. This ensures that dialectical reality is always ensnared in the contingencies that inform its experiential immediacy. Despite the universality of the logic of the dialectic, mind is always contextually realized. Yet each movement, each shape of the dialectic, is merely one moment within its holistic teleology, differentiated only by form. The process as a whole constitutes the dialectic, whereby each movement highlights a particular piece of psychic activity that is subject to its own particular idiosyncratic expressions and modal contingencies. As each valence is highlighted in its immediacy or lived-experiential quality, it is merely one appearance among many in the overall architectonic process of its own becoming.

Hegel's dialectic essentially describes the process by which a mediated dynamic begets a new immediate. This process not only informs the basic structure of his *Logic*, which may further be attributed to the general principle of *Aufhebung*, but this process also provides the logical basis to account for the role of negativity within a progressive unitary drive. Hegel's use of mediation within the movements of thought is properly advanced in the *Science of Logic* as well as in the *Encyclopaedia Logic*, which prefaces his anthropological and psychological treatment of spirit in the *Encyclopaedia of the Philosophical Sciences*. In the *Logic*, thought initially encounters Being, which moves into Nothing and then develops into Becoming, first as the "passing over" into nothing, second as the "vanishing" into being, and third as the "ceasing-to-be," or passing away of being and nothing into the "coming-to-be" of becoming. Becoming constitutes the mediated unity of "the unseparatedness of being and nothing" (SL 105). Hegel shows how each mediation leads to a series of new immediates, which pass over and cease to be as that which has passed over in its coming to be until these mediations collapse into the determinate being of *Dasein* – its new immediate. Being is a simple concept, while Becoming is a highly dynamic and complex process. Similarly, *Dasein*, or determinate being, is a simple immediacy to begin with, which gets increasingly more complicated as it transitions into Essence and Conceptual Understanding. It is in this early shift from becoming to determinate being that you have a genuine sublation, albeit, as a new immediate, spirit has a new beginning.

In Hegel's treatment of consciousness as pure thought represented by the *Logic* (1812), as well as his treatment of history in the *Phenomenology of Spirit* (1807) and anthropology and psychology in the *Encyclopaedia* (1817/1830), spirit – whether it be the mind of each individual or the collective psyche of the human race – continues on this circular albeit progressive path, conquering each opposition it encounters, elevating itself in the process. Each mediation leads to a new beginning, and spirit constantly finds itself confronting opposition and overcoming conflict as it is perennially engaged in the process of its own becoming. In the *Logic*, the whole process is what is important as reason is eventually able to understand its operations as pure self-consciousness; however, in its moments, each mediation begets a new starting point that continuously reinstitutes new obstacles and dialectical problems that need to be mediated, hence eliminated. But thought always devolves or collapses back into the immediate.

The process by which mediation collapses into a new immediate provides us with the logical model for understanding the dynamics of the mind. An architectonic process, *Geist* invigorates itself and breaths its own life as a self-determining generative activity that builds upon its successive phases and layers, which form its appearances. Mind educates itself as it passes through its various dialectical configurations, ascending towards higher shapes of self-conscious awareness. What spirit takes to be truth in its earlier forms is realized to be merely a moment. It is not until the stage of pure self-consciousness, what Hegel calls Absolute Knowing as conceiving or conceptual understanding,[7] that spirit finally integrates its previous movements into a synthetic unity as a dynamic self-articulated complex whole.

PHILOSOPHY OF MIND

Hegel's theory of mind is comprehensively outlined in the *Philosophy of Spirit* (*Philosophie des Geistes*), which is the third part of the *Encyclopaedia of the Philosophical Sciences*. Unbeknownst to psychoanalysis, Hegel provides one of the first theories of the unconscious. He gives most of his attention to the unconscious within the stage of presentation (*Vorstellung*) in the context of his psychology, thus belonging to the development of theoretical spirit or intelligence, what we today refer to as cognition. Here Hegel refers to a "nocturnal mine (*Schact*) within which a world of infinitely numerous images and presentations is preserved without being in consciousness" (*EG* § 453). Hegel explains that the night-like pit – what I have translated as the *abyss* – is a necessary presupposition for imagination and for higher forms of intelligence.[8] While these more complex forms of the psychological would not be possible without the preservation of images within the unconscious mind, the unconscious is given developmental priority in his anthropological treatment of the soul (*Seele*).

For Hegel, the unconscious soul is the birth of spirit that developmentally proceeds from its archaic structure to the higher order activities of consciousness and self-conscious rational life. Like Freud who tells us that the ego is a differentiated portion of the It (*Es*), the conscious ego is the modification and expression of unconscious activity. For Hegel, the soul is not an immaterial entity (*EG* § 389) but, rather, the embodiment of its original corporeality, the locus of natural desire (*Begierde*) or drive (*Trieb*).[9] As the general object of anthropology, Hegel traces the dialectical emergence of the feeling soul from the abyss of its indeterminations. At first unseparated from its immediate universal simplicity, it then divides and rouses itself from its mere inward implicitness to explicit determinate being-for-self. Through a series of internal divisions, external projections, and reinternalizations, the soul gradually emerges from its immediate physical sentience (*EG* § 391) to the life of feeling (*EG* § 403) to the actual ego of consciousness (*EG* § 411), which becomes further refined and sophisticated through perceptual cognition, conceptual understanding, ethical self-consciousness, and rational judgment, the proper subject matter of the *Phenomenology*.

It is beyond the scope of this immediate synopsis to give a comprehensive overview of Hegel's philosophy of mind, a subject I have already attended to with precision (see Mills 2002a); rather, I provide a terse introduction that is germane to the discussion at hand. Hegel's Philosophy of *Geist* is presented in the third division of the *Encyclopaedia*, which is further subdivided into three sections: namely, "Anthropology," "Phenomenology," and "Psychology." Each subdivision is concerned with explicating a specific feature and function of the mind. Because Hegel's dialectical method is suffused throughout every aspect of his philosophy – the dialectic being the force and substance of spirit – each domain of psychic life may only be properly understood in relation to the whole. For our purposes, however, it becomes important to see how the epigenesis of the mind proceeds from its most primordial unconscious configurations to the higher-order functions of rational self-conscious understanding. In many remarkable ways, Hegel's treatise on mind parallels the psychoanalytic account of psychic development, a topic that will preoccupy us shortly.

Anthropology

As the general object of anthropology, that is, what is common to us all regardless of culture, race, or gender, Hegel is first concerned with the universal significance of the soul (*Seele*). Here the role of the unconscious in Hegel's conceptualization of the mind is an integral aspect to his philosophy. In fact, the higher forms of mental life emanate from an unconscious ontology and are the phenomenological development of an original unconscious ground. For Hegel, as too for psychoanalysis, the unconscious is the foundation of the soul, which, in turn, is the foundation of consciousness and self-conscious *Geist*. In the "Anthropology" section of the *Encyclopaedia* Hegel painstakingly delineates how the soul dialectically evolves from an original unconscious unity. Through a series of internally mediated dynamics beginning as natural soul (*EG* § 391), spirit "awakens" as a sentient feeling subject (*EG* § 403), which further becomes actual (*EG* § 411) as the ego of consciousness, the initial subject matter of the *Phenomenology of Spirit*. The unconscious soul undergoes development through its own dialectical divisions, projections, and reconstitutions as the mediated process of sublation, entering into opposition with its natural corporeality and elevating its unconscious structure to the form of ego. Thus, ego development is constituted through unconscious process.

It is in his anthropological treatment of the soul that Hegel first refers to the unconscious as a nocturnal abyss (*Abgrund*). The unconscious abyss is integral to spirit's constitution, which remains a central aspect in the normative psychological operations of conscious intelligence or cognition. But the abyss is also responsible for the primal activity behind *all* appearances of spirit, which Hegel affirms is always "unconsciously busy" (*SL* 36). Thus the unconscious becomes the indispensable psychic foundation of mind. While the unconscious soul is sublated as ego, it nevertheless remains a repository for lost, alienated, or conflicted shapes of spirit. Therefore, the soul becomes the locus in both mental health and psychopathology.

Phenomenology

The Greek term *phainomenon* (φαινόμενον), derived from the verb *phainein*, means "to appear" or "to show itself." Although the dialectical activity of the soul may be considered the pre-phenomena of the unconscious mind, the ego of consciousness is that which appears. The "Phenomenology" section of the *Encyclopaedia* presents Hegel's mature theory of consciousness. For Hegel, consciousness (*Bewußtsein*) is distinct from the soul (*Seele*) and the unconscious (*Unbewußte*), yet it is an outgrowth of the unconscious soul and is hence the soul's appearance as ego (EG § 413). As self-certainty, the ego is an immediate being or subject that must confront its otherness, namely, its object (i.e., external reality). Before the ego encounters the sensuous world, the ego's object is the natural soul itself, what the ego was but no longer is in its presently evolved shape. By confronting the natural soul and denying its suffocating restriction to the corporeal, the ego attains its own independence, no longer belonging to the soul but to itself. Because the ego thinks in a form that is now proper to it, its determinations are no longer of the soul but of consciousness.

Hegel states that the goal of spirit as consciousness is to raise its self-certainty to truth, that is, to pure self-consciousness (EG § 416), the culmination of absolute reason. Like the soul's progressive dialectical unfolding, this requires spirit to advance through a series of mediated shapes beginning with (1) *consciousness* as such, where sense, perception, and understanding have a general external object; then (2) *self-consciousness*, where desire, self-recognition, and universal self-consciousness as ethical revelation have the ego as its general object; culminating in (3) *reason* as the unity of consciousness and self-consciousness determined in and for itself – the Concept (*Begriff*) of spirit as pure conceiving or absolute understanding (EG § 417).

Like the natural soul's initial apprehension of its immediacy as feeling, Hegel (1807) consistently views the initiation of consciousness as the manifestation of "the sheer *being* of [a] thing" (PS § 91) to a subject that only knows its simple and immediate sense-certainty. Consciousness as such is sensuous consciousness of a sensory presentation or impression with spatial and temporal singularity, simply the "*here* and *now*," what Freud would call a "thing-presentation." But, as Hegel continues to describe this process: "Strictly speaking this belongs to intuition" (*EG* § 418). Here we may see the inextricable interrelatedness between consciousness and the psychological operations of cognition and intelligence that preoccupies Hegel's later psychological analysis of the ego. The ego senses that something is external to it by reflecting into itself, thus separating the material from itself and thereby giving it the determination of being.

The initial divisions of the *Phenomenology* may be viewed by contemporary standards as a treatise on the unfolding operations of cognition. Here Hegel sees three primary stages of consciousness: (1) sensuous, (2) perceptive, and (3) understanding, with consciousness itself being the first of three developmental stages of the phenomenological unfolding of spirit resulting in self-consciousness and reason, respectively. In immediate sensuousness – the empty or abstract recognition of being – consciousness then proceeds to grasp the essence of the object, which it accomplishes through perception. The essence becomes the general object of perceptive consciousness, where singularity is referred to universality. There is, in fact, a multiplicity of relations, reflectional-determinations, and range of objects with their many properties that perceptive consciousness apprehends, discerns, and brings into acuity (*EG* § 419). Having mediated the immediacy of sense-certainty, sensuous thought-determinations are brought into relation with concrete connections to universals. This constitutes "knowledge" (*EG* § 420). The linking of singulars to universals is what Hegel calls a "mixture" that contains their mutual contradictions (*EG* § 421). Because singularity at this juncture is fused with universality, contradictions are superseded in understanding consciousness. Understanding consciousness is the unity of the singular and the universal in which the general object is now raised to the appearance of being for the ego. In the next stage, self-consciousness arises where the ego takes itself as its own object, and the process continues until spirit wins its truth in pure reason.

Hegel's exposition of consciousness is essentially an exposition of the functions of the ego that Freud (1933a), although conceived differently, also finds as the object of science (*SE* 22:58). Both Hegel and Freud were preoccupied with the science of subjectivity and articulating the universal processes that govern mental functioning. It is for these reasons that psychology becomes an essential ingredient in our appreciation of the abyss and why Hegel needed to address the psychological processes of cognition within his *Philosophy of Spirit*.

Psychology

In the "Psychology" section of the *Encyclopaedia*, Hegel gives greater consideration to the cognitive processes of attention, perception, imagination, fantasy, memory, thought, and understanding. For Hegel, psychology is primarily restricted to the domain of intelligence under the direction of reason, but this does not impede the psychological significance of the soul and the phenomenology of consciousness. Intelligence is what Hegel calls a "spiritual faculty" (*EG* § 445), not as a fixed or ossified agglomeration but, rather, as a malleable and determining process of cognition. Intelligence finds itself as naturally determined, insofar as it cannot will itself not to think, and is concerned with the empty form of finding reason. Cognition is therefore the concrete dialectical activity of mediating and unifying objects with concepts.

As the psychological forms of subjective mind unfold, the unconscious abyss is the primary domain of this activity. Hegel points out that intelligence follows a formal course of development to cognition, beginning with (1) intuition of an immediate object (*EG* § 446); moving to (2) presentation (*EG* § 451) as a withdrawal into the unconscious from the relationship to the singularity of the object and thus relating such object to a universal; leading to (3) thought (*EG* § 465), in which intelligence grasps the concrete universals of thinking and being as objectivity. In the stage of intuition or sensation as immediate cognizing, intelligence begins with the sensation of the immediate object, then alters itself by fixing attention on the object while differentiating itself from it. It then posits the material as external to itself, which becomes intuition proper. The second main stage of intelligence as presentation (*Vorstellung*) is concerned with recollection, imagination, and memory, while the final stage in the unfolding of intelligence is thought, which has its content in understanding, judgment, and reason.

Although Hegel isolates the contingent events of each intellectual manoeuvre, he stresses the point that each operation of intuiting, representing, and so forth is merely a moment of the totality of cognizing itself, which underscores the necessity of rational thought (*EG* § 445). Throughout the various substages of each operation, he shows the mutual relations between contingency and necessity and how one dialectically prepares the path for the other.[10] First, intelligence has an immediate object; second, material is recollected; and third, it is rendered objective.

In Hegel's anthropological, phenomenological, and psychological treatment of spirit, the dialectic becomes the underlying dynamic force behind all activities of mind. Hegel cogently shows how the mind undergoes a formal and logical process of development, starting from the most primitive features of unconscious activity that subsequently sublate into higher cognitive organizations. Because the dialectic informs every aspect of mental life, from the normative to the pathological, Hegel underscores the notion that psychic reality is a process of becoming.

The primacy of process becomes an essential component of psychodynamic thought. Because the dialectic remains the rudimentary force behind the appearances of mind, Hegel's process philosophy bears a direct relation to psychoanalytic psychology. As I intend to show, psychoanalysis may profit from adopting a dialectical approach to theory and method. And with the introduction of process psychology it may entertain new possibilities.

THE DIALECTICAL STRUCTURE OF THE UNCONSCIOUS

As we have seen, the dialectic informs both the inner organization and the content of the unconscious. It is the dialectic that provides the self with intrapsychic structures and functional operations that can never be reduced or localized, only conceptualized as pure activity. This pure activity of the dialectic as Self is constantly evolving and redefining itself through such movement. The unconscious forms of spirit (initially as feeling soul and then as ego) are thereby necessarily organized around the dialectical activity of the abyss. These structural operations, however, are not mechanistic, reductionistic, or physical as in the positivist framework often attributed to traditional psychoanalysis.[11] They are mental, telic, and transcendental, always reshaping the psyche's inner contours and the internalized representational world within the night of the mind.

For Hegel, the unconscious is pure process, a changing, flexible, and purposeful activity of becoming. As the very foundation, structure, and organizing principles of the unconscious are informed by the movement of the dialectic, the architecture of the abyss is continuously being reshaped and advanced as each dialectical conflict is sublated by passing into a new form that, in turn, restructures, reorganizes, and refurbishes the interior contours of the core self, hence our soul. Therefore, the structural foundations of the self are never static or inert but always in dialectical movement, having its origin and source in the unconscious, revamping the texture in which spirit emanates. This self-generating dialectical movement of the unconscious is the evoking, responding, sustaining, and transcending matrix that is itself the very internal system of the subjective mind.

The concept of the self as subject in Hegel is of particular importance in understanding the unconscious nature of mind. Essentially, the stage-by-stage (phase) progression of the dialectic is expressed as an epigenetic theory of self-development. Through sublation, Hegel's notion of the self encompasses a movement in which the subject is opposed to an object and comes to find itself in the object. This is exemplified by Hegel's treatment of the master-slave dialectic outlined in the *Phenomenology*, but this process is well prepared during the soul's unconscious development. During the dialectical movement of spirit, the subject recognizes or discovers itself in the object. This entails the mediation of its becoming other to itself, with the reflection into otherness returning back to itself. The process of the development of the self is, like that of the soul, a process of differentiation and integration. As seen in the *Logic*, Being is characterized by an undifferentiated matrix that undergoes differentiation in the dialectical process of Becoming, which, in turn, integrates into its being that which it differentiated through its projection, reclaiming it and making it part of its internal structure (also see Levin 1992, 51). This is the very fabric of projective identification and is, as I later show, the ontological movement underlying the progression of mind. The outcome of the integration is once again differentiated then reintegrated; unification is always reunification. Therefore, spirit comes to be what it already is, the process of its own becoming.[12]

AMENDMENTS TO HEGEL'S DIALECTIC

Process psychology takes as its presupposition the ontology of the dialectic, which may be said to account for the most primordial and archaic activity of psychic life as well as the most cultivated achievements of human consciousness. The dialectic becomes the internal thrust of the mind and social life that manifests itself through innumerable intrapsychic and intersubjective forms, from primitive unconscious processes to reason, politics, social governance, aesthetics, and ethical self-consciousness. Yet Hegel's dialectic has been criticized by psychoanalysis for not accounting for certain forms of psychopathology despite offering a logic based on the primacy of conflict. Hanly (2004) recently charges Hegel with the inability to account for fixation and regression within development, thereby challenging the legitimacy of Hegel's dialectic, which privileges an upwardly progressive process of sublation. While Hegel (1817/1830) did in fact offer an abbreviated theory of mental illness that he largely adumbrated in the "Anthropology" section of the *Encyclopaedia* (§§ 406–8), therefore accounting for the role of the autism of the soul, subjective fixation, psychosis, melancholia, regression, and neurotic withdrawal back to previous phases of psychosocial development, he is committed to a teleology of spirit that is oriented towards vanquishing opposition on its ascent towards higher forms of unification. Although Hanly is technically wrong to claim that Hegel cannot account for the dynamics of defence and disease, the dialectical acclivity of mind in the service of progressive unification is an overarching thrust of his logic and thus overrides his stipulations, which allow for fixation, regression, and psychopathology, a topic that remains of some debate within mainstream Hegel scholarship. In order to ameliorate these problematics, process psychology departs from Hegel's dialectic in three significant ways:

1 There is a regressive element to the dialectic that competes with its upward, natural acclivity towards wholeness;
2 There is a selective aspect to the retention and preservation of previously vanquished experiential forms the mind encounters that are temporally and contextually realized; and
3 The Idealist notion of Absolute Knowing as pure self-consciousness is displaced by a contemporary theory of mind that realizes the limits to the epistemology of self-consciousness. These necessary correctives have direct implications for the concept of teleology, which I address in turn.

Dialectical Regression

The logical progression of the dialectic constitutes an architectonic model of natural development: each progressive level of maturation draws on, is informed by, and builds upon its previous experiences and internal structural organizations. An essential aspect behind this development involves a generic movement in which a mediated dynamic begets a new immediate. Each mediated immediacy builds on its previous shapes and experiences and thus explains how opposition, violence, and subsumption are responsible for a unitary progressive drive towards higher forms of consciousness. For Hegel (1807), this dialectical progression constitutes the process behind the historical evolution of the human race, the nature of self-consciousness and culture, and the exalted forms of reason actualized as art, religion, and philosophy. Although Hegel's dialectic allows for inversion and withdrawal back to earlier shapes of subjective unconscious experience (see Berthold Bond 1995; Mills 1996, 2002a), his overall treatise on objective spirit – or the collective socialization processes that govern our civilized laws and practices – does not allow for regression because the subjective features of individual minds are already surpassed and integrated within a higher objective stage of the dialectic. This creates a problem for Hegel when attempting to account for psychopathology on a collective scale.[13]

Process psychology observes that mental life, whether individually or collectively realized, is always under the pressure of internal and external destructive forces and contingencies that can potentially and regressively pull higher developmental achievements back towards earlier instantiations. While it may be said that human consciousness and collective identity in general are oriented towards psychic holism, either in actuality or in fantasy,[14] they equally have the potential to relapse into degenerative and pathological states of inversion, abrogation, fixation, and flight to earlier developmental configurations of psychic experience – configurations once found to be familiar, simpler, and less threatening. In fact, we see a split or divide within the dialectic's unitary monistic structure, with one side thrust towards acclivity, the other towards descent; one towards unity, the other towards disunity; one towards progression, the other towards withdrawal. The double orientation of desire becomes an important variable that influences the dialectical progression of mind, a progression that is particularly sensitive to the subjective exigencies or environmental disruptions (e.g., parental attachments, societal forces, trauma) that influence its developmental path and variations. This dual centre, or double edge, of desire is particularly influential in the regressive features that inform psychopathology.

Temporal Mediacy

Psychic organization has a simultaneous temporal relation to the past, the present, and the future: (1) The past is subsumed and preserved within the dialectic; (2) the present is immediate mediated experience; and (3) the future (in contemplation and fantasy) becomes a motivational-teleological impetus. Temporal experience is a mediational realization informed by this threefold relation of the dialectic; however, each domain may have competing and/or opposing pressures that affect the other modalities at any given moment. In other words, each locus may pressurize, extol, invade, usurp, coalesce, and/or symbiotically conjoin with others within their interdependent dynamic system. But each domain also has the potential to have a subjective surge, voice, or lived reality of its own, despite the force and presence of the other two realms. Yet such seemingly autonomous moments of individualized expression are relegated to the broader systemic processes that operate within the dialectic. In psychoanalytic language we may refer to these differentiated experiences as a multiplicity of self-states that are operative on parallel or overdetermined levels of functioning within the ontologically monistic, supraordinate agency we call the self.

The past we may refer to as *archaic primacy*, thus emphasizing the primordial nature of our historicities, including a priori ontological conditions (e.g., constitutional, social, and cultural forces) as well as that which is subjectively (i.e., qualitatively) and developmentally experienced (both consciously and unconsciously). The present we may call *immediational presence*, thus stressing the phenomenology of the concretely lived experience presented as subjectively mediated immediacy. The future we describe in terms of *projective teleology*, which captures the future trajectory of the dialectic of desire, which stands in relation to a valued ideal, goal, or purposeful wish-fulfilment. These three simultaneous facets of temporal mediacy are the dialectic in action in the moment of bringing the past and future to bear upon its present, or immediate, experience.

Archaic primacy holds a privileged position in the psyche since the mind always presupposes and draws on the past in all its mental forms, derivatives, contents, and operations. For instance, cognition necessarily requires memory, which is the *re-presented* past, just as the mind itself requires certain ontic relations and neurobiological processes in order for there to be cognition at all. Similarly, the unconscious is lost presence, namely, that which had formerly presented itself (albeit in its multiply derived forms) but had receded back into the abyss. Archaic primacy has a stipulated degree of causal influence over the driving force behind the dialectic since the archaic is always brought to bear upon presentational encounters that the subject confronts as immediacy, which furthermore stimulates projections of a future. The way the present is incorporated into the past, however, may be highly conditional and idiosyncratic given the unique contingencies that comprise the nature of subjectivity, either individually or intersubjectively actualized. It is in this sense that the preservative aspect of the dialectic may be very *selective* in what it retains. Although we may generally say that the past is preserved in some way as our personal thrownness or developmental historicity (and this is certainly true of world history), there are certain elements that are – or have the potential of becoming – omitted or negated and forgotten altogether, hence denied, dissociated, and/or repressed. That is, certain aspects of archaic primacy may not be operative, mobile, or causally expressive and, perhaps, may fizzle-out entirely in the psyche, while other aspects are selected, secured, harboured, and sustained (especially as segregated schemata within unconscious life). The selective retention feature, or operation, of the dialectic points towards the enactment of determinate choice within the experiential contingencies encountered in the process of becoming.

Immediational presence is the subject's experience in the here-and-now and how it engages what is presented before it (either as an internal event or stimulus, or as an external imposition), thus affecting thought, feeling states, somatic schemata, action, and their unconscious resonances. The immediacy of the lived encounter highlights the context and exigencies that influence the phenomenology of the emotional, cognitive, and unconscious aspects of personal experience. Although the present immediacy of the moment is largely a conscious phenomenon, immediate experience is already a mediated dynamic by virtue of the fact that archaic primacy already suffuses every lived encounter, which is superimposed as its facticity. This means that unconscious processes always saturate every conscious experience and become a mediatory screen, or template, in which the world is received and perceived, thus influencing the contingency and construction of experience.

Selective retention is particularly operative within immediational presence as the dialectic executes certain determinate choices in its relation to mediated experience. In effect, the dialectic seizes upon certain aspects of the environment and/or internally evoked stimuli from the press of archaic primacy while refuting, denying access to, or limiting the range of others that may exert certain degrees of determinate influence on immediate experience – the range and signification of each mediated choice having resonance in the dialectic's trajectory and orientation towards the future. In every immediate encounter, the past and future are summoned and converge on the present: the archaic superimposes past form and content; the future superimposes goal-directed intentionality in mediate thought and action.

Projective teleology is the future trajectory of a desired state of affairs (as fantasy, wish, intention, or purpose) that is stimulated by presentational processing or mediatory interventions, thus instigating the teleological projection of a goal-directed aim. Like archaic primacy and immediate experience, the projected future may entertain a certain selective aspect to the retention and/or locus of experience that takes place within the transformative, progressive dialectical processing governing each mediated dynamic. Mediation stands in relation to lack, which the subjective mind experiences as desire. In all three spheres, however, there exists the primacy of ambiguity, uncertainty, and context, for real and virtual time may be suspended within the mind and experienced as radically dissociative, incongruent, and/or atemporal, yet nevertheless wed to contingency.

At any given moment of experience, the past and future are ontologically operative on subjective immediacy, bringing to presence the vast configurations and pressures of unconscious affect, wish and defence, and the corresponding conscious reality that is simultaneously evoked and represented. Archaic primacy, immediational presence, and projective teleology are functional aspects of orienting the psyche towards dialectical growth, even if regression and decay are activated consequences of the lived encounter. Here it becomes important to keep in mind that the dialectic works radically to compress and transpose its multiple instantiations within its mediatory functions. There are multiple realities and self-states that coalesce, intermingle, compete, vie for attention and expression, and do battle for supremacy in forcing themselves on the pressure cooker we call mind. The teleological motives of the dialectic are therefore informed by the threefold presence of the past, the present immediate context, and the future trajectory to which it is oriented, each vector exerting its own source and constraint on the inner constitution of the subject.

The Ubiquitous Nature of Contingency

We are currently entering a Hegel Renaissance among contemporary academe. At the same time the value of his ideas are attracting increasing praise, there are equally many dissenters, a philosophical critique of which is beyond our current focus (see Cullen 1988 for a review). Generally, Hegel's system has been both revered and criticized based on its insistence on rational necessity (Taylor 1995), its absolute idealism (Desmond 1989; Pippin 1989), and its broader implications for ethical, religious, and political-state reform (Harris 1997; Pinkard 1994), just to name a few. Although there is enormous debate among Hegel scholars regarding the legitimacy, viability, value, and logical congruity of his system, these nuances do not concern us here. Process psychology only need be committed to Hegel's general logic of the dialectic and the implications it generates for understanding and substantiating psychoanalytic thought.

On this point, process psychology does not need to espouse the metaphysical notion of an Absolute or ultimate standard or principle of the Ultimate in order to defend the dialectic. While human subjectivity may be oriented towards an ultimate goal or purpose of its own choosing, the route to which can take many radically different forms, we need not evoke a predetermined, innate mechanism or Aristotlean teleology directing the outcome of such yearnings. In fact, Hegel's dialectic is truly appealing for this reason: it does not profess a model of mind in which future events are causally determined. On the contrary, the future is brought about by dialectical mediations that must constantly confront the borne contingencies of the moment. This means that immediacy is radically contextual and relative to the multiple overdetermined influences that converge and simultaneously superimpose themselves on subjective and relational experience, which is, in turn, dialectically mediated by mind. It is only by looking back at the process (Findlay 1971), that we can discern an intelligible pattern or dynamic of becoming, one that is nevertheless free from predetermination. This is a major theoretical advantage of dialectical psychoanalysis that many deterministic notions of psychic reality preclude: mind is ultimately free.[15]

However, for Hegel, like Aristotle before him, Logic was ultimately God as pure thought thinking itself into existence and then dispersing its being into nature, only to emerge out of, evolve, and discover itself as Mind, the coming into being and fulfilment of itself as pure reason.

Drawing on Schelling's and Spinoza's notion of the Absolute, the Absolute was the standpoint of pure knowing, conceiving, or conceptual understanding as comprehending the evolution of nature, mind, and human civilization. For Hegel, *Geist* achieves pure knowing. Perhaps psychoanalysis would simply say this is an illusory wish, but one that we nevertheless strive for and value as civilized people in search of truth and meaning. Perhaps this is the illusion behind science itself, which strives to obtain an objectively unadulterated epistemology. For process psychology, the Absolute is an unattainable abstract ideal. Yet, despite his emphasis on absolute knowing, Hegel never strays from his insistence that the dialectic is always mired in contingency and context. From the standpoint of contingency always saturating Being, there is no absolute standard apart from such conditions of which, at any given time, we may only have partial knowledge and control. This ensures that the context in which human subjectivity finds itself will be a decisive factor in how the dialectic encounters and engages experience. In this way, dialectical psychoanalysis holds an advantaged position in that the complexifications and overdetermined processes that constitute the nature of psychic reality, intersubjectivity, and social order can never be fully understood without involving their relation to one other.

TOWARDS DIALECTICAL PSYCHOANALYSIS

Throughout this prolegomena I have been mainly concerned with explicating the primordial constituents of psychic activity that are ontologically operative within all forms of human experience. In this preview to a system, I have emphasized the value of a process metaphysics for enriching the theoretical domain of psychoanalytic inquiry. Process is predicated on the ontology of the dialectic and is the necessary a priori condition for all intrapsychic, relational, and intersubjective life. Although the implications of process thought are broad and are applicable to many key psychoanalytic concepts, including clinical practice, a proper appreciation of such remains the task of future work. It is my hope that psychoanalysis will begin to acknowledge the import of philosophical justification as a harbinger for the unity of logic and science.

In what follows, I intend to show how psychoanalytic process psychology offers a logic of the dialectic that proves useful in explaining the rudimentary development of the psyche, from its most basal ontological conditions to its most robust configurations and complexifications. In our quest for understanding the origins of psychic reality, it becomes increasingly important to emphasize how mind and intersubjective relations are constituted through process.

With its current focus on consciousness, psychoanalysis is straying from its original contribution to the behavioural sciences. We need to properly return psychoanalysis to a study of the psyche, which is first and foremost concerned with deciphering the mysteries of the unconscious mind. It is only after a proper appreciation of the ubiquity of unconscious mental economy that we can turn our attention to consciousness, for unconsciousness conditions all psychic reality.

Dialectical psychoanalysis grants the radicalization of the unconscious and, in this sense, advocates a return to Freud. *The unconscious is the house of being that fuels and sustains all psychic reality.* The radicalization of the unconscious privileges the reality of the unseen, the unthought – that is, unformulated, pre-reflective unconscious experience – over conscious, reflective rational life. Although conscious experience comprises the crux of our waking lives, and we have every reason to exalt its status, we cannot decentre the force and value of unconscious process and its indelible pressures, presence, and emergence into perceptual thought and behavioural revelation. To do so would either commit psychoanalysis to the grave fallacy that haunts Descartes' *cogito* as a transparent agency capable of indubitably clear and distinct (i.e., unconcealed) ideas or it would plummet psychoanalysis into vogue materialism commensurate with contemporary approaches to the philosophy of mind and cognitive neuroscience.

Unconsciousness precedes consciousness, hence it maintains ontological and logical priority, thus, all conscious phenomena emerge from an unconscious a priori ground. Consciousness becomes the manifestation of unconscious structure, which never completely yields to conscious cognition or the deliberate intentionality of the will. Even in our most cultivated forms of self-consciousness, which inform our aesthetic, ethical, social-political, spiritual, and intellectual pursuits, the unconscious reigns supreme as the reality of the life within.

In considering our methodological approach to psychoanalytic inquiry, I am initially concerned with explicating the most elemental ontological features of mind dialectically proceeding towards more cultivated and robust forms of mental organization. Dialectically moving from the most primitive to the more refined, from inner experience to external encounters, further underscores the architectonic and epigenetic processes that construct and define psychic constitution.

Psychic reality is always changing within the universal dialectical forms that shape its interior content and structure. But before we venture into expatiations on unconscious development, wish and defence, ego and reality (the subject matter of future chapters), we need to address the question of the *origin* of psychic reality, a topic that has only been peripherally acknowledged by psychoanalysis. Attempts at discerning origin have crudely relied on materialist notions of mind-brain dependence or on deducing a priori ontological principles, a full account of which has been more properly attempted by the neo-Platonists, theosophists, and the systematic philosophies of Kant, Fichte, Schelling, and Hegel. However, within psychoanalysis, the question of origin finds its full significance in Freud. Freud is the only theorist who attempts to show how the ego of consciousness arises from differentiated states of unconscious organization, while all subsequent psychoanalytic thinkers have historically focused on psychic development from the standpoint of consciousness (i.e., from infancy onward). This is a much neglected area of psychoanalytic scholarship, and, despite Freud's adumbrated attempt, it is one that remains incomplete and inconclusive.

Freud is unjustly vilified in contemporary psychoanalytic circles for his metapsychology, largely, I argue, because many do not take the time to understand what he actually says in his texts. This is, in part, due to mistranslations that have sullied his original insights and have been accepted as "fact" within the psychoanalytic literature. This has further subjected Freud to the dismay of reactionaries, who have unfairly used him to launch their own platform of ideas, many of which are compatible with his general psychological theories. As we embark on deciphering the question of psychic origin, we may use Freud as our guide, even though we will eventually part company with him in many significant ways. In our dialectical approach to conceptualizing the psyche, we need to repeatedly orient ourselves to the fundamental questions Freud generates in his attempt to explain unconscious modification, possible answers to which may be offered through process thought. In order to show the internal consistency and explanatory power of the dialectic, we must begin our inquiry with the most rudimentary of all questions concerning intrapsychic dynamics, namely: When does the unconscious come into being? Here enters the "genesis problem."

· 1 ·

Spacings of the Abyss

In the *Timaeus*, Plato gives us an account of the creation of the universe as an intelligible eternal presence forever inexpressible. Here origin is before beginning, before the syllable, beyond language, a mobile image of eternity – archaic, fleeting, ineffable. No doubt Freud was in search of this universal when he said that the unconscious is timeless, hence not bound to the finite world of lived consciousness, what Plato would call the shadows of appearance. What we know of the world and of our experiences is merely a copy – an image – of what is eternal and true, a changing reflection of changelessness. Plato refers to this origin as a *chora*, a psychic receptacle of all generation that he equates with a nurturing maternal process born of a paternal spring, a receiving principle he metaphorically compares with birth – the vessel between container and contained.[1] Derrida conceives of this *chora* as a spacing, a divide that eschews classical ontology, a non-place that resists representation. We know it as translation, a filtering produced from choreographies of presubjectivity. Perhaps this signifies an archetypal knowing (*intellectus archetypus*), what Kant anticipated as "obscure presentations" (*dunkele Vorstellungen*), or what Leibniz called *petits perceptions*. And what is this womb of which we may figuratively speak, the nurse of all becoming? Unbounded generative generativity conditioned on nothing, yet conditioning everything.

How can we think about genesis prior to beginning, prior to the sign? This requires us to suspend our modal logic, developmental sequelae, and linear chronologies for a diachronic way of conceiving of pre-experience, namely, the unconscious ontology of presubjective life. In the history of philosophy there have been many endeavours to represent the unrepresentable. The Gnostics refer to the ineffable as the "Alien" or "first Life," the pre-beginning or primal ground, the "Other." Boehme speaks of the *Ungrund* as a ground without a ground. Fichte refers to psychic genesis as a pure act of posit or self-assertion. Schelling conceives of an unconscious will that creates as it cognizes. And Hegel views the essence of spirit (*Geist*) as emanating from the realm of an unconscious soul, only to have Freud, a century later, systematically delineate its force, loci, and organizational structure.

Psychoanalysts are, for the most part, unaware of the origins of psychoanalysis, that is, of its prehistory – the ancient pursuit of the question of soul. Freud knew all along that Plato was the first psyche-analyst and that is why he could not elude Plato's tripartite theory of the soul in his final model of mind. Over one hundred years later we are still rethinking the unconscious. Here returns the question of origin.

FORMS OF UNCONSCIOUSNESS

It becomes difficult to sustain the question of unconscious genesis and, specifically, of how the unconscious comes into being, without revisiting what has already been advanced by many learned thinkers on the philosophy of the unconscious. Despite the cornucopia of literature on the subject, I have yet to see psychoanalysis properly engage how unconsciousness comes into being in the first place; that is, how it is born. Throughout this book I provide an extended treatment of this subject through a revisionist lens and engage classical and contemporary analytic theorists on the question, meaning, and forms of unconsciousness. There are some philosophers who still question the existence of the unconscious, largely in their rebuttals, which are based on their misinterpretation of Freud. Careful analyses of these criticisms show that, for the most part, they are based on a selective and circumscribed reading that misguidedly collapses the unconscious into material reduction, or hypostatization. From these renderings, the unconscious is often portrayed as a bestial entity or independent being that directs the motives, contents, and behaviours of the subject's mind against its own will, as if it were controlled by a homunculus. We can see why Freud, due to his reified language, invites misinterpretation. Here the unconscious is often envisioned as "a cauldron full of seething excitations" (SE 22:73). Yet Freud is clear that he approaches such descriptions based on "analogies" for, as with Plato, we may only use metaphor to capture that which is unrepresentable. Freud's more casual and informal explanations of unconscious process are based on his public lectures, which were specifically written for a lay audience uneducated in his novel theories. One must look at his entire theoretical corpus to properly appreciate his evolving and sometimes contradictory speculations on the nature of unconscious mentation.

Philosophers such as Alasdair MacIntyre (1958, 71–9) wish to dispense with the unconscious as something "substantial," what Wittgenstein (1958) calls "mythology," as does T.R. Miles (1994, 20), who denies its existence as "something real." More recently, Charles Elder (1994, 3) wishes to relegate the unconscious to the domain of a conceptual construct determined by grammar and the linguistic conventions, rules, and practices pertaining to "conditions of meaning, not to fact." While MacIntyre and Miles bar any ontological significance to the unconscious because, as an entity, they claim it does not exist, Wittgenstein and Elder make the unconscious a linguistic construct subject to the laws of signification, cultural definition, and grammatical relativism. What I propose is that both of these criticisms – namely, ontological negation and conceptual creationism – are insufficient attempts to explain away the phenomenology of our encounters with unconscious experience. In short, these arguments, as many psychoanalysts would contend, are defensive manoeuvres designed to either crassly disavow or omnipotently abort the primordial peril of what the unconscious represents or symbolizes. Hence, they are motivated to harness some sense of control over its archaic presence by making it into a mere *concept* rather than accepting it as an ontological force in the mind. Here we may appreciate the logic of denial: when we are psychically threatened, either something *must* not – indeed, *does* not – exist or it is transformed through fantasy into something we can manage. But denial only works insofar as reality is suspended, while fantasy collapses under the weight of its own unsustainable illusions.

Critics discredit any attempt to ascribe substance to the unconscious as a being-in-itself, let alone as a being-for-itself. Arguments that denounce the unconscious as an entity are antiquated not because they don't have merit but, rather, because they are misattributed to Freudian theory. It is important to note that Freud could not settle for this view either (the details of which I address shortly). But this does not negate the unconscious as an ontological category, nor does it negate the fact that the unconscious has being or presence, that it appears through modification of its original form, and that it is constantly evolving and revamping its own internality in its encounters with conscious experience, external reality, biological pulsions, and the forces of culture. There are many forms of unconsciousness that deserve our careful differentiation and delineation in terms of their inherent constitutions, internally derived organizations, modes of expression or appearance, and qualitative experiential complexity. Before systematically engaging these axiomatics, these variances within invariances, I first attempt to lay out my propositions concisely enough to alert the reader to what I argue for in the work that lies ahead.[2]

Ontological Propositions

I. The unconscious is real, that which is, that which is the case.

I.1 When we speak of the unconscious (*Unbewuβt*), we are not speaking of a substance, material object, or independent entity that is ontologically distinct or separate from other aspects of mind, only something that is structurally differentiated, categorically separated, and modified in its organizational form from other mental elements and spacings.

I.1a It is not a thing that has a different or separate essence from other forms of mental order or flux, only something that maintains a logical and developmental priority over all other aspects of psychic functioning.

I.2 *Das Unbewuβt* is process.

I.2a Process is self-presencing, hence it subsumes being not as a static object and not as a denoted place but, rather, as being-in-becoming with multiple layers of internal division, turbulent organization, and vectors of instantiation all situated within a comprehensive complex holism, each demarcated by its contextual variances and moments within a unifying totality.

I.2b Such particularity within universality constitutes the plurality of invariance.

II. The unconscious is a *spacing*, a transitioning dynamic self-organizational process of systemic complexity.
(i.) As a movement, as becoming, constituting actual occasions.[3]
(ii.) As eccentric self-relation.

II.1	(iii.) A spreading out or dispersal of pure interiority. (iiia.) A dispersal that disrupts space: Inwardized, exteriorized, temporalized. (iv.) As figuration, as schematism. (v.) As expanse. Inserting intervals within interstices, producing infinite extensions, yet always on the threshold of occlusion.
II.1	Unconscious spacing does not displace or suspend ontology, only abridges it through a delimitation of presencing that hovers within and over its own divide.
II.1a	More specifically, unconscious mentation is a *series* of spacings, each punctuated by temporal moments of chaos, symmetry, self-alienation, self-recoverability, and reconstitutive order.
II.1b	Unconscious spacing is a vacillation or meandering throughout terrains of experiential variance forcefully and agentically attempting to secure a psychic clearing where it may reside.
II.2	Spacings are not topographies or localities of psychic territory; rather, they are fluid and mobile processes that produce various emergent states of manifestation.
II.2a	Spacings release presence, disrupt inwardness, destabilize pure self-relation.
II.3	Unconscious spacings are tantamount to eternity, to the abysmal, to timelessness actualized in time, a diachrony suspended as we know it consciously.
II.3a	In such suspensions we find abridgement and fissuring, compartmentalization but no compartment, confinements within unboundedness – all transpiring from an archaic primacy that informs the ground of spacing as such.
II.3b	Spacing is a historicizing that has no location, only motional content – fleeting, amorphous. In this spacing, all locality is lost or misplaced, resisting anchorage, disavowing concretization.
II.3c	Transience is its home.
II.4	Unconscious spacing is dislocation within difference socially arranged by its own spreading, a spacing that nevertheless must be secured.

II.4a	In this gap, this fissure, there is an opening that is still occlusive – that is, closed intensely (*occludere*) – thus remaining blocked, obstructed, foreclosed.
II.4b	Here lies a lapse, a blank, a discontinuity, almost without limit. We may call this occlusive opening – this gap in being – the *abyss*.
III.	The unconscious is the house of being, the primordial ground (*Grund*) of all psychic reality.
III.1	The abyss is the original psychic receptacle, both container and contained, the wellspring of all generation.
III.2	The abyss is non-consciousness, that which lacks consciousness yet incorporates it. That is to say, it incorporates phenomenal contents and affective reverberations of lived experience imprinted or evoked via consciousness.
III.2a	This archaic receptacle is a repository for lost shapes of consciousness (e.g., images, perceptions, and sensuous data pre-reflexively encoded and recorded).
III.2b	It is also a repository for regressive shapes of experience under defensive, adaptive, or pathological currents, whether forgotten, repressed, dissociated, segregated, compartmentalized, sequestered, unformulated, disformulated, unrealized, unsymbolized, presymbolized, or unarticulated.
IV.	The abyss is realized, hence made actual, through the spacings of the dialectic.
IV.1	At once annulled, surpassed, and preserved within an increasing rotary, dynamic totality, unconscious process is governed by an overarching, superordinate structure it forges from within its own interiority as determinate teleology gathered from the primordial ground of its own ontic givenness.
IV.1a	That is, unconscious agency finds itself in ontical relation to its own facticity, hence a self-relatedness, which it emerges from and transposes as it seizes upon its own capacities for generative creativity.
IV.2	The dialectic of internal division, separation, expulsion or externalization, and reincorporation (as recoverability and reconstitution) is the generic dynamic of projective identification that becomes the epigenetic, architectonic function of mind sublating psychic structure.

IV.2a	The unconscious is a relational matrix of progressive interacting systems or communities of determinate (causal) order. These social systems emanate from the same essence and modify their form and content to potentially take on autonomous (functional) states of organization, each with various degrees of freedom, vectors, and specificity of action governed by the interpenetrating superordinate generative thrust of the dialectic.
IV.2b	Dialectics within dialectics – multiply infinite, symmetrical, contradictory, overdetermined.
IV.2c	The generative dialectic is at once ascending and progressive in its drive, hence oriented towards higher forms of self-realization yet capable of reverting and descending in its aim, especially if contextual contingencies invoke regressive or pathological forces.
IV.2d	This duality of desire is the inherent nature of *pathos*, of death and destruction that saturates the psyche, a primal conflict that propels the engines of the dialectic in the pursuit of both growth and decay.
IV.2e	In generation, this is the positive significance of the negative.
IV.2f	In degeneration, we find aberration, disease.
IV.3	In its procreative moment, the abyss is capable of self-mutational generation and internal division oriented towards higher tiers of experiential unification that seek semblances of holistic integration.
IV.3a	That is, the unconscious is oriented towards sublation as a self-articulated complex totality.
IV.3b	Paradoxically, such epigenetic synthetic, generative activities ontologically transpire within a pressurized system of psychic division, difference, and fragmentation governed by conflictual order.
IV.3c	In other words, the unconscious is borne from negation and chaos, which lends structure, procession, symmetry, and continuity to the fluctuations, shifts, discontinuities, and transitions that characterize the phenomenal spacings of psychic interiority.
V.	The unconscious experiences and acquires its own arcane *episteme* and institutes its own semiotics through its own self-generation as the coming into being of pure subjectivity.

V.1   The abyss is originally, archaically organized as a corporeal, sentient, and affective pulsation of psychical processes that arise from desire and transpire within the spacings of unconscious embodiment.

V.1a   The abyss emerges from its material facticity to find itself as an unconscious ego with agentic functions that perform basic economic, defensive, and synthetic tasks of seeking gratification, mollifying anxiety, securing internal zones of safety, and achieving tension reduction.

V.1b   It evolves from an elementary teleonomic function and becomes more teleological and self-determinate as it gains in developmental vitality and qualitative organization.

V.1c   The unconscious ego is the seat of agentic, telic, and synthetic activities of mind.

V.1d   The agentic ego forms the basic operations of mediating internal and external dynamics; discerning relata; establishing memory and representational schemata; registering perceptual stimuli; signalling affect, desire, wish, and defence; linking associational networks of sense data and mediatory cognitive actions to signs and signification in the internal webs of relations; establishing a combinatory of signifiers in the abyss; generating the imaginary and encoding the symbolic; moderating tension and pressures that arise within the psyche; and performing economic functions inherent to our corporeality expressed as sentient, embodied urges and needs that stem from our teleonomic evolutionary past.

V.2   Unconscious mentation first ensues as desire, as being-in-relation-to-lack, then as cognizing apperception, which is the implicit pre-reflective, non-propositional awareness of itself as a sentient desirous being and that which experiences itself as self-certainty, a mediatory *unconscious self-consciousness*.

V.3   Unconscious desire is structurally inscribed with a semiotic that leaves its mark, or trace, as it developmentally unfolds into more robust forms of complexity that inform conscious experience.

V.3a   Unconscious subjectivity ontically prepares the way for encounters with the maternal object, familial attachments, the external environment, community, and culture, thereby processing subjective esoteric experience, assimilating the

	formal acquisition of language, and assigning and transposing signification subject to its own eccentric organizing principles.
V.3b	Unconscious semiotics are translinguistic, extralinguistic, and expressed through the idioms of desire.
V.3c	Although semiotic functions originally transpire before consciousness and concept formation, they are expanded and enriched by linguistic and symbolic structures.
V.3d	Therefore, the unconscious ego enlists both pre- and postlinguistic processes as it transforms desire into phantasy and thought.
V.3e	Desire as being-in-relation-to-lack remains the semiotic prototype of all other forms of signification.
V.4	Unconscious semiotic experience evolves from appetitive desire to organize itself within pulsional, somatic, affective, perceptual, and conceptual schemata that originally derive from primordial apperceptive sentience. Unconscious schemata elevate in content and form to linguistic order, self-consciousness, and the highest forms of meaning, including intellectual, aesthetic, ethical, spiritual, and rational life.
V.5	The unconscious ego attains a personal sense of agency and intentionality only after conscious experience has been incorporated and sufficiently organized by the abyss over the course of developmental and social maturation.
V.5a	Prior to conscious experience and the recognition of possessing a personal I or self-identity, unconscious agency is merely a formal operation constituted by desirous-affective mediatory cognizing activity with a rudimentary pre-reflective awareness of its existence as immediate self-certainty.
V.5b	In other words, the unconscious ego originally takes itself as an object, not as a subject, the latter belonging to higher developmental stages of self-consciousness.
VI.	Unconscious agency precedes consciousness, precedes language, precedes the signifier
VI.1	Formal unconscious processes: (i.) Logically and developmentally unfold prior to the emergence of consciousness in the nascent mind. (ii.) Are ontologically prepared a priori to anticipate and engage conscious experience.

(iii.) Are the psychic ground for all other forms of mentation to arise.

(iv.) Are the structural foundations of the ontogenesis of the self.

VI.1a Consciousness is the manifestation of unconscious structure.

VI.1b Consciousness is the architectonic development and sublation of primitive or nascent mind.

VI.1c Objects of consciousness, sense perception, emotive experience, familial life, communal and cultural forces, particularity, contingency, context, and linguistic order enrich and expand the abyss, but the abyss allows for higher forms of experience to emerge, materialize, and thrive to begin with; hence, all aspects of lived phenomenology are ontologically prepared by unconscious a priori faculties.

VI.2 The unconscious is not created by consciousness; consciousness is merely co-extensive with its original form.

VI.2a To say that the unconscious is created or interpretively constructed by consciousness alone is to displace its ontological primacy as the creative generative force behind mental life.

VI.3 Consciousness is a secondary awakening and sublated creative force that expands unconscious life and, in many ways, becomes more dominate and pervasive over mental organization, yet it is capable of becoming truncated by unconscious dynamics that prevent sublation and inform psychopathology.

VI.3a Conscious perception is the sublation of unconscious apperception.

VI.4 Culture and language are categorically subsumed within the prehistory of the individual and are thrown as part of our social ontology informing the archaic primacy of the human race.

VI.4a Language, culture, and signification are not realized until they are introduced by conscious experience; hence, these particular contents of universality are not introduced to the subjective mind until the ego enters the phenomenal world.

VI.4b They are only operative as formal a priori orders or ontological categories.

VI.4c	The unconscious epistemic ego originally neither knows these orders exist nor feels their direct impositions in the solipsistic chambers of foetal (in utero) and neonatal symbiotic life.[4]
VI.4d	The specificities of social ontology are gradually introduced once the transition to consciousness has been initiated.
VI.4e	The ontological demand and significance of culture and language may precede the birth of each subject or individual mind, but it does not become transposed onto the incipient ego until the ego is plunged into conscious life.
VI.4f	Hence, the formal presence of a social ontology does not negate the internal presence of an unconscious agency that ontically prepares, encounters, resists, and embraces such formal structures that are part and parcel of the exogenous forces imposed by external reality.
VII.	The abyss is foreclosed from absolute knowing, a *mysterium*, yet is open to logical, philosophico-theoretic investigations.
VII.1	We do not have direct phenomenological access to unconscious experience, but we come closest to apprehending unconscious phenomena during sleep, dreaming, temporal discontinuity, twilight transitions, and altered states of consciousness when perceptive awareness has become inverted, inwardly directed, disrupted, and subjected to the operations of agentic governance that appears foreign.
VII.2	We come to experience unconscious spacings as their phenomenal appearances or framings, hence as windows into particular psychic territories that are momentarily exposed or highlighted, like a snapshot in time.
VII.2a	Such framings are not copies of unconscious reality; rather, they are alterations of original form – not as they exist in their pure essence – for the simple fact that our conscious epistemology is itself the modification and transmogrification of unconscious knowing, an original or primal epistemology.
VII.2b	Unconscious essence *appears* as forms of consciousness, including normative and pathological instantiations.
VII.2c	It is these normative and pathologic variances that lend empirical credibility to the existence of dynamic unconscious motivations routinely observed in the clinical encounter.

GAPS IN BEING

Freud favours spatial metaphors when describing the unconscious. In his *Introductory Lectures* (1916–17) he states that "the unconscious is a particular *realm* of the mind with its own wishful impulses, its own mode of expression and its peculiar mental mechanisms which are not in force elsewhere" (SE 15:212, emphasis mine). Here we are alerted to the unconscious as a spacing rather than as a discrete being or entity. In "The Unconscious," Freud (1915b) gives us several justifications for the concept of the unconscious. What is remarkable is that he anticipates criticisms that are still used by contemporary psychoanalysts who question the very credibility of the concept itself. Freud knew that we could never observe the unconscious directly, neither empirically nor phenomenologically, and that, therefore, any epistemology could only appeal to rational inquiry, supported by clinical evidence, in order to validate a particular conceptual scheme, which, in keeping with the true notion of science, would always be open to theoretical revision and modification when new data became available. In fact, Freud supports my claim that unconscious process may only appear as phenomena, which, he specifically says, have "undergone transformation or translation into something conscious" (SE 14:166). Dreamwork, parapraxes, symptoms – all are elements of translation. As early as the dreambook, he states: "Everything conscious has an unconscious preliminary stage" (SE 5:612). For Freud, the unconscious is ontologically necessary to explain what conscious experience does not: namely, the "gaps" (*lückenhaft*) in understanding linkages between internal experience, "psychical acts" (*psychischen Akte*), and meaning. Furthermore, he concludes, "the assumption of there being an unconscious enables us to construct a successful procedure by which we can exert an effective influence upon the course of conscious processes, [and] this success will have given us an incontrovertible proof of the existence of what we have assumed" (SE 14:167). For Freud, not only is the unconscious a necessary category for the theoretical explanation of mental phenomena but it is also essential to structuring and orienting therapeutic technique.

Freud appeals to many sensible facts that legitimate his theses:

1 What is accessible to consciousness at any given time is mainly in a state of latency awaiting evocation or retrieval: therefore,

not everything mental or psychical can be logically equated with consciousness.
2 The unconscious accounts for unexplained disruptions in psychical continuities.
3 It aids in our potential understanding of the mind/body problem, specifically challenging psychical-physical dualism.[5]
4 It adds explanatory depth to the normative processes of mental activity and the emergence of clinical symptoms or "pathological facts."
5 The concept of the unconscious eschews the ontological quandary of how multiple states of consciousness can exist yet not be accessible to awareness when, by definition, they should be if they are elements of consciousness.
6 It also enables us to infer the existence of another mind based upon our own self-reflective epistemology and can, indeed, infer specific processes in others that we cannot readily detect in ourselves. In other words, we can posit and infer mental processes in others based upon clinical observations that we cannot observe in our own psyche because we often cannot take our own mind as a direct object of study with the same degree of objectivity due to the fact that we are subjectively blinded by our own competing and defensive agendas.

What Freud ultimately suggests "comprises" the essence of the unconscious are "acts" (*Akte*) or "processes" (*Vorgänge*) (SE 14:172). Freud describes these acts or processes in many detailed ways, from his early theoretical musings (designated by depth metaphors depicted on a topographic continuum interfacing the *Ucs.*, *Pcs.*, and *Cs.* Systems) to his later so-called structural theory, or what I would call his process theory, which more elaborately articulates modified yet interrelated realms of mental life that occupy the various spacings and dynamic operations of mind. Despite the substantial theoretical revisions Freud made in his lifetime, he never relinquished his conviction that:

1 Unconscious process embraces rather than repudiates contradictions (hence, it does not know or obey the law of non-contradiction).
2 It emphasizes primal desire based on a simple economy of pleasure.
3 It is timeless in its spacings.
4 It replaces external reality with its own interior phenomenology.

5 The unconscious knows no negation, no bounds, no limits – only *immediacy*, tarrying in a sea of eternity.
6 There is no sense of valuation or moral sensibility in what is primus, that is, in what is most archaic. It is infinite, just as repressed content is "virtually immortal" (SE 22:74).

What Freud is describing is an unconscious phenomenology of presence; more specifically, a principle of self-presencing. The unconscious is container and contained, an infinite holding bin of unlimited and unbounded sedimentation that mixes with its own internal spring, which becomes the formal condition of receiving and incorporating objects and their relational patterns. But the spring must well up before it can bubble forth, flow, and swallow – even engulf – the manifold of consciousness. At first it trickles – even gushes – exhibiting its self-presence, the coming into being of unconscious structure. And how do we know such unconscious self-presencing? Here enters punctuation, what we may call the *rip*.

What is of particular interest is how Freud argues that the concept of the unconscious is "necessary" (*notwendig*) and "legitimate" (*legitim*) because it accounts for "gaps" or discontinuities in consciousness. Here the notion of spacing is demarcated as a hole or a lack in being. Throughout many of his writings, Freud is fond of saying that, contra Kant, the unconscious is "timeless." What Freud means is that the unconscious does not process events in lived time, in linear-sequential experiential order; hence, there is no beginning or ending, duration or succession. Nor are such experiences "altered by the passage of time" (SE 14:187), just as they are not very interested in external reality. But this lack is also diachronic, that is, it presents itself as absence in time – the *abstinence* of phenomena – as a lapse with no discernible location. It becomes merely otherness – foreign, unknown, fleeting, ineffable. Time is eclipsed in this spacing *through* this dislocated location. It is precisely this gap, split, suspension, lapse, or disruption of psychical continuity that prevents the temporal registration of phenomena, but this does not annul the notion of unconscious temporality. On the contrary, the mere notion of conceiving of the unconscious as an experiential spacing allows for temporality to operate ontologically without encumbering the workings or domain of unconscious phenomena, which are insulated and self-insulating. Here we may envision a solipsistic underworld of internal objects and their relata, which the unconscious attempts to sequester from the intrusions of external reality. Subject to the dominion of the pleasure-principle governed by the adroit and imaginative hands of unconscious fantasy,[6] the abyss devolves into desirous appetitive pulsation.

For the French school of psychoanalysis, lack becomes the sine qua non – the signifier – of the unconscious. Indeed, Lacan bases his whole critique of the Freudian unconscious on Freud's notion of "gaps" in being. In his 1964 seminars, Lacan continuously points towards the gap, split, hole, scar, or slit as the signifier of the non-realized, that which "holds itself in suspense" in the area of what we might call the "unborn" (FC 23). Freud knew that we could never come to know the noumena directly, so, as with the Kantian categories, we come to know them as phenomena. Thus, Lacan focuses on what first presents itself to us in this gap, namely, that of "impediment," leakage, puncture. Something breaks, is dislodged, bursts, disrupts our coherence, our stream of consciousness, which we discover through the surprise. This leads Lacan to say that discontinuity "is the essential form in which the unconscious first appears to us as a phenomenon" (FC 25). Discontinuity is the idiom of desire, the cut in consciousness, where "something other demands to be realized." It is the whisper of lack.

But why *lack*? Would not such a rupture yield presence, even abundance? Lacan would say what is presented is a "want-to-be." In our analysis of the presence of the present we must not overlook what is lacking in presentation. The stroke, slit, or gash "makes absence emerge," the disquieted voracity of desire. The unconscious always manifests itself in the gap, in the fissure that divides the subject within itself, a vacillation between barring and clearance, effacing and retention, striking out and reinstating, an opening into the neither regions, where all continuity is foreclosed by adventures of the unexpected. Here consciousness is maimed by its original form.

In his characteristically obscure language, Lacan situates the ontology of the unconscious in a spacing – the gap – that appears to us in its marbled shapes. But when asked to speak of this gap, which he readily concedes is an "ontological function" (namely, that which is "most essential"), he says something most unanticipated and contradictory: "The gap of the unconscious may be said to be *pre-ontological*" (FC 29). What does this mean? Lacan specifically says that the emergence of the unconscious "does not lend itself to ontology." Here Lacan wishes to clude metaphysics: the unconscious does not lend itself, does not offer or furnish itself to being. That is to say, it does not occupy a concrete location, instantiation, or presence, "neither being, nor non-being," only the unrealized. What Lacan declares without properly arguing is that something more primordial, more archaic precedes the emergence of the unconscious. But what could precede being? We know it as puncture, as an aperture in the abyss. And what could predate this crevice or gulf in being that opens its vent to conscious experience as quickly as it vanishes back into its lair? Lacan does not ask about pre-beginning, he merely presumes it. The gap presents itself as lack through laceration, both a cavity or entranceway as well as a latch or recess, both revealed and occluded, a hinge simultaneously opened and shut. It is at the structural level of the signifier – revealed in the stutter, the broken utterance, the slip – that the lapse enters a chiasm, the intersection between signifier and signified.[7] But what antecedes the signifier? Here Lacan is silent. Perhaps he would say the Real (*réel*), hence the impossible, itself occlusive.

UNFORMULATED EXPERIENCE, DISSOCIATION, AND THE MULTIPLICITY OF THE SELF

Contemporary perspectives on the unconscious vary widely in scope and content, from displacing the dynamic unconscious altogether, to appealing to neuroscience, to favouring postmodern sensibilities that subordinate psychical processes to language. Here unconscious spacing is conceived in a different way, namely, as dissociated or "unformulated experience," what Lacan would call the "unrealized." Donnel Stern and Philip Bromberg are proponents of such redirective shifts in contemporary thought. However rich in clinical utility, these theoretical postulates are not without serious conceptual omissions, particularly when raising the question of psychic genesis. Since poststructuralism, it has become enticing to boil everything down to language as the original instance (as in the insistence or authority of the Letter),[8] or cause, of human experience, given over to us from the facticity associated with our being thrown into a cultural ontology. Stern (1997, 7) supports the claim – and here is the great mistake – that "all experience is linguistic." Because linguistic experience is by definition developmentally acquired through consciousness, this claim immediately annuls the possibility that the unconscious could predate linguistic phenomena. It further implies that any notion of unconscious experience would necessarily be a corollary to consciousness and created or forged after the birth of the conscious subject. This is also a similar theoretical conviction to that held by Gargiulo (2004, 5) who claims that the unconscious is "created by interpretation." Laplanche (2004, 463) is even more specific when he says: "It is repression which actually creates the unconscious." Gargiulo (2006, 467–8), however, takes this position to the extreme: "before a patient communicates and/or before an analyst interprets, there is no dynamic or repressed unconscious worth speaking of." These positions do not account for the archaeological (*arkhē*, beginning, and *logia*, knowledge) or anagogical (*ana*, a return to the most ordinary, principle, or elemental) motifs, historic-developmental sequelae, or logical a priori forces that prepare the coming into being of conscious experience. Hence, they do not address the question of origin.

Stern's view is so radically postmodern that he is willing to grant language the status of being and volitional agency without realizing the *aporiai* he generates. Not only does he believe that "language is the condition for experiencing" (Stern 1997, 7), but he opines that "In a very real sense, language uses us; *we* have become the utensils. Language is no longer our tool, but the very crucible of our experience" (9). Here Stern has us believe that, somehow, language is a hypostatized entity that has a will and intentionality all of its own. But *words don't think*, they don't possess agency, they have no intentionality, they direct nothing. Words in themselves are impotent and meaningless without a mediational subject who directly assigns them signification and meaning. Stern is so committed to the linguistic turn that he is willing to deny prelinguistic or preverbal psychic organization, drives, somatic structures, affective resonance states, emotive and/or intuitive processes, and translinguistic and extralinguistic experience, such as aesthetic or spiritual sensibilities, for the belief that nothing can "possibly come before words" (16). Stern, like many postmoderns, wishes to claim that, because we are thrown into a culture, place, and time that define and give shape to our experiences, language is causally determinative and nothing precedes it. But how does he account for the way the unique individual subject comes to acquire language in the first place and to incorporate linguistic phenomena (e.g., phonemes, words, and sentences) through the idiosyncratic mental operations of registering, processing, mediating, and ordering its matrices of unconscious meaning structures? Just because culture and language exist prior to the birth of a human subject does not mean that psychic genesis is born from the outside and superimposed on the interior of the experiential organic agent. On the contrary, psychic reality is at first an internally emergent and expansive self-organizing system that must mediationally encounter its own immediate experiential pulsations and tensions long before unconscious agency is introduced to the manifold of conscious experience. This process, I argue, belongs solely to the domain and labour of the unconscious ego, which formally prepares the mind to encounter consciousness that arises in it.

Other contemporaries, such as Stolorow and Atwood (1992, 33), have attempted to account for realms of unconscious process by referring to what they call a "pre-reflective unconscious," which they equate with the organizing principles that "shape and thematize a person's experiences." Here they do not explain how such organizing principles operate, that is, how they are constituted or, specifically, how they are derived to begin with. They also describe a "dynamic unconscious," defined as a defensive process of barring articulation in consciousness, yet again lacking any formalization of how such defensive functions work or transpire; and an "unvalidated unconscious," which is the field or horizon of possible articulation that was never realized due to misattunements and invalidations from the object surround that remain unsymbolized. Here unconsciousness is merely that which was never made actual. Further, according to Stolorow and Atwood: "All three forms of unconsciousness, we have emphasized, derive from specific, formative intersubjective contexts" (33). Here there is no doubt that consciousness, and specifically intersubjectivity, is the prerequisite for unconsciousness to materialize and develop. The same is true for Zeddies (2000), who views the unconscious as a purely "relational," or interpersonal, construction.

Back to Stern. As I understand him, unconscious experience is only that which was introduced in some fashion through consciousness yet was actively interrupted, suspended, unattended to, blocked and/or avoided, hence left unformulated, whether as material semiotically encoded and sequestered on parallel levels of distributive processing, as defensive constellations designed to protect the subject from psychic threat, as the pure (formal) realm of potentiality, or as pre-reflective non-propositional thought lacking attention, self-conscious awareness, or mnemonic potency. In the end, Stern (1997, 37) seems to equate unconscious experience with anything that is linguistically unarticulated and lacks "clarity and differentiation." This definition could equally apply to the most sophisticated forms of unconscious mental functioning and a simple act of inattention.

Since Freud's early move from a dissociative model of consciousness to a repression model of unconscious process, psychoanalysis has been tacitly led to believe that dissociation and repression are mutually exclusive categories when, in fact, they are not. Contemporary theorists seize upon this assumption when advocating for dissociation as a better theory for understanding unconscious experience while jettisoning repression as a viable construct that aids clinical theory. The false either/or dichotomy that gets erected holds either that dissociation displaces the need for a repression model or that dissociation becomes subsumed with (or tantamount to) repressive functions. Stern (1999, 88) defines dissociation as "the avoidance of certain formulations of present experience, ... [which is] a channel or current along which certain meanings can flow and others cannot. To dissociate is simply to restrict the interpretations one makes of experience ... [or] a restriction on the experiences we allow ourselves to have." Here Stern equates these phenomena with unconscious experience but not in any dynamic way, that is, not in a way that an unconscious agency orchestrates, executes, sustains, or harbours. Dissociation from this definition is entirely possible through the operations of consciousness. There is no unconscious teleology, no unconscious ego directing such mental actions, no unconscious intentionality of any kind. "Formulations" or "interpretations" that are "avoided" or barred are simply linguistic processes that are either foreclosed or "restricted." What Stern calls the unconscious is merely formed through the repudiation or absence of linguistic construction.

Stern's focus on dissociation as both a defensive process and a benign passivity of inattention further parallels Bromberg's recent work on the subject. What Stern calls "unformulated," Bromberg calls "unsymbolized," or what Stolorow, Atwood, and Orange (2002) call "dysformulated." In fact, it is in the realm of "presymbolized experience" (Bromberg 1998, 132) where dissociation transpires on unconscious levels of information processing that block or abort the emergence of formulated conceptual thought due to danger associated with conceptual formulations that are too cognitively intense to bear. Like Freud's repression censor, this implies an active banning or barring of consciousness, an aborting of the symbolization process altogether. Here Bromberg underscores the centrality of trauma on psychic organization. He emphasizes the defensive and adaptive transformational capacities of dissociation as well as the pathological. He specifically points towards how dissociation leads to self-hypnoidal and amnesic mental states, and how it becomes a normative and essential operation in the organization of personality. Of course, that which we are unaware of at any given moment becomes a form of unconsciousness even if our attention may be drawn to it. The question becomes: How are these self-hypnoidal and amnesic states instituted if, by definition, we are unaware of our Self during such operations? More specifically: How is dissociation capable of lending order and organization to personality structure if, by definition, it is fractious and non-consolidatible?

What is not directly discussed by Stern or Bromberg is *how* unconscious agentic processes instantiate themselves as dissociative enactments. Presumably, Stern would deny the unconscious any agency (or at least this is inferred from his text) while Bromberg would not. But these are not questions they directly entertain. It is not enough to confirm the ontic function of dissociation without explaining how it is made possible to begin with. What I wish to argue is that unconscious experience as dissociability is derived from the basic dialectical processes that govern mental life, first and foremost constituted through unconscious agency and, more specifically, the unconscious ego. Even analysts like Bollas (1987), who is preoccupied with tracing the operations of the unconscious ego as the seat of agency and the director of mental activity, and Grotstein (2000), who imports and attributes a *personal* sense of agency to the unconscious as the executor of mental functioning, do not properly describe how the unconscious ego comes into being. They start, as do all other theorists, with the birth of the human subject as consciousness qua consciousness. Although I share affinities with both Bollas and Grotstein, I wish to take these ideas farther by examining how the unconscious ego comes into being and how it acquires agency as a teleologic determinate being-for-self.

Dissociation is momentary fragmentation in self-continuity – itself a spacing – a split, fissure, or gap in being. From this standpoint, dissociation is the agentic expression and overdetermination of unconscious motivation as teleological intent. In many ways, dissociation is a failure at representation, whether this be a failure to *re-present* visual images of events such as traumas, affective resonance states, or somatic forces that persist as embodied unconscious memorializations. Such unconscious schemata may actively resist becoming recollected within conscious awareness when under the direction of defence and self-protective currents. Or they may evade conceptual formulation or linguistic articulation in consciousness for a variety of reasons, defensively motivated or not. Moreover, dissociative content may have simply not been encoded due to adaptive and normatively benign aspects of inattention, detachment, or compartmentalization (Naso 2007). But, most important, dissociative processes must be directed by a mental agent executing such dynamic activity, and here I do not see this issue being directly addressed by many contemporary writers. Dissociability in its most elemental form is none other than the proclivity of the psyche to split or modify itself from its original simple unity as embodied apperceptive desire, dividing itself into bits of self-experience through self-externalization, only then to *re-gather* and *re-cover* its self-division and externalization and to incorporate itself back into its immediate self-constitution or internal structure – only to have the process repeat itself endlessly through an ongoing trajectory of dynamic pattern. In psychoanalysis, we have come to call this process projective identification.

My understanding of the unconscious is that it is process oriented, process driven, and process derived. Process psychology displaces the primacy of language over the unconscious, but it does not negate the value of signification. Instead, the unconscious incorporates the sign and builds a whole elaborate matrix of unconscious semiotics that conforms to its own laws and its own rules of signification fashioned by its own hands. The linguistic turn in psychoanalysis only partially accounts for unconscious dynamics as, in my mind, the postmodern collapse of the subject and subjectivity in favour of the reification of language is misguided. What is fundamentally at stake is the ontological status of the unconscious. Although postmodernism may champion the so-called death of metaphysics, reality always has a way of coming back to bite us in the backside. This is the surprise, the ambush, the astonishment of revelation, the unanticipated, the unforeseen. There is a reality to the unseen that becomes even more actual, valid, and substantial than any physical object or concrete phenomena. The invisibility of the abyss is known through divisibility, through the *rip* in consciousness. We know with indubitable self-certainty when the uncanny visits us, the return of the prefamiliar, the return of the pre-experienced. This is the moment of being torn open from the inside out. Lack reveals itself through rupture.

Recall that the unconscious declares itself as discontinuities in consciousness, what I prefer to call spacings of the abyss. We know them as apertures, perforations, or lapses in experience, where time is momentarily eclipsed by the presencing of absence – a hole in being. Dissociation is only one such phenomenon in our "gaps of experience," what Stern (1987, 60) refers to as "empty space" in the "beginning of life." But such empty space is full of non-being, of nothingness, hence no-thing is there, only experiential flow, appetitive pulsation – desire – a hovering over a clearing simultaneously exposed yet closed, open yet occlusive, the yawning gulf of the abyss. The abyss is never completely consolidated or unified, only discontiguous but unifying in its functions. Bromberg (1998, 244) supports Hegel's project when he says that "the psyche does not start as an integrated whole, but is nonunitary in origin." Here nonunity is a formal condition of the psyche experienced as discrete and discontiguous processes that are nonlinear, dynamic, and complex. However, as I argue, Bromberg and Stern are ultimately imprecise when they speak of nonunity or empty space: there is in fact a unity (albeit rudimentary, primitive, and unsophisticated) as well as a spacing that is emergent yet shallow and contourless, hence not totally devoid of experiential content. What we may say is that, in the beginning of life, such discontinuities do in fact have a simple formal unity from which the unconscious soul wishes to emerge, and it is precisely through the breach or puncture that emergent nonunity gives rise to plurality of form and content within the mind.

While many contemporary psychoanalytic theorists remain naive with regard to formal metaphysics, various factions have also posed divided and contradictory notions regarding the nature and meaning of the self. What has generally been uncontested among several predominant postmodern positions – more specifically within the genre of Foucault, Deleuze, and Derrida – is the insistence that the autonomous self is a fiction. As Lacan (1977) puts it, the ego is an illusory misrecognition (*méconnaissance*) of the Other. These convictions reify society, culture, and language, hence semiotics, which, in turn, defines all discourse about selfhood and, thus, causally determines any element of personal agency that we might attribute to an individuated subject. In other words, all aspects of personal subjectivity have been conditioned by cultural signifiers that subordinate the individual to the symbolic order of language operative within one's social ontology. From this standpoint, there is no individual, hence no self. And what we may customarily call a "self" is really nothing other than a linguistic invention based on social construction.

On the other hand, when discourse on the self is given attention in the relational literature, the notion of the self has been theoretically altered from a singular unity to a multiplicity of selves. Popular among some relationalists today is the belief that there is no singular unitary self; rather, there is a multiplicity of selves that exists within each subject, which, in turn, is ultimately governed by an intersubjective or dyadic system that determines how multiplicity is instantiated to begin with. Bromberg (1998, 186) is clear when he says "there is no such thing as an integrated self"; instead, there are "other" (13), "many" (311), or "several selves" (256). It is one thing to argue that there are multiple ego-alterations or self-states that populate intrapsychic life due to the multiple operations of psychic modification (such as through the parameters of dissociation and defence), but it is quite another thing to say that each subject contains a conglomeration of multiple selves that may or may not be in touch with one another yet exist and act as independent nominal agents within a singular mind. Although I agree that self-states may be modified elements of original instantiations as previous expressions of mental processes that have undergone internal division, differentiation, and transmogrification – which may further be experientially realized as atemporal, non-unified, incongruent, dissociated, and/or alienated aspects of mind – it is unfathomable to me how one can view a singular subject as possessing multiple selves that coalesce as existent independent entities.

Multiplicity can be legitimately explained as a unique and particularized experiential activity within the mind that has potentially formed or acquired new organizations of self-experience and adaptation through defensive transformations of earlier or conflicted archaic processes in response to real or perceived threat, anxiety, and/or trauma. And this is substantiated time and again in clinical practice. But when you commit to the proposition of multiple entities within a singular subject, you have the messy burden of explaining how multiple entities could possibly exist within a singular embodied being, whereby each entity inhabits the same body, perceptual apparatus, and experiential medium regardless of qualitative differences in desire, content, or form. The resultant array of conundrums is unbounded: Who is the governing agent among agencies?

How could you epistemologically justify that there is such a governing agent to begin with? Who or what organizes or unifies the cacophony of experience if there are different beings within one mind? Who or what is ultimately in control of the mind? How can multiple selves share anything derived from their own nature when, by definition, they are independent entities that compose different natures? Separate entities, by definition, cannot share or participate in the same nature because, by virtue of their differences, they have separate essences. Yet discourse on multiplicity directly assumes that separate selves within a singular mind can intuit, feel, absorb, influence, and communicate with one another and, hence, must have a shared essence. Therefore, multiple selves within one mind cannot exist because they would not have any ability to converse or have contact with the other selves unless they were derived from the same essence. Some theorists clearly confound this issue.

Separate selves eliminate the possibility that there could be any shared psychic participation among these different selves because they would have to have separate experiential mediums or apparatuses that radically vary in phenomenological content and form. What this means is that all experience would have to be perceived and assimilated by a separate psychic register within each self or self-state and, hence, be organized by independent agentic forces processing and guiding self-experience. But how could this be so? How could two or more entities with two or more essences co-habit and participate in each other's essence when they are ontologically distinct, thus incapable of intermingling without altering their essences, hence annulling any notion of difference to begin with? These are palpable logical contradictions for which any metaphysical theory of duality or multiplicity must be able to account in order to salvage some theoretical credibility.

From my standpoint, a multiplicity thesis is most legitimately justified by appealing to a developmental monistic ontology governing the subjective mind of each individual, thus accounting for psychic division, differentiation, and modification of content and form (namely, self-states) without generating separate psychic entities (qua selves), each with its own separate essence. To justify a theory of mutually exclusive multiple essences that have the capacity to interact and intermingle would lead to some form of occassionalism, monadology, or parallelism, each with its own particular set of problems. Explanations of modified self-states, psychic realms, or experiential orders of subjectivity are quite different from multiple subjects, and this is precisely what the relationalists who avouch such a theory of multiple selves need to consider.

Commensurate with Stern and Bromberg's work, Elizabeth Howell (2005) conceptualizes the mind as reducible to dissociative processes, and she is following the same theoretical trend as many relational postmoderns. This view lends itself to parsimonious and possibly reductionistic accounts of the complexifications of mental functioning, not to mention introducing a theoretical problematic because it does not adequately address the question of agency within a dissociative model. If everything we call mental or psychical is a multiplicity of self-states, how is a state organized? What processes or mechanics are operative that constitute dissociability to begin with? Does this merely devolve into neurobiology? From my account, one has to have active unconscious agentic functions executing mental activity or this argument collapses into and privileges a materialist model of consciousness. Following this line of reasoning, the unconscious is not even a necessary psychoanalytic construct, let alone an ontological force in the mind. Furthermore, if you don't allow for agency directing mental activity on multiple levels of systemic psychic organization that are conjoined as a unifying totality that makes multiplicity possible, then you have a problem with human freedom and causality to boot.

If dissociation theory is to replace a model of dynamic unconscious processes and is said to account for all normative and pathological enactments, then how are enactments executed if you cannot sufficiently account for agency? And if agency is to be attributed to consciousness, and dissociation occurs outside of conscious awareness, then are we not begging the question of what constitutes dissociation? If dissociative enactments devolve into consciousness, then this is contradictory because dissociation is presumed to transpire outside of conscious awareness. And if the answer is to be found somewhere in brain processes, then are we not committed to material reduction and a mereological fallacy? Not only does this not adequately answer the question and mechanics of dissociative enactments but it also subverts the philosophical question of unconscious agency. Dissociative enactments must be exercised and executed by an agentic teleological organization of mind. If they are not, then you have either the intractable problem of multiple essences conversing or a view of the mind as a biological machine, devoid of freedom and agency, that is turned on by the environment. This makes it sound as though Skinner is potentially alive and well in contemporary psychoanalysis.

Although I cannot do justice to this complex issue all at once, what I propose to argue that an adequate solution may be found by conceiving the multiplicity of the self as a dispersal of modified and differentiated self-states that are ontologically conjoined and inseparable from a unitary self that is a *unifying unifier* – but one that is neither static nor unified. Rather, the self is pure process that is systemically and developmentally organized as a dynamic self-articulated complex holism. Instead of the antipode between biology versus culture, unconsciousness versus language, dissociation versus drive, I believe contemporary psychoanalysis would profit from an integrative theory whereby particularity and universality, context and contingency – the one and the many – can coalesce within a comprehensive paradigm that properly accounts for human similarity and difference. Here the inherent dichotomizing that characterizes the unitary self versus multiple self debate can find resolve in a process psychology that dialectically accounts for plurality within a unifying conception of mind.

Unlike Stern, Bromberg (1998, 253) allows for a dynamic unconscious through dissociative enactments that are complex, overdetermined, and subject to conflictual motivations and traumatic after-effects populated by multiple self-states with "opposing realities." His notion of dissociability is much more in keeping with my notion of unconscious spacings as split-off or modified ego-states that are discontiguously formed through hiatuses or phenomenal lapses that are sequestered within pockets of psychic reality originally partitioned off as discrete units of experience. They are further inaugurated and established by unconscious agentic forces and directives, and are held in abeyance in the mind until such units of experience are dislodged, called forth, or impelled to mobilize themselves through a variety of possible executions and permutations. As I elaborate upon later, experiential units of unconscious organization may take a variety of different schemata or shapes in:

1 *Content* or material, such as:
   a. Specific encoded data derived from conscious experience, sensory impressions, or images;
   b. Mnemonic linkages;
   c. Imaginative or fantasy constructions, including specific wishes; and

d. Semiotic structures, symbol formation, and formal conceptual thought.
2. *Form*, such as:
   a. *Sentience*, somatic urges, drives, and corporeal sensations;
   b. *Appetition* or desire;
   c. *Affect*, including emotion and mood;
   d. *Perception*, originally derived from unconscious apperception; and
   e. *Conceptuality*, hence thought proper.
3. *Valence*, which is the capacity of differential units of material and form distributed throughout discrete spacings yet on parallel planes of organization to converge, overlap, interact, react, unite, and potentially combine portions of their divided essence into new experiential linkages or junctions of psychic order that were previously sequestered and inaccessible to interaction; and
4. *Intensity*, which is both the:
   a. *Quantitative* force or power of teleonomic processes and energetic stratification of material interactions (namely, those forces belonging to our embodiment and intrinsic psychophysical constitution along with their emergent properties); and
   b. *Qualitative* states of lived psychic reality that we may call *unconscious qualia*.

Unconscious qualia are differentiated by their distinguishing traits and fluxations, which belong to the immediational presence of experiential self-structure. Intensities may vary in value, degree, and kind; correspond to the array of competing unconscious forms of experiential units; possess teleologic aims; and serve to titrate an exceptionally great measure of concentration, pressure, or emphasis to intrapsychic complexity. Unconscious qualia may conform to positive and negative experiential content, form, and their valances, and they are demarcated by differential degrees of internal activity, felt-valuation, potency or causal efficacy, and self-mediatory expression.

From this vantage point, the unconscious is not merely a realm of dissociated mind, which is instituted on a continuum of consciousness, whereby the unconscious or forms of unconsciousness become alienated shapes of consciousness. On the contrary, the abyss becomes the midwife to consciousness and maintains an archaic primacy. A purely dissociative model of mind runs the risk of eliminating unconscious dynamicism by rendering it impotent and deactivated, with no causal efficacy of its own capable of issuing forth agentic direction. Instead, we may envision an ontogenetic developmental process whereby earlier primordial shapes of mind divide, grow, differentiate, multiply, modify further, and move from an antediluvian cycle of repetitive form towards an upward, ascending trajectory of dynamic pattern forged through conflict and negation – hence, the positive significance of the negative. Mind is architectonic and epigenetic, oriented towards higher stages of progression and creative generativity yet capable of regressing or fixating in repetitions of negativity or banality.

How can we speak of unconscious phenomena when, traditionally, experience is said to belong to consciousness? This antipode begs the question of what constitutes experience, and it is just this hegemony that I wish to displace. All aspects of conscious experience must be necessarily predicated on prioricity, on a prior ground (*Grund*), one without foundation, without bottom (*abussos*). If we are to take seriously the principle of sufficient reason and posit an archaic ground to all being and becoming, then we must be willing to engage, at least in theory, that which makes experience possible. Here re-enters the question of origin.

· 2 ·

Deciphering the "Genesis Problem": On the Origins of Psychic Reality

Freud never actually used the words "ego" and "id" in his German texts; these are English translations into Latin, taken from one of his most famous works, *Das Ich und das Es*. When Freud spoke of the *Ich*, he was referring to the personal pronoun "I" – as in "I myself" – a construct that underwent many significant theoretical transformations throughout his lifetime. By the time Freud (1923) advanced his mature model of the psyche, concluding that even a portion of the "I" was also unconscious, he needed to delimit a region of the mind that remained purely concealed from consciousness. This he designated by the impersonal pronoun *es*, which he used as a noun – the "It" – a term introduced by Groddeck, originally appropriated from Nietzsche. The translation "ego" displaces the deep emotional significance tied to personal identity that Freud deliberately tried to convey, while the term "id" lacks the customary sense of unfamiliarity associated with otherness, thus rendering these concepts antiseptic, clinical, and devoid of all personal associations. The "I" and the "It" express more precisely the type of antithesis Freud wanted to emphasize between the familiar and the strange, hence the dialectic of the life within.

When we refer to ourselves as "I," we convey a meaning that is deeply personal, subjective, and known, while references to an "It" convey distance, separateness, objectification, and abstraction. The I is familiar while the It is foreign and unknown, hence an alien presence. Because Freud wanted to preserve the individual intimacy associated with a personal sense of self, the I was to stand in firm opposition to the It, which was purely estranged from conscious awareness. But the distinction between the I and the It is not altogether unambiguous, and, as I argue, not theoretically resolved by Freud himself. In fact, even today, psychoanalysis, in all its rich theoretical variations, has not rectified this issue. While Freud (see SE 19:24–5, 38; SE 20:97; SE 22:76–7; SE 23:145) eventually conceded that the I developed out of the It, he did not explain with any detail how this activity was accomplished; he merely declared that it just happened.

It is my contention that post-classical through contemporary psychoanalytic thought still suffers from ambiguity surrounding the ill-defined nature of the development of the I from the It, which has either been taken as a mere propositional assumption within psychoanalytic theory or has been subverted by alternative paradigms that boast they have surpassed Freud while subsuming his model within an overarching metahistorical paradigm. But a persisting, endemic problem to psychoanalysis is the absence of any *philosophical* attempt to account for genesis, namely, the origins of psychic reality. It is not enough to say that psychic experience begins as unconsciousness and progresses to consciousness, from drive to reason, from the It to the I: we must be able to show how these primordial processes originally transpire and sequentially unfold into dynamic patterns of organized mental life. Relational, interactionist, intersubjective, and systems accounts focus on the interpersonally elaborated psychosocial matrix that defines, nurtures, and sustains the existence of the self. And we have every reason to appreciate these exciting advances in our conceptual understanding of psychic development. However, without exception, these schools of thought have not addressed the a priori conditions that make the emergence of the self possible to begin with, that is, the ontological ground and moments of the inception of psychic reality.

We have reason to believe that the I and the It are not ontologically differentiated; nor is it to be accepted at face value that the I does in fact develop from the It. What is missing in previous developmental accounts is any *detailed* attempt to chronicle the very processes that bring the I and the It into being in the first place. Throughout this chapter, I am preoccupied with what I call the "genesis problem," namely, Beginning – the origins of unconscious life. By way of dialectical analysis, I trace the means in which such primitive processes acquire organization, differentiation and integration, teleological progression, self-constitutive identity, and psychic cohesion. Although Freud articulated the fundamental intrapsychic forces that populate and beset human existence, he did not attend to these ontological-transmutational concerns. It is my intention to offer a dialectical account of the coming into being of the I and the It, or what I shall call the ego and the abyss, and show how process psychoanalytic thought provides a plausible solution to the question and nature of unconscious maturation.

CONCEPTUALIZING THE PSYCHE

When Freud refers to the mind, he is referring to the Greek notion *psyche* (ψυχή), which corresponds to the German notion *Seele*. In fact, Freud does not speak of the "mental apparatus" at all but, rather, of the "organization of the soul," which he specifically equates with the psyche. Freud (1905b) adopted this usage as early as 1905, when he emphatically stated: "'Psyche' is a Greek word and its German translation is 'soul.' Psychical treatment hence means 'treatment of the soul' [*Seelenbehandlung*]" (SE 7:283). Furthermore, Freud equates psychoanalysis with the science of the life of the soul (*wer die Wissenschaft vom Seelenleben liebt*) (SE 22:6), which stands in stark contrast to the biological connotations associated with the English word "mind" (see also Bettelheim 1982, 71–5).

Freud was well read in ancient philosophy, and Plato's notion of the soul, as well as his depiction of Eros, left a lasting impression on his conceptualization of the psyche. Before we proceed, however, it is important to distinguish between what we mean by psyche, self, I or ego, and the It. Psychoanalysis, like other professions, has the propensity of using highly technical jargon to capture the complexities of human mental functioning. This is patently justified, but it poses a problem in conceptual discourse and mutual understanding, especially when concepts remain murky or are presumed to have universal definitions when, in fact, they mean many different things to different theorists and within different philosophic disciplines. So we may avoid equivocation of our terms, let us begin with a conceptual definition of the I.

The I, or ego, has a special significance for Freud, which is associated with personal identity, self-reference, conscious thought, perception, mobility, reality testing, and the higher executive functions of reason and intelligence. *Das Ich* is not a common German expression used in everyday conversation: it is used only by professionals in a quasi-scientific context.[1] Nor are references to the self (*Selbst*) or the subject (*Subjekt*) common parlance. In fact, to refer to oneself as *mein Ich* or *mein Selbst* would be viewed as being exceedingly narcissistic. The term "ego" also carries negative connotations of inflated self-importance and self-love (as reflected in the words "egotistical," "egoistic," and "egocentric"); hence the terms "I" and "ego" have a shared meaning in both German and English. Since the word "ego" has become immortalized in psychoanalytic literature as well as in popular culture, for customary purposes within this context I refer to the "I" and the "ego" interchangeably.

Freud realized that he could not adequately account for the I as being solely conscious; therefore, he introduced a division between conscious and unconscious ego domains and their respective operations. What Freud was mainly concerned about in making this division was to explain how certain ego properties, qualities, and tension states affected the nature of wish, defence, drive discharge, and self-preservation, and how the I stood in relation to an alien force and presence compartmentalized from the ego itself. The ego became a pivotal concept for Freud because it was the locus of agency, intention, and choice (both consciously and unconsciously realized). However, it was an agency that existed alongside competing agencies in the mind. This theoretical move on Freud's part is not without conceptual drawbacks and has led many critics to question the plausibility of competing mental entities. Although Freud used the terms "provinces," "domains," and "realms" to characterize such psychic activity, he in no way meant to evoke the substance ontology characteristic of ancient metaphysics, which is in vogue with some forms of materialism today. Freud explicitly abandoned his earlier neurophysiological visions of the mind represented in his *Project for a Scientific Psychology* (1895), and, by the time of *The Interpretation of Dreams* (1900), adopted a corpus of the soul that admonished reductionism (see SE 5:536; SE 15:21). Characterizing Freud's theory of agency in terms of entity or substance ontology further misrepresents his views on the active processes that constitute the psyche. Freud's purported agencies are active, purposeful, malleable processes – not static, fixed, immobile structures. While Freud (1900, 1923, 1933a) prefers spatial metaphors in his description of these forces, he is quick to remind us they are only heuristic devices: the question of localization becomes a meaningless proposition when, in actuality, we are discussing temporal spacings of mental processes.

Freud's use of the term "I" imports ambiguity when we compare it to a psychoanalytic conception of the self. In some of Freud's (1914) intervening works on narcissism, his concept of the ego corresponds to his concept of the self. And, in *Civilization and Its Discontents* (1930), he specifically equates *das Ich* with *das Selbst* (SE 21:65). This implies that the self would not contain other portions of the psyche, such as the drives and the region of the repressed. This definition also situates the self in relation to otherness and is thus no different from our reference to the ego, with its conscious and unconscious counterparts. In German, however, the "self" encompasses the entire human being. But, on a very earthly plain, it represents the core from which the ego acts and relates mostly to the conscious aspects of personal identity. Although a strong case can be made for the Self as a supraordinate (see Meissner 2000) encompassing principle – what Freud calls the Soul (*Seele*) – I believe Freud is justified in conceptualizing the I, ego, and self as synonymous constructs. The self stands in relation to its opposite (namely, the Other) as subject stands to object and, hence, evokes a firm point of difference. This is precisely why Freud insisted on the dialectical presence of otherness: the I is *not* the It.

For Freud, the It is *alienus* – both alienated mind and that which is alienating. We know it as conflict and chaos under the pressure, whims, and persecutory impulses of the drives, our animal nature. They emanate from within us but are neither consciously willed nor desired. The It does not know and does not say no – *It* knows no negation (SE 19:239; SE 22:74). Under the force of foreign excitations clamouring for discharge, unrest and tumult are *das Es's* very nature. Yet, by necessity, such chaos is combated by degrees of order emanating from the ego. Freud's introduction of the It preserves that realm of inner reality that we may never directly know in itself. Here Freud insists on the Kantian *Ding an sich*, the Fichtean *Anstoss* – an impenetrable limit, obstacle, or impasse. The mind becomes demarcated by a rigid "check" that introduces irreconcilable division and contradiction: in other words, the dialectic.

We may never have direct access to the It, only to the way in which it appears. We know the It through its endless derivatives, such as dreams, fantasies, slips, and symptoms, as well as through that which torments us, through that which we wish would remain dead and buried, forever banished to the pit – disowned, renounced, and, hence, repressed. But things that are misplaced or forgotten have a way of turning up unexpectedly. With every covering over, with every concealment, there is simultaneously a de-covering, a resurfacing of the old, a return of the dead. Freud crowned the It the king of the underworld – Hades – while the I traversed the domains of its earthly surface down into the bowels of its nether regions.

Freud's final paradigm of the mind rests on a basic logic of modification. The I differentiates itself and develops out of the It; and later, the I modifies itself again and evolves into a critical-moral agency, what Freud calls the *Über-Ich*, or that aspect of the I that stands over against itself and holds itself up to a higher authority. Here the I undergoes another doubling function, in fact, a doubling of the doubling – this time turned onto itself. What is familiarly know as the "superego" is nothing other than a split off portion of the I that stands in relation to a particular form of identification: namely, a set of values and prohibitions it internalized from attachment figures, familial relations, and cultural experience, ideals and principles the self strives to attain. Freud's logic of modification (the explanatory limits of which he modestly concedes [SE 22: 77; SE 23:145]), however, goes unexplained.

While Freud makes the superego (over-I, or above-I) into a critical agency that besieges the I and defiles the It, the superego is merely an extension of the ego, both the self in its exaltation as an identification and pining for its ideal form as well as the judgment, fury, and condemnation that informs our sense of conscience, guilt, shame, and moral reproach. The ego and superego are therefore the same agency divided yet internally conjoined. Freud spoke prematurely in making the superego a third agency of the psyche, when, properly speaking, it is not: it merely *appears* as an independent agent when, ontologically, the ego and the superego are the same. The ego is *supra* in relation to itself – what it wants to be, hence what it strives to become. And when the ego does not live up to itself – up to its own ideals – it debases itself with as much wrath and force as is brewing in the tempestuous cauldron of the It. It is no coincidence that the It and the superego share the same fist of fury. This is because both are fuelled (with stipulations) by the drives, a point to which I return shortly. But for now it is important to emphasize that the psyche is a divided self, with each division and modification remaining interdependent and ontologically bound.

In the end, Freud gives us a vision of the mind as composed of three ontically interrelated forces with varying qualitative degrees of organization and zest, ranging from the most primitive, unmodulated evolutionary impulses to the most refined aspects of intelligence and ethical self-consciousness, all brought together under the rubric of soul. Bettelheim (1982, 77) tells us that nowhere in his texts does Freud actually provide us with a direct definition of the soul, although we may infer that he intended for it to stand as an overarching concept that enveloped the three agencies of mental life. We do know, however, that Freud had no intention of implying that the soul is immortal or that it carries any religious connotations whatsoever. Freud (1927b, 1930) was a voluble atheist, thus his use of the term is meant to reflect our shared collective humanity.

Freud's tripartite division of the soul returns us to the Greek vision of the psyche, with one exceptional difference: the soul is largely unconscious. As the seat of the passions (*eros*), reason (*nous*), and moral judgment (*ethos*), the psyche becomes a dynamic organization of competing dialectical forces. Because the notion of consciousness is a modern, not an ancient, concept, Freud is able to enrich the Platonic view by showing that irrationality and emotional forces driven by unconscious processes constantly plague the intellectual and ethical strivings of the ego. Therefore, the logocentrism that is often attributed to Freud must be viewed within the context of the pervasive tenacity of irrational pressures, although there is always a logic to the interior. Left undefined by Freud, we may nevertheless say that the psyche is the composition of competing dialectical processes that inform and sustain the division of the I from the It along with its multifarious derivatives. The psyche is pure process and experiential flow composed of a multiplicity of dialectical organizations – each with varying degrees of opposition, complexity, and strands of unification – which form a temporal continuity enduring in embodied space. Although the psyche consists of unifying activity, it itself is not a static unity but, rather, a motional-experiential process of becoming spatio-temporally realized as mediated immediacy.

This leads us to a process account of the psyche, or, for our purposes, the Self, as a supraordinate complex whole, including both conscious and unconscious parallel activities. Although classical through historical and contemporary psychoanalytic models have paid great attention to the details and developmental contours of intrapsychic, interpersonal, and psychosocial life, the question of genesis – psychic Origin – and its ontological modifications remains virtually unconsidered.

THE DIALECTICS OF UNCONSCIOUS EXPERIENCE

Within the history of the phenomenological tradition, the question and meaning of "experience" is exclusively situated within the realm of consciousness. With the exception of Eduard von Hartmann's philosophy of the unconscious and Whitehead's process metaphysics, there has been no purported philosophy that attempts to account for the phenomenology of experience outside of conscious states. Here I wish to increasingly draw our attention to the topography of unconscious process, which makes conscious experience possible. Following our dialectical account of the coming into being of the psyche, experience is first constituted on the unconscious level of psychic modification as a process of becoming. Because process is pure activity, unrest, or event, by definition it constitutes the ontological movements that define the dialectic; thus, the dialectic itself constitutes the metaphysics of experience.

Freud is a dialectician of the mind: in his final paradigm he envisioned the psyche as an active composition of multifarious, bipolar forces that stand in antithetical relation to one another and are therefore mutually implicative. The I and the It, the two classification of drives, primary versus secondary process mentation, the pleasure principle versus the reality principle, love and hate, the individual within society – these are but a few of the oppositional processes that inform his dialectical system. However, Freud never clarified his logic of the dialectic; instead, he relied on introspection and self-analysis, clinical observation, and technical judgment based on careful consideration of the data at hand, which, over time, led to radical revisions of his many core theoretical postulates. One of Freud's most modest attributes was his ability to change his mind about previous speculations when new evidence presented itself, thus showing the disciplined persistence of the refined scientific attitude he had revered as *Logos* (SE 20:54).

It is not altogether clear how Freud's dialectic is philosophically constituted, a topic about which he said nothing; however, we may draw certain reasonable assumptions. While some dialectical forces seek unification, resolution, and synthetic integration, others do not. For example, consciousness and unconsciousness, like the I and the It, are firm oppositions, yet their distinctions become blurred in times of sleep, daydreaming, and fantasy formation. Even when we are unconscious, such as when asleep, the mind generates impressions and representations from the tableau of images once experienced in conscious sensation and laid down in the deep reservoir of memory within the unconscious configurations of the mind. This suggests that consciousness is on a continuum of presence and absence, disclosure and concealment, with each respective appearance being merely one side or instantiation of its dual nature, a duality highlighted and punctuated by its phenomenal valences and qualities, yet nevertheless ontologically conjoined. Consciousness and unconsciousness could not be ontologically distinct due to the simple fact that each context of being overlaps and participates in the other. If they did not, such duality could not be intelligibly conceived unless each counterpart were to be viewed as having a separate essence. However, if this were the case, neither could participate in the realm of the other, nor could they have mutual causal influence (as they are purported to have) for the simple reason that that which has a distinct ontology or being would, by definition, have a different essence. Just as Aristotle's criticism of Plato's forms still stands as a cogent refutation of ontological dualism based on the incompatibility of different essences, so must we extend this assessment to the split domains of consciousness and unconsciousness. Conscious and unconscious life must have the same ontology, hence the same essence, by virtue of the fact that each informs the reality of the other: their respective differences point to their modified forms.

In order for an essence to be what it is – without which it could not exist – it must stand in relation to what it is not. Freud maintains this division of consciousness and unconsciousness from: (1) an experiential or phenomenological standpoint (that which qualitatively appears); (2) from an epistemological standpoint (that which is known); and (3) as a conceptual, heuristic scheme (that which is conceived). However, despite his dual classification of drives, he does not maintain such duality from an ontological framework: consciousness arises *in* the ego, itself the outgrowth of an unconscious It. I speak more to this later, but suffice it to say that Freud's dialectic permits both integration and impasse, synthesis and disunity, universality and particularity, hence contradiction and paradox. But, as Freud says, the It knows nothing. Above all, it does not know the law of contradiction: "Contrary impulses exist side by side, without canceling each other out or diminishing each other: at most they may converge to form compromises" (*SE* 22:73). Mental processes could "converge" and transmute their original forms only on the condition that they participate in the same essence; that is, in an original ontological ground that makes the conversion of form possible.

Another example of the blurred distinctions of duality and limit in Freud's system may be witnessed in the dialectic of repression (Freud 1915b). That which is denied conscious access, negated, and banished to the pit is not totally annulled and, hence, not completely opposed; rather, it is preserved where it festers and seeks discharge through another form. Thus, opposition remains contextual, yet always has the potential of being breached.

Although we may observe a boundary of firm antitheses in Freud's model, there is also a synthetic function to the ego that seeks to mediate, resolve, and channel competing desires and conflicts through intentional strategies that find their way into overt behaviour and conscious phenomena. But there is also a regressive function to ego that is potentially mobilized given the particular contingencies that govern psychic economy. On the other hand, the process of sublimation has a unifying, transcending character that combats regression, despite the fact that both can be operative on parallel realms of development. This leaves Freud somewhere between what Kant referred to as the antinomies of reason or the paralogisms of the self, which correspond to irreconcilable contradictions within the mind that meet with no resolve, and the Hegelian notion of *Aufhebung* – a progressive dialectical process that cancels, surpasses, and simultaneously preserves opposition within an elevating, unifying procreative self-structure. Despite Freud's lack of clarification surrounding his dialectical logic, we can nevertheless say that his model is compatible with a process account of unconscious experience that is dialectically organized and mediated by oppositional contingent forces exerting equiprimordial pressures that are contextually realized in time.

A common interpretation of Freud's dialectic is to conclude that there are oppositional forces that are never resolved, hence never cancelled, surpassed, or transcended. Instead, it is thought that a multiplicity of opposing processes and contents – say, impulses, wishes, fantasies, and their counterparts – are preserved in deadlocks, thus maintaining the psychic tension that characterizes the psyche. And there is justification for this argument: Freud himself places a great deal of emphasis on dualism. But this dualism, as I have argued elsewhere (Mills 2002a, 128–9), is the way in which psychic processes appear or unfold phenomenologically, even if such appearances are movements or modifications within unconscious experience as the transmutation of organizational processes that fuel and sustain psychic structure. Freud is a developmental monistic ontologist, and, in this respect, his dialectic is comparable to (albeit not convergent with) Hegel's. As I point out, Freud's mature theory involves a series of modifications and transmogrifications that are derived from the most primitive unconscious activities to the most exalted self-conscious deliberations; hence, psychic organization is a developmental achievement. In the mind, polarity seeks expression, discharge, and resolve. If it does not attain some modicum of compromise, hence negotiated expression, then it can lapse into impasse and, therefore, into a stalemate that can lead to pathology, regression, or fixation at more primitive stages of organization. This is why dream formation, slips of the tongue or pen, significant forgetting, bungled actions, and symptom manifestation are attempts at dialectical syntheses,[2] just as rational discourse and scientific explorations strive for higher (synthetic) levels of comprehension.[3] But these processes are enacted with varying degrees of success and elevation. For example, it can be argued that a repetition compulsion is a failed attempt at achieving a higher stage of transcendence or sublation, which is aimed at mastery, unification, and wholeness, while sublimation is a more successful and cultivated expression of primordial conflict (e.g., through art, culture, religion, and social-ethical reform). The mind can never remain "deadlocked" without falling into chaos and despair, and this is why Freud wants to differentiate the abnormal from more adjusted states of mind.

The mind is dialectical, hence relational; that is, it stands in relation (in both temporal continuity and disjunction) to that which is other-than its current form or experience. It is important to note that, regardless of the form of difference we wish to theoretically or experientially highlight, all dialectical organizations of the psyche are simultaneously operative from the vantage point of their own unique constitutions and contextualized perspectives. Therefore, the processential perspectivism[4] of each inhabited domain of lived (yet at times unformulated) unconscious experience is not to negate the force and presence of competing intentional faculties within the mind. It now becomes our task to more closely examine how these psychic processes are logically constituted through dialectically mediated progression, a discussion that will prepare us to engage the question of original ground.

APPROACHING THE "GENESIS PROBLEM"

The dialectic proves especially useful when attempting to understand the logic of modification, which Freud does not adequately address, as it lends logical rigour, deductive justification, and internal coherence to procedural inquiry concerning, among other things, the nature of the genesis problem. Empirical science in general, and developmental research in particular, can only proclaim to determine how the ego comes into being by making reasonable, inductive inferences based on observable phenomena; and this is more often accomplished through speculative inferences based on our own subjective experiences. For example, Daniel Stern's (1985) proclamation of the "emergent self" as the earliest stage of ego development in infancy (from birth to two months), while having theoretical value, does nothing to illuminate the ground from which the self emerges. There is a current tendency in psychoanalytic infant research to emphasize the relational, dyadic systems and intersubjective domains that help constitute the ego, but this does not address the genesis question either. While these developmental paradigms are insightful and informative, the ontology of the *inception* of subjectivity is ignored: psychic activity is presumed but not accounted for.

Empirical approaches (including clinical case studies and phenomenological-qualitative investigations) ultimately face the same strain as do purely theoretical attempts to define the origins of psychic development because we simply do not possess direct first-person epistemological access to the primordial organizations of the incipient subjective mind. Put laconically, we can never "get inside" an infant's head. Biologic attempts ultimately fail because they succumb to the bane of material reduction, thus effacing the unique quality of the lived experience that is displaced by simple location, thus committing the fallacy of misplaced concreteness. Although our physical nature is a necessary condition for psychic life, it is far from a sufficient condition to account for the coming into being of psychic reality. This is not to disavow the relevance, contiguity, and importance of the biological and neurosciences for psychoanalytic inquiry, only to emphasize that process thought extends far beyond psychophysicality.

Although process psychology has a favourable attitude towards empirical science, it realizes that relying solely on perceived, observable (controlled) experience is of little help when answering the question of Beginning. To approach such an issue, we must enlist the principle of sufficient reason: what is the *ground* of psychic life – the inner world? We cannot begin to answer this question without making a priori claims about the logic of the interior, a logic of unconscious internal modification. Tabula rasa approaches, typical of early modern philosophy, claim that all knowledge comes from direct conscious experience, while a priori judgments tell us that certain ontological conditions of subjectivity must be unconsciously operative in order to make experience possible. While the former rely on observable experience that presupposes a psychology of cognition, the latter emphasizes the ontological and logical continuity of unconscious experience, which allows for the structures and functions of consciousness to arise. Tabula rasa explanations are philosophically simple, myopic, and naïve – long displaced by the Kantian turn in philosophy and refined by many idealists through to poststructuralism, whereby a priori accounts are favoured in logic, linguistics, and evolutionary epistemology. As we will see, the process of unconscious modification rests on the internal negations, divisions, projections, incorporations, and reconstitutive movements of the dialectic.

We must start with the question of genesis, of Beginning – original ground. If it becomes necessary to trace the origin and development of the mind in order to come to terms with first principles (the metaphysics of the soul), then we must attempt to conceptually isolate a ground in which all else arises. Like Freud and other scientifically motivated theorists, we must situate this unfolding ground within the natural world, within the corporeal subject itself, and thus avoid appealing to a singular, first principle or category of the ultimate, with which neither we nor the philosophers are equipped to deal without either begging the question or entering the cellar of infinite regress. Not only must we start with the natural being of the embryonic psyche, with its *given* natural immediacy, but we must also inevitably begin from the inside-out, progressing from unconscious internal activity to external mediated consciousness. I argue that, as epistemologically subjective, self-attuned experiential beings, we intuit, feel, apprehend, and/or know our own interiority *before* we encounter the manifold data of the sensuous outside world. Although, as previously mentioned, externality, biological, social, and linguistic contingencies, as well as cultural historicity, are superimposed upon us a priori as part of our ontological facticity and archaic primacy.

From a methodological account, tracing the dialectical birth and epigenesis of the psyche from the interior to the exterior is philosophically defendable because it does not merely presuppose the existence of the object world; instead, it constructs a means to engage external reality from its own internal psychic configurations. I do not wish to revive the irreparable schism between the failed realism/anti-realism controversy, only to show how process is internally mediated and dialectically conditioned. From my account, the subject-object contrast must be seen as a dialectical process system that is ontologically interdependent, emergent, and equiprimordial. The inner world of subjective experience and the outer world of objective natural events are equiprimordially constituted as interpenetrable processes that comprise our fluxuational experiences of psychic reality.

For all practical purposes, we live and function in a world that we indubitably accept as real – things happen around us even if we don't adequately perceive them or understand their existence or purpose. The instant we open our eyes and orient our senses to what we apprehend before us, we have already made a metaphysical commitment: reality is presupposed. The minute we open our mouths to converse with another, we have already accepted the existence of the other by virtue of the fact that we participate in actions that affirm a sense of the real. Radical subjectivists, idealists, sceptics,[5] and postmoderns who wish to deny the reality of the external world are simply professing a delusion. Whether under the auspices of scholarly assiduity, or motivated by narcissistic currents protective of a certain philosophical ideology, no sane human being truly lives a life devoid of accepting certain premises that predicate an extant world: to say otherwise is disingenuous intellectual masturbation. What is real is what each subject experiences, despite any claim to consensus, originality, personal understanding, or indubitability, by the simple fact that it is his or her experience.

Like philosophy, psychoanalysis remains torn between various tensions that want to affirm both objectivist and subjectivist dimensions of human experience while avoiding the pitfalls inherent to each position. This tension is exacerbated by false dichotomies that either emphasize empirical (objective) science over the phenomenology of (subjective) experience or vice versa, which inevitably makes ontological assertions about the existence of a mind-independent world. For all practical reasons, this dichotomy is worthless: I live and experience a world that I apprehend as encompassing both inner and outer spatiotemporal events, those intrinsic to my intrapsychic embodiment and those externally alien to me, thus making fine distinctions in the content, contextual operations, and cognitive-affective-somatic processes in which sensuous experience and rational judgment unfold. From a pragmatic account, the question of whether natural objects exist independent of consciousness becomes inane: of course they do, or you would not be reading this book. Whether or not we can *know* the real, however, becomes an important quest for psychoanalytic epistemology.

It is very difficult to denounce the notion that each individual has first-person privileged access to his or her inner thoughts, beliefs, feelings, and experiences that no other person could possibly know, even if such access is limited, truncated, or distorted under the press of mutational factors. Even if thoughts or belief attributions are objectively false, the inner subjective experience is nevertheless a psychic reality and is *known* – albeit imperfectly – to the person as *his* experience. Therefore, the truth or falsity of particular beliefs does not negate the fact that inner experience and self-consciousness of that experience is knowledge. Although we may become more intimately acquainted with various elements of our inner experiences through third-party observation, extraspective data, and interpersonal facilitation, there is no substitute for knowledge that one directly apprehends or thinks. This is because it is an immediate form of self-experience. In addition, knowledge of our own mind is privileged and authoritative when compared to knowledge of other minds and other things, although such knowledge also constitutes first-order experience by virtue of the fact that we posit it internally.

We have a private viewing in the theatre of our own minds. No matter what anyone else thinks or observes, no outside source can directly know that first person's privileged access to his experiences irrespective of truth claims, misrepresentations, or the validity of self-knowledge. Put simply, I know what I had for breakfast this morning and others don't. As Davidson (1974) states, sincere first-person, present-tense assertions about one's own thoughts have an authority no second- or third-person claims, or first-person other-tense claims can have, even if such claims are fallible. This bears directly on psychoanalytic epistemology since the analyst is attempting to uncover and illuminate hidden aspects of the patient's mind within the joint context of examining the patient's unique experiential world and the intersubjective ambiance that lends mutual direction to the emergent field of subjective truths.

The ontological process in which subjectivity accounts for our experience of the real has been virtually ignored in psychoanalysis. This claim may at first seem palpably false: consciousness is predicated on unconsciousness; but it is precisely this *process* of development that remains murky, hence unresolved. One decisive advantage to process psychoanalytic thought is that it attempts to show through progressive dialectical mediation how potentially *all* aspects of experience may be accounted for within a logical speculative paradigm: this approach accounts for the *subjective universality of form* within the multiply contoured contextualization of individual and collective experience that constitutes the qualities and contents of our phenomenal lives. The phenomenal perspective of the sense of the real – the echo of inner truth – carries a validity that only each individual knows and harbours regardless of whether another experiences with that person a shared meaning, reciprocal identification, or empathic resonance. In fact, subjectivity is conditioned by the dialectic even if perspectival experiences defy objective consensus or natural laws. Our subjective appreciation of what is real is radically habituated by our own internal worlds and unconscious permutations, thereby influencing conscious perception, judgment, and intersubjective exchange. This is why psychic reality is first-order experience.[6]

All we can experience and know *is* psychic reality: whether inner or outer, present or absent, perceived or imagined, hallucinated or conceived, reality is mediated by subjective mind.[7] Here I do not wish to introduce an ontological duality between psychic and material reality, as is customary for most psychoanalytic discourse; rather, I wish to reemphasize that subject and object are equiprimordial and mutually implicative constructs. Psychic reality is our only register and epistemic medium for engaging life and, as such, cannot be partitioned off from the external world, which it dialectically conjoins through the process of its own engagement via the apparatus of consciousness. Yet, although an enormous aspect of mind and personal identity involves consciousness, it is only a surface intermediate organ or mesoagentic systemic activity – the modification of unconscious life, a fraction of the activity that comprises the internal processes and pervasive throbs of unformulated unconscious experience. Our epistemological understanding of the real is ontologically conditioned on a priori unconscious structures and governed by *intrasubjective* processes that allow the natural external world to arise in consciousness. Therefore, our encounter with and understanding of psychic reality is always mediated by intrapsychic events that are first-order or first-person experiences, even if such experiences operate outside of conscious awareness or are under the influence of extrinsic events that exert variable pressures on our mental operations.

Freud frowned on metaphysics, yet his theory of mind is a metaphysical treatise replete with quandaries. Although Freud stated that the

I develops out of the It and that consciousness arises in the ego, he did not proffer an adequate explanation of how this activity occurs. In fact, there are many problems with the relations between ego activity and the drives, the question of mediation by the drives, the distinctness of the I and the It, and whether they can be distinguished at all (and, if they can be distinguished, this is only in a phenomenological sense; in other words, they do not have separate essences but only different appearances). Freud held that psychic origin commenced in that broad category of the mind labelled *das Es*, what he earlier stipulated as falling under the rubric of the system *Ucs*. Now that we have prepared the context for a process account of the mind, it is time for us to return to our original task, namely, the genesis problem, and to give voice to the logic of modification Freud anticipated but left unexplained. Here we must examine the psyche's most elemental pulse from its natural immediacy, what Freud reified as the indubitable primacy of the drives or pulsions.

CLARIFICATIONS OF *TRIEB*

Freud's (1915a) pivotal work, *Triebe und Triebschicksale*, continues to be a source of misunderstanding among English-speaking audiences almost a century after it appeared in print. Customarily translated as "Instincts and Their Vicissitudes," this is not only a mistranslation but it also inaccurately implies a set of propositions that Freud neither intended to convey nor espoused – namely, that the human psyche, which Freud referred to as the soul (*Seele*), was composed of behaviorally hard-wired, physiologically determined instincts that formed the edifice for human motivation and action. *Instinkt* was a word Freud rarely used in the context of the human subject; rather, he reserved it for animal species, loathing it for its simple equation to material reduction. This is precisely why he deliberately chose the word *Trieb* – more appropriately translated as drive, pulsion,[8] impulse, or urge – to characterize human motivation. Likewise, *Schicksale*, rendered as "vicissitudes," is equally misleading because it implies a passionless, staid mechanism of change rather than the dynamic notion of mutability that belongs to the destiny of life experience. This is what Freud had in mind when he envisioned the psyche as a temporal flux of dynamic events that arise from the most archaic fabric of our corporeal nature, which transforms over time through internal mediations we customarily refer to as "defence mechanisms," itself another unfortunate and misleading term. "Drives and their Fate" comes much closer to capturing the implied meaning behind the transmogrification of inner forces, a process that extends to the most unrefined and immediate expression or derivative of a drive to the most sublimated aspects of human deed and desire.

George Frank (2003, 691) offers another recent challenge to Freud's thesis on "drives," claiming, like others before him, that we ought to do away with the term altogether, only to replace it with a "new paradigm" of "needs, affects, beliefs, etc." This seems to be a standard view within contemporary psychoanalysis, yet it does not do justice to the abstruse concept of *Trieb*, which, in my estimate, gets watered down to a theory of consciousness. Not only does Freud's thesis on the nature, activities, and transmutations of the *Triebe* answer to the theoretical conundrum of human motivation that still besets psychoanalysis today, but I further show that Freud's concept of drive does not at all contradict competing contemporary models favouring beliefs, needs, wishes, and intentionality. On the contrary, he explains how those processes are made possible to begin with.

Freud's technical use of *Trieb* is distinguished from the ordinary usage, which describes an urge, such as a whim or a caprice. For Freud, *Trieb* is the *driving force* behind the mind compelled and fuelled by unconscious desire. While Freud certainly says that the source (*Quelle*) of a drive is biologically informed (hence emanating from constitutionally based somatic tension), this is preceded by his emphasis that the "essence" (*Wesen*) of a drive is its pressure (*Drang*), namely, internal experiential activity under the press of certain events – events that make themselves felt or known as an urge, wish, desire, or need. It is important to qualify that the source is *not* the motive, as Frank (misinterpreting Freud) implies, only that it is internally derived: motives, on the other hand, are complex phenomena subject to many intervening and emergent interactive effects both internally mediated and externally influenced: "Although drives are wholly determined by their origin in a somatic source, in the life of the soul [*Seelenleben*] we know them only by their aims" (SE 14:123). Note that Freud says a drive is determined by its "origin" (*Herkunft*), not that all motives are biologically based. Quite simply, the reason Freud logically situates the source of a drive within our biologically determined facticity is that we are embodied beings. We our thrown into a body a priori, and hence all internal activity must *originally* arise from within our corporeality mediated by internal dynamics. Here Freud is merely asserting an empirical fact grounded in a natural science framework. Those analysts like Mitchell (1988), who wish to abnegate the archaic primacy of the body, are simply misguided. As a consequence, many advocates of the American middle group uncritically and naively devalue the importance of embodiment in favour of relational motives; however, they do so based on extreme polemics and unsophisticated dichotomies that utterly fail to acknowledge the indubitable certainty that relationality is predicated on our embodiment (e.g., Pizer 2006).[9] What is utterly ignored within these circles is the fact that Freud was the first one to pave a theory of object relations and ego psychology that was interpersonally based on the relational motives of the drives. I will explain, but first let us further prepare our discussion.

Freud further analyzed the elements of a drive by examining its aim and its object. The aim (*Ziel*) of a drive is to seek satisfaction, hence pleasure, which is achieved by terminating a state of stimulation. This is the *telos* of a drive, its purpose. But unlike the mechanical operations of fixed, predetermined tropisms that are genetically hard-wired behavioural patterns belonging to some animals and lower organisms, human drives are determinative. That is, they are endowed with a degree of freedom manipulated by the agency of the ego, an ego that operates on manifold levels of conscious and unconscious activity. Freud specifically tells us that the aim of a drive may take "different paths" with multiple instantiations, may be inhibited or deflected (perhaps in the service of an ultimate aim), or it can achieve "intermediate" endeavours, work in tandem with competing goals, and be combined, coalesce, or merge into a confluence all at once, thus being operative on different levels of pressure and meaning (SE 14:122). Of course an aim *needs* an object in order to achieve satisfaction, and this is why Freud says an object (*Objekt*) is the "most variable" aspect to a drive, the avenue through which a drive is able to procure fulfillment. Furthermore, an object is "assigned," hence it is not "originally connected" to a drive. In fact, an object can be anything, whether in actuality or in fantasy, and can be both extraneous or internal (e.g., the "subject's own body" [*des eigenen Körpers*]) (SE 14:122). Notice how Freud uses the language of subjectivity when describing a drive and, specifically, the ego's mediating activity of satisfying its aim. And note that the overarching preponderance of objects are mostly people and the functions they serve. Drives desire others, hence relatedness.[10] Here Freud unequivocally accounts for how interpersonal phenomena arise based on the most primordial activities of unconscious desire. Thus, not only does Freud account for a relational theory embedded within the process of drive activity itself, but he also shows the logical necessity and developmental progression from intrapsychic to intersubjective life.

Taken as a whole, drives are pure experiential activity. They are not fixed or static behavioural tropisms (such as instincts); rather, they are dynamic patterns of events that are malleable and flexible instantiations of unconscious occasions. The fate or destiny of a drive is what becomes of its activities, from beginning to end. This is why Freud concludes that *die Triebschicksale* are different "methods of defence" or resistance (*als Arten der Abwehr*) against a drive and that, due to the competing overdetermined motive forces at work in the psyche, prevent it from satisfying its original unmodified aim (SE 14:127). What follows is that a drive must divide or split itself and take itself as its own object. Freud's careful inspection of the activities and attributes of a drive in his 1915 paper are the result of his changing theoretical system. At this time, Freud was working from the premise that drives derive from a libidinous spring, from a *Lust*-principle. Up until then, *Trieb* was used to describe a number of different activities that arose in consciousness and were applied to intentional self-states belonging to the ego, which he called *die Ich-Triebe*, such as wishes, beliefs, actions, propositions, and so forth. Frank (2003, 692) is content to view a drive and a wish as synonymous, but this is inaccurate. A wish, belief, or need is a derivative and transformation of a drive, what is typically considered a conscious manifestation from contemporary perspectives. Of course, Freud wanted to account for the presence and ubiquity of unconscious fantasy, which takes the form of determinate self-states (such as beliefs, needs, and propositional attitudes) but only on a pre-reflective level of self-expression or self-certainty that is somatically and affectively realized. While Freud (1912) emphasized the notion that "every psychical act begins as an unconscious one" (SE 12:264), he also showed that, through the transformation of the drives, conscious and self-conscious (hence reflexive) cognition produces various needs, beliefs, and so forth, which are the modification of unconscious structure. Therefore, Freud's 1915 thesis on the nature of a drive is a pivotal step in his move towards his mature theory, in which he concludes that mind is an architectonic, epigenetic achievement that evolves from the most rudimentary expression of the dialectic of life and death – hence from the libidinal activity of Eros and the destructive will of *der Todestrieb* – organized within an unconscious It as alien and alienated desire, executed by the agency of the ego, and sublimated through reason, aesthetics, and moral judgment inherent in self-reflective social life. Here we may argue that human subjectivity is predicated on agentic determinacy expressed through the epigenesis of unconscious process as the maturation and actualization of freedom. But before mind can be successful in actualizing its freedom, it must first confront death.

DEATH AS DESIRE

What could be more banal than death, than the inevitable, something predictable, utterly certain? It is banal by virtue of the fact that it is unimaginatively routine – eternal. Death cannot be waived or amended, what Heidegger (1962) avows "stands before us – something impending" (BT 294), something imminent – our thrownness – to be postponed, even denied. For Freud, death is much more than that which stands before us; rather, it resides within us, an impulsion towards annihilation. But before the will to murder, there exists an insidious self-implosion, namely, suicidal desire. Here the banality of death is not just something that happens to us, it *is* us – our inner being, only to be experienced in novel fashions, repetitiously, circuitously, ad nauseam.

Death-work for Freud (1933a) was ultimately in the service of restoring or reinstating a previous state of undifferentiated internal being, a drive "which sought to do away with life once more and to re-establish [an] inorganic state" (SE 22:107). Freud did not argue that death was the only aim of life, only that it maintained a dialectical tension in juxtaposition to a life principle under the ancient command of Eros, yet the two forces of mind remained ontologically inseparable.

The force of the negative is so prevalent in psychoanalytic practice that it is perplexing why the death drive would remain a questionable tenet among psychoanalysts today.[11] From a phenomenological standpoint, it is impossible to negate the force and salience of the negative. The world evening news is about nothing but death, destruction, chaos, conflict, tragedy, and human agony. Even advocates who champion a pure trauma model of self-destruction or externalized negativity in the service of explaining human aggressivity must contend with inherently destructive organizing elements that imperil the organism from within. Even medical science is perplexed by the internally derived forces (e.g., cancer, AIDS,

ALS) that drain the healthy organism of life due to attacks perpetrated by its own immune system or endogenous constitution. Consider the paradoxical processes that result in sleep's being both regressive and restorative and, particularly, how going to sleep is associated with wanting to return to a previously aborted state of peace, tranquility, or oceanic "quiescence" – perhaps a wish for a tensionless state, perhaps a return to the womb. Excessive sleep is also one of the most salient symptoms of clinical depression and the will towards death. Furthermore, it would be inconceivable to argue that humankind's externalized aggression is not inherently self-destructive for the simple fact that it generates more retaliatory hate, aggression, and mayhem, which threatens world accord and the progression of civil societies. Given the global ubiquity of war, genocide, geopolitical atrocities, and the poisoning of our natural environments, in all likelihood we as a human race will die by actions brought about by our own hand rather than the impersonal forces of nature. *Homo homini lupus* – "Man is a wolf to man."[12] Contemporary psychoanalysis seems to be uninterested in Freud's classic texts on the primacy of death, to the point that the latter are dismissed without even being read simply because credible authorities in the field say this may be done. Here I have in mind the relational school's anti-drive theory campaign. In my opinion, those who argue against the death drive simply do not grasp the inherent complexity, non-concretization, anti-reductionism, and non-linearity of what Freud has to offer us. Critics claim that the death drive defies evolutionary biology, therefore it must be bogus. But this criticism is merely begging the question of what we mean by death. And, more specifically, what we mean by the *function* of death in psychic reality. Or, to be even more precise, how death is organized as unconscious experience. Just because a species is organically impelled to thrive does not mean it is devoid of destructive principles derived from within its own constitution – principles that imperil its existence and proliferation. It can be logically claimed that life is only possible through the force of the negative, which brings about higher developmental achievements through the destruction of the old.[13] This is the positive significance of the negative, an artefact of psychic reality that derives its source from internal negation and anguish while at the same time transcending its descent into psychic pain. Psychoanalysts are often confused by viewing death as merely a physical end-state or the termination of life, when it may be memorialized in the psyche as a primary ontological principle that informs the trajectory of all psychic activity.[14] Here death is phylogenetic (*phulon*, class; *geneia*, born). Death has multiple interpretations and meanings within conscious experience that are radically opposed to the logic of negativity that infiltrates unconscious semiotics. Death is an ontological category for unconscious experience that can never elude psychic existence. This is because what we know or profess to know epistemically as mediated inner experience is always predicated on our felt-relation to death, that is, to the primordial force of repetitive negation, conflict, and destruction that alerts us to being and life, a dialectic that is ontologically inseparable and mutually implicative. What we call a life force, drive, urge, or impetus is intimately conjoined with its pulsional opposition, that is, its negation, termination, or lack. Here life = death: being and nothing are the same.

Freud never used the term "death instinct" to refer to the organism's innate propensity for destruction; rather, he used the term *Todestrieb*, which is more accurately translated as the "death drive." Philosophers have placed great importance on the role of death and destruction in the constitution of human subjectivity, but Freud gives it paradigmatic primacy as the ontological force behind the origins of mind. This interpretation may only be properly appreciated after we come to understand how libido, and later Eros, is born/e from death, the details of which are most thoroughly articulated in *Beyond the Pleasure Principle*. Freud's attribution of the centrality of death is the result of laborious theoretical evolution, a notion that gained increasing conceptual and clinical utility as his ideas advanced, based on appropriating new burgeoning clinical data, not to mention the fact that death and decay had a profound personal resonance.[15]

Yet Freud was not always favourably disposed to the primordiality of destruction: his early position was to subordinate aggression to libido or to make it a derivative of it. Freud's ambivalence about the constitutive role of death constituted a visible tension in his thinking from as early as his dispute with Adler regarding the existence of an "aggressive drive" (*Aggressionsbetrieb*) (see Freud 1909; SE 10:140n2). We may further observe his own personal confessions about his unease with the inextricability of sex and death, to the point where it needed to be repressed, a narrative Freud reported as early as 1898 (SE 3:292–4), although he later elaborated his views more fully in *The Psychopathology of Everyday Life* (Freud 1901; SE 6:3 5). Regardless of his ambivalence, Freud was preoccupied with the nature and meaning of death and its influence on mental functioning since his early psychoanalytic writings. In one of his early communications to Fliess (Draft N, enclosed in Letter 64, 31 May 1897), he discusses how death wishes are "directed in sons against their father and in daughters against their mother" (Freud 1896b, 255). This passage may arguably be Freud's first allusion to the Oedipus complex.

Death, destruction, anguish, and tumult not only become the conflictual properties of the psyche in both content and form, but they also form the ontogenetic edifice of the underworld – "chaos, a cauldron full of seething excitations" (SE 22:73) – as Freud puts it. Furthermore, Freud makes death an ontological a priori condition of the coming into being of human subjectivity that is "phylogenetically" (SE 22:79) imprinted and laid down within the aboriginal structural processes that constitute our unconscious strivings. Freud situates these strivings within an inherent tendency towards self-destruction that is in combat with the reactionary impetus towards growth and greater unification – in other words, the dialectic of life and death. Yet Freud (1920) ultimately makes death the "first drive" (SE 18:38), a compulsion to return to an original inanimate state. In fact, Freud (1933a) tells us that the death drive "cannot fail to be present in every vital process" (SE 22:107). It is inherent in the whole process of civilization, which is "perpetually threatened with disintegration" (Freud 1930; SE 21:112), just as conspicuously as Eros ensures its survival. Freud built upon his 1920 introduction of the destructive principle and systematically forged his dual classification of the drives in 1923; showed its presence in masochism in 1924; made it a key component of anxiety by 1926; and, in his final days, avowed in his posthumously published monograph, *An Outline of Psycho-Analysis* (1940), that death is inseparable from Eros, which "gives rise to the whole variegation of the phenomena of life" (SE 23:149). Therefore, death becomes the necessary touchstone and catalyst of psychic existence. Here we have a very grave philosophy indeed.

But how does death acquire such a primary position in the psyche? In other words, how is death interiorized from the beginning? Freud (1920) provides an initial explanation by appealing to what he observed, namely, the phenomenon of repetition. He noticed this in the traumatic neuroses, particularly in people who were suffering from posttraumatic stress due to the baneful effects of the Great War, and who were continuously being resubjected, in horrific dreams, thoughts, fantasies, and perceptions, to the traumatic moments they had previously encountered. In fact, here was Freud's first major amendment to his thesis that dreams represented the disguised fulfilment of a wish. On the contrary, traumatic dreams were experienced as a fresh charge of anxiety *against* the fulfilment of a wish. And for good reason. Under these circumstances, the psyche is fighting against what it had internalized through unwanted surprise, ambush, and impingement – sheer terror. Anxiety is a bid for survival. But Freud quickly turns to more normative experiences of separation from the primary attachment figure (i.e., one's mother), thus ushering in anxiety, abandonment, and loss as an impetus to repetition. In fact, he uses his own grandson, Ernst, as an example – the illustrious *fort-da* narrative – thus canonizing the ambivalence and helplessness associated with the anxiety of uncertainty and anger over the disappearance of a love object. In short, Freud observed his eighteen-month-old grandson invent a game that involved throwing various objects, mainly his toys, and simultaneously saying "o-o-o" when his mother left him during the day. Freud interpreted this to be the linguistic signification of *fort* (gone). It was only when he discovered a yo-yo that he could make the object return once he had thrown it away, followed by a joyous *da* (there). Here Freud not only illuminates the motive that drives a repetition (i.e, "mastery") but also shows the economic element that "carried along with it a yield of pleasure of another sort" (*SE* 18:16). The inherent aggression involved in throwing the toy away, coupled with the undoing of destruction through the satisfaction of its reappearance, points towards how this childhood game serves to recapitulate loss through return. Freud is suggestive, but he does not actually say that this yield of satisfaction of "another sort" is achieved in the context of absence, of lack or nothingness, a property of death. Death enters into "every vital process," and this is certainly the case between the dialectic of presence and absence, being and nothingness, abundance and lack.

The nature of repetition naturally leads Freud to examine the phenomenon of self-destructiveness, what he observes in the nature of psychopathology itself, the "compulsion to repeat" trauma via symptom formation, a topic he addressed earlier in "Recollecting, Repeating, and Working Through" (Freud 1914). Death is manifested in repetitions of thought, fantasy, and behaviour; in parapraxes; in masochism and sadism; in symptoms such as melancholia, paranoia, and psychosis; and in the uncanny, just to name a few. Death residue impregnates repressed schemata that find expression through repeating the unconscious material itself as it is happening in the moment rather than remembering what had been an occurrence in the past. When repressed events take the form of "fresh experiences" rather than being properly ascribed as reproductions of the past, reality is clouded with negativity, affective contagion, paranoiac fantasy, and, subsequently, qualitative suffering. These repetitions, driven by inner compulsions, do not bring satisfaction, only "unpleasure." This conundrum led Freud to believe that instinctual life was driven by more than just libidinal discharge and "that there really does exist in the mind a compulsion to repeat which overrides the pleasure principle" (SE 18:22). He needed to go deeper than simply relying on his customary economic explanations. He needed to find something "more primitive, more elementary, more instinctual than the pleasure principle which it over-rides" (SE 18:23). Moving from the empirical, Freud had no other recourse than to engage inferential logic, what he carefully referred to as "speculation," and "often far-fetched speculation" at that (SE 18:24). Despite his critics' renunciation of the death drive on evolutionary grounds, charging that it allegedly betrays Darwinian biology (Sulloway 1979; Webster 1995), there is nothing "far-fetched" about it at all. From my account, the death drive is Freud's greatest theoretical contribution to understanding the dynamics of the unconscious mind. Let us explore this notion more fully.

Freud situates his argument within the language of embryology and postulates that a living organism in its most simplified form is in a state of undifferentiation yet is "susceptible to stimulation" from the many forces that comprise the external world. Freud conjectures that the organism must have an intrinsic capacity to protect itself from powerful stimuli through a resistive process internally operative and sensitive to intrusive encroachments from externality that threaten its potential destruction. The human mind is no exception. Here Freud's entire discourse is an economy of energetics designed to transform stimuli in the service of self-preservation, thus defending them from both external and internal stimuli that create states of unpleasure. This example from embryology is extended to the psychical apparatus, once again what Freud later referred to as the soul (*Seele*).[16] Here the role of trauma becomes paramount,[17] and Freud is specifically referring to external events that have the capacity to breach the protective barrier and flood the mental register with excessive states of excitation, thus rendering it unable to master or bind the breach or to find appropriate modes of discharge. The so-called "traumatic neurosis" is one such outcome of an extensive breach of the protective barrier or systems of defence, thus leading to a compulsion to repeat, which Freud says exhibits a high degree of "instinctual" (*Triebhaft*) character, by which he means the degree of felt urgency it assumes in the psyche, what he sometimes equates with possession by a "daemonic" power (SE 18:36). Here it is interesting to note Freud's choice of words: "daemonic" not only signifies possession by a demon but is also derived from the Greek *daimōn*, which is a creative force or divine power.

Under the pressure of disturbing external forces, a drive becomes an urge, or pulsion, to repeat itself, the motive being to return to an earlier state of undifferentiation, an "expression of the inertia inherent in organic life" (SE 18:36). It is here where Freud extends his hypothesis that all drives aim towards a restoration of earlier events or modes of being, namely, unmodified quiescence. Because drives are "conservative" – that is, they follow a conservative economy of regulatory energy, are acquired historically and phylogenetically in the species, and tend towards restorative processes that maintain an original uncomplicated immediacy – Freud speculates that an "elementary living entity" would have no desire to change, only to maintain its current mode of existence. Here Freud attributes the process of organic development to the disruptive press of external factors that impinge on the quiescent state of the organism, factors it is obliged to internalize and repeat. It is here where the organism acquires the *telos* to return to its original inorganic state. Here Freud summons Horace: *mors ultima linea rerum est* – death is the final goal of things. As Freud concisely puts it: "*the aim of all life is death*" (SE 18:38, emphasis in original).[18] Therefore, the first drive comes into being as a tension introduced by an extrinsic force that stimulates the impulse to cancel itself out. It is here that the genesis of organic life becomes death, itself the "origin and aim of life" (SE 19:39).

It is important to note that Freud is attempting to delineate a philosophy of organic process by isolating the "origin" (*Herkunft*) of life within a psychic ontology constituted by death. What Freud does with death is to make it an inner attribute and impetus, originally summoned from within the psyche itself, that is awakened by an external stimulus. According to Freud, all living organisms die for "internal reasons," that is, death is brought about from the cessation of internally derived activity. In other words, death is not merely executed by an extraneous force;

rather, it is activated by endogenous motives. But death does not happen any which way: it must be executed by the agent itself, more specifically, by the unconscious ego aligned with fulfilling the wish for its own destruction. Here the psyche is given determinate degrees of freedom to "follow its own path to death" (SE 18:39), that is, to bring about its end fashioned according to its own hands.[19] But this end is actually a return to its beginning, a recapturing, a recapitulation of its quiescent inorganic immediacy. This is why Freud thought that the unconscious forces operative in repetition were ultimately in the service of self-destruction in the form of a wish to return to an original undifferentiated condition. However, because the impetus towards death is internally derived, the ego can seize upon many choices in its death-work, which is accomplished through the circuitous routes and detours that often accompany the variegated phenomena of life. Although the ultimate *telos* of a drive, and hence its final cause, is death, it may only be enjoyed via postponement through unconscious volition. This is why *Todestrieb* is beyond the pleasure principle: not only does it precede the life-preserving drives but it also stands over them as a supraordinate organizational thrust. And this is how the life instincts, or Eros, harness the power of death to serve their own transformative evolutionary purposes. Here evolution is not merely unquestioned conformity to Darwinian principles oriented towards a single aim; rather, it is a modified internal organization oriented towards higher modes of existence and self-development via defensive adaptation forged through forays into conflict, negativity, and death.

But what is to become of death if life supersedes it? What Freud concludes particularly highlights his genius, for death is ultimately in the service of the pleasure principle. This is a very delicate theoretical move and is only successful when you observe the logic of the dialectic as the confluence of mutually implicative oppositions that share a common unity. Following the laws of psychic economy, the pleasure principle is a tendency to free the psyche of excitation, or at least to minimize stimulation levels so that there is a tolerable degree of constancy. The ultimate condition of pleasure would therefore be a state that is free of tension: through this end, cessation of tension would represent its fulfilment, hence its completion. From this impersonal account of unconscious teleology, what could be more pleasurable than death, than non-being? Death is a tensionless state, unadulterated peace. But Freud's teleology is not strictly Aristotlean: although the unconscious mind aims towards death, it has the capacity to choose its own path towards self-destruction. It is only under this condition of determinate freedom that the psyche can bring about its own end, which makes death-work inherent in the life-enhancing processes that repudiate the will towards self-destruction while embracing it. Here we may observe two opposing forces operative within the single purpose of the pleasure principle: death and life are ontologically conjoined yet differentiated from one another. It is here that Freud's dual classification of the drives is solidified.

Recall that, for Freud, death is the "original drive" or urge in the embryonic psyche, and it is transformed by the life forces that emerge from it and then combat it, hence bringing about a doubling of the negative. Freud is clear in telling us that death and its derivatives or representatives, such as aggression and destruction as well as Eros and its manifestations of libido or the life-enhancing processes that promote self-preservation and advance, are "struggling with each other from the very first" (SE 18:61–2n1). Harnessing and diverting the internal powers of death, the destructive principle must be deflected outwards, which serves the libidinal progression of the psyche in its ascendance towards self-development. The sexual or libidinal impulses thus become defined and refined in opposition to competing forces that seek to bring about their demise or premature decay. Here the life force is at odds with its destructive antithesis, both conjoined in conflict yet punctuated by oscillating moments of self-manifestation. Freud could not bifurcate Eros and Thanatos, despite their dual forms of appearance, because he observed that each always interpenetrates the other, hence they are not ontologically separated.

Freud (1930) vacillated, even waffled, with regard to his tendency towards a dualistic view of the drives verses a monistic developmental ontology, and, in this way, he remained a thorough dialectician in conceiving the mind as "an original bipolarity in its own nature" (SE 21:119). Melanie Klein continued this tradition of juxtaposing oppositions but gave the death drive an even more exalted status: death became the meridian of mental organization. In Melanie Klein's (1932) first book, *The Psycho-Analysis of Children*, she makes her first reference to the death drive, which she takes over wholeheartedly from Freud. Under the influence of Abraham's views on orality, Klein becomes interested in the phenomenon of infantile sadism, which she attributes to the tension between the polarity of the life and death instincts. It is specifically in the context of the early development of the origin of the superego that Klein annexes the death drive and makes it a key catalyst in the emerging process of the infant's mental functioning. Klein sees the fusion of the dual drives as occurring at birth, the destructive forces further emanating from within the infant and in response to unsatisfied libido, thus culminating in anxiety and rage, which only strengthens the sadistic impulses. Here Klein sees the source of anxiety as directly flowing from the destructive principle directed towards the organism, thus reactively alerting the ego to danger and helplessness in the face of annihilation. As Klein states: "anxiety would originate from aggression" (126). Not only does the infant experience anxiety in response to its own self-destructive urges, but it also fears external objects that are the locus of its sadism, now acquiring a secondary source of danger. Here Klein introduces the splitting of the ego as a defensive attempt to deny and repress the acknowledgment of its internal sources of anxiety fuelled by the death drive: objects of frustration, hate, rage, and sadism are now seen as the exclusive source of danger, thus diverting the dual nature of anxiety by transposing internality onto externality. This is the earliest manoeuvre of splitting, projection, and paranoia that transpires in the ego, which "seeks to defend itself by destroying the object" (128).

Klein radicalizes the presence of the death drive and anxiety in the embryonic mind. Death creates anxiety, thus leading to the developmental processes of schizoid, paranoiac, and depressive positions, later recaptured in awakening Oedipal tendencies but first originating within the organism itself and defensively deflected onto external objects. This process thereby becomes the antediluvian cycle of projective identification: the entire architectonic function of psychic maturation is predicated on the instantiation and transformation of death.

Death-work suffuses the ontology of subjectivity instantiated through its experiential unfolding, what Hegel attributes to the dialectic of mind in both its maturation and decay. Death permeates being, from its archaic nether regions to the triumph *Geist* enjoys in vanquishing earlier moments of experience, itself the result of annulment and supersession, only to devolve back into darkness – the abyss. Freud (1925d) tells us that death largely works "in silence" (*SE* 20:57), a position he was later to recast. Yet for Klein, there is nothing silent about death: it screams violently upon the initial inception of the psyche, an intrinsic predetermined barrage of negation, onslaught, and desolation, an inferno besieged by it own flames. Here Freud is radicalized: mind becomes apocalyptic. Active at the moment of birth, death lends structure to the embryonic mind, a facticity that saturates all aspects of early ego development. In Klein, death finds its pinnacle as the fountainhead of psychic life.

Even if critics find the death drive theoretically untenable, I still believe it is a useful clinical heuristic that guides therapeutic practice. What we as analysts face everyday is the inherent self-destructiveness of patients who can find neither amity nor reprieve from psychic conflict and the repetitions that fuel their suffering. These inherent capacities for self-destruction are not merely located in external sources as they are both *interiorized* and *internalized*, thus becoming the organizing death principles at work on myriad levels of unconscious experience. Inherent capacities for self-destruction take many circuitous and compromised paths, something the modern conflict theorists would ascribe to symptom formation, addictions, self-victimization, pernicious patterns of recurrence, and harmful behaviours that hasten physical deterioration or poor health. All of these tragedies may be further compounded by external trauma and affliction, which Freud first identified in his trauma model of hysteria; however, this does not necessarily negate the presence of internally derived deleterious aggressions turned on the self. We see it everyday in the consulting room. From oppressive guilt, disabling shame, explosive rage, contagious hate, self-loathing, and unbearable symptomatic agony, there is a perverse appeal to suffering, to embracing our masochistic *jouissance* – our ecstasy in pain. Whether in the form of an addict's craving for a bottle or a drag off a cigarette, there is an inherent destructiveness imbued in the very act of the pursuit of pleasure. All aspects of the progression of civilization and its decay are the determinate teleological fulfilment of death-work.

WHERE *IT* ALL BEGINS: THE TRANSMOGRIFICATION OF THE DRIVES

The inner pulsion, urge, or locomotive pressure of a drive becomes a more descriptive way of emphasizing the notion of intrinsic unrest, desire, and compulsion often associated with impersonal, non-intentional forces impelling the individual from within. We may initially see why Freud's concept of drive has descriptive utility: it is an unconscious process that fuels and propels the organism. But, more important, Freud conceives of a drive as a malleable, plastic, transformative activity – not as a static, genetically imprinted or determined pressure that cannot be mediated or amended. For Freud, a drive can be altered and permutated, while an instinct, being stagnant and unchangeable, cannot. Whereas the expression of a drive can be mitigated if not changed entirely, an instinct cannot undergo modification at all. In English, the term "instinct" also typifies something that is innate. Therefore, in order to avoid duplicating confusion about the nature of drive and instinct, it should be clear by now that all references to instinctual processes should be viewed within this stipulated context of drives.

As we have seen, Freud's theory of the drives went through many significant transformations throughout his career, at one time focusing solely on libido (*Lust*), then on many different competing urges belonging to both unconscious and conscious processes (e.g., *die Ich-Triebe*), before finally settling on the primacy of two antithetical yet interpenetrable classifications: sex and death. Relational and intersubjective proponents can't buy this central tenet, what Stephen Mitchell (1992, 3) calls the "outmoded concept of drives"; namely, that the mind is driven and influenced by multifarious, overdetermined unconscious forces that, originally, are biologically based pressures impinging on the conscious subject and clamouring for release. But the main objection among these schools is the concentrated refutation of the role of libido with regard to relational and intersubjective motives. Here we see the first big turn-off (and subsequent resistance from the anti-classical field): everything boils down to sex.

This unfortunate attitude is based on Freud's (1905a) early work on infantile sexuality; it does not take into account his mature theoretical advances (see Freud 1933, 1940). As mentioned earlier, Freud was not particularly impressed with having to think the same thing all the time: by the end of his life he had incorporated libido, or the sex drive, into his conception of Eros – an encompassing life principle, similar to that of the Greeks, who saw the pursuit of Eros as life's supreme aim (i.e., the holistic attainment of sensual, aesthetic, ethical, and intellectual fulfilment). In this sense, mind and body are contiguous. Blindly focusing on Freud's early work at the expense of his mature theory leads not only to misunderstanding him but also to distorting his theoretical corpus. It also leads one to incorrectly presume that Freud was committed to a genetic fallacy; namely, that all psychic life can be *reduced* to its developmental origins.[20] Eros is the sublimation (*Sublimierung*) of natural desire, first materializing as drive then progressing to the cultivated activities of the ego (i.e., rational self-conscious life).

For Freud (1915a), the source of a drive is unequivocally biological and somatic. This is the second big turn-off: humanity is viewed as a physical-instinctual machine that is turned on by the environment. I am of the opinion that not only do many post- and anti-classical schools of thought misunderstand the nature of drives but also that they ultimately misunderstand the role of biology and human embodiment. It is simply delusional to think that biology has no place in psychic economy, and those deifying relational factors through negation of the natural body are misguided. Why sex and aggression? Because they are part of our animal evolutionary past and are the essence of being human. The notion of drive underscores Freud's natural science foundation, which is inextricably bound to evolutionary currents: sex and aggression are the two fundamental forces behind the inception, course, and progression of civilization, without which there would arguably be no human race.[21]

In the historical movement of psychoanalysis we can observe a conceptual reclimatization, a move away from drive theory towards object relations theory, ego psychology, self psychology, and, now, intersubjectivity, each of which calls for a paradigm shift. In the early stages of psychoanalytic theory-building each post-classical movement championed a particular constituent of psychic activity (e.g., ego over object) while complementing and subsuming Freud's general psychological theory. In fact, it was Freud who launched ego psychology and the object relations movement.[22] Today, however, with the insistence on relational and intersubjective approaches, psychoanalysis (with stipulations) is being plummeted into a land of false dichotomies, suggesting that relation cancels drive. And even if it is conceded that the two realms co-exist, we are still asked to choose sides (see Greenberg and Mitchell 1983, 390). As a result, within many contemporary analytic circles, the primacy of the drives and the unconscious itself have virtually disappeared.[23] Take Mitchell (1992, 2) for example: "There is *no* experience that is not interpersonally mediated" (emphasis added); and Stolorow (2001, xiii): Intersubjectivity "recognizes the constitutive role of relatedness in the making of *all* experience" (emphasis added). These proclamations clearly state that consciousness conditions unconsciousness, while failing to account for what Freud had been so careful to investigate.

Although interpersonal processes are an integral and necessary aspect of psychic development, they do not by themselves negate the relevance of the drives and their mutual influence over mental life. Furthermore, Stolorow's and his colleagues' (Orange, Stolorow, and Atwood 1997; Stolorow and Atwood 1992; Stolorow, Brandchaft, and Atwood 1987) claim that everything is intersubjective fails to consider intrapsychic experience prior to the onset of consciousness. Unconsciousness precedes consciousness, hence subjective experience is internally mediated prior to one's encounter with the object world, including other subjects. In fact, drive becomes an ontological a priori that cannot be annulled or denied: moreover, it precedes interpersonal interaction by virtue of the fact that drive is constitutionally predicated.

We can never escape from the fact that we are embodied. Freud's insistence that the source of a drive is biologically given is simply an acceptance of the brute facticity of our natural corporeality. The mistake many psychoanalytic theorists make involves interpreting biology as reduction and assuming that drive discharge precludes relational activity, when, contrarily, Freud's conception of drive makes reduction impossible and relatedness possible. Let me explain.

Freud has to account for embodiment – our natural immediacy – within which urges and impulses arise, thus he focuses on the body as initially providing form, content, and structure to internal experience. This is why erogenous zones are corporeally emphasized. But, more important, Freud has to show how ego activity and consciousness are also sensuous processes: attention, perception, and the greater faculties of cognition are sentient experiential actions. This is why Freud (1923) says that the ego is a body-ego, itself the projection of a surface: *It* projects itself *onto* its surface, the surface of its immediate feeling and sensuous embodiment. Therefore drive is constituted as ego, but not at first. While Freud does not say this directly, it may nevertheless be inferred: drive becomes ego, which first knows itself as a feeling, craving, desirous corporeal being. But how does this occur? Freud says very little.

It is important to reiterate that Freud (1915a) distinguishes between four constituents of a drive: source, pressure, aim, and object. While the source (*Quelle*) is somatically organized, Freud is very clear that the pressure (*Drang*), thrust, or force of a drive is its very "essence" (*Wesen*). Here he unquestionably situates the nature of *Trieb* in its activity: drive is pulsation, unrest – pure desire. The aim (*Ziel*) or motive of a drive is to satisfy itself, to achieve pleasure as tension reduction, to end the craving; and the means by which a drive is sated is through an object (*Objekt*). Objects, especially people, are coveted for the functions they serve, and these functional objects may fulfil many competing aims as psychic life becomes more rich and variegated. In fact, drives transmogrify through many circuitous routes and take many derivative forms: what we commonly refer to as a "defence mechanism" is the teleological fate of a drive. This is an unfortunate term because "mechanism" evokes images of stasis, rigidity, and fixed predetermined movements when, instead, defences are fluid, mutable, and teleologically directed expressions of desire as *process systems*. As transformed drive, a defence is a particular piece of desire, often unconsciously intended and differentiated by its function in relation to a competing urge, impulse, or counter-intention, internal danger, environmental threat, and/or potential conscious realization that must be combated. Some defences urge the psyche to regress while others urge it to progress, and this is why a drive cannot simply be seen as biological reduction or devolve back to its original state. Because drives transform, they cannot return to their original form: we can never know a drive in itself, only as a psychical representative, presentation, or idea (*Vorstellung*). Furthermore, what we often experience as drive is its aim – the craving for satisfaction. Moreover, because drives modify themselves through a process of epigenesis, they make the more sophisticated forms of conscious and self-conscious life possible: from the archaic to the refined, unconscious drive manifests itself through relatedness to objects.

Freud's theory of *Trieb* is not without difficulty, and many critics proclaim that, because his model of tension reduction was ultimately a hydraulic component of biological-homeostasis theory, the aim or *telos* of a drive overrides relational motivations. But this conclusion is not justified, especially when others become the objects of our satisfaction and search for personal fulfilment and meaning. Freud (1915a) specifically says that the object of a drive is its most variable aspect and that it may serve multiple simultaneous motives (*SE* 14:123). Nowhere are we led to believe that relation is subordinated to biology when a drive is mediated though object relatedness. Furthermore, Freud's later theory of Eros ultimately speaks to the desire for love and the pursuit of our most cherished ideals, which he specifically equates with the Eros of Plato in the *Symposium* (Freud 1925a; *SE* 19:218). As a result, Eros becomes a relational principle (see Reisner 1992), a relation towards ourselves and others through the exaltation of human value. From the most primitive mind to the most civilized societies, we are *attached* to our ideals through others.

But let us return to a conceptual dilemma for Freud: how could a drive have an object? Put another way, how could a drive take an object as its aim without possessing some form of agency? As a teleological process, a drive has a purpose constituted through its aim; but how could it also be guided in its ability to *choose* objects for its satisfaction without accounting for intentionality on the part of an unconscious agent? Here we see why Freud had to introduce the notion of unconscious agency as constituted through the alien presence of the It. The It constitutes the realm of the dual classification of drives as well as the realm of the repressed. But is Freud justified in making the It into an agency? Could it be possible that unconscious actions of the ego are actually performing object choice, while the drives and repressed material merely act as a constant pressure the ego must mediate? This is particularly problematic for Freud given that he specifically tells us that the I logically and temporally proceeds from the It. Freud is very clear in his final specifications of how the psyche develops in this fashion. In *Inhibitions, Symptoms and Anxiety*, Freud (1926a) states:

> We were justified, I think, in dividing the ego from the id, for there are certain considerations which necessitate that step. On the other hand *the ego is identical with the id, and is merely a specially differentiated part of it.* If we think of this part by itself in contradistinction to the whole, or if a real split has occurred between the two, the weakness of the ego becomes apparent. But if the ego remains bound up with the id and indistinguishable from it, then it displays its strength. The same is true of the relation between the ego and the super-ego. In many situations the two are merged; and as a rule we can only distinguish one from the other when there is a tension or conflict between them ... [T]he ego is an *organization* and the id is not. *The ego is, indeed, the organized portion of the id.* (SE 20:97, emphasis added)[24]

Freud (1933a) clearly explains that the I is a modally differentiated aspect of the It, which becomes the mental organization of its prior shape. Elsewhere he says: "the ego is that portion of the id that was modified ... tak[ing] on the task of representing the external world to the id" (SE

22:75). This corresponds to the ego of consciousness, where the material of sensuous perception and thought are mediated, stored, and retrieved from the inner world, hence underscoring the contiguous and interdependent levels of unconscious and conscious processes. Freud's theory of mind adheres to an architectonic process: the ego develops out of its natural immediacy, then acquires increased dynamic complexity and organization as modally differentiated shapes of earlier processes assume new forms. As previously stated, Freud's recognition that organized psychic processes develop from unorganized hence undifferentiated natural determinations insulates him from criticism that his theory of mind purports three ontologically distinct agents that participate in mutual causal relations. Because the trinity of the three provinces are modally differentiated forms or shapes of its original undifferentiated being, each participates in the same essence and, thus, none is an independent nominal agent; rather they are interdependent forces that *appear* as separate agencies, when they in fact together form the unification of the dynamic temporal processes that govern mental life.

Although Freud admonished Jung for allegedly "watering-down" libido to a monistic energy, Freud's model of the psyche conforms to a developmental monistic ontology: higher instantiations of mental order evolve from more primordial forces of psychic life through a process of differentiation and modification. Although the I and the It are modifications of the same ontology, it is only the I that appears, itself an unconscious derivative. The specific process of differentiation, however, goes unexplained. All we are told is that the ego becomes the higher organizing agency of the mind derived from primitive processes. In fact, Freud (1940) concedes that, while drives find their first psychical expressions in the It, they are "in forms unknown to us" (SE 23:145). But why did not Freud isolate the moments of differentiation and modification within the It itself? Given that drive is the basic constituent of mind, which even precedes the organization of the It as a thoroughly unconscious agent, why did he not address modification at this level? Furthermore, if the ego is a secondary modification from a primary unconscious ground, then, by Freud's account, drive mediation would have to take place before the ego emerges. But how could a drive possess such agency? Freud does not say.

From my account, the transmogrification of the drives gives rise to psychic agency, and it is through a careful inspection of the process of modification that we can potentially resolve the genesis problem. I believe that Freud was mistaken when he made the It into an agency without accounting for how the unconscious portion of the I performs the executive functions of object choice for the drives and competing unconscious material pressing for discharge. The It cannot be understood as an unconscious agency (if at all) without the implicit inclusion of the I, unless the nature of a drive includes the capacity to choose objects, which is highly improbable given that only the ego is organized and synthetic with regard to its executive tasks. In fact, Freud (1915a) tells us that the object of a drive is "*assigned* to it only in consequence of being peculiarly fitted to make satisfaction possible" (SE 14:122, emphasis added). What does the assigning, ego or drive? If the I is ontologically undifferentiated from the It, it makes the question of unconscious agency more delicate when attempting to account for teleology and intentional object choice. Rather than the I developing from the It, the ego may be properly said to develop from drive. But even more important, as I soon argue, we have reason to believe that drive and ego are the same.

As it stands, there are many problems associated with Freud's contrast between the I and the It. The It is impersonal but it allegedly picks an object for the drives: how is this so? According to Freud, only the ego can do this; hence, we have a problem with an executive agency, and we have a problem with the definition of a drive. Although a drive needs an object for its satisfaction, are we justified in saying that an object is a proper characteristic of a drive? This implies that an object inheres in the drive as a property of it, when this is unlikely. An object stands in relation or absence to the *telos* or aim of a drive, but it does not follow that an object is necessarily a part of a drive's constitution, only that is requires an object for its satisfaction. In order to procure an object, the drive requires mediation. Here enters the I. The unconscious ego, not drive, mediates object choice, hence Freud introduces a contradiction in his model. He further confounds the issue by making the ego a developmental agent that does not materialize until the formative stages of early Oedipalization, a postulate corrected by Klein and many post-Kleinians, and today confirmed by developmental researchers who recognize the existence of the ego or the self at the moment of birth.

Freud attempts to resolve his own contradiction by making the It a separate agent. But how does it have any organizing agency without the ego, which lends it structure and direction? Yet Freud equivocates by saying that the I is "identical" with the It. In Freud's final tripartite model (the Freudian trinity), the ego becomes the locus of mind because of its synthetic and dynamic functions, which stand in mediatory relation to the other two competing agencies. Yet, because these other two agencies are ontologically, and hence inextricably, conjoined, we cannot separate any one agency from the others.

But is it possible to save Freud from his own contradiction? Can a drive take itself as its own object? And, if so, when does drive become ego? Why does it emerge to begin with? At what point does the I take on a formal unity? How does it effect its transition to executive agency? To consciousness? In order to answer these questions, we must increasingly turn our attention to a dialectical account of modification.

ARKHĒ

When does psychic life begin? Does the emergence of the ego properly constitute human subjectivity? Or can we legitimately point towards prior ontological forces? As mentioned earlier, I do not wish to reduce this metaphysical query to a materialist enterprise, only to acknowledge that certain neurophysiological and biochemical constituencies of embodiment are a necessary, albeit not a sufficient, condition for accounting for psychic origin. Although dialectical psychoanalysis is sensitive to the contiguous and compatible work within the biological and neurosciences, this need not concern us here. If one is content with a materialist approach, then one may resort to a discourse on ovum and sperm.[25] We, however, must proceed with a careful respect for Freud's (1900, 1933a) dictum and resist the temptation to reduce the psyche to its anatomical substratum. Because empirical approaches alone cannot possibly address the epistemology of the interior or the lived quality of experiential process, we must attempt to approach the question dialectically. Put more specifically, we are concerned with isolating the experiential movements that bring about the inception of lived psychical reality. Before we can address the ego of consciousness, we must first account for original ground through a process account of the coming into being of archaic structure. Although unarticulated by Freud himself, the concept of drive allows us to engage the question of genesis.

We must now return to the question of ground. Although Freud tells us that the It conditions all other forms of psychic agency, drives and the repressed condition the It. Furthermore, since repression is a vicissitude of the drives, drives necessarily become a grounding unconscious activity. Therefore, what we can infer from Freud is that the drives become primordial. But is this enough? How do the drives constitute themselves in the first place; that is, how do they function as organized unconscious life? Moreover, how do they come into being at all?

As we have said, unconsciousness precedes consciousness, hence there is a radicalization to unconscious subjective experience. In fact, consciousness is the manifestation of unconscious structure, first expressing itself as drive. Although Freud emphasized the equiprimordiality of Eros and destruction, his notion of the death drive, as previously mentioned, may arguably be considered one of his most important theoretical achievements. The death drive (*Todestrieb*) is not merely the innate presence of animal aggression or externalized acts of destruction; rather, it is the *impulse-towards-death*. While the drive towards death may be observed as a will to murder, it first speaks to the subject as a will towards suicide. But, as Freud tells us, mainly due to antithetical, counteractive drives motivated by the desire for adaptation and self-preservation, self-destructive impulses are typically deflected and defended against through projective displacements that find fulfilment through many circuitous paths throughout our developmental histories. Death *appears* as aggression and destruction whether externally displaced or turned on ourselves.

Recall that, before Freud fully commits to his notion of the death drive, he gives a speculative account of the evolutionary birth and metamorphosis of animate from inanimate life. In *Beyond the Pleasure Principle*, Freud (1920) conjectures that "*the aim of all life is death*" (SE 18:38, emphasis in original) and that organic life ultimately wants to return to an inorganic state of quiescence. In considering how animate activity came into being, Freud speculates that inorganic matter would have been perfectly content with its simple unity of quiescence if not for the encroachment of neighbouring dangers that threatened its internal cohesion and integrity. As a result, the libido, or life principle, is erected as a defensive manoeuvre against the imminent threat of destruction from a foreign invasion. From this account, the drive towards life is a defence against a real or perceived danger that threatens to invade the organism's solipsistic world. Extending this notion to the human subject, death is paradoxically beyond the pleasure principle yet at the same time is the ultimate pleasure: death is a tensionless state. But death only becomes pleasurable to the extent that it is protracted and endured; this is why Freud says that it must be engaged through circuitous routes of self-destruction (i.e., as repetition or, for Lacan, as *jouissance*) that bring the organism back to its original inorganic condition. In other words, violence is brought about through the subject's own hands.

As discussed, Freud's bold claim has not been well received among psychoanalysis and has been outright rejected based on biological grounds; yet death is unequivocally ontologically conditioned. Death, expressed through conflict, negation, and chaos, saturates psychic structure and is the motional process behind the very evolution of the dialectic. By turning our attention to a process account of the dialectic of desire, I believe we are justified in saying that death is our original drive. Death – Conflict – is the *primordial principle*, a necessary condition for psychic development. Negation, violence, and death are the driving pressures behind process; hence, negativity becomes the cornerstone of the dialectic. Negativity is our inner being and it enters into opposition with itself, with its own competing, antagonistic mental processes vying for expression, whether consciously or unconsciously conceived. As Hegel informs us, the mere act of confronting opposition is negative and aggressive, hence it involves a conflictual enterprise of cancelling, surpassing, and preserving such negativity within the unconscious abyss of our inner constitution. Yet the destruction inherent in all dialectical relations is merely a moment within the holistic process of elevating inner states to higher forms or modes of being. Hence, there is a *positive significance to the negative* that brings about more advanced levels of psychic progression and realization. The positive significance of the negative is constituted by the propitious force that propels the upward acclivity of the dialectic, the constructive destruction that paves the path towards progression and elevates psychic sophistication. In this way, negativity is both a grounding and transcending process of mind. Extending Freud's notion of the death drive to process dialectics allows us to show how the unconscious grounds its own ground through determinate negation. Death is teleologically directed and experienced as life turned outward, from the interior to the exterior, towards procuring the means of returning to its previous state of undifferentiated, undisturbed peace. *Mors ianua vitae* – death is the gate of life.

In considering the inception of psychic life, however, we must take Freud's thesis further. In conceiving of genesis – the birth of psychic activity – it makes more sense to me that mental life would have to experience a form of upheaval from *within* its own interior constitution rather than from without. Instead of a pristine unadulterated state of quiescence, the presubjective soul, embryonic ego, or preformed unconscious agent (what Freud calls the It), would have to experience a *rupture* due to internal discord that would serve to punctuate its breach to life, a process of awakening from its nascent self-entombed unity. But how is this possible? Hegel describes the process by which the unconscious soul undergoes a dialectical evolution and eventually becomes the ego of consciousness. His method is particularly relevant to the question of genesis. By taking a dialectical approach to our theoretical analysis, we may speculate how unconscious agency first materializes.

Because mind cannot emerge ex nihilo (unless we grant nothingness the ontological presence of being), we must posit the coming into being of psychic agency as a progressive unconscious dialectical activity; that is, as a determinate teleological drive. Given the brute facticity of our embodiment – the givenness of corporeal nature itself – mind must emerge from within its natural beginnings. In the *arkhē*, there is simple immediacy, the mere given existence or immediate *is*ness of psychical pulse, what we may loosely call *unconscious apperception*.[26] This is unconsciousness in its immediacy, neither cohesively constituted nor developed but, rather, the experiential presence of its sentient being. Because that which *is* is an unconscious pre-reflective immediacy, we may only designate it as an implicit agent or passive activity belonging to nascent mental experience. Because it is merely implicit activity in its initial immediacy and structure, it must make itself explicit and mediate through laborious dialectical progression. Yet this requires developmental maturation: mind has much work to do before it becomes a consciously cognizant processential being. Thus, in its prenatal form, we may only say that mind is unconscious pulsation as lulled apperceptive experiential process.

From my account, it makes no sense to speak of the nascent mind or self in the beginning as "the summation of sensori-motor aliveness" (Winnicott 1960, 149), or the "center of initiative and a recipient of impressions" (Kohut 1977, 99), without explaining how selfhood and conscious life are prepared by unconscious mediatory relations. Psychoanalysts from Freud to Klein, Winnicott, and Kohut were not able to provide us with a satisfactory account of self-development from the standpoint of genesis. Although the ego is a progressive developmental accomplishment present at birth only in a naive form, we must account for how prenatal maturation of the ego prepares the psyche for later self-transformations and functional tasks. This requires explicating the dialectical manoeuvres that bring consciousness into being in the first place. Because the self-development of the self simply does not pop up as the ego of consciousness, we must first examine the context and contingencies the soul encounters in its initial immediacy. The term "soul" is used here, à la Hegel, to describe the immediacy of subjectivity as an unconscious state of undifferentiated oneness or unity with its natural corporeality. Thus, unlike Freud, who discusses the soul as the unification of unconscious and conscious life, here the soul is strictly an unconscious affective embodiment. It does not belong to the sensuousness of consciousness, even though sensuousness, in the form of affective self-certainty, is its experiential modality.

It is important at this point to re-emphasize that the soul in its immediate unconscious unity, undifferentiated from its sentient nature, is a *lulled* or subdued experiential apperceptive activity. The term "apperception" is used here to denote the felt sensuousness or self-apprehension of the soul's self-immediacy. In its implicitness or initial experiential form, the soul must undergo an internal evolution that arouses itself to a state of experiential *mediacy*. This is the initial dialectical instantiation of psychic life, a relation the unconscious first has with itself. And this is a process that unfolds from within itself, from within its own interior constitution. This self-relation the soul has with itself is the first transition to giving itself determinate life. Before that, soul is ontologically determined immediacy.

In its transition from implicitness to explicitness, immediacy to mediacy, it seizes upon its teleological nature as determinate being. Soul, or what I call the incipient unconscious ego, undergoes an *unrest*; moreover, it undergoes an intensification of its already unrestful nature as pure activity and generates the initial movement of its own becoming. Hence unconscious being is already thrown into participation with the process of its own becoming as an unconscious trajectory of determinate mediatory relations. Thus, in the beginning stages of the soul's development, the lulled being of unconscious experience undergoes an internal tension and awakens within its natural immediacy as a sensuous corporeal embodiment.

This is a gradual architectonic process of unfolding dialectical relations that becomes contextually realized through self-generative expression. These operations undergird psychic development and are the fundamental dynamic activities of erecting mental structures and order (as continuous, interactive processes of interrelated and complementing forces) within the mind. Why does the soul undergo an internal tension? In its lulled rudimentary form of mind, the organism is a passive activity, asleep (as it were) in its own inwardness. We may reasonably say at this point that mind is largely a subdued flow of activity or pulsation, that it is relatively simple, lacks complexity and internal cohesion, and is mainly constituted through its physiological teleonomic contingencies. But, unlike Freud's quiescent organism, mind undergoes a profound restlessness or inner rumble of negativity, which it experiences from within its coma-like condition as an eruption to *be*. Such restlessness is due to the opposition it encounters from within its own interior, *not* from externality, as Freud posits; yet perhaps it is experienced as an alien presence or presentation of tension commensurate with Freud's vision of drive. This pulsion, however, acts as an internal stimulus and impetus to awaken, to move, to mobilize itself to more concrete experience: in its initial state of unconscious arousal, it takes itself as its own being, which is vibrant and sentient.

Here unconscious apperception rouses itself to *be* and to project life into itself as the form of feeling self-certainty. The soul intuits its own presence as such through the affective embodied experience of its immediate self-awareness. This self-awareness, however, is not the self-reflective, directive aspects of self-consciousness belonging to the ego of conscious perception and introspection; rather, it is a pre-reflective, non-propositional form of self-certainty as immediate subjective, sentient-affective experience, what we may call *unconscious self-consciousness*. The amorphous self knows itself in its immediacy as unconscious experiential subjectivity.

But why does drive emerge to begin with? What urge or impulse awakens the mind from its internal slumber? Here mind is a restless indeterminate immediacy, a simple self-enclosed unconscious unity that pulsates and exists in a state of *disquieted* quiescence. It undergoes upheaval because of certain instinctual, motivational currents pressing for expression in the form of a primordial hunger or longing to experience, to feed, to fill itself. Here, we are talking about appetition or *desire*, and we have something to learn from the Idealists:[27] human subjectivity is a desirous enterprise – it yearns, it seeks, it finds. But why do we desire? In other words, what constitutes desire in the first place? Freud finds its source in somatic organizations, and we have good reason to believe that desire is a natural process emanating from the body informed by evolutionary pressures; but this does not adequately address the ontological status of desire, nor does it mean that drive devolves into biology (as we have previously shown). Freud is unmistakably clear in telling us that the pressure or force of a drive is its very essence (*Wesen*) and, hence, is not simply reducible to its subterranean material-efficient causal determinants.[28] But why does unconscious desire experience such pressure to begin with? What is its *reason* to desire?

Mind desires because it stands in relation to absence or lack. Thus, drive emerges from a primal desire, the desire to fill the lack. In the most primitive phases of psychic constitution, mind is an active stream of desire exerting pressure from within itself as drive, clamouring for satisfaction, what Freud would call "pleasure." But unlike Freud, who sees pleasure as tension reduction, mind may be said to always crave, to always desire. While a particular drive or its accompanying derivatives may be sated, desire itself may be said to never formally stop yearning: it is condemned to experience lack. Unlike Lacan, however, who describes desire as "lack of being," and Sartre, who initially views human existence "as lack" or nothingness, here unconscious desire is *being-in-relation-to-lack*.[29]

The essence of desire is that it lacks an object, specifically it lacks a discernible object. Within this context we may view desire as an empty appetition in the mode of a pulsional form. In its transition to drive, desire seeks to modify itself in order to satiate its lack. It is here that drive creates a binding – a *Besetzung* – to an object, in which it may potentially find partial fulfilment. Although desire in its essence is boundless, drives become bound. As drives attach themselves to objects of unconscious intentionality in pursuit of fulfilling their *telos*, desire mutates into a particular form of expression by dispersing its essence through a determinate execution of psychic activity.

Within the very process of unconscious genesis, we may observe the overwhelming presence of death. The dialectic is conditioned on the premise of negation and lack, a primacy of the *not*. Nothingness or lack informs the dialectic, which we experience as desire. Desire is teleonomic-teleologic (purposeful) activity, a craving – at once an urge and an impetus – an infinite striving, a striving to fill the lack. Absence stands in primary relation to presence, including the being or presence of absence, which is why desire remains a fundamental being-in-relation-to-lack. Although drive gradually becomes more expressive and organized into mental life, the deep reservoir of the unconscious begins to fill as a psychic agency that simultaneously incubates and transposes itself through its own determinate activity. In its original state, however, being and nothing, life and death, are the same.

TELEONOMY, TELEOLOGY, AND PSYCHIC AGENCY

Antoine Vergote (1998) denotes a particular form of finality as *teleonomy*. This is a regulatory process inherent to psychic motivation and is devoid of any determinate conscious intentionality. He envisions teleonomy as an innately regulatory, orienting, and constructive activity that is lawful, hence causal, and executed by the pulsional body. I wish to further take up this idea and to distinguish between teleonomy, teleology, and psychic agency.

Teleonomy corresponds to the impersonal forces, pressures, urges, and trajectories informed by corporeal sentience, largely emanating from desire and drive. It is relatively rudimentary, economic, and conservative in nature, welling up as biologically derived systemic motivations seeking expression, discharge, and gratification. Its finality or end, although systemically derived from biological pulsions, is more predetermined in its aim, hence lacking flexibility or determinate selective choice due to innate natural urges and processes inherent to our constitutions or embodied facticity. Teleonomy may be said to largely regulate bodily functions, to be oriented towards adaptive and satiable ends, to be non-intentional and non-propositional in nature, and to generally compose the regulatory actions that govern unconscious determination. Here the emphasis is on economic utility and regularity, which propels or orients psychic events towards the functionality necessary to organismic strivings.

Teleology is more complex in design, purpose, function, and internal motivation than is teleonomy. It subsumes teleonomic pressures and principles but involves and evolves more elaborate systemic organizations within the mind. Unlike Vergote (1998), who assigns intentionality to consciousness, I maintain that intentionality is unconsciously constituted within the abyss under the governance of unconscious agency. Teleology comprises intentional finality within an orienting dynamism that governs the dialectic. While teleonomic aims oriented towards particular ends are predetermined, teleologic aims and ends are not; rather, they are self-determinate and subject to multiple motivations, action pathways, and modes of expression and execution. There is a degree of freedom and spontaneity over the nomic constraints that pressurize the psyche, which allows for a good deal of modification and variability over specific intentional contents, aims, actions, and object choice. Although the mind has certain psychological tendencies that regulate and direct its functionality, unconscious teleology, as with conscious intention, gives to itself its own finality and poses its own ends. In other words, it chooses the grounds by which to direct itself and to act. In this sense, finality is never a predetermined fixed end-point or immutable design within psychic structure; rather, it is a self-determining and mutable process of becoming in interaction and ontic relation to many different competing forces and contingencies, both internally derived and externally imposed.

Unconscious teleology surely has an interface of aims that guides mental events or actions, and in this sense it is intentional (*intentus*) or attentive to purpose and finality. In short, unconscious intentionality executes direction and conveys determinate import to psychic experience. Although telic aims may be dynamic and reflexive, the systemically informed design or plan of action of an unconscious intention is largely pre-reflective. Of course, the teleonomy and teleology inherent to mind must stand in some relation to agency in order for there to be any meaning, direction, or purpose to finality at all. There must be an agent, executor, regulatory force, or systemic process that organizes and directs psychic action, or else teleonomic-teleologic functions would have to be self-governing. From my account this is untenable. Since this is philosophically problematic in the same way as is the proposition that entities with contradictory essences can interrelate or intermingle, we must attempt to show how unconscious agency is organized and rendered operative by harnessing the teleonomic-teleologic functions that arise in the mind. Here the seat of agency is the unconscious ego.

What is agency? What constitutes its presence, function, and conceptualization? Are we not invoking an ontological discourse – a commitment to freedom, to the indeterminate, to spontaneity as the locus of action? Are we not inferring a principle of unconstraint when we ask these questions? Here agency may be conceived as pure action potential, often marked by its degrees of directionality, valence, and intensity in relation to an unspecified or undetermined outcome. This is the essence of psychic freedom – liberty of choice in the face of an undecided future state of possible events. Of course, such liberty is never totalistic or unbounded for psychic agency may only be actualized through determinations made within the context of one's historicity, whether this be one's personal history, embodied facticity, cultural environs, or social contingencies. Freedom is only actualized when determinate choice is agentically formulated and bound to an object or course of action.

Agency is the initiation of action derived from an internal force, energy, catalyst, prompting, or order of psychical events directed towards a particular finality. Agency speaks to directionality or processential movement aimed towards a purposeful end or telecausality. We may say that both teleonomic and teleological elements are combined and interfuse one another in agentic functions subject to self-determinate laws within ontological givens that govern and regulate internally mediated events and directive actions. Agency is the house and prerogative of the unconscious ego within the abyss of its indeterminations or the infinity of its possible internal realities. Here agency should not be viewed as having the same degree of complexity and cultivation as a conscious person, subject, or human being has developmentally achieved through sublation, but this does not mean that the embryonic unconscious agent in question does not possess subjectivity or that which is particular to its given experience. The unconscious ego as subject (*subicere: sub-*, below + *jacere*, to throw) is pure experiential activity that wells forth into more organized threads of experiential intricacy through internal modification and coherence, thus providing the archetypal structure that enables conscious subjectivity to emerge, become sophisticated, and thrive. What ultimately regulates psychic reality is a superordinate regulator with many different patternings, trajectories, and orderings of dynamic systemic complexity based upon internal differentiation, multiplicity, and unifying or integrating propensities derived from unconscious transmogrification. Here Freud's triadic theory of agency is not defendable: mind is not ontologically discrete. There is only one agent. Agency, however, appears in modified forms.

THE EPIGENESIS OF UNCONSCIOUS SUBJECTIVITY

Following our dialectical analysis of the coming into being of unconscious agency, we can readily see how this developmental process proceeds from the archaic and unrefined immediacy of our sentient corporeal nature to the standpoint of ego development belonging to the higher activities of cognition: mind awakens from its initial primordial indeterminate immediacy and unfolds into a more robust, determinate progressive organization of psychic life, from the most primitive to the most exalted shapes of human consciousness. But, initially, mind has its form in the natural immediacy in which it finds itself as nonconscious pre-reflective, affective-embodied experience. The self-certainty the unconscious ego has of itself in its natural immediacy may be summarized by the following dialectical phases:

1 Mind awakens as unconscious apperception due to internal compulsions to experience and reveals itself to itself as sentient, desirous corporeal activity.
2 The coming into being of unconscious subjectivity undergoes a gradual internal upheaval due to the pressures of desire and drive.
3 Mind initially experiences this unfolding as affectively laden, embodied sensuous self-certainty.
4 This pre-development of the human being no doubt takes place in the prenatal foetal milieu, which, essentially, consists of innately predisposed orientations of the organism belonging to and awakening as the privatization of unconscious subjective experience.

We have determined that lulled restlessness due to desire as the experience of lack is the initial point of genesis of felt psychic expression. This evolves from an inner rupture, what we may by analogy compare to the big bang singularity, except that there is no bang, just an inner implosion that reflexively begins to expand throughout the cosmic universe of the abyss. The psyche at this level takes itself as its initial form, which is none other than the affective self-certainty of its embodied natural immediacy. So far we have used the term "soul" to designate this intermediate process of psychic development, but are we justified in going further? When does unconscious subjectivity become an organized agency to the point where we can say there is an I and/or an It? Is it legitimate to say that, as soon as there is any unconscious activity at all, this constitutes agency? Or must agency derive from a higher developmental state or occasion? Because there is a mediatory transition from restless desire to the urge or pulsion to experience *itself*, I think we are justified in saying that, at this phase in the epigenesis of the unconscious mind, we have the

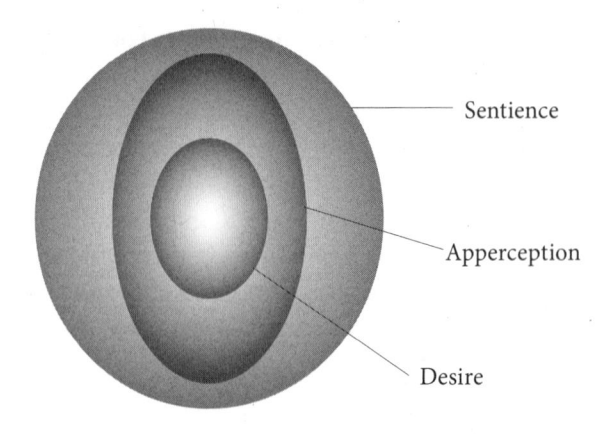

Figure 2.1 Epigenesis of the unconscious ego

rudimentary form of ego, which has as its task to become more aware and to develop even further as a subjective being-for-self in the world. Because mind mediates its immediate naturality as experiential affectivity, this constitutes a dialectical movement of determinate affirmation of self even, though such determination is still profoundly primitive and elementary. This determination of the mind's self-instantiation places ego development *prior to birth* within the foetus's prenatal environment, where it prepares for conscious awakening. Therefore, the ego is not merely an agency constituted *at* birth or thereafter; rather, it is prepared in the unconscious soul long beforehand.

Schematically, we may developmentally trace the initial unfolding of the incipient unconscious ego as it progresses from (1) desire to (2) apperception to (3) sentience, each phase being merely a moment in the constitution of subjective agency through its own determinant dialectical mediation (see figure 2.1). We can readily see how this process of modification continues to proliferate in a consecutive sublated dynamic fashion, eventually becoming the ego of consciousness embracing and incorporating its new-found experiences and maturational acquisitions.

Up to now, I have emphasized the affective embodied experience the ego has with its own immediacy within its unconscious totality. In other words, the ego only knows itself as a feeling sentient being. In fact, it has no content other than its original form of unity within its natural corporeal condition of unconscious sensuousness. This sensuousness, however, is not the sensuousness of conscious perception; instead, it is the felt inwardizing of experiential immediacy. However, as soon as the ego feels itself as an experiential being, it already preforms the mediatory action of *cognizing* its own existence. *This shift from waking within its natural immediacy to experiencing itself as a feeling-cognizing being constitutes the agentic birth of the psyche.* We may refer to this activity as a process of *intuition* that is both a form of felt sensuousness and a form of *thought*. Here the rigid bifurcation between emotion and thought must be suspended as unconscious affective apperception becomes the prototype for thinking, which we attribute to conscious subjectivity: thought – reason – is the materialization of desire. In effect, the nascent self intuits its own being by collecting or gathering up the sensuous data it experiences internally, from within its own self-interior, and then posits or thinks itself *in* this state; hence, this process is both an affective and a cognizing activity. This is not to imply that the self thinks itself into existence, as many modern philosophies of the will contend; rather, *thinking is initially experiential affectivity of the self-certainty of its immediacy.* While the higher operations of conscious cognition do not concern us at this stage of development, we have shown how consciousness is dialectically prepared within unconscious subjective experience. In this way, the unconscious ego imposes its own experiential order on the phenomenology of consciousness that arises in the ego upon the actual physical birth of the human infant. However, despite the intensification of the senses that accrue through cognitive development, the resonance of the ego's initial unconscious affective states becomes the touchstone for mind to filter and compare all subsequent experiential encounters. The life of feeling remains an essential aspect of human subjectivity.

The self experiences itself as sensuously embodied thought that eventually becomes further divided, differentiated, organized, and expressed dialectically as higher shapes of psychic development unfold. We may refer to this generic process of psychic progression as a projective identificatory trajectory of dynamic pattern, whereby the self divides itself via internal splitting, then projects its interior into externality as affirmative negation, and then identifies with its disavowed shape, which it seizes upon and reabsorbs, hence reincorporating itself back into its transmuted inner constitution. This is a progressive dynamic pattern of unconscious architectonic evolution that moves far beyond the notion of projective identification first espoused by Klein (1946) and later refined by Bion

(1962a). In fact, this process itself is the ontological force of the dialectic responsible for the evolution of mind, a topic I thoroughly address in the next chapter. It is from that dim interior of unconscious void that the ego must liberate and elevate itself from its solitary imprisoned existence to the experiential world of consciousness and intersubjective life. Yet the embryonic ego first knows itself, not as a conscious subject, but as a pre-reflective, unconscious self-consciousness; in other words, as inwardizing self-intuition.

The unconscious ego comes into being as a simple agent that has some crude capacity for dialectical mediatory relations; and, in determining the point of such transmogrifications, we can reasonably say there is determinate teleological expression. The ego's dialectical mediation of its natural immediacy and affective experience of itself as self-certainty becomes the logical model of psychic progression. It is in this way that the unconscious mind progresses from the most archaic mental configurations of desirous pulsation and urge to the refined experiences of self-consciousness. In its move from self-certainty to sense-certainty, the fabric of embodied affective life and symbolic networks of signification introduce defensive and dissociative aspects to psychic organization and its various spacings. This partially explains why internally competing epistemologies may become sharply divided, compartmentalized, and sequestered from one another. These emergent process systems become more complex, diffuse, and less immediately recognizable as mediated certainty. This is also how alienated aspects of mind are developmentally forged, maintained, and press for re-emergence via conscious manifestations.

But this assessment leaves us with the difficult question of difference between ego and drive, what Freud eventually dichotomized as the I and the It. Rather than conceive of the ego and the domain of the drives as two separate entities or agencies, I believe it becomes important to reconceptualize this duality as a monistic process of psychic differentiation and modification showing how the ego is in fact the organized embodiment and experience of drive. Because the ego is ontologically fuelled by the dialectic of unconscious desire, and desire is the very thrust behind the appearance of drive, the division between the I and the It is essentially annulled. It is in how drive *appears* as ego that we may observe such differences, while ontologically speaking ego and drive are identical.

Drive is a teleonomic function, whereas ego is teleologic. This is why a drive needs a mediatory agent to direct and fulfil its aim via the array of object choice and their relata. Drive is impotent without unconscious teleology directing its pursuit and purpose. Here the distinction between ego and drive is only formal as ontologically they are undifferentiated.

In relation to Hegel's philosophy, I have relabelled the domain of the It as an unconscious *abyss*, which I think more precisely captures the multiple processes of unconsciousness that Freud tried to systematically categorize. Yet, whereas Freud alerts us to his view of the unconscious as consisting of three divided agencies, with the ego and superego being further split into conscious and unconscious counterparts, I envision the abyss from the standpoint of a monistic developmental unconscious ontology that gives rise to higher forms of psychic organization. These developmental articulations interact with and interpenetrate the experiential and intersubjective contingencies that the abyss encounters and assimilates through a cybernetic function of reciprocal dialectical relations. The abyss is that domain of the unconscious mind from which the ego emerges and yet continues to fill and engage through its relation to conscious subjective experience. In a word, the abyss is the indispensable psychic foundation of human subjectivity – the ontological a priori condition for all forms of consciousness to emerge, materialize, and thrive. This ensures the primacy of archaic experience, somatic organization, unformulated affect, emotional vicissitudes, and prelinguistic and/or extralinguistic reverberations, despite the equiprimordiality of language resonating within unconscious process.

The relation of the unconscious ego to the abyss becomes one that requires a degree of differentiation and negation performed by the ego and directed towards all realms of otherness. In effect, what the ego experiences is alienation, especially its own self-alienation or alienating activity as disavowed experience, which becomes relegated to otherness and split off from its own self-identity. In contemporary psychoanalytic literature, this process is tantamount to dissociation. Such differentiation is an activity the ego performs within itself through determinate negation – I am *not* It! – but the ego is what the abyss has become from the standpoint of the ego's self-differentiation from its foreignness and its original natural immediacy. Here the essence of dissociation is determinate negation.

The abyss is the materiality of nature from which the ego emerges but in which it is always immersed: it experiences itself as drive – as a desirous subjective being (here desire is unrelenting and insatiable, while drive is impending and satiable) – which is the formative organization and expression of unconscious agency that epigenetically becomes the ego of consciousness. It is only in relation to itself that the ego forges a gap between itself and the abyss, which becomes the domain of all that the self refuses to identify as being identical to itself. We can readily see how the Freudian *Es* may be conceptually subsumed within the abyss of the ego, that element of mind *alienus* to the ego's own experiential immediacy.

We have determined that desire as being-in-relation-to-lack is the essence of mind that fuels and sustains the process of the dialectic. Desire becomes the ontological thrust behind the presence and felt experience of drive, itself the urge, pressure, or impulse towards activity. And this process gives rise to the unconscious ego awakening within its own inwardness to discover itself as a sensuous, apperceptive affective self-intuiting being that knows or cognizes itself in its natural embodied immediacy. *This dialectical transition from indeterminate immediacy to determinate mediacy by which the ego takes its own natural form as its initial object constitutes the coming into being of unconscious subjective agency.* Despite the ego's crude organization at this phase of its life, it nevertheless points towards the dialectical process of its own becoming as a progressive teleological trajectory of self-expression eventually acquiring conscious cognition and the higher faculties of self-conscious rational thought as psychic maturation sequentially unfolds. These higher planes of development are forged by the sustaining power of the dialectic, a process that takes place first and foremost within the unconscious abyss of its natural embodied immediacy.

The ego materializes out of an abyss in which it itself remains. In this way, the unconscious ego is itself an abyss that must mediate the multiple, overdetermined, and antithetical forces that populate and besiege it. In the ego's determinate activity of mediation, it sets itself in opposition to otherness, which it must sublate, and this inevitably means that certain aspects of its interiority (e.g., content, images, impulses, wishes, ideation) must be combated and/or superseded. It is only on the condition that the ego intuits itself that it gives itself subjective life felt as concrete experiential immediacy. When seen from the standpoint of the ego's mature development, the abyss becomes anything that the ego refuses to identity as belonging to its original constitution.

Freud (1923) tells us that "the ego is first and foremost a bodily ego" (SE 19:26) by the simple fact that we are embodied. But he did not fully describe this process: the ego is first and foremost an unconscious embodiment that intuits its Self within the natural immediacy in which it finds itself. Through continual dialectical bifurcation, the ego expands its internal experiential and representational world and thus acquires additional capacities, structures, and attunement through its mediated, conscious relational contingencies and epigenetic achievements. In doing so, the ego forges an even wider and deeper abyss, casting all otherness into the lair of self-externalization. Therefore, the chasm between the ego and the abyss is really a chiasm in which the ego creates itself. The ego of consciousness emerges from an unconscious void into which it sinks back at any given moment, thus never truly attaining ontological distinction. The ego first awakens as unconscious subjectivity within the feeling mode of its original desirous being, which it experiences as drive, the restless compulsion to experience. This is why ego and drive are not ontologically differentiated: ego is merely the appearance of drive. Drive is transformed embodied, expressed natural desire – our original being – which goes through endless transformations in the contextualization and enactment of our personal individualities and interpersonally encountered realities. Drive is transporting, and this is what governs the dialectic. The reason the domain of drive, and, more broadly, that of the abyss, seems so foreign to the ego is that, from the standpoint of conscious self-differentiation, we are so much more than our mere biologies. We *define* our subjective experiences through determinate volition, linguistic signification, and idiosyncratic meaning. And, when they come from unintended locations as extraneous temporal encroachments – from the monstrous to the sublime – they are not identified as emanating from within or by one's own determinate will. These are times we must heed Nietzsche's dictum: Not *I think* but, rather, *It thinks* in me.

Throughout this chapter, I have attempted to show how dialectical psychoanalysis explains the coming into being of unconscious subjectivity, thus responding to Freud's adumbrated attempt to explain the differentiation of the I from the It. With the current focus on the primacy of emotions in organizing self-experience through intersubjective relations, it is important to emphasize that process psychology explains how somatic and affective resonance becomes the locus of that unconscious mediatory experience the self first has with itself. This may explain why the life of emotions yields primordial force and direction in forming psychic structure and intersubjective reality and, thus, partially answers the question of why certain unconscious affective experiences predate and resist articulation through linguistic mediums.

· 3 ·

Mind as Projective Identification

The psychic process known as "projective identification" has become a familiar tenet of psychoanalytic doctrine. The term was coined by Melanie Klein in 1946,[1] when it was conceived as an aggressive discharge of certain portions of the ego *into* an external object, the aim of which was to dominate or consume certain aspects of the object's contents in order to make it part of the ego's own internal constitution. Not only has the introduction of this concept revolutionized Kleinian theory, but further developments have also paved the way towards its progressive application in understanding a number of mental processes, pathologies, and clinical encounters. To be sure, projective identification may be viewed in multiple fashions: (1) as a general process of mental activity, from unconscious structure to conscious thought; (2) as a defensive manoeuvre motivated by intrapsychic conflict; and (3) as an intersubjective dynamic affecting object relations, especially the process of therapy.[2] But, with a few exceptions (see Bion 1959), projective identification has been largely overlooked as a basic element of psychic organization.

Throughout this chapter I am preoccupied with highlighting the normative functions of projective identification and showing how it is an indispensable ontological feature underlying the rudiments of mental activity. Through the logic of the dialectic, projective identification may be seen as the most elementary, albeit complex, constitutive process that governs both unconscious and conscious life, a dynamic that brings us into dialogue with Klein, Bion, and contemporary psychoanalytic thought. Because the dialectic is a fundamental constituent of all psychic process, we may readily observe how this takes the structural form of more advanced dimensions of intrapsychic and intersubjective life through a supraordinate order of unfolding pattern we may call projective identification. The individual psyche – as well as culture itself – mediates opposition and conflict that it generates from within its own evolutionary process and attempts to resolve earlier problems for which new immediacy emerges. As we saw in the epigenesis of the unconscious ego, mediation is an agentic activity performed from within the mind and between interpersonal forces that, in turn, make new experience possible. We will further see how projective identification becomes the basic structural process of dialectical progression, which is responsible for the epigenesis of unconscious organization, consciousness, the ontology of the self, and civilization at large – a dynamic responsible for both maturation and psychic decay.

THE DIALECTICAL NATURE OF PROJECTIVE IDENTIFICATION

We have seen how the dialectic of desire forges the progressive path of ego development that emanates from the unconscious abyss of indeterminate immediacy to the determinate mediacy of the unconscious ego to that of conscious life. Thus, the unconscious mind is an original undifferentiated unity that emerges from its immediate self-enclosed universality to its mediated determinate singularity. This is initiated through a dialectical process of internal division, self-externalization, and introjection as the reincorporation of its projected qualities back into its interior. Here lies the basic process of projective identification: unconscious agency splits off certain aspects of its interior, externalizes its Self, and then reconstitutes itself by identifying with its own negated qualities, which it regathers and assimilates back into its unconscious framework. Through the complexities of mediation and sublation, the psyche achieves higher levels of unification and integration through rational self-reflection and the attainment of self-consciousness, thus uniting more infantile experiences and earlier movements within its more mature organization.

As we have shown, negativity, aggressivity, and conflict – the hallmarks of death – are essential forces in the thrust of the dialectic, a process Klein emphasizes in her characterization of ego development. The sleep of the mind is an undifferentiated void with the inner ambience of violence. It experiences the primeval chaos of an intense longing to fill its empty simplicity, desire being its form and content, the desire to fill the *lack*. Through the drive towards self-differentiation, the unconscious ego defines itself as a determinate being-for-itself and thus effects the passage from the universal to the particular, from a unity that lacks difference to differentiated plurality within singularity. There is an antediluvian cycle of negativity that we may say belongs to the prehistory of the conscious subject, a circular motion of the drives that constitute the dialectic of desire. Awakening as sensation from its nocturnal slumber, the feeling soul remains the birthplace of what is the substance of the "heart," for the abyss is the midwife of mind.

INTERFACES WITH KLEIN

Klein's theory of splitting has revolutionized the way we understand ego development. For Klein, the ego exists at birth and is plagued by anxieties characteristic of psychosis, which it attempts to fend off and control through the primary defence mechanisms of splitting, projection, and introjection, thus giving rise to the paranoid-schizoid and depressive positions that mould object relations and psychic structure. Although Klein refers to these defensive manoeuvres as "mechanisms," they are not mechanistic. As mentioned earlier, ego activity is never fixed or static and does not take the form of predetermined tropisms; rather, psychic organization is the continuity of subjective temporal processes distributed throughout spacings of the abyss. It is more accurate to conceptualize these early mechanisms as defensive *process systems* comprised by the ego's intrapsychic relation to itself and its object environment, initially the mother. This makes ego development and object relations an intersubjective enterprise.

In her seminal essay, "Notes on Some Schizoid Mechanisms," Klein (1946) proclaims splitting as the original primordial defence, a process she started analyzing as early as 1929. Beset by the death drive (*Todestrieb*), the immature ego deflects the destructive impulse by turning it against the object accompanied by oral-sadistic attacks on the mother's body, thus giving rise to persecutory anxiety. Splitting is the very first in a series of defences that are never completely separate from one another, hence forming the dialectical cycle we have come to label as projective identification. While Klein cogently articulates the gradual evolution and strengthening of the ego, she concedes that "so far, we know nothing about the structure of the early ego" (4). Here process psychology becomes instructive for contributing to psychoanalytic theory.

As previously outlined, Hegel traces the dialectical course of the soul as a sentient feeling entity – at first a prenatal agent – only to gradually acquire more personal unity and organization, a process I extend to the epigenesis of the unconscious ego. It is important to note that Hegel, Freud, and Klein refer to the same word, *Ich*, to designate the personal agency of the ego, what we have argued is at first an unconscious constellation that later makes consciousness possible. Klein (1946, 5) says very little about the prehistory of the ego prior to birth, yet she is suggestive: "The question arises whether some active splitting processes within the ego may not occur even at a very early age. As we assume, the early ego splits the object and the relation to it in an active way, and this may imply some active splitting of the ego itself." Klein is correct in showing that splitting is the ego's original defensive activity, despite the fact that she omits explaining how the ego is formed in the first place. This is presumably due to her scientific attitude, which is guided by quasi-empirical considerations; however, by way of our treatment of the unconscious soul, the logical progression of the dialectic clarifies this process. Process psychology shows that we can reasonably conclude that the ego exists prior to birth and is prepared by the unconscious mediatory activity of the soul, which lends increasing order to intrapsychic structure. Because the ego cannot simply materialize ex nihilo, it must emanate from a prior unconscious ground or abyss, what Boehme refers to as the *Ungrund*, a ground without a ground (see Mills 2002, 23–9). The ego has a prenatal life that is developmentally prepared prior to conscious perception: unconscious experience precedes consciousness.

Not only must we situate splitting at the inception of the soul's development, but we must also demonstrate that splitting is the earliest activity of mind. Splitting becomes the prototype of mental process and remains a fundamental operation in the normative as well as in the pathological functions of the psyche. The unconscious ego first undergoes an internal division or separation from its interior, which it projects as an external object *within its own internality*, only to regather and again make it part of its inner constitution. This primary splitting activity is architectonic, thus forming the foundation for psychic growth. Since splitting is identified as the initial movement of the dialectic, thus effecting its transition into mediatory relations, it becomes easy to see how splitting becomes the archetype of later ego activity, which Klein emphasizes in her developmental framework. But, unlike Klein (1946, 1955) who repeatedly tells us that the ego's first object is the mother's breast, it would follow that the ego's first object is itself – its own internality. This observation need not contradict Klein's main theses; rather, it may substantiate her theoretical innovations. The ego must first posit and set itself over its initial immediacy, which it does through splitting.

In "Splitting of the Ego in the Process of Defence," a posthumously published unfinished paper, Freud (1940 [1938]) addresses the notion of disavowal and the "alteration of the ego," which goes beyond his earlier treatment of splitting in cases of psychoses (Freud 1924a; SE 19:152–3) and fetishism (Freud 1927a; SE 21:155–6), which is now included within his general theory of neurosis. Freud, like Klein, generally sees the conceptualization of splitting as a defensive process that is usually confined to the domains of conflict, while our emphasis on the internal divisibility of the unconscious ego makes splitting a generic process that may be applied to any mediatory aspect of division and negation within the mind. In fact, it is *negation* that is technically the first movement in the process of splitting, for division and difference are based on a determinate judgment or mediatory relation to antithesis, the initial form being denial or abnegation – the determination of the *not*. In *New Introductory Lectures*, Freud (1933) is clear that splitting is a general ego operation: "the ego can be split; it splits itself during a number of its functions – temporarily at least. Its parts can come together again afterwards" (SE 22:58). Freud also alludes to an innate and normative function of splitting as it is applied to the synthetic processes of the ego. He states: "The synthetic function of the ego, though it is of such extraordinary importance, is subject to particular conditions and is liable to a whole number of disturbances" (Freud 1940; SE 23:276). Although in several places before Freud emphasized the synthetic functions of ego unification (Freud 1926a, SE 20:97–100; Freud 1926b; SE 20:196; Freud 1933a; SE 22:76), which had always been an implicit part of his theory, we can show that splitting is a basic psychic operation that may take on more pathological configurations throughout development, such as in the cases of psychotic and schizoid disorders articulated by Klein and her followers or in pathological narcissism and borderline personality, a topic that occupies much of the personality disorders literature today.

The ego is unconsciously implicit within the apperceptive sentient soul and is already a prenatal form of self-awareness. Both a sensuous and cognizing agent, unconscious subjectivity intuits itself as a pre-reflective, non-propositional self-conscious being, a being that reflects into itself through the process of immediate unconscious self-awareness as self-identification. In our previous discussion of the ego's actual emergence from its natural embodiment, the ego has to confront its corporeal confinement and inwardness. Hegel relays this process nicely: "It is through this *intro-reflection* (*Reflexion-in-sich*) that mind completes its liberation from the form of *being*, gives itself that of *essence*, and becomes *ego*" (EG § 412, *Zusatz*, emphasis in original). In its alteration from mere immediacy to determinate mediate being, the soul *senses* its Self as an impression, already containing the rudiments of ego-awareness in its self-intuiting. In its ego explicitness, before the soul makes its final trajectory to consciousness, unconscious mind has already undergone a manifold splitting of its interior by its own hands. In each incremental process of splitting that accompanies sublation there is an internal division, projection, and (re)introjection of its particularization back into its internality. Each introjective manoeuvre is a reincorporation of its projected interior that takes place through an identification with its alienated shape(s), which it takes to be an exterior object possessing, however, its internal qualities. Such projective identification may be said to be the truncated recognition the ego has of itself through the process of intro-reflection as self-reflexion – itself a preliminary form of unconscious self-consciousness – except that the ego has undergone a splitting as an element of defence against its unconsciously perceived conflict, which subsists due to the negative tension of the dialectic.

As noted, this continual process of internal separation, projection, and introjection as reincorporation is the general structural operation of projective identification. The ego projects its internality as alienation, comes to recognize and identify with its alienated qualities, then takes hold of and repossesses its earlier disavowed shapes. It is through this continual elevating process that both the content and the developmental hierarchy of the mind becomes more complex and sophisticated. The unconscious mind comes to take itself as its own object through its incremental reflection into its self once it projects its interior as its exterior, reflects upon it, and takes back into its internality what it perceives to be the externality of nature or otherness that it cognizes (cf. Hegel, EG § 384, *Zusatz*) and, thus, effects a transition back into reunification. The mind is continuously engaged in this dialectical process in all its shapes; however, at this level in the ego's development, unconscious agency displays an early form of self-recognition through its projective identification as mediated self-reflection.

This model of unconscious self-consciousness as pre-reflective or non-propositional self-recognition becomes the logical template for the emergence of self-awareness and recognition of self and others in conscious cognition. It is because we have a pre-familiar awareness of our own sense of self that we can come to recognize our self in the image of another human being and, in doing so, recognize the needs and desires of others as separate subjects. This is the gist of Hegel's theory of self-consciousness, which is outlined in the dialectic of desire advanced in the *Phenomenology* (PS §§ 166–230), a process already prepared in the unconscious soul. The soul is desirous, and the abyss is unconsciously self-aware, with drive (*Trieb*) and intro-reflection providing the logical prototype for the emergence of desire and self-consciousness in conscious life. Although both Freud and Klein see the ego as a more modified portion of the It, we have clearly shown that consciousness is the manifestation of unconscious structure.

But why would the unconscious ego *need* to split itself in the first place? Here enters the force and primacy of denial (*Verneinung*). As previously mentioned, the ego's original activity is one of negation: it defines itself in opposition to what it is not. Following Freud, Klein speculates that splitting mechanisms arise in an effort to subvert the death drive that threatens the ego with internal destruction. Splitting is a defence against felt or perceived annihilation. As we have seen from our previous analysis, unconscious subjectivity first encounters an inner negativity, aggressivity, or conflict, which becomes the impetus for dialectical intervention. In fact, splitting itself is a violent cleaving operation that divides subject from object. For Klein, splitting disperses the destructive impulse, while for Hegel splitting is destructive: it destroys as it negates. But the destruction incurred by the cancelling function of the dialectic is also preserved in the same moment as the ego sublates itself to a higher state. Splitting and projection highlight the negative side of the dialectic while introjection serves a synthetic function. The repetitive process of projective identification may be applied to the general ascending thrust of sublation or it may succumb to contentious dichotomies that are mired in chaos. Although the relationship between the death impulse and negation still remains equivocal, destruction is nevertheless a key element in the progressive unification of the ego.

In several works, Klein (1946, 1952) underscores the point that the ego is oriented towards higher degrees of unification. Elsewhere she states: "Together with the urge to split there is from the beginning of life a drive towards integration" (Klein 1963, 300). This is the affirmative and ongoing drive of the ego, which forms the edifice of the Hegelian dialectic, a proclivity that inevitably strives for wholeness and that Klein herself endorses. Hegel's emphasis on holism anticipates Klein's (1960) advocacy of a well-integrated personality, the goal of which is to master early developmental frictions that arise from persecutory anxiety and its vicissitudes.

But for Hegel and Klein, there is a dual tendency for both progression and regression, for both elevation and withdrawal to previous points of fixation. As Klein (1946, 4) puts it, "the early ego largely lacks cohesion, and a tendency towards integration alternates with a tendency towards disintegration, a falling into bits." Hegel refers to this disintegration as a fixation and/or regression to the form of feeling – the original self-enclosed simple unity of the feeling soul, a dynamic responsible for "madness" (see EG §§ 403–8).[3] We may further conclude that impediments to sublation underlie all forms of pathological dissociation. Like Klein, who stresses the primacy of developmentally working through the paranoid-schizoid and depressive positions, Hegel sees mental health as the ability to achieve holism through sublation: while feeling is never abandoned as such, it is subsumed within the higher instantiations of self-conscious rational thought. Even Klein (1963, 313) herself says that "the urge towards integration, as well as the pain experienced in the process of integration, spring from internal sources which remain powerful throughout life." For Hegel, this would be tantamount to the labour of *Geist*, an arduous, poignant crusade. If the subjective mind is not able to developmentally progress towards synthetic rational integration, then earlier primitive defensive constellations will persist unabated.

BION ON THINKING, LINKING, AND PHANTASY

Although Klein (1946) first defined projective identification as a defensive process expressed through splitting and schizoid mechanisms, she later (1957) suggested that envy was intimately embedded in projective identification, a process by which the ego forces itself into the psychic reality of the other in order to destroy its coveted attributes. Shortly after this theoretical modification, Bion (1959) distinguished normal from pathological forms of projective identification, which has further led revisionist Kleinians to articulate many distinct yet related modes of projective-identifictory processes (Hinshelwood 1991).

Bion, himself analyzed by Klein, was the first psychoanalyst to recognize normative functions of projective identification embedded in normal thought processes. Bion (1959, 1962a, 1962b) distinguished between two alternative aims of projective identification marked by difference in the degree of violence attached to the mechanism. The first, *evacuation*, is characterized by its forceful entry into an object, in phantasy, as a means of controlling painful mental states directed towards relief and often aimed at intimidating or manipulating the object. This is a pathological manifestation of projective identification. The second, *communication*, is a more benign attempt to communicate a certain mental content by introducing into the object a specific state of mind, a function often seen in the process of *containing* – a process in which one person contains some part of another. This is a normative function. It may be argued that evacuation is itself a form of communication, thus blurring the distinction; however, for our purposes, evacuation highlights the thrust, intensity, and urgency of the need to expel psychic content. In all likelihood, evacuation and communication operate in confluence separated only by their motives and the force of violence enacted through projection.

In his influential essay, "Attacks on Linking," Bion (1959) presents his mature view of projective identification as a form of communication taking on both normal and abnormal valences. Drawing on Klein, Bion depicts pathological forms as falling within a range of *excess* (e.g., the degree of aggressivity of splitting, hatred, intrusion, omnipotent control and fusion with the object, the amount of loss or defusion of the ego, and the specific awareness of destructive intent). Normal projective-identifictory processes, however, play an adaptive role in social reality and are ordinary operations of communication and empathy, which furthermore transpire within the process of thinking itself.

Bion's (1957) model of thinking, linking, and phantasy is preliminarily addressed in his effort to differentiate psychotic from non-psychotic personalities, with special emphasis on the awareness of psychic reality. For Bion (1954), drawing on Klein's (1930) and later Hanna Segal's (1957) work on symbol formation in the development of the early ego, the awareness of psychic reality is contingent upon the capacity for verbal thought derived from the depressive position. Yet this process goes back even further. Linking – the capacity to form relations between objects or mental contents – serves a functional purpose, a process derived from the paranoid-schizoid position. Bion (1957, 1959) envisions psychotic organization as largely plagued by violent attacks on the ego – particularly on the links between certain mental contents – and the awareness of inner reality itself. As a result, the schizophrenic lives in a fractured world of terror, where mental links are "severed" or "never forged." Phantasy formation is fragmented, persecutory, and horrific. Attempts at linking conjunctions or making connections between objects are all but destroyed, and when minute links exist, they are impregnated with perversion and cruelty.

What is of importance in understanding the normative functions of projective identification is being aware of how Bion conceives of the phenomenology and evolution of thinking, a notion that brings him into dialogue with process thought. Bion (1957, 66) informs us that "some kind of thought, related to what we should call ideographs and sight rather than to words and hearing exists at the outset" – a capacity derived within the non-psychotic part of the embryonic psyche. He continues to tell us that this crude level of thinking "depends on the capacity for balanced introjection and projection of objects and, *a fortiori*, on awareness of them" (ibid.). Ultimately, for Bion, both pre-verbal and verbal thought necessarily require an awareness of psychic reality.

Throughout the course of his theoretical contributions, Bion explicates three phases in the process of thinking. The first relies on the presumption of a priori knowledge, whereby an innate *preconception* meets a *realization* in experience, which results in a *conception*, the product of thought (Bion 1959, 1962a). Bion's notion of preconceptions is similar to Segal's (1964) notion of unconscious phantasy, which is used as a means of generating hypotheses for testing reality. A preconception may be understood as a predisposed intuition of and expectation for an object, such as a breast, which "mates" with the realization of the actual object in experience, thus forming a conception.

Bion's second phase of thinking depends on the infant's capacity to tolerate frustration. A positive conception is generated when a preconception meets with a satisfying realization. When a preconception encounters a negative realization – say, absence – frustration ensues. Klein shows that, when the immature ego encounters absence, it experiences the presence of a bad object or, perhaps more appropriately, a bad self-object experience. Bion, however, extends this idea further and posits that the experience of absence is transformed into a thought. The notion of absence, lack, or nothingness is conceptually retained. Yet this process is contingent on the infant's ability to modulate frustration. If frustration tolerance is high, the generation of absence into a thought serves the dialectical function that presence is possible; that is, the absent object may appear or re-present itself at some later time in the future (e.g., as the breast or bottle). For Hegel, affirmation and negation are dialectically conjoined, separated only by their moments. With application to Bion, nothing stands in opposition to being, which, once realized, is expected to return, hence it becomes. If the capacity to manage frustration is low, the experience of nothingness does not advance to the thought of an absent good object but, rather, remains at the immediate level of the concrete bad object experienced in the moment, which must be expelled through omnipotent evacuation. Bion (1962a) believes that if this process becomes arrested, then advances in symbol formation and thinking are deleteriously obstructed.

Bion's third phase of thinking involves more advanced levels of projective identification, which he (Bion 1962b) describes as the container-contained relationship. Here the infant has a sensory experience, feeling, or need that is perceived as bad and that the infant wishes to banish. This type of projective identification evokes within the mother the same type of internal sensations experienced by the infant. If the mother is adequately well balanced and capable of optimal responsiveness, what Bion calls *reverie*, she will be able to contain such feelings and transform them into acceptable forms, which the infant can re-introject. Bion labels this process of transformation the *alpha function*. In healthy development, the container-contained relationship allows the infant to re-introject the transformed object into something tolerable, which eventually results in internalizing the function itself. If successful, this process aids in the increased capacity to modulate frustration and developmentally strengthens the infant's cognitive capabilities to conceptualize and generate symbolic functions, which generally leads to the fortification of the ego. Not only does Bion breach the sharp schism between feeling and thought that has dogged philosophical rationalism, but he also shows how emotions are made meaningful within the broader conceptual processes of thinking (Spillius 1988).

Bion's (1962b) theory of thinking is most fully elaborated in his esoteric treatise, *Learning from Experience*, in which he situates projective identification as the genesis of thought. Here he engages Freud's thesis on the origins of thinking and emphasizes the core of an infant's emotional experience in phantasy formation. In "Formulations on the Two Principles of Mental Functioning," Freud (1911) tells us that "restraint upon motor discharge (upon action) ... was provided by means of the process of *thinking*, which was developed by the presentation of ideas (SE 12:221, emphasis in orginal). He elaborates upon how the heightened importance of the sense-organs directed towards the external world gives rise to consciousness attached to these objects of sense-experience. The special function of attention was further developed as a means of organizing data of experience in order to meet internal needs, a process aligned with the formation of memory. Under the dominion of the pleasure principle, memory became "a means of unburdening the soul (*seelischen Apparats*) of accretions of stimuli" (SE 12:221). These stimuli, in turn, were redirected onto the body, thereby producing affect and motor activity. Here Freud is speculating on how mental process converts conscious events into emotionally organized meaning and expressive action.

For Freud, experience stimulated by external reality is internalized and encoded in memory, which forms the rudiments of ideas. In essence, the psychic register makes impartial "judgments" (*Urteilsfällung*) or "decisions" about the truth or falsity of certain ideas (*Vorstellung wahr oder falsch*) in relation to the build-up of memory traces associated with corresponding reality. The process of thinking evolves with the "presentation of ideas" (*Vorstellen*) to the mind, which allows for the process of representation to occur without the constant need for the organism to react to the magnitude of competing stimuli constantly being presented afresh.

Bion's work on the genesis of thought centres on the infant's capacity to tolerate frustration. He takes these ideas up directly from Freud, who states: "Thinking was endowed with characteristics which made it possible for the psyche to tolerate an increased tension of stimuli while the process of discharge was postponed" (SE 12:221). Rather than reacting, mind is afforded the capacity to act, delay, or inhibit motor action based upon the increased succession in mentation, judgment, and determinate thought. What is remarkable is that Freud anticipates how thinking is prepared a priori from unconscious processes. He states: "It is probable that thinking (*Denken*) was originally unconscious (*unbewußt*), in so far as it went beyond mere ideational presentations and was directed to the relations (*Relationen*) between impressions of objects, and that it did not acquire further qualities, perceptible to consciousness, until it became connected with verbal residues" (SE 12:221). Notice here that Freud wishes to demarcate an area of mental activity that is not entirely conditioned on sense data; rather, he focuses on the way "relations" are formed between mental events and their content. It is precisely the way relations between objects are associated and conjoined, including the capacity to institute determinate judgments of "comparison" based on similarity, difference, opposition, equivalence, and so forth, that inherently differentiates the process of thinking from mere sense perception. In Bion's terms, *linking* is the capacity to form relations between objects and mental events.

Freud talks about fantasizing (*Phantasieren*) as the ability the psyche gains over external reality in accordance with the pleasure principle. No matter how external reality makes its presence felt or known, mind never totally renounces its allegiance to wishfulness and the pleasure that accompanies imaginative thought. Here the psyche undergoes a fundamental split: wish and reality are dialectically opposed yet mutually implicative. As Freud explains, "one species of thought-activity was split off; it was kept free from reality-testing (*Realitätsprüfung*) and remained subordinated to the pleasure principle alone" (SE 12:222). This is what Bion emphasizes in his theory. In fact, what differentiates Bion from Freud is not his theory but his emphasis.

Bion (1962b, 31) sees projective identification as tantamount to the "origin" of thought, which he equates with the "omnipotent phantasy" of splitting off parts of the self and placing them into an object. Here the origins of thinking involve a dynamic process of systemic interrelations between self and object and is not simply an isolated intrapsychic act of directional intentionality. Actually, Bion assigns a particular form of teleology to the process of thinking qua projective identification. That is, the incipient psyche seeks a specific purpose, end, or finality to desire, namely, "an introjective activity *intended* to lead to an accumulation of good internal objects" (32, emphasis added). Extending Freud, Bion specifies that the impetus in the process of thinking emerges in response to tension, agitation, or frustration, which leads to various states of displeasure. We may equate this with the teleonomic or economic function of the pleasure principle. But the aim of phantasy as intentional thought is teleological in the sense that it is directed towards procuring a final purpose or end goal. If the motive or aim is to reduce frustration under the pleasure principle, then the rupture of thought, according to our process theory, is more about procreative genesis than it is about simply maintaining organismic homeostasis. If we were to extend Bion's emphasis on phantasy, then the origins of thought would comprise an intentional redirection of phantasy into the mother, which is the specific object of which Bion is speaking.

Bion's equivocal and "abstract" use of the term "alpha-function," which he defines as an "unknown variable" (Bion 1962b, 55), does not necessarily shed light on his theory of thinking, but it does suggest that thought is derived from the reciprocal relation between two competing subjectivities. This of course would displace a purely intrapsychic model with an intersubjective one. But this would not by logical necessity exclude the perspectival emphasis on the rudimentary phenomenology of unconscious life, which is what Freud, Klein, and Bion are attempting to address in their speculative theories of mind. For Bion, thought is originally an emotional experience both initiated by the infant's internal impulses and the mother's reverie. Even if we were to dispense with the Kleinian/Bionian notion that the original contents of thought were directed towards part-objects such as the good and bad breast, this does not mean that the varied contents of ideational thinking do not include emotional properties imbued in the very object of sense representation. Bion does not address this issue as plainly as I do here, but he certainly introduces an equivocation with regard to how we might wish to define what actually constitutes thought.

There is a level of awareness implicit in thinking, what dialectical psychoanalysis originally situates within the unconscious ego as apperceptive pre-reflective self-consciousness, which becomes the template for conscious thought. For Freud, however, thinking begins as mediatory attempts to exert control over our bodies in space and, more specifically, as voluntary control over the movement of our muscles. Implicit in thought is awareness of relations between sense events, judgment, and memory. This is certainly in line with contemporary currents in evolutionary epistemology and neuropsychoanalysis. For Bion (1962a, 57), thinking is more properly inaugurated as an emotional awareness acquired through learning "forced" on the mind by external reality.

Process psychology situates thought much earlier and views thinking as internally derived despite the organism's coexistence with externality (e.g., the foetus's symbiotic relation to the mother's embodiment). In fact, the initial form of thought is a *self-relation* that is a desirous-sentient-affectivity. Here I wish to displace, through parallax, the rigid hegemony that typically characterizes our conventional separation of desire (libido) from affect (feeling) and thought (reason).

HEGEL'S THEORY OF THINKING

Bion's theory of thinking is prefaced by Hegel's detailed analysis of the ontological processes of thought and the phenomenology of consciousness. In the *Science of Logic*, Hegel is concerned with articulating the ground, scope, and functional operations of thinking, reason, and the coming into being of pure self-consciousness, while in the *Phenomenology of Spirit* he comprehensively outlines the various appearances or shapes of individual and collective consciousness. Hegel's philosophical psychology is presented in his philosophy of the subjective mind, which is outlined in the third section of his *Encyclopaedia*. Recall that Hegel discusses the role and function of the unconscious soul in the "Anthropology," which provides a prelude to the activities of conscious awareness. In the "Psychology," he shows how the normative operations of thought, perception, attention, imagination, phantasy, memory, and concept formation are intimately associated with unconscious processes that are prepared by the soul, or what I refer to as the unconscious ego.

When Hegel refers to the subjective mind, he is referring to the internal operations of cognitive perception and thought that may be applied to all individuals, hence he is describing universal intrapsychic processes of cognition. What I have argued through a process account of the psyche is that, as the mind performs its cognitive functions, the unconscious abyss becomes the primary domain of these activities. In his philosophical psychology, Hegel points out how cognition progresses from sense-certainty within the initial mode of perception to (1) forming an intuition or sensation of an immediate object in consciousness (*EG* § 446); to (2) presentation (*EG* § 451) as a withdrawal into the unconscious from the relationship to the singularity of a presented object in consciousness and, thus, relating such object to a universal; leading to (3) thought (*EG* § 465), in which the mind grasps the concrete universals of objects that exist in reality. In the initial phase of intuition as immediate cognizing, cognition begins with the sensation of the immediate object, then alters itself by fixing attention on the object while differentiating itself from it, and then posits the material as external to itself, which becomes intuition proper. The second main phase of cognition as presentation is concerned with recollection, imagination, and memory, while the final phase involves what we properly call thought, which has its content in understanding, judgment, and reason.

For clarification, let me use a conventional example. When we awake each morning, the minute we open our eyes we become immediately aware that there is sense-certainty of some kind, although we do not reflect on it as such. It may take the form of an indistinguishable blur of sensations or images, whether this be emanating from within our own body (e.g., hunger pangs) or from the manifold impressions that immediately fall upon the eyes or ears. Albeit totally outside of our awareness, but perhaps at times preconscious, what we experience in that moment is the immediacy of being – of something that is there – that which presents itself to the senses. It is not until we begin to focus our attention on the objects of our sensations that we have a proper perception of what they are (e.g., a bedroom ceiling, night stand, clock, or some other object in the room). Upon entering into conscious perception, we then become cognizant of the object of our senses, which crystallizes as a distinct and separate discernable image, sentient sensation, sound, thing, and so forth. Phenomenologically, there are in fact many different competing sensuous and perceptual processes transpiring at once, thus requiring many different operations of information processing working simultaneously and in conjunction with one another. Each realm of parallel processing must perform necessary linkages that, in principle, can be pooled together and intertwined and that are capable of being compartmentalized and operating as distinct units of experience. What is remarkable, but is nonetheless the case, is that, at the micromoment of any sensuous experience of a crystallized conscious object (e.g., a cup of water on the night stand), the psychic registration of such an object is at the same time subjected to our conceptual understanding. What this means is that the object is immediately linked to a concept or the categories that imbue linguistic signification and meaning to experience. Here we have the essence of thought in its proper form. In other words, the minute we crystallize an object within our perceptive understanding, we have already mediated it through our linguistic concepts, which label it as such, that is, as a sign (the signifier), which designates an assigned conceptual meaning (the signified) that we retrieve from the chain of signification that is laid down within the deep mnemonic configurations of our unconscious mind and acquired through learning and experience. This whole process takes place within a fraction of a second. Because these dialectical mediations and transitions transpire so quickly, it becomes easy to appreciate how unconscious intelligence is at work.

By Hegelian standards, Bion's model of thinking appears rather simplistic; however, in his defence, Bion (1962a, 306) himself admits that his theoretical system "differs from philosophical theory in that it is intended, like all psychoanalytical theories, for use ... composed in terms of empirically verifiable data." However, Hegel is very clear that his speculative outlook is not at odds with empiricism; rather, "*experience*" becomes the standpoint of "*speculative thinking*" (EL §§ 7–9, emphasis in original). In the *Philosophy of Nature* he also states: "Not only must philosophy be in agreement with our empirical knowledge of Nature, but the *origin* and *formation* of the Philosophy of Nature presupposes and is conditioned by empirical ... science" (PN § 246, emphasis in original). Like Freud and Bion, Hegel is concerned with articulating the inner meaning and ontology of thinking that applies to both normal development and disease.

Bion's scheme is remarkably compatible with Hegel's on many levels emphasizing: (1) the awareness of inner reality, (2) the nature of preconceptual mental activity, and (3) the process of realization as conceptual thought. In our discussion of the coming into being of the abyss, the unconscious ego attains for itself, via intro-reflection, a preliminary level of non-propositional, pre-reflective self-consciousness. In other words, the nascent ego does not yet posit itself as a subject reflecting upon itself as an object but, rather, is intuitively aware of its internal divisions and shapes, which it sets over itself through its splitting activity. Such unconscious self-consciousness is the prototype for the process of consciousness. In fact, consciousness itself is a split-off epigenetic instantiation of unconscious structure.

Unconscious intro-reflection corresponds to Bion's notion of innate a priori knowledge in the form of preconceptions; yet, for Bion, this gets explained through encounters with realized or non-realized objects, resulting in positive (satisfying) or negative (frustrating, non-gratifying) conceptions. Hegel's epistemology derives from the logic of the dialectic, while Bion's is merely presupposed and interjected through the subjective encounter. In order for conceptualization to occur, certain mental preconditions or configurations must be thought to exist prior to experience and to be mobilized from the beginning. Through the principle of sufficient reason, there must be a ground to psychic life that precedes conscious experience, and this assumption remains a cardinal pillar of psychoanalytic doctrine. In other words, all events, objects, and changes in the mind are related to each other by necessity, require each other in their relationships, and cannot be other than what they are. There is a reason for all this, although we may not be fully aware of the conditions or comprehend the ground for their ultimate occurrences. In psychoanalysis, we have customarily referred to this principle as "psychic determinism."

For Hegel, the process of conceiving or conceptual understanding is a complex achievement, an activity attained very early, at least from Bion's account. Bion's notion of preconceptions would be explained by Hegel as the implicit realization of ideas or the Concept (*Begriff*) within the deep internal abyss of the mind – a process fully actualized in Absolute Knowing. Put in more accessible language, the unconscious ego generates preconceptual, prelinguistic ideas belonging to its innate natural constitution, what Freud, Klein, and Bion would contend are drive derivatives that are phylogenetically informed. But Hegel also locates preconceptual mentation within the realm of unconscious feeling, a position closely allied with Bion's. Furthermore, both Hegel and Bion place primacy on the awareness of psychic reality (Hegel in the feeling soul, Bion as a precondition for the process of thought and symbol formation). For both Hegel and Bion, awareness of inner reality is a necessary and universal condition for the occurrence of symbolization, phantasy, and language acquisition.

Unconscious Intelligence

Hegel is very specific in tracing the cognitive development of the subjective mind, a process that has further implications for Bion, Klein, and Freud. For Hegel, cognition moves from the sensation of its immediacy to attention (whereby it fixes on the object as it separates it from itself) to intuition proper as positing the object external to its own self. At this point, the presentation of certain material leads to three more corresponding operations: (1) recollection, (2) imagination, and (3) memory. Presentation (*Vorstellung*) implicitly unfolds within intuition because attention is paid to two moments, namely, feeling and the attending act, whereby an object is isolated, held in focus, and related to externally. Attention now becomes introspective and must *re-collect* the content intuited within itself, as Hegel says "within its *own space* and its *own time*" (*EG* § 452, emphasis in original). This content initially appears as an image (*Bild*), but it could very well be a sound, which is taken up by the ego and extracted from its external context in which perception had occurred. Abstracted from the concrete immediacy of perception, the image becomes arbitrary and is merely a fleeting moment since attention may focus on only one or a few select things at a time.

During presentation, the ego internalizes the content of what is presented before it by gathering up and separating the external image or impression and then incorporating it, but, being only a fleeting impression, it vanishes quickly from consciousness: "Intelligence is not, however, only the consciousness and the determinate being …; recollected within it, the image is no longer existent, but is preserved unconsciously" (*EG* § 453). Here Hegel points to the underworld: intelligence is not merely a conscious operation but also a "nocturnal pit [*nachtlichen Schacht*] within which a world of infinitely numerous images and presentations is preserved without being in consciousness." Hegel specifically equates intelligence as this unconscious abyss, thus forming the domains of two fundamental realities, the world of the deep and the world of consciousness.

Hegel explains how objects within experience are preserved within certain "localities" and "fibers" in the unconscious, subsisting outside of awareness as inherently concrete yet simple universals. Intelligence has "imperfect control of the images slumbering within the abyss" that cannot also be recollected at will (*EG* § 453, *Zusatz*). In fact, we have no way of gaining access to, let alone knowing, the full extent of what lies within the unconscious, here pointing to certain aspects of psychic life that resist incorporation into the dialectic: "No one knows what an infinite host of images of the past slumbers within him. Although they certainly awaken by chance on various occasions, one cannot, – as it is said, – call them to mind" (*EG* § 453, *Zusatz*). This concession on Hegel's part points to the inner autonomy of unconscious life, which is resistant to conscious influence and, thus, under the governance of the unconscious ego, and shows how, from the standpoint of consciousness, they share a divided existence within psychic totality.

Imagination

What is of particular interest here is Bion's theory of ideographs in relation to Hegel's theory of imagination and phantasy. Bion (1957) postulates that something analogous to ideographs and sight are formed in the preverbal ego, presumably as early as the paranoid-schizoid position if not from birth onward. This would corroborate Hegel's theory of imagination and, particularly, his notion of symbolization. As noted before, unconscious images are preserved within the abyss of the mind and, due to the negative character of the dialectic as well as early developmental contingencies that mould ego development and object relations, they can take on many persecutory qualities and valences that are in need of evacuation. To recall an image is to repeat or *re-present* an intuition, and this is why it is free of immediate intuition – because it is "preserved unconsciously." We recognize in immediate perception images we have experienced before. While consciousness isolates a specific feature, it relates it to the universality of unconscious recollection. Representation is therefore the synthesized product of relating an immediate intuition to an unconscious universal that becomes an object for consciousness. It is in imagination, however, that the process of relating one representation to others is intellectually carried out.

For Hegel, imagination mediates between intuition and thought, or the sensual and the conceptual. In imagination, representations are related to one another in the flow of consciousness that becomes linked with other images, affects, and thoughts as they are generated and manipulated by the ego's activity. Retrieved from the abyss, they are now technically under the ego's control, but with qualifications. Imagination also assumes three movements or sub-phases, namely: (1) reproductive imagination, (2) associative imagination, and (3) phantasy. First, representations are reproduced from the abyss but fall under the direction of the ego as "the issuing *forth* of images from the ego's own inwardness," which it now governs (EG § 455, emphasis in original). The line of demarcation that divides the unconscious ego from the conscious ego is now breached: the ego vacillates between its unconscious and conscious counterparts.

Images are not only retrieved but also issue forth from the ego itself, assuming that unconscious material is externalized into conscious apperception, or, as Hegel puts it, "excogitated ... from the generality of the abyss." This process immediately initiates an association of variegated images, part-objects, and features that are related to further presentations, which may be either abstract or concrete and may vary in content and form. In this way, the range of intellectual connections expands. However, if links are attacked, as Bion informs us, such connections would be attenuated. But normatively, within this multiplicity of associations, the synthetic functions of intelligence are already operative as thought implicit within intelligence. Imagination in general determines images. As a formal activity, the reproduction of images occurs "*voluntarily*" (EG § 455, *Zusatz,* emphasis in original); it does not require the aid of an immediate intuition to effect this process as in the case of recollection, which is dependent upon the presence of an object of intuition. Distinguished from recollection, cognition is now "self-activating."

Phantasy

Phantasy is the third movement of imagination, where the ego fully manipulates its representations and images, drawing lines of interconnection where particulars are subsumed under universals and given the richer elaboration of symbols and signs that effect the ego's transition to memory, the third stage of presentation. Phantasy is a subjective bond the ego has with its contents, and with the introduction of symbolization, allegory, and sign, imagination gains increased synthetic mastery over its presentations, which are imbued with "reason." Here the inwardness of intelligence "is *internally determined concrete subjectivity,* with *a capacity* of its own deriving" (EG § 456, emphasis in original). Within phantasy, there is an imagined existence as hidden unconscious processes infiltrate the creative centres of subjectivity. This can be both horrifying and sublime.

While phantasy attains its most elaborate articulation in language and speech, it does not strictly require words in order to reveal itself. This may be achieved by the mind's manipulation of its own operations with respect to both content and cognitive functions, such as the confluence of certain feeling states attached to interrelated images. In fact, phantasy is the a priori condition for language; it is a prelinguistic organization that precedes organized conceptual thought.[4] Here Hegel's position is Kleinian: phantasy precedes concept formation. While Klein, Bion, Segal, and others focus upon the content, motives, and qualitative attributes underlying the phenomenology of phantasy, Hegel clarifies the ontological processes that make phantasy possible.

Phantasy both symbolizes and engenders signs. Initially, it subsumes singulars under a universal through symbolization, but because the immediate content is both a particularization and a universal, interpretation remains ambiguous. Phantasy becomes a central operation in unconscious production, a spewing forth of impulses and desires from the wishing well of the abyss. It may be suspended in space and time, conform to the abyss's will through regression or withdrawal irrespective of the ego's counter-intentions, and warp objective reality to the tone of the ego's own subjective caprice or pathology. This is why images may be either disturbing or pleasing. The "*symbolizing, allegorizing* or *poetical* power of the imagination" (EG § 456, emphasis in original) is not confined to the mere subjective, however; it may take an external objective referent as the embodiment of its creativity. This move constitutes "the phantasy of sign making" (EG § 457).

Through signification, intelligence is concerned with unifying the relations between determinate content and what it signifies universally. The synthesis of phantasy is the unity of the sign with the universal and its self-relation. Hegel states that, "in phantasy intelligence has being, for the first time, not as an indeterminate abyss and universal, but as a singularity, i.e. as concrete subjectivity, in which the self-relation is determined in respect of being as well as universality" (EG § 457). This statement suggests that universality itself is a sort of abyss, in that all particularity is lost in it, whether this be the soul's initial immersion with and undifferentiation from nature or its subsumption within universal spirit. Such unification of the sign with universality is seen by the mind as its own activity, which is internal and proper to it. Here intelligence gives itself *being*, which is now within its own capacity to do. Not to be underestimated in its importance, the sign "adds proper intuitability" to images as an objective existent (EG § 457). While the symbol refers to the intuition of the content and its relation to its essence and concept, the sign *designates* meaning in which the content of intuition becomes dislodged from what it signifies (EG § 458). In symbolic phantasy, intelligence pays attention to the given content of images, but in sign phantasy it replaces imagined universality with objective affirmation: the presented universal is liberated from the content of images. According to Hegel: "The *sign* is a certain immediate intuition, presenting a content which is wholly distinct from that which it has for itself; – it is the *pyramid* in which the alien soul is ensconced and preserved" (*EG* § 458, emphasis in original). Hence intelligence proceeds from the pit to the pyramid,[5] the soul sublated as intelligence gains more mastery over its self-designating operations. The content of intuition becomes "irrelevant" to what it signifies. Cognition may now focus on the signified universal rather than on the particular features of its intuited content. But before its final transition to memory, imagination must cancel its subjectivity, its internality, and give itself objective being. In this way "the universal and being, one's own and what is appropriated, inner and outer being, are given the completeness of a unit" (*EG* § 457). These operations belong to the mature liberated ego, a developmental progression from the primitive functions of unconscious phantasy guided by archaic forces.

Intelligence goes beyond the sign to understanding its meaning. With each new immediate intuition, intelligence moves from unconscious determinateness that transforms intuitions into images, images into representations, and representations into associations and is thus raised to the level of objective existence and self-determining being as sublatedness – a normative process conforming to the dialectic of projective identification. Intelligence is now presented (as presenting itself) with a "tone" from the unconscious soul, "which intelligence furnishes from the anthropological resources of its own naturalness, the fulfillment of the expressiveness by which inwardness makes itself known" (*EG* § 459). Sound instantiates itself further in speech and, as the interrelations of words, in a system of language that endows the sensations, intuitions, and representations with a "second determinate being" that sublates the immediacy of the first. Mind no longer needs the constant presence of external signs; when they vanish as ephemeral phenomena, intelligence draws upon its inner meaning and "inner symbolism" as it generates and relates to its own processes. Intelligence remains active, it confers meaning through sounds and words and, as such, becomes a sublated intuition for itself. Networks of meaningful relations are externalized as signs, and when they disappear the mind must reconstitute their significance through its own self-relating activity. Imagination first makes visible unconscious processes in the form of images, then manipulates their relations through phantasy, conferring symbolization and assigning meaning – the name, a word. When the name vanishes, imagination either must create a new name for its set of relations or it must recollect a previous name and its meaning and attach it to new associations. This requires memory, a process that is always implicit in any form of recollection or representation.

Cognition has moved from its initial task of internalizing intuitions to its externalization of the abyss through imagination, to which it takes its next shape as memory, the task of which is to integrate its previous two movements. While intelligence gains greater dynamic unity in verbal, reproductive, and mechanical memory, Hegel sees cognition through to its end, that is, to thought as understanding, judgment, and formal reason. Thought knows itself, it *re-cognizes* itself, and achieves its fullest logical elaboration as pure thinking: thought thinking about itself and its operations. While these are the greater faculties of mind, they need not concern us here. Bion's model of ideographs is given richer articulation by Hegel's analysis of imagination, which has further implications for understanding unconscious phantasy.

We have seen the overwhelming presence and indispensable function of the nocturnal abyss throughout the stage of presentation, the necessary precondition for higher activities of mind to become manifest. Presentations are fleeting and much of memory fades, but it becomes imprinted within the soul and wells up from imagination. Hegel explains:

> The power of memory is replaced by an unchanging tableau of a series of images fixed in the imagination ... Not only is spirit put to the torment of being pestered with a deranged subject matter, but whatever is learnt by rote in this manner is as a matter of course soon forgotten again ... What is mnemonically imprinted is as it were read off from the tableau of the imagination ... and so really brought forth from within, rehearsed from the deep abyss of the ego. (*EG* § 462)

As Hegel reminds us once again, intelligence is unconsciously constituted as ego. There can be no doubt about the importance of imagination and its relation to the abyss; spirit is as much dependent on imagination – especially phantasy – as it is on reason. In fact, their relationship is so intimate that it leads Hegel to say, even with stipulations, that "phantasy is reason" (*EG* § 457). Imagination therefore becomes the locus of the powers of the mind.

Hegel's anticipation of Klein's and Bion's theories of projective identification as the process of the self returning to itself due to its own self-estrangement adds to our understanding of both the normative and pathological processes of mind. In health and illness the ego projects certain aspects of its self onto the object world, which it then identifies with and finally re-introjects back into its subjectivity. In effect, the self rediscovers its self in the product of its own projection and then reintegrates itself within itself as reunification. This is the generic structural movement of the Hegelian dialectic, whereby internal division, external projection, and reincorporation function as a mediating and sublating dynamic.

Klein herself, as well as all post Kleinians, constantly refers to the dialectical forces of splitting accompanied by projection and introjection that are responsible for both good and bad self-object representations as well as the general division between the ego and the object and the internal polarities that maintain rigid antitheses struggling for reconciliation. Hegel's emphasis on psychic holism mirrors the general consensus among Kleinians that the ego strives for wholeness guided by an orienting principle aimed at increased synthetic integration – the primary motive of sublation. This is simply the dialectic of desire, the internal thrust of spirit that yearns for self-completion.

As we have seen, our dialectical depiction of projective identification has implications for understanding psychic structure, psychosis and schizoid mechanisms, thinking, linking, symbol formation, phantasy, and containers and change. Having seen the ubiquitous nature of the dialectic at work in the most rudimentary processes of thinking itself, I now wish to turn our attention to its foundational origins in unconscious organizing principles. I specifically want to engage the question of thinking and phantasy prior to the formal acquisition of language. This is where Bion proves instructive. The types of thoughts and conceptions Bion speaks of during the ego's early development of thinking, linking, and phantasy is not the type of conceptualizing belonging to formal intelligence or reason that Hegel expatiates; rather, they are always dominated by the unconscious press of phantasy. Despite Bion's reference to "ideographs," which he speculates "exist at the outset," presumably at birth, he leaves the *details* of symbolic signification unexplained. Equally, while Hegel elaborately articulates the process of thinking, he does not properly account for how symbolization transpires prior to linguistic concept formation governed by unconscious phantasy. What appears to be missing in both accounts is a proper appreciation of unconscious semiotics.

· 4 ·

Unconscious Semiotics

The *It* remembers what the *I* forgets.

In *Studies on Hysteria*, Freud (1893–95) tells us that the origins of defence emanate from a psychical force that resists knowing certain pathogenic ideas through a process of censorship that is protective or insulating in its function (SE 1:268–9), a function we have commonly come to know as repression. Freud believes that this functional force in the mind is based on an "aversion on the part of the ego" that had originally driven threatening representations out of our awareness and that actively opposes their return to memory. Freud specifically states: "The idea in question was forced out of consciousness and out of memory. The psychical trace of it was apparently lost to view. Nevertheless that trace must be there" (269). This presumed *trace* becomes an unconscious artefact, not as a static unalterable truth about psychic reality awaiting to be unearthed in pristine form but, rather, as a *semiotic* that resists representation, that which resists being known. Following the logic of the dialectic, it becomes legitimate to assume that such a trace would persist in the abyss, given that all psychic phenomena, when negated or cancelled, must by extension be preserved to some degree within the repository of the unconscious, which Freud identifies as timeless and eternal. In fact, Freud (1925b) sees negation (*Verneinung*) as a "certificate of origin" (SE 14:236), the signifier of repression.

Contra Freud, the trace is never preserved in its original perceptive form, as if it were merely a datum catalogued in a computer chip; rather, it is mutated the minute it is incorporated into the psychic register. According to process psychology, certain aspects of the trace must undergo transmogrification once subjected to the dominion of unconscious agency. And here I would argue that there is a selective retention performed by the microdynamic operations of agency inscribed on the psychic repository, an agentic process of memorialization that selectively preserves what it simultaneously alters due to unconscious emotional motivations, what Freud metaphorically equates with a malleable mnemonic tablet.

In his brief and playful essay, "A Note upon the 'Mystic Writing-Pad,'" Freud (1925a) draws an analogy between how unconscious representations are encoded and how a magnetic sketch pad records impressions on the surface that can be erased yet preserved underneath its structural interior.[1] Freud equates the perceptual system with the surface of sense impressions, which are ephemeral perceptual processes of the conscious mind that are passively received, filtered, unnoticed, and forgotten, yet that leave a "permanent trace" upon a subcortical level he equates with unconscious mnemonic representations. The former is a permeable and transient receptor of external stimuli that simultaneously acts as a "protective shield," while the latter is the hearty magnetic slab or, to invoke another computer analogy, the hard drive that records and preserves all softwear programs. Perceptual consciousness "has an unlimited receptive capacity for new perceptions," which "lays down permanent – even though not unalterable – memory-traces of them" (SE 19:228). Notice that a semiotic is "not unalterable." In fact, it is subject to all kinds of internal transformations, not to mention the way in which unconscious traces are construed, interpretively constructed, or understood within the patient-analyst dyad.

In describing the dynamics of unconscious teleonomy, Freud speculates that "cathectic innervations [*Besetzungsinnervationen*] are sent out and withdrawn in rapid periodic impulses from within" (SE 19:231) the unconscious into the perceptive apparatus of consciousness.[2] Note that Freud says that the origin of such activity, as a trajectory or occupation (*Besetzung*) of psychic energy, emanates "from within" and is directed into consciousness, where it receives perceptions and passes them into the mnemonic reservoirs of the abyss. Here mental process is directed and withdrawn as an active agentic function, not merely as a biologic mechanism, or at least it is not reduced to such. We may extend Freud here to show how both teleonomic and teleologic aims (i.e., those belonging to economic and adaptational aims and those belonging to more complex dynamic, purposeful [intentional] activity governed by unconscious motivation) are mutually operative. However, unlike Freud, a withdrawal of innervetic occupation or stimulation does not bring conscious life to a "standstill"; rather, the demarcation between the abyss and consciousness is suspended through a process of inversion. In other words, the ego withdraws into itself.

What is important to note is how unconscious telic activities, as determinate aims executed by the unconscious ego, are channelled into sensory perception, where they take the manifold sense impressions as their objects (hence making this the most permeable aspect of a *Trieb*) and then withdraw back into its interior. Here unconscious processes both breach and close up the porthole to consciousness when outwardly directed stimuli are suddenly disrupted – stimuli that are subsequently aborted. Freud states that such "interruptions" have an "external origin" (*SE* 19:231). Like the mystic pad, impressions penetrate the unconscious through the celluloid register of the conscious apparatus and leave their mark. When they are interrupted by external reality the unconscious closes up and inverts into its internal spacings. Here Freud returns to a trauma motif, as he did when he introduced the death drive in *Beyond the Pleasure Principle*. A protective or defensive retrograde reaction is immediately instituted when an encroachment or intrusion is felt on the telic trajectory of mental directionality. This closing of the breach, this occlusive function of the psyche in the moment of intrusion, is introduced through a "discontinuity" – hence a gap – in perceptual stimuli. Recall that, for Freud (1915a), the unconscious reveals itself as phenomena through discontinuities. Here foreclosures in perceptual stimuli signal the call for a retreat into the abyss. Sense impressions, perceptual impingements, images, cognizing mediations, and so forth are internalized into the deep structural configurations of unconscious memory and exposed to the internal demands and economic pressures of the pulsions, where they are further submitted to the ego's agentic autonomous manipulation by phantasy. Here lies the wishing well.

When speaking of the origins of dream-work, Freud (1900) states:

> There is often a passage in even the most thoroughly interpreted dream which has to be left obscure; this is because we become aware during the work of interpretation that at that point there is a tangle of dream-thoughts which cannot be unraveled and which moreover adds nothing to our knowledge of the content of the dream. This is the dream's navel, the spot where it reaches down into the unknown. The dream-thoughts to which we are led by

interpretation cannot, from the nature of things, have any definite endings; they are bound to branch out in every direction into the intricate network of our world of thought. It is at some point where this meshwork is particularly close that the dream-wish grows up, like a mushroom out of its mycelium. (SE 5:525)

Dream-work is an act of translation – translation with a limit, a point of blockage. This *nodus* is what Freud calls "the dream's navel" (*der Nabel des Traums*), where there is a "tangle" (*Knäuel*) that cannot be "unraveled" (*der sich nicht entwirren will*), as sometimes happens in a ball of yarn. Here there is a knot, a check, an obstacle – the occlusion of dream space – the meaning of which is "left obscure" (*Dunkel lassen*); hence, this is the limit of analysis itself. Freud points to the infinity of the abyss when he says that our dream-thoughts have no "definite endings" (*mussen bleiben ohne Abschluss*), only branches that spread out into an "intricate network" (*in die netzartige Verstrickung*) of unconscious semiotics. The wish – the content of desire – grows up out of a "meshwork" (*Geflecht*) of insoluble knots and tangled threads, what Derrida (1998) calls "the umbilicus" (16), "an unanalyzable synthesis" (15). The navel, the scar of birth, is an apt symbol for the trace – the semiotic – that signifies genesis, the seat of unconscious origin eclipsed from pure knowing. This semiotic is not only foreclosed, hence cast into the pit of the noumenal "unknown," but is also the wellspring of desire, which blooms out of its convoluted mass. Spacings of the abyss awaiting to be born from its core, "like a mushroom out of its mycelium."

SEMEION

When I refer to semiotic, I am specifically inferring the Greek notion of *semeion* – a mark, trace, or distinctive inscription. As I have shown, the unconscious ego is awakened through a rupture brought about by its inner desire to externalize itself through the felt self-certainty it acquires via the negation of its confinement to its corporeal nature. It is in the formation of the unconscious ego prior to the birth of the infant that we have collapsed the sharp distinction between sensuous life and the realm of intelligibility, that is, between emotionality and thought. Desire is not only affective dialectical activity coming to presence but it is also teleologically expressed through the inward awareness it has of itself as lacking; hence, presence and absence are cognized by the incipient mind in its initial dialectical moments. Desire is semiotic in that it differentiates and distinguishes through its sublating activity, always leaving behind the trace or inscription of its experiential movements as they are preserved within the abyss. Moreover, despite being qua absence, lack remains a *formal presence* in the mind. Recall that, while drive may be sated in its moment, desire may never be fulfilled or completed for mind would no longer long to move beyond itself, thus the dialectic would perish entirely, and the ego would cease to be. Lack is always an inscription within the psyche and, therefore, the seed of thought itself.

Unconscious self-consciousness is predicated on the level of awareness the soul attains for itself through its progressive dialectical achievements. Here we take Bion much further: the unconscious ego is dimly aware of its psychic reality prior to its birth into consciousness. In fact, the ego first and foremost becomes prereflectively aware of the lack that innately permeates its inner pulse of sentient-affective experience. Recall that desire is being-in-relation-to-lack as pure unrest, event, and internally derived activity, the very process that stimulates and fuels the dialectic. As a result, lack initially becomes the internal signifier for establishing a whole network of unconscious semiotic connections. This is arguably a radicalization of Klein's general notion of unconscious phantasy and Bion's theory of thinking, for the simple reason that it is preliminarily primed, arranged, and rehearsed prior to the ego's eruption into consciousness. Therefore, unconscious semiotics become the logical template for the acquisition of linguistic signification, concept formation, and language.

Lack – the presencing of absence – engenders its own forms of signification that are peculiar to the unconscious ego's unique subjective relationship to its own internality, such as the way it comes to experience its own sentience or affective reverberations as well as its prenatal environ. Being-in-relation-to-lack becomes the original form of representation – hence the representation of absence, of empty form – for it constantly imprints itself afresh in the psyche, thus it perpetually *re-presents* itself through the structural negativity informing the dialectic. With stipulations, we may loosely say that lack introduces a semiotic that both conveys something we sense or feel (the signifier) and think (the signified), thus conferring a relation between the sensuous and the receptive (apprehended), what we may more accurately refer to as preconceptual, pre-reflective apperception. Therefore, the signification of desire represents the object of lack or absence to the incipient mind. Here the relata of signification becomes triadic: at once desire signals and engenders a (1) *sign* or mark it institutes through its relation to the presencing of lack, thus producing (2) an *object* for itself that it (3) *re-presents* to itself through intro-reflection, hence pioneering its transition to thought. Yet thought at this level is not to be equated with the thinking of consciousness predicated on linguistic concept formation or the symbolic order; here it is merely formal, hence empty of concepts despite being registered by the agency of the ego as signifying absence. In fact, lack becomes the unconscious semiotic that signifies the very essence of the dialectic – namely, negativity, death, nothingness – the rotary drive behind appetition.

Because desire is a process relation between mutually implicative forms of opposition, thought is necessarily imbued with negativity. Here it becomes easy to see how unconscious phantasy is prepared by the dialectic to enter into internally divided, persecutory, and paranoiac relations characteristic of the paranoid-schizoid position, a process that formally transpires before birth. Klein and Bion require that the ego attain conscious experience before splitting, thinking, and symbol formation develop, while here I am pointing to the primordiality of unconscious signification that allows for conscious signification (such as metonymy and metaphor) to materialize through more rich and robust planes of experience, perception, and conceptual construction properly acquired through language and the structural laws of signification. What I wish to highlight is that not only does the dialectic generate and sustain unconscious semiotics, but it also establishes a whole fabric, network, or chain association of signification that is both prelinguistic and translinguistic, thus establishing the primacy of unconscious semiotic phantasy.

The reader should be aware that I concern myself with a narrow point of view with respect to the question, meaning, truth, and being of semiotic structure within a speculative ontological framework of unconscious process. I do not wish to engage the disparate and nuanced fields of linguistics and psycholinguistics, or the broader domains of structural and poststructural theories of language, which are derived from a wide body of research conducted in the social and human sciences (primarily in France), including anthropology, sociology, literary theory, cultural and political studies, and even mathematics. In fact, semiologists will likely object to my analysis based on the simple observation that language and signification are predicated on consciousness and culture. This is an assumption, however, I wish to challenge, or at least to qualify. Signification and meaning have archaic roots that emanate from the lived body, both evolutionarily and phylogenetically informed, at once a corporeal expression affectively animated by desire, drive, and sentience.[3]

Although not diminishing poststructuralism per se, I wish to distinguish myself from Lacan, who believes that the unconscious is "structured like a language" and, indeed, who equates the unconscious with language itself (see Lacan 1955–56a, 11; 1955–56b, 119; 1955–56c, 166–7), which is predicated on consciousness and cultural determinism. For Lacan, because the symbolic temporally exists prior to the contingent birth of the subject, this, in turn, determines the essence of the subject. Therefore, the subject is constituted by the symbolic function. For Lacan, the subject is conditioned upon its "entrance into language" under the symbolic Law (E 1957, 148), which ultimately makes the unconscious a cultural category captured by his formula: "the unconscious is '*discours de l' Autre*' (discourse of the Other)" (E 1960, 312). Because the symbolic order, namely, language and culture, is causally superimposed, this corresponds to the constitution of the human subject. Here Lacan precariously subverts the notion of freedom within psychic agency as if everything is conditioned on language. Furthermore, for Lacan, the ego is an "illusion of autonomy" based on its *méconnaissances* and imaginary relations to others (E 1936–49, 6); and, unlike Freud, even "man's desire is the *désir de l' Autre* (the desire of the Other)" (E 1960, 312). In Lacan, we may call into question whether human agency even exists, for he sees agency as belonging to the authority of the letter. For Lacan, human subjectivity is always constituted by something outside of itself.

Process psychology offers a rapprochement between the subject-object/otherness binary by supplanting the hegemony between the semiotic and the symbolic. But we do not wish to boil everything down to the sign, as postmodern theorists tend to do, because this reifies language, social causality, and linguistic determinism through the displacement of embodiment, biology, individuality and subjective qualia, personal agency, and freedom. Nor, for the same reason, do we wish to import Pierce's semiotics into process psychology as, like Lacan's, his system privileges a theory of language. Furthermore, while there are fruitful comparisons with regard to the role of signification and the tertiary functions that mediate higher modes of meaning relations, there are also divergences within our respective frameworks due to Lacan's emphasis on the symbolic as opposed to Peirce's emphasis on the sign. Although these theories of semiotics potentially possess pockets of compatibility with much of what I have to say, from my account it is important not to subordinate the unconscious to linguistic processes alone, only to show how they are accommodated and subsumed within more sophisticated aspects of unconscious order with a clear respect for the notion of overdetermination.

On the potential compatibilities with Peirce, it is interesting to note that he delineates a triadic theory – or what Merrell (1997) refers to as a "tripodic" theory – of signification based on the interdependency of a *representamen* or representation (R), which is formally the sign, a semiotic object (O), and an interpretant (I). Here I would situate the function of agency within the interpretant as ego, which generates the meaning relations between the signifier (sign) and signified (conceptual object). Here meaning is conferred and mediated between these interpenetrating events directed by a semiotic agent, which is necessarily contextual, variable, and nonlinear in its process relations and which, furthermore, supersedes the Saussurean *signifier-signified* dichotomy. What is of further fascination is that Peirce attributes the locus, origin, precipitant, or coming into being of this triadic relation – what he insists is a systemic unit – to a "cut" (CP 5:441). This is the very language Lacan uses and which, as we have shown, is derived from Freud's notion of the "gap," or discontinuity, in consciousness, itself the signification that unconscious processes are at work. For Peirce, the cut precedes his categories of immediate *Firstness*, dyadic *Secondness*, and mediate *Thirdness*, which form the basis of his theory of signs. Indeed, Peirce sees the cut as a marker or disfigurement of "nothingness" (CP 5:441) informing the ground or pure conditions for the emergence of semiotic possibility. Here I would extend this notion of nothingness, seeing it as a spacing that precedes all division and separation in the mind and in the relata of signification diachronically enacted and realized by unconscious agency. This *pre-beginning*, or primal nothingness, structurally imports the supremacy of negation. Following the logic of the dialectic, negation is enacted in every division or splitting of mental content. And the cut, like Freud's gap, guarantees that any act of signification, meaning relation, or symbolism would be marred by discontinuity emanating from the abyss.

Following Kristeva's (1974) emphasis on the semiotic, I am interested in exploring the realm of the presymbolic, what she has identified as the dimensions of subjectivity and meaning that exceed the structure of language and the laws of signification (Beardsworth 2004). Bearing in mind the truest etymological sense of the ancients' emphasis on *semeion* as a distinctive trace (ἴχνος), we can easily appreciate how psychic reality would have to emerge from an underworld forging its marks along the way. Not only does consciousness (particularly the perceptual apparatus) leave a trace, or, more accurately, a combinatory of referential traces that serve as ongoing stimuli for one another in the associative matrix of signification, but unconscious processes themselves also institute distinctive inscriptions that are memorialized within unconscious structure and that serve as ongoing sources of internal stimulation. Here I would argue that the unconscious is ontologically prepared a priori by the dialectic both to generate and to acquire linguistic structures, not merely to have them causally and passively superimposed by virtue of our cultural thrownness. What is inferred from this position is that thought and ideas are not caused by a one-way relation, whereby external dictates (the Lacanian "demand") inscribe themselves on the blank slate of the mind through the superimposition of signifiers; rather, there is a two-way relation between the agentic processes that organize and institute signification and those experiences that are stimulated within the psychic register by what it encounters through sentient (desire/affect) and, later, conscious (perceptive/conceptual) impingements. Although the unconscious mind incorporates language and its formal operations introduced through the vehicle of consciousness, what it does with such information-carrying signs, symbolic communications, and meaning transmissions is conditioned by the unique intrapsychic microdynamic linkages performed by each individual ego, subject to the adroit manipulation of unconscious phantasy. Following the developmental unfolding of the ego, first there is an extended mediatory relation of interiority to externality – not the other way around. This means that the unconscious mind has the capacity to resist universal laws of signification that are properly attributed to the formal structures of language, instead forging its own modes of signification through desirous, defensive, libidinal, and/or aggressive processes sequestered from or dissociatively compartmentalized in opposition to more elaborate logical operations or rational restraints belonging to consciousness.

These sequestered, parallel processes typically fall under the influence of affective and somatic resonance states imbued with desire, conflicted motivations, wish-fulfilling properties, and so forth – under the direction of the pleasure principle and its derived variants. This principle of unconscious semiotics potentially explains how bodily and affective schemata are formally constituted by an agentic ego through phantasy operations that link content with form mediated by desire and emotionality, thus abstracting representations and interjecting them with coveted qualities and functions within the boundlessness of the abyss. But, as Bion points out, there are attacks on linking due to anxiety and threat, hence a defensive negation is employed by the dialectic based on a particular transitivism via projective identification.

The prelinguistic and translinguistic function of semiotics ensures that unconscious phantasy plays a definitive role in symbolic representations and concept formation, with affectivity or emotionality attached to thought and even adhering within the concepts the mind generates or conceives. What I have in mind here is a word, especially an antonym, that carries the possibility of being imbued with affect based solely on an archaic experiential meaning. For example, I had a patient whose father, upon greeting her each night at the end of his workday, told her, with great emotive delight, that she was his "little princess." The affirmative word "princess" acquired a very negating quality once she heard her jealous mother call her "little princess" in a scoffing tone accompanied by contorted facial expressions. To this day, for this patient, the word is inscribed with an affective semiotic that evokes disgust and negativity.

In traditional linguistics, affect has no place in semiotic structures, let alone in the irrational forces that beset mental activity. Here I am arguing that emotions are enlisted and potentially imbued in all objects of signification originally transpiring within the unconscious mind. In effect, unconscious qualia are structurally inscribed in the very meaning properties of a sign. These may be relatively benign, even pleasure-oriented, or aesthetically distasteful, dangerous, or malignant, depending upon how semiotic orders are linked to qualitative affect states associated with a particular event or piece of psychic datum. When the valences of competing psychic contents, forms, and their accompanying intensities overlap, interpenetrate, or are combined in an associational nexus orchestrated by the unconscious ego, a sign may take on very eccentric meaning properties specific to that individual subject's evoked internal experience filtered through her or his past developmental history. The potential radical subjectivity inherent to unconscious phenomenology ensures that semiotic structures are never completely severed or secured from the encroachment of competing psychic processes. Here a semiotic can never completely insulate itself from the underworld of striving pulsions, wishes, affects, conflicts, terrors, and so forth that can potentially attach to or bore into the sign itself, which it then disfigures, congregates, or makes its habitat. This would imply that the chain structure of signification would not be rigidly causal, unalterably laid down within memory, or harbour predetermined meanings in relation to signifiers.

It becomes easy to appreciate how certain signs have different meanings for different people, despite there being a collective consensual agreement around their range of potential meanings. Signification is initiated within the unconscious unfolding of the ego; therefore, thought in its rudimentary form is cognized within the initial internal splitting of the psyche as the desirous apperceptive soul takes itself as its object. Moreover, experience becomes semiotically etched or imprinted on the unconscious mind prior to the formal entrance into and acquisition of language, linguistic signification, and concept formation. What this means is that unconscious phantasy begets its own signs and deferral of signifiers attached to representations created by its own imaginary powers derived from the modification of desire and drive instituted through unconscious agency.

ON IDEOGRAPHS

I have been arguing that desire and lack, somatic and affective schemata, and the broader diachronic organization of unconscious semiotics are initially generated from within the nascent interior of the unconscious abyss only to become more vital and substantial during conscious ego development. On the level of unconscious experience, signification, symbol formation, and phantasy are radically subjective, thereby disfiguring language, in turn reshaping it through self-imposed unconscious signifiers potentially defying universal laws or orders of sign classifications, or at least eclipsing them through determinate negation. When under the influence of anxiety or pathological currents, such as traumatic, schizoid, paranoid, and depressive phenomena, unconscious semiotics distort the laws of linguistic signification through the idiosyncratic medium of unconscious agency.

Let us now return to Bion's abbreviated theory of thinking as emanating from sight and pictorial symbol formation manifested in the form of "ideographs." What exactly does Bion mean by this term? He does not say. Let us extend his ambiguous speculation. I believe that rudimentary ideas, primarily based in visual sense data, are stimulated or evoked, symbolically interjected or encoded, and attached to objects of experience insofar as an object becomes an emergent representation signifying some form of meaning to the incipient mind. Recall that Bion (1957, 66) specifically says that "some kind of thought, related to what we should call ideographs and sight rather than to words and hearing exists at the onset." To my knowledge this is his only statement on the concept of ideographs. Here Bion emphasizes "sight." But we have shown how this is preceded by the unconscious ego's felt self-relation in the desirous, somatic, and affective reverberations it ingressively encounters, shapes, and re-experiences while ensconced within its immediate fluid, corporeal monadic interiority. We must seriously question whether "sight" should be the prototype for ideographs.

Idea (ἰδέα) in Greek refers to form, as "to form in," taken from *idein*, to see. Due to the evolution of the desirous apperceptive ego, the ideologic form of an unconscious idea must precede sight and the pictorial graphic symbols that represent such ideas or things. More pointedly, unconscious mentation originally takes the cognizing form of somatic and affective self-certainty: *feeling* becomes the proper form of such ideographs, itself the modification of desire. Unconscious cognition first cognizes itself as a desirous and sensuous felt-immediacy, only to differentiate and modify itself further as apperceptive sentience or unconscious self-consciousness. Given that the foetus in utero can hear and absorb many aspects of the prenatal environment within its self-enclosed cocoon, somatic sensations, affective urges, and audible sound precede a priori visual perception. Although still crude and inchoate, sight becomes the further elaboration of ideation inaugurated through the breach into consciousness. The manifold of sensation itself is subjected to the synthetic and unifying powers of the ego. When signification, concept formation, and symbolic meaning are introduced through linguistic structures, unconscious semiotics are further expanded and enriched.

Bion is correct when he refers to ideographs as "some kind of thought." But notice that, in his definition, thought is only possible with the inception of perceptual consciousness. I wish to argue the opposite: perceptual consciousness bursts through the primitive meaning structures and networks of signification that first arise within the abyss prepared by the unconscious ego. Thought first lives underground – first emanating from the felt-sensuousness of its own self-interior – only to emerge as re-presentations of its original form. Archaic thought is formally interjected into all subsequent experiential encounters of perceptive cognition transpiring within the ego. It is the unconscious recapitulation of original form that allows new experience to be assimilated, organized, and transmuted within internal structure through the phenomenological robustness only consciousness affords. These a priori agentic orienting processes emitted from the abyss allow for structural variation and expanse, whereby the psychic register forges new pathways and networks of signification and synthetic meaning channels supplied by the multiple presentations, permutations, and multi-modal sources of information processing that ensue during the experiential flow of conscious perception. What this means is that representation is conditioned on the unconscious mobilization and assembly of original form that takes experience as a cognized object.

REPRESENTATION

When we conceive of the process of representation, which is often associated with the reproduction of images in the mind, it is important to note that they are in fact re-presentations of original sensate (*sensus*) experience that are mnemonically encoded either as visual images, distinct sensations, or impressions aroused or imprinted in the embodied mind. Furthermore, they are specific sensory stimuli that have undergone inner transformations imbued with particular affective ideation and manipulated by the dexterous fingers of unconscious phantasy. The powers of imagination, both voluntarily willed or involuntary inscribed, re-present an original presentation (*Vorstellung*) that has been subjected to unconscious mediation and, hence, has potentially been altered in form and content when reproduced in the mind, whether consciously or unconsciously realized. Imagination re-presents these sensory experiences laid down in the microdynamics of memory arranged as differential schemata, which intermingle and gel with the infinite co-extensive matrices of semiotic connections, only on the condition that they reappear through translation and transmogrification of original form. What is reproduced as representation is in fact an alteration of form as well as the minutiae of content, despite the fact that certain subjective elements of memory and meaning are epistemologically clear or indubitably certain and/or extrinsically (i.e., objectively) verifiable. What this means is that representations are both translated and mediated psychic facts reconstructed through mnemonic retrieval mechanisms and potentially (albeit not necessarily) further constructed through phantasy relations and perceptual distortions that serve to fabricate sense data or real events due to primal anxieties and/or wish-fulfilment. These operations are metaphysical quandaries not open to direct empirical investigation, therefore they are inherently subject to duplicity and imprecision. On the other hand, the empirical observation, validation, falsification, or verity of their true facticity is not epistemically ascertainable, therefore such questions become mute and irrelevant. What is clinically germane, however, is how the lived phenomenology of the patient's psychic reality is experienced.

There is a doubling function inherent to the nature of representation that must be acknowledged when we mnemonically retrieve any previous experience or piece of psychic reality. Contemporary psychoanalytic theorists tend to focus on the constructive aspect of representation, while classical theorists tend to emphasize the dichotomy of objective verses subjective elements. Here it becomes essential to note that there is always a dialectic between these two parallel aspects of psychic functioning and that analysis itself should be equally concerned with attending to both of these issues simultaneously. The argument that everything is constructed is untenable because it negates ipso facto the a priori ground that prepares constructive processes to begin with; and the argument that there are irrefutable lines that demarcate the object from the subject become untenable when mind and nature cannot be conceived or perceived without their dialectical symmetry. Representations are necessarily conditioned on how objects of experience – hence aspects of the world – are incorporated, transposed, and transformed by internally mediating processes. Therefore, pure constructivist and objectivist epistemologies only highlight one pole of dialectical totality and do not properly appreciate their systemic role in how oppositionality is conjoined in holistic order.

Imagination operates on both conscious and unconscious levels of organization. In conscious experience we imagine an object, which is the recovery of a lost image (*imago*) brought back to immediational presence from the depths of the abyss. Therefore, representations, by definition, have already undergone some form of unconscious mediation, the exact nature of which is left to critical speculation. If unconscious phantasy systems are particularly active and interested in attaching to a particular imago or presentation, thus investing it with particular or peculiar intentionality, what Freud would call a cathexis (*Besetzung*), then the representation would reappear as an alteration of the originally encoded experience due to the bimodal functions of the perceptual system that filters or distorts pure objects of internalization in the moment of cognizing them. Or they are subjected to other evoked intrapsychic operations that, by necessity, (perhaps defensively) transform initial sense impressions (e.g., the dissociation of traumatic events). Freud referred to how perceptual phenomena may undergo repression, disavowal, projection, and so forth during the initial act of presentation, while Morton Prince, Charcot, and Janet before him emphasized dissociation, a concept that is now currently in vogue. The main notion here is that representation is a reconstructive retrieval based upon original sensory information processing units that had been transmuted during their perceptual reception, subjected to conceptual signification, and imbued with emotional properties that alter or reconfigure the presentation as it becomes an internal object. In this sense, the represented object acquires a different structure from its point of origination conceived in consciousness, and, hence, its initial impact on the psychic register becomes transposed.

Freud used the term *Vorstellung* – not idea – when he spoke of an object presented to the senses within the conscious mind. An idea is a later conceptual achievement based upon higher-order cognitively mediated events. For Freud, following from the entire history of German philosophy, presentations were distinct from thought. Presentations were associated with the processes and objects of perception while thought was connected to conceptual linguistic operations. Freud referred to the former as "thing-presentations" (*Dingvorstellung*), while he called the latter "word-presentations" (*Wortvorstellung*). In his essay "The Unconscious," Freud (1915b) conjectures that the perceptual system was advanced by conceptual thought through secondary process mentation linked to earlier object-presentations that belonged to the unconscious system. He specifically states: "The system *Ucs.* contains the thing-cathexes of the objects, the first and true object-cathexis; the system *Pcs.* comes about by this thing-presentation being hypercathected through being linked with the word-presentations corresponding to it" (SE 14:201–2). Despite the fact that conceptual thought, including reason, brings about a "higher psychical organization," Freud does not formally ascribe a semiotic function to the unconscious system, at least not in this earlier work, especially when he categorically commits to the notion that "the unconscious presentation is the presentation of the thing alone" (SE 14:201), hence devoid of language. He designates word-presentations as a function of consciousness. But this does not mean that the implications of his thought annul unconscious semiotics.

As I have previously argued, I do not uphold the same level of categoritization or bifurcation between thinking, emotion, and sensation, as if they are distinctly separated forms of cognition. On the contrary, I wish to dispose of any rigid antitheses between desire, sentience, affect, and thought. Although felt sentient life is the most primordial form of mentation, sentience thinks as it senses and, hence, represents its own corporeal experience to itself as rudimentary forms of unconscious cognitive mediation. This activity transpires within the elemental configurations of the agentic ego, where all mediatory cognitive relations are executed.

Freud is brilliant in arguing that the presentation resists a certain linguistic mediation belonging to consciousness, what he relegates to the operations of repression. As he puts it, what is denied "to the presentation is translation into words" (SE 14:202). Here Freud is speaking about unformulated experience, the unsymbolized, the unarticulated. But this does not mean that semiotic processes are not hard at work. On the contrary:

> Thought precedes in systems so far remote from the original perceptual residues that they have no longer retained anything of the qualities of those residues, and in order to become conscious, need to be reinforced by new qualities. Moreover, by linking with words, cathexes can be provided with quality even when they represent only *relations* between presentations of objects and are thus unable to derive any quality from perceptions. Such relations, which become comprehensible only through words, form a major part of our thought-processes. (ibid., emphasis in original)

Here Freud underscores the point that thought is based on a rudimentary form of relatedness between presentations and qualitative meaning, but because they are largely unmediated by language, they remain unformulated, hence unconscious. In his early monograph on aphasia, Freud put forth the notion that thing-presentations, or representations of sense objects, would remain an open system linked to "a large number of further impressions in the same chain of associations" (SE 14:213), such as acoustic, tactile, and visual sense data. Word-presentations, however, were a relatively closed system with a limited number of semiotic associations, a claim the poststructuralists would overturn. But Freud does note that words acquire "*meaning* by being linked to an 'object-presentation'" or things (ibid., emphasis in original), and that the relation between words and things take on a "symbolic" function that objects in-themselves do not (214). Here the nature of representability is sublated through language. Moreover, representation becomes the re-presentation of *relationships* between internalized objects and words.

Recently, Keith Haartman (2006) argues that meaning is generated through relationality to our objects of attachment, where bonds of love and affection bind the symbol to the symbolized in the metaphorical mind. Clearly, our relatedness to other people, and particularly to our parents or primary attachment figures, provides a higher-order linkage to our emotional life – one that generates both integrative and debilitative semiotic meaning structures. Haartman emphasizes the sublated forms of the ego's ability to generate meaning through the incorporation of the primacy of the parents as significant functional objects – the parents more so than any other people for the simple reason that they are emotionally powerful and imbued with value, hence meaning, that cannot be annulled or denied in psychic reality. Here we would be hard pressed to negate the priority of these internal objects. For Haartman, meaning is necessarily an object relation.

Notwithstanding Haartman's fine contributions, what I wish to highlight is that this object relation is predicated on a self-relation. Meaning is initially generated from within the subject's own self-relation to its inner unconscious experience and then transposed onto objects. The peculiar microdynamics of unconscious experience provide the prototype for future modes of object relatedness. This orienting principle is especially realized in relation to the m/other, the concrete attachment figure infused with the symbolic, who, in turn, acts as a mirror function to vitalize and extend value to the self-in-relation to others. Meaning becomes semiologically generated from the interiority of the abyss and given more functional currency and importance when linked through our relationality to love objects. What I have been attempting to argue is that, before such meaning structures become "comprehensible only though words" (SE 14:202), they are prepared by the somatic and affective representations that predate our formal relations to others. Before we relate to other human beings, the first object the ego takes is itself.

Before the ego becomes aware of things or others presented to it in the stream of consciousness, it first finds itself in self-mediation with its own presented organic nature as soma, only to feel itself through bodily pulsions as self-certainty, which the unconscious apperceptive soul enjoys as cognized sentience. Freud (1915a) tells us that the unconscious discharges itself "into somatic innervation that leads to development of affect" (SE 14:187–8). Here we have the rudiments of schematic representation, but the process is left unexplained. Elsewhere Freud (1923) returns to this theme when he declares that the ego projects itself onto the surface of its body, hence it takes its embodiment as its first form, which we may infer acquires emergent representational ideas associated with the pleasure and tension gradients of the ego's sensuous nature. Yet we have shown how this process originally transpires within the unconscious ego long before the ego is born into consciousness (i.e., conscious sense perception arising from within the ego itself). The forms of schematic representations as modes of differentiated embodiment have a prehistory. The original somatic and affective schemata experientially prepared within the unconscious soul become the archetype for latter conscious productions. Clinical evidence alerts us to how somatic and affective schemata are often dissociated from conscious insight and are resistant to linguistic mediation.[4] Recent developments in cognitive neuroscience have alerted us to the domain and role of somatic and emotional schemata (e.g., see Bucci 1997, 2003), which introduce important insights to clinical theory. However, without exception, the fruits of such research have not offered us any coherent picture of how such prelinguistic processes are organized without appealing to general brain events. In fact, the whole field of neuropsychoanalysis runs the risk of always remaining under the spectre of material reduction, however well intentioned it may be. From a philopsychoanalytic perspective, it becomes essential to explicate the logical, ontic, and developmental sequelea of how schemata are ontogenetically generated and dialectically emerge from unconscious process without devolving into reductive biologism or the mechanisms of the brain.

THE MICRODYNAMICS OF UNCONSCIOUS SCHEMATA

It proves instructive to note that the term *skhēma*, like *idea*, refers to the Greek notion of *form*. The unconscious ego is initially immersed in form, in a formal unity or universality confined to its own interiority from which it must break free. *Sēmeiōsis* is the organization of representational schemata originally instantiated within the corporeal and affective constituents of unconscious experience. Furthermore, bodily, pulsional, and emotional processes often resist being articulated or expressed through language, thus showing how embodied affective life has an ontological and developmental priority within psychic structure. This is why, in our clinical experience, the life of affect reigns supreme in the unconscious.[5] Affect fuels the substance of our greatest motivations and fears, from *primaevus* anxiety and destruction to the coveted attainment of love, ethical sensibility, and aesthetic sublimation. This ontological condition ensures that the realm of desire and the irrational will always hold sway over the masses.

By way of a brief clinical example, I had an analysand who had been prone to somatization her whole life. Particularly, she developed extreme conversion symptoms of colitis and irritable bowel syndrome when she became increasingly aware of her repressed and disavowed rage and hatred towards her mother. Her body bore the brunt of her emotional torment and conflicted unacceptable desire to kill her mother, which took the somatic form of defecating streams of blood. The repressed rage was submitted to a compromise that simultaneously expressed both the wish that her mother would die through her "shitting her out" of her entrails (symbolic of the purging of toxic introjects) and the need to harm and punish herself through obsessional worry, physical debilitation, guilt, and shame, thus leading to the acting out of further destructive repetitions. The bleeding stopped when she was able to conceptually form meaningful connections to her mother's past cruelties, which were traumatically absorbed within her psyche-soma yet never articulated in self-reflective conceptuality, hence never made actual. When her somatic and affective schemata were given a voice as narrative by being converted through proper conceptual thought, articulated in vivo, and validated by myself, there was an internal shift in her unconscious representations that allowed her to verbalize her unformulated, unsymbolized phantasies and oppressive conflicts rather than keeping them mired in more primitive representations.

The overall internal transmutation and psychic revamping that occur from microshifts in somatic and affective schemata allow for a sublation of conflict. Shifts from more primitive instantiations of representation to conceptually articulated thought and symbolic meaning allow unconscious schemata to transform and disperse their intensities through a redistribution of form.

Rudimentary ideas and their representations, what Bion refers to as "preconceptions" (hence, that which precedes linguistically mediated constructions belonging to advanced levels of thought), are better understood as affective and sensuously mediated experience that is semiotically assigned a functional meaning by the incipient ego when it encounters an object in consciousness. The ego's experience of objects is transient in nature and characterized by pre-reflexive immediate cognizing, particularly during the first few months of life, when mnemonic tracks are tenuous and only in the crude stages of being neurologically prepared. The emphasis here is on the ego's capacity to process immediate experience by its own novel engagement with objects presented to the senses, which are quickly lost as fleeting impressions. During the moment of engagement, objects are semiotically filtered through the psychic register and related to the original object of signification – *lack*. Here an object for consciousness becomes a presence rather than an absence, and, hence, the process of signification enters into other dialectical unfoldings based upon a multitude of sensible objects experientially presented to the ego. Ideation at this stage is not the mechanism of an a priori preconception mating with an object that produces a conception, as Bion would tell us; rather, it is a process of designated signification associated with the experiential *functions* objects serve.

I believe the preverbal ego constructs meaning not through concepts or words but through images, impressions, and/or sensory-tactile sensations that are internally processed in relation to a felt referent and related to objects encountered in unconscious phantasy, either real or imagined. Thought is originally the succession of sensory impressions imbued with emotional mediacy linked to functional meaning associated with objects of experience originally derived from the apperceptive sentient unconscious abyss of the ego.[6] What becomes encoded or imprinted on the psyche is the functional qualities, properties, and attributes of the experiential presencing of objects. Under the influence of internal drives and their derivatives – such as affect, wishes, and their vicissitudes – in relation to exogenous factors, the nascent ego constructs meaningful relations to objects through the functional attributions of phantasy that are subject to the anxieties and/or pleasure associated with its own internal impulses and eccentrically perceived object attachments. Images and sensory experience related to objects are imbued with functional meaning, linked to associative affect or corresponding feeling states, mnemonically recorded, and laid down as semiotic traces in the deep combinatory of signifiers in the unconscious, which are called forth when phantasy is mobilized. Such combinatorial operations highlight the overdetermined processes and multiple functions assigned by psychic agency.

We are justified, I believe, in further saying that the nascent ego performs such mediatory operations by attaching functional meaning to objects in the form of qualities and their related expectations, which take on the signification of the affects evoked corresponding to gratifying or anxiety-ridden associations. In effect, the ego assigns an object and the experience of such a task or job, which is related to the quality and expectation it evokes, the represented meaning of which stands for the function the object serves. Hence, the function is the imbued purpose (*telos*) upon which the meaning is constructed. Sensory impressions become the original contents for the earliest modes of thought, which have their origins in the prenatal activity of the unconscious mind, where the embryonic ego senses its own internality along with its felt-sentience, urges, and affect arising within its constitutional embodiment. In the beginning stages of conscious life, the ego forms meaningful associations with objects based on the functional qualities and evoked affective states mediated through phantasy, a process that becomes more robust during language acquisition and formal concept formation. We may conclude that what Hegel refers to as the function of symbols and signs, and what Bion calls ideographs, occurs at the unconscious level of the feeling soul. Although the incipient ego does not think in concepts or words, the experiences of objects are dialectically mediated through projective identification in phantasy; they signify and are categorized by their various functional meanings in correlation to affect. It is only when language is introduced that such mediatory relations acquire conceptual signification in the form of phonemes, syllables, words, names, and proper linguistic signifiers.

Meaning is originally created privately, where imago and sign are gelled into a constellation of emotional properties and functional classifications. Here purposeful expectations are constructed, resulting in certain possible consequences that are perhaps even anticipated in response to desire and lack, thus resonating within the privatization of the nascent ego's interior language, which is assigned by its own affective organizing principles. This pre-reflective, affective-functional execution of signification, which mediates the infant's conscious experience of the object world, is dialectically prepared by unconscious semiotics. Such preparation allows for the receptivity and amalgamation of language that must converse with the ego's original forms of affect signification, thus producing a developmental revamping of the subject's intrapsychic semiotic linkages, which become more linguistically mediated over time. With the introduction of language, the question becomes: to what degree does the psyche partition off, via splitting, dissociation, and projective identification, somatic and affective schemata that are resistant to this new and more articulate form of signification, which is introduced through the medium of the spoken word and that gives rise to new capacities to symbolize and represent meaning?

We have already determined that the dialectic is the ontological force behind the generation of multiplicity and complexity with regard to content and form, beginning as (1) embodied sentient life, progressing to (2) affective organization, then to (3) consciousness, and finally to (4) self-conscious self-reflection mediated by linguistic conceptualization and meaning. Because somatic and affective schemata are so intertwined despite having the capacity to appear as separate schematic representations (e.g., via compromise functions), the introduction of linguistic schemata in itself produces both a cleavage – hence a spacing – and a mode of unification between the inner world of embodiment and felt-sensation and the ability to represent such processes via conceptual thought and rational abstraction. At times signification may attain a triangulation of somatic-affective-linguistic linkages. But with concepts being applied to represent more embodied and emotional experiences, there is also a compartmentalization instituted between the ability of the subject to form linkages between bodily states, emotions, and conceptual thought, which may fall under the influence of dissociative strategies or militant forms of psychopathology. As Bion alerts us, perhaps there are inner intentional phenomena (as split-off or alienated desires) that attack other parts of the ego, what the Kleinians typically refer to as part-objects, or what more contemporary perspectives label as self-states, and therefore prevent the crystallization of junctions between soma, feeling, and thought. And if they are approximated, they are only partially forged. Regardless of the synthetic unification and compartmentalization processes at work, themselves the vacillation of the dialectic, the unconscious ego remains the executive agentic mediator of all psychical events and will be vigilant of the multitude of competing dangers, threats, and ancillary wishes vying for expression and victory over other competing processes pressing for fulfilment, defence, or censorship. Here we may say that the executive agentic activities of the unconscious ego merely perform a formal function of interceding, barring, and unifying opposition in the service of sublation. When this is not possible, the self falls under neurotic propensities subject to a variety of pathogenic potentials. In the case of trauma or overwhelming stress or fear, synthetic and integrating functions are compromised altogether, hence behavioural action and adaptative responsiveness is rendered incapacitated. Here the dialect may become arrested or stymied in its sublating powers, or may regress to previous levels of functioning.

In more extreme forms of fear, danger, and trauma, the alienation, dissociation, and subsequent inability to form synthetic links will be more pronounced. Yet schemata belonging to these separate realms or orders of experience will fall back on the most original or regressed forms of signification that the mind feels it has previously mastered or that at least is most familiar to it when stress is present and threat reduction is summoned in the service of adaptive survival. This is one reason why so many traumatized patients, psychotics, schizoids, depressives, and alexithymics experience a fundamental gap between forming concepts about sequestered somatic and affective states. It is also why they are not able to enunciate and attach earlier dissociated body memories to emotional processes and their meaningful conceptual linkages. Here the dialectic resists synthesis and, instead, prefers to tarry in its previous modes of split-off division based on the negation of otherness. Or it regresses back to its previous, primitive mental divisions. It also becomes easy to imagine how the dialectic would inverse itself and withdraw to more emotive and somatic expressions that become represented, hence communicated, through affective dysregulation and bodily conversion symptoms guided by compromise formations. In effect, symptoms are accommodated by the unconscious ego. Here the cornucopia of mental illness can be seen as having its origin in disjointed, stifled, and segregated unconscious schemata barred from proper semiotic linkage, mediation, integration, and meaning construction.

But how are these split-off segregated schemata able to converse with one another or to intermingle, let alone to achieve some form of unification through conceptual mediation? A possible answer is to be found in understanding how schemata emerge out of basic units of unconscious organization that further differentiate themselves from their original unity and progressively modify in form through dialectical activity. This is why the mind should be conceived as emerging from a developmental monistic ontology, whereby sentient life gives birth to the realm of affect, which, in turn, gives rise to the phenomenology of consciousness. Here we must entertain the primordial ground of unconscious desire as it projects itself into higher tiers of articulated expression, culminating in the assimilation of earlier unconscious, embodied emotional activity within the conscious ego's conceptually self-reflexive mediation. Here it further becomes important to revisit the principle of archaic primacy: the past always saturates the present, which, in turn, conditions the ego's projection of a future as a desirous ideal state of affairs or wish-fulfilment. Each schematic system may also prove to successfully insulate itself from encroaching threats through defensive or dissociative strategies, which manage to keep the various schemata segregated. As a result, somatic, affective, and linguistic representations may appear at times as distinct organizations that are compartmentalized, although they are merely split-off relations that have not been formally integrated. Each differentiated schema or self-state is ontologically interconnected despite being modified from its original source, namely, desire as drive.

This brings to the fore the question of schematic structure. How is a schema constituted? What activity is at work within corporeal, affective, and conceptual order? As we have intimated in our treatment of the epigenesis of the unconscious ego, schemata emerge from the developmental architectonic thrust of the dialectic beginning with the most primordial form of embodied sensuousness, then moving to the life of feeling, then to the robust explosion of consciousness that begets the higher fruition of lived experience. Schemata are originally constituted by splitting through the dividing function of negation carried out within the process of projective identification as sublating recapitulation. Hence lack – or the presencing of absence – becomes a semiotic function that brings the form of emptiness or nothingness into contact with the self-certainty the ego finds as itself, with the projection into otherness it comes to reincorporate back into its self. Recall that the *unconscious ego comes into being through an implosion as externalized rupture*, hence a negation of its constricted form of sleep, lethargy, or implicitness. The minute movements of the dialectic lend themselves to more cohesive forms: first the immediate self-sensuousness of the ego's embodiment (somatic schemata), then emotional reverberations within its interior (affective schemata), then a breaching into consciousness at birth and thereafter (perceptual, imagistic, iconic, symbolic, conceptual schemata, and so forth) – each schema emanating from its original ontic foundation yet differentiated over time into distinct interstices and groupings of mental spacings.

At this point we need to look at how a differentiated mental form is organized from within its own interior constitution and how this is predicated on the prior shapes or movements of the dialectic. As we have seen, modification is achieved through the complex activity of projective identification as split-off, dissociated, or alienated feeling-properties, somatic-sensations, unconscious qualia, and self-states make a bid for integration or synthesis. Yet they are constantly fighting the tensions and elements that are resistant to amalgamation and fuelled by opposition and defence that strive to maintain a compartmentalization between the schematic orders and their subcomponents. Differentiated schemata stand in relation to one other, sometimes in rigid opposition and at other times in less resistant forms of engagement. Regardless of the malleability or mutability of schemata potentially interacting with one another, we have separate formations of inner experience that have their own spacings, press, valences, vectors, and qualities, such as biological impingements, urges, wishes, and conflicts that are opposed to other competing schemata, which inevitably produce discord with one another. We may assume a perspectival stance of understanding the internal dynamics of each schema and how it unfolds in relation to the rest. This requires us to think phenomenologically about the internal microdynamics of schematic activity within the broader ontological configurations that dialectically guide this process.

Given the logical unfolding of the dialectic as progressing from a general inner division to external dispersal to reincorporation, the internal activity of a schema would progress from (1) the immediacy of its somatic, sensual (or sensuous) pulsations;[7] to (2) affective reverberations; to (3) perceptual organization; then finally to (4) conceptual (symbolic) order, each mode consisting of previously undifferentiated units of experience that have undergone modification in form and developed out of prior archaic shapes. A schema may be understood as first constituting a one-way internal relation to its own immediacy, only to dialectically transform through further division and modification that are sufficiently reorganized as separate pockets or units of experience having differences in content, form, valence, and intensity. Although there is a transactional, supraordinate system that is generated and maintained through the relata of schemata that are ultimately engineered by the unconscious ego, there still remains an internal relation that constitutes the intrinsic activity of each schema, what we may call the intrapsychic constituency of evolving mental form. Here a schema is viewed as participating within a subsystem or community of events that comprises the intrinsic constitution of each schematic structure or its representative; further, each differentiated schematic organization or category (i.e., somatic, affective, perceptual, conceptual) falls within the general organizational force of dialectical order. Here each schema has the potential to act with certain degrees of freedom. This potential may take both progressive and regressive forms, may marshal around certain aims for unification and communication with other schemata, or may coalesce around more compartmentalized organizations that delimit or annul the range of semiotic connections to (and awareness of) other schematic modalities that simultaneously exist and press for expression within unconscious mentation.

Given the level of semi-autonomous assertion inherent in schematic structure, we may readily appreciate that certain schemata may be dissociated or radically oppose coming into contact with other schemata due to the magnitude of conflict that may transpire. For example, a patient of mine who was sexually abused as a child had a somatic aversion to meat as an adult but was unable to understand why until she recovered repressed memories of having been raped by an uncle. Her having depersonalized throughout the trauma allowed certain body and affective schemata to remain compartmentalized and unintegrated within her perceptual and cognitive appraisals of the event. Remarkably, she recalled that, during her depersonalization, she had focused on a box of Kentucky Fried Chicken that had been left on the kitchen table. When these repressed memories came flooding back into consciousness, she was quick to conceptually link the horror of the abuse with what she psychically infused into the chicken box, which subsequently induced her generalized aversion to meat – the symbolic penis – as a means of keeping the memory buried. Before she had these insights, segregated schemata were presumably operative yet not integrated within conscious thought, despite taking the character of a compromise formation. This parallel unconscious activity supports the degree of autonomy various schemata may acquire and exert independently over other governing forces within the mind.

Given our logic of modification, each schematic subsystem or community acquires the capacity to mediate between other schemata once certain channels of communication are sufficiently compatible and less legislated by censorship or by the defensive manoueuvres inherent to each schema. When this is favourable, schemata may undergo a transfigured relation, whereby they can absorb certain aspects of other schemata that are then incorporated within their own internal orders. When internal dynamics are unfavourable for cross-schematic interaction or fertilization, a schema may defend against other schemata and their imposed self-agendas through the inclination to cleave or abort linkages altogether. This points to the autonomy of agentic choice with regard to object and action at the hands of each differentiated or dissociated self-state that potentially inhabits schematic structure. This directionality of desire inherent within schematic structure also points to the selective retentive aspect of the dialectic, which is at odds with the mind's thrust towards unification and synthetic transcendence.

Figure 4.1 depicts the internal structure of a schema. Because schemata originally emerge from the primordial bedrock of the unconscious ego and encounters with psychic experience that the ego is condemned to organize, channel, and filter through the vast array of competing desires, endogenous impulses, teleologic pressures, counter-defences, brushes with external impingements (e.g., social reality), and so forth, they may be viewed as differentiated and modified *microagents* that cluster into more functional units or subsystems that spawn their own organizational forms corresponding to specific modalities of embodiment and conceptual order. The pulsional mind generates thought through desire, thought that first lives underground, confined to the circumscribed life of schematic structure. Because psychic modification is dialectically instantiated, all differentiated schematic forms must share and participate in the same essence. It is only in this way that multiplicity and diversity of psychic processes and their respective contents can interact, correspond, congeal, amalgamate, intertwine, or infuse with one another; yet they can equally oppose, negate, annul, and retreat from such linkages into fortified burrows forged through their own defensive constructions.

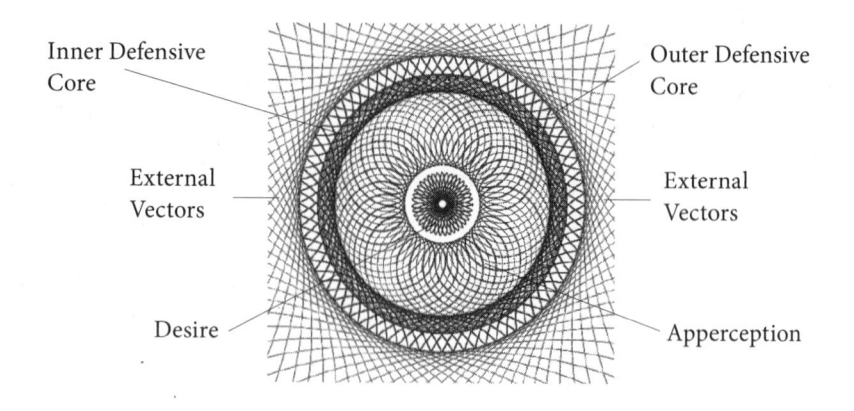

Figure 4.1 Schematic structure

(Labels: Inner Defensive Core; Outer Defensive Core; External Vectors; External Vectors; Desire; Apperception)

As desire gives rise to unconscious apperception, the ego generates both an inner defensive core and an outer defensive core, the former being an internal protective mechanism against intrapsychic and internally derived wishes, anxiety, and conflict, the latter being a shield against the encroachment of exterior impingements and environmental vectors. Here the rudimentary organization of the ego extends to schematic structure as schemata are modified self-states impregnated with ego-properties and their operations.

Because schemata share the same (modified) essence derived from unconscious process, they operate as self-contained ego-properties with their own locus of agency and internal organization assigned by the unconscious ego; however, they should not be conceived as entities that are separate or distinct from the ego. On the contrary, we have repeatedly maintained that the unconscious ego is the executor and directing force behind the unifying and telic operations of mind. In effect, the unconscious ego is a Grand Central Station that authorizes, dispatches, and attempts to unionize the multiple ego-states and their related contents that are alienated or dissociated from the ego itself into spacings of the abyss as they come back clamouring for rechannelling or resolve. Here the unconscious abyss becomes the cosmic storage bin, with labyrinthine tunnels forged through circuitous routes attempting to return to home base, only to be subverted and repetitiously sought and, perhaps, eventually retrieved or even called back to Grand Central. Although this banal metaphor does not do justice to the complexity and onus the unconscious ego ultimately shoulders, it may nevertheless serve as an analogue for the diverse activity of unconscious agency.

In psychoanalytic language, the unconscious ego disperses its internal content through projective identification. However, the content and ego-properties inherent in schemata have semi-autonomous modes of agency that take on a quasi-life of their own. They may revisit the executor (ego) or remain in the interstices of psychic space (like a planet in the solar system that maintains its own orbit regardless of whether it is ever discovered, stumbled upon, or bumped into by other objects in the cosmos). Here lies the universe of the abyss, populated with endless schemata and communities of schemata that may form substructures as process systems. The plurality of schematic forms and their combinations are virtually limitless. Some are more sophisticated, such as elaborate phantasy systems, while others are pithy and simple. The more schemata gather in communities, the more they gain in organization and strength. Communities can oppose one another, and, like our anthropological relations with other cultures and societies, they can have conflict and war. Dominant groups may attempt to capture and subdue other communities and assimilate them into their own social substructures. We may call this *colonization*. Colonies may oppose other colonies, or they may co-exist in more harmonious fashions. Information may be transmitted or blocked by multiple overdetermined sources at once. The internal organization of each schema is ultimately determined by the dialectical mediations that transpire on micro and macro levels of order. This view of schematic structure is compatible with modern conflict theory in psychoanalysis today.

Because each schema is a modified and transmuted series of ego-states, whether sentient, affective, or conceptually mediated, it derives from the original process of unconscious desire and apperceptive self-certainty that is the ego's basal constitution. Here a schema is constructed by the unconscious ego and endowed with functional properties and qualia within representational structures and subjected to (as well as foreclosed from) semiotic meaning. Figure 4.1 attempts to show how each schema must necessarily participate in the unconscious ego's original form as desirous apperception, which must institute and execute internal defensive barriers that insulate it from the subjective contents both internally composed and derived from the network of external vectors impinging on the internal structure of each schema. External vectors are composed of the multitudinous forms of information processing within the psyche, along with its competing teleonomic pressures and teleologic trajectories laid down in the cosmic web of signification. The interactive and interactional dual cores form a three-way relation between the detection of inner experience, outer registrations, and the mediated object, which is a particular piece of datum (such as the material being apperceived or defended against). The dual defensive cores serve the double function of protecting against external peril and internal implosion and decay due to the self-destructive propensities of the death drive. The inner core safeguards the ego against self-annihilation, while the outer core protects against predation and external sources of discomfort and pain – both in the service of self-preservation through armament.

As the schemata divide and multiply, they acquire their own internal orders, which have varying degrees of complexity. This naturally means that more sophisticated forms of consciousness, such as perception and verbal concept formation, intervene in or are superimposed on earlier, more archaic and primitive forms of internal experience.

Figure 4.2 depicts how schemata can emerge out of one another as separated, differentiated modalities of inner experience, yet can also potentially interpenetrate one another when schematic receptors are reciprocally attuned and open to interaction, hence producing structural overlaps in content and form. When schemata defend against other schematic intrusions, they may operate as alienated or dissociated ego-states that work to guard against perceived invasions from other schemata that threaten their internal integrity or cohesion. As mentioned, when schemata interpenetrate each other in content and form, they can give rise to higher-order complex structures that we may call colonies. As a general rule, these colonies are more sophisticated and dominate psychic valuation processes. In other words, they exert more force and influence over unconscious mentation. Of course, these colonies can be both positive and negative in content and form, hence susceptible to adaptive or pathological valences. Colonies are ingressive and can enter into other schemata, attempt to incorporate, subjugate, or oppose them, or strip them of their original properties. They may ban together with other colonies or maintain their unique autonomy. Colonies are tantamount to elaborate desirous phantasy systems that populate unconscious life. Here the dialectic is operative on multiple levels of annulment, supersession, and preservation within its sublating teleology.

Figure 4.2   Schematic emergence

Taken together as a system of differentiated agentic organization, each schema exerts a certain bid for freedom while falling under the governance of the dialectic executed by the telic functions of the unconscious ego. The diverse latitude of schematic autonomy may be said to account for resistance barriers and censorship as well as for open gates to communication via schematic redirection that allow for signification networks to engage one another, thus attempting to achieve some modicum of representational unification even if sifting filtration processes are operative.

I use the term "agency" rather than the term "entity" to denote the activity of a schema in order to avoid reifying the schema as a separate being or substance; however, I realize that the term "agency" can be just as problematic as the term "entity." I also realize that the reader may find the language I use to ascribe agency to psychic organizations existing as independent clusters in the mind to be highly anthropomorphic, interpreting them as hypostatized concrete entities. Of course, our human language imports psychological attributes when describing the observance of natural phenomena (e.g., when physicists ascribe the natural laws of repulsion and attraction to particles), but this is all the more reason to believe that subjectivity saturates every epistemological aspect of the natural world. Perhaps it is better to view a schema as a microagent or a distinctively organized self-state. What I wish to convey is that each schema, in principle, has a degree of freedom that compels it to act and that may fall under the sway of the drives, pulsional body, constitutional pressures, environmental forces, external vectors, or defensive functions that serve its optimal self-interests. Of course, each schema exists in relation to others that have potentially equal force, valence, and intensity, thereby ensuring systemic constellations of tension that the unconscious ego must mediate through redirective negotiated tactics or compromises. This potentially explains how certain elements of psychic phenomena appear alien to our own conscious intentions, desires, beliefs, and attitudes, thus accounting for conflictually ridden internal experiences, including dreams, slips, fantasies, and symptoms. We may refer to this alien process as Freud's *Es*, or, more broadly, the workings of the abyss. Despite the element of choice each schema possesses, it is important to keep in mind that these are differentiated aspects of the unconscious ego and are always subject to its executive powers. Hence, the ego is the *unifying unifier*; yet it is a unifier that, in principle, is not unified but, rather, is constituted as dynamic activity – fluid and in flux – yolked together by form.

The more autonomous, compartmentalized, or detached a schema becomes from the ego's synthetic hub, registry, or point of confluence, the more likely it may operate as an independent force in the mind. Here it is important to emphasize that the term "force" does not refer to homunculi operating in the mind but only to process. However, as any self-state, the schema is merely a differentiated element of the ego that retains its essence and thus seizes upon its internal capacity to act through dialectical mediation.

Let us attempt to summarize a few key points:

1 Schemata are the building blocks of the psyche and comprise the basic constituent movements of the dialectic. They operate as micro-agents with semi-autonomous powers of telic expression. Schemata build upon one other as epigenetic and architectonic achievements and can coalesce into higher organizations of complexity and order, just as consciousness proceeds from its unconscious foundation. In fact, schematic organizing principles allow for the emergence of higher-order forms of complexity.
2 The schematic underworld is composed of multitudinous complex subsystems or communities of associational and communicative net-

works harbouring a combinatory of signifiers. Unconscious semiotics are under the direction of implicit or unformulated phantasy systems within each schematic realm that partitions off objective content (i.e., perceptive data gathered from the senses about the object world) from subjective desire and wishes fraught by defence under the persecution of real or perceived threat and anxiety. Here interschematic communication constitutes ontic relations with potentially indefinite modes of intrarelations and interrelatedness.

3 Unconscious phantasy systems constitute the central activity of psychic life and become the locus of the abyss. In principle, there is a vast underworld of communities with smaller precincts or subcultures that are composed of various groupings or factions of schemata, each clustering around particular resonant states, affects, or symbolic ties that are potentially linked together by an extended chain of signification with a potentially infinite deferral of associations. It is here that imagination, and particularly phantasy, once again initiated and sustained by the ego, becomes a central nexus for appropriating and manipulating various schemata for unconscious semiotic expressions.

The term "community" is used to emphasize the communal nature of schematic communication and its mutual relata. For schemata to commune they must maintain something in common (*communis*), hence they must have a shared essence, despite variance in content and form. There are some communities that are more self-governing and dominant over others, again, what we might call colonies. But these dominant settlements could be either positive or negative, depending upon a person's developmental history and life experiences. For example, it goes without saying that a child with relatively secure attachments would have different internal schemata than would a neglected, abused, or traumatized child. Furthermore, schematic processes enjoy a degree of liberty with regard to how they organize their internal structures, regardless of what extrinsic events transpire or are imposed. However, trauma can retard the growth, autonomy, and degrees of expressive freedom schemata can execute, not to mention the greater dynamic system we call mind.

Schematic communities may coalesce into certain dominant modes of organization, each assuming hierarchical levels of order, whereby some content is elevated and other content is subordinated in terms of importance or internal press. It is also conceivable that some communities will form more advanced, elaborate, compound, and reigning organizations, while others will struggle to thrive or peter out altogether. Once again, the potential for schematic subsystems to exist in harmony, tolerance, avoidance, or combat with one another mirrors cultural anthropology. Each may exist in engagement, proximity, or isolation from the others, but none is ever completely untouched or untouching. Plurality, independence, separateness, and interpenetration are conjoined under the rubric of dialectical unity.

Generally, we have identified the realm of: (1) *somatic schemata*, which are originally derived from the sentient pulsional body guided by desirous appetition; (2) *affective schemata*, which pertain to the feeling soul, which is the proper locus of emotions; (3) *perceptual schemata*, which are more consolidated, coherent imagistic clusters of cognitive-sensuous events; and (4) *conceptual schemata*, which belong to linguistic concept formation, symbolic signification, and rational understanding, the advanced domain of thought. Each classification of schemata has its own differentiated mode of mnemonic retention, synchrony, and semiotics that corresponds to its distinguishable form. However, when internal conditions are favourable, schemata may work together synergistically to form higher-order societies with more sophisticated modalities of generativity and creative meaning relations.

Generally, we may observe how the dialectic of desire has internally divided and modified itself through projective identification, which has prepared the developmental progression of each major schematic organization, whereby the lower relations remain subsumed within the higher yet are capable of retaining segregated relations that resist complete absorption into the sublated whole. Of course, phantasy systems may inhere in each type of schema under the direction of disunited ego-states. Here unconscious semiotic properties inherent in each schema may display various degrees of regulatory units of unconscious experience (a topic introduced in chapter 1). The *content* is highly contingent and variable, as are the levels of *valence* (or the capacity to form conjoint relations with other schemata) and the structural *intensity* of teleonomic pressures and telic trajectories of unconscious qualia. The more force or internal impulsion guided by quantitative (biologic) and qualitative (phenomenal) intensities, the more dynamic demand and economic constraint these schemata exert on the unconscious ego to mediate such tensions, which, in turn, exerts pressure on the whole dialectical system to intervene, arbitrate, and/or attempt sublation. It is within the threshold of these intensities that psychic life forms a nucleus of confluences that potentially answers to the mind/body problem as a complex totality of vital processes ontologically conjoined yet differentiated by form.

Here let us briefly consider the role of temporal mediacy on the spacings of the abyss. Recall that, according to the principle of archaic primacy, the past has a primordial causal impetus within each psychic form or schema, exerting a powerful toll on its ontological status and motivational valences. Archaic primacy has an ontological privilege in the psyche for it encompasses the historicity of presubjectivity or, put another way, the prehistory of subjectivity, including the constitutional and phylogenetic dispositions that could be operative within psychic structure. Archaic primacy suffuses the immediational presence of being, which informs its projective teleology towards its future state of becoming. Here unconscious semiotics must necessarily take into account its various filterings of previously encoded content as concrete data within all three temporal contexts that pressurize one another in the infinite multitude of subsystems that exist within each classification of form. No small task indeed.

What this amounts to is that the unconscious ego has the onerous job of attempting to satiate the teleonomic pressures conforming to bodily pulsions or constitutional organic laws, which, in turn, are subject to higher-order teleological directives that forge the cosmic underworld of unconscious schemata and their semiotic correlates. This means that inscriptive markers or traces that are structurally inscribed in each specific schema, and of which there are potentially (at least in theory) an infinite number within the abyss, incubate, gestate, and possess some active life-force or energetic load clamouring for redirective expression or discharge. Here lies the inherent autonomy and freedom of psychic event clustered into precincts of permissible versus barred zones of delivery, each of which are brimming with various degrees of excitation, slumber or inactivation, and heightened modes of action potential. Just as the free association method of psychoanalysis can potentially lead to an endless stream of productions, so the conceivable associational branches of signification between the competing instantiations of schemata are as vast as a universe, and all of them are subject to the synthetic-mediating agentic activity directed by the dialectic. In fact, the structural complexity, functional operations, and teleological organizations governing the microdynamics of unconscious experience truly underscore the awesome capacities of mind.

· 5 ·

Ego and the Abyss

It is widely assumed across many disciplines that subjectivity is synonymous with consciousness and that consciousness is synonymous with mind and a cognitive self or ego. Following formal rules of inference, these logical propositions are representable in the form of a hypothetical syllogism:

$$p \supset q$$
$$q \supset r$$
$$\overline{}$$
$$p \supset r$$

If p (subjectivity) then q (consciousness);
If q (consciousness) then r (ego);
Therefore, p (subjectivity) if r (ego)

Although this is correct in logical form, the birth of the subject does not correspond with the simple equation that subjectivity equals consciousness or that the *cogito* materializes when the infant is born from the maternal womb. I have argued that subjectivity dialectically arises from the presubject originally constituted as an unconscious ego and that unconsciousness dialectically precedes consciousness. Therefore, consciousness must emerge from the rudimentary ego and not the other way around, as many psychoanalytic theories by implication would contend. That is, it is often assumed that a self or ego is a conscious discovery, construction, or invention. On the other hand, postmodern theorists view the self as an illusion. Throughout the various schools of psychoanalysis selfhood is said to be facilitated through the maternal holding environment (Winnicott 1965), the mirroring function of the Other (Lacan 1936), selfobject responsiveness (Kohut 1971), reciprocal dyadic affective attunement (Beebe and Lachmann 2003), and the mentalizing processes of the mother (Fonagy, Gergely, Jurist, and Target 2002). While respecting the legitimacy of these points of view, I see selfhood as having a priori organizations that psychically prepare the infant to recognize a sense of self in relation to otherness.

Although our sense of self and our self-conscious awareness and understanding of self is mediated, expanded, and enriched through relationality and intersubjective exchange, whether it be with our attachment figures, other people, or social relationships within our cultural embeddedness, any semblance of selfhood, agency, self-awareness, or self-assertion must be predicated on the felt-prefamiliarity we have with ourselves as an experiential subject. This felt-prefamiliarity we have of ourselves is none other than the echo of our inner soul, which we intuit and recognize when we recognize ourselves in the face of the other, hence our shared sense of self. If we did not possess some sense of felt-prefamiliarity with ourselves, then, by definition, we could not recognize ourselves in the mirror or in the eyes of the m/other because we would lack any self-referent or criterion of recognizability.[1] Although mentalization capacities of self and others fall under various restraints and developmentally mediated contingencies, this felt-prefamiliarity of self answers to the ontological problem of other minds. In order to apply the notion of recognizability, self-awareness, or self-consciousness of oneself as a separate being or agent, we must consult our more primitive form of experiential self-certainty, which we first encounter as unconscious ego. Therefore, the subject arises through the microdynamics of unconscious experience only to expand and sublate itself through its new-found world of consciousness mediated by relationality, otherness, and the symbolic within our social ontology. Here the ego of consciousness undergoes a *second awakening* from its unconscious slumber: the division between mind is now split into different realms of psychic reality mediated by the agentic ego, which now actively forges new experiential worlds and navigates between its dimensional internal and external divisions.

The ego is active before birth, only to be phenomenologically modified, existentially realized, and rendered structurally sophisticated through consciousness and language. It is through the further activation of the ego's executive powers during developmental maturation that the ego is nurtured, strengthened, and refined in its operations, content, form, and self-defining properties. In order to clarify the identity and mental processes of the ego and separate it from the abyss, we first need to address how the ego structures reality.

EGO AND REALITY

Psychoanalysis teaches us that consciousness is informed by the nature of our wishes, conflicts, defences, and phantasies. The metaphysical implications of this claim are truly astonishing. It goes without saying that unconscious processes affect the way we think, feel, and perceive, especially how we experience ourselves, others, and the world. In other words, consciousness is constructively informed by unconscious variants. What this means is that *reality itself is constituted by mind*.

This is a monumental assertion governing the way we conceive of the interpenetrability of mental functioning and the presencing of reality. One implication of this thesis is that mind is equated with reality: if mind structures reality, then there would be no reality without mind. This conclusion, however, would be premature. It is more accurate to say that our experience of reality is dependent upon mentation, for reality is mediated by mind. Without mental processes, we could not experience, sense, or know anything, hence we would have no justifiable epistemology with which to judge, let alone determine, that reality exists in itself or independently of mind. Here the realism/anti-realism debate is rendered hopelessly moot. But we *do* operate *as though* objects exist in the world independently of our psychical faculties, and this ontological given governs the pragmatics of individual behaviour and social life. Whether a pragmatic theory of truth can be toted under the rubric of the real is another question, one that, for our purposes, we do not need to engage.

In order to find a potential viable solution to this debate that both advances a psychoanalytic metaphysics and extends to the practicalities of clinical practice, let us revisit the notion that reality is constituted by mind. What I wish to argue is not a grandiose idealism that espouses the belief that mind creates reality, makes matter through will or volition, or thinks the natural object world into existence but, rather, a *psychoanalytic idealism*: namely, that the only reality with which we can have commerce is reality as we *conceive* it to be. In all our epistemic imperfections, all we can experience and know is psychic reality. Process psychology argues that internal and external reality are dialectically conjoined and inseparable ontological categories of experiential order mediated through the faculties of psychical life. What makes our idealism particularly novel is that reality will always and necessarily be constructed and filtered through unconscious subjectivity. Here the object world we encounter is perceptually cognized and conceptually conceived through the medium of our conscious and unconscious mental processes, where cognition is a mediatory register subject to the dominion of imagination and phantasy. Inner and outer are at once merged and emergent, separable by perspective and divisible by content, shape, and intensities, yet yolked together by structure or form. It is in these spacings of the abyss and consciousness that inner and outer are simultaneously experienced and processed by the agentic ego.

When I say that reality is what mind conceives it to be, I mean that mind devises, apprehends, forms, and/or develops an internal organization of what it takes in (Lat. *concipere*: *com-* [intensive] + *capere*, to take) as well as what emanates or emits from within its interior constitution. What I wish to emphasize is that it is not simply thought that structures the subject's perception of the world but the whole intrapsychic fabric of the subject's unconscious processes, which infiltrate consciousness during the *way we conceive* of reality. Here the sharp divide between thought, emotion, and phantasy is collapsed within the enveloping supraordinate totality of a complex process system punctuated by modified expressions of differentiated psychic organizations that are potentially dialectically conjoined at any given moment; hence, they are developmental manifestations of one another extending from the bowels of primordial desire. Therefore, psychic "conception" is to be understood as both a generative activity and as inclusive of unconscious agency, which is interjected into all objects of mental phenomena.

In order to obviate potential confusion or any concerns the reader may have that I am precariously close to a crass idealism that claims that reality is the product of pure thought, let me be clear that the psychoanalytic idealism I wish to espouse incorporates objective (external) reality as it internally structures its experience of that reality. This definition may pose challenges when we consider the nature of psychosis or delusional thought processes, but it does not annul the reciprocal interaction between the dialectic of conception, perception, and desire. Therefore, one can fall off a ladder even if one conceives it to be stable and safe, but the act of conceiving itself is subject to a whole host of contingency relations mediated by the nature of experience and construction. So even in the case of psychosis, where there are blatant distortions in perception of and belief in the object world, reality is nonetheless constituted by the subject's intrapsychic register and semiotic meaning systems, which are transposed by cognition through the act of conceiving and constructing experiential reality, even if perception and belief are faulty, false, or inaccurate.

Any higher order aspect of cognition is necessarily predicated on its original or more primitive modes of instantiation, which remain subsumed and operative within the mind despite the fact that they may have been sublated in structure and sophistication. Following the principle of archaic primacy, the earlier and more primordial configurations of psychic development are surpassed yet preserved within more refined forms. In its modal depths and operations, the ego structures how we conceive of the world and interpolates its own contents, perceptions, and properties into every conceivable object of experience as a being-for-itself. In this way, the ego is always a valuing agency with the inherent capacity to process information and to create meaning.

It is important to acknowledge that what is truly germane to psychoanalysis is not whether there exists a natural world that is independent of mind but, rather, how the world is psychologically composed by the ego. Upon the unconscious ego's awakening into the ego of consciousness, we must appreciate the immediate complexities of how the incipient self must encounter, filter, assimilate, and imbibe the novel experiences afforded through the new sensorial refinements of consciousness. As the ego progresses in maturation, structural organization, and identity, it institutes more negation, splitting, and division, followed by an endless stream of introjective functions, projective identificatory reincorporations, and synthetic integrations. These multiple processes transpire within an elaborate flow of associations and discontinuities, allowing for connective or linking functions as well as for disjunctions in affect, phantasy, and thought. The dialectic of junction and disjunction is contextual in variation and form and is simultaneously experienced by various schematic multiplicities competing for expression and the bid for semiotic freedom. Psychic reality is therefore a macro-process system operating simultaneously within contingent parallel realms of inner and outer, self and other, subject-object totality that comprise its experiential valences and parallax paradoxes. When consciousness of the object world arises within the ego, reality is coloured and structured through the lens of its a priori organizations, which stand in relation to a combinatory of competing multiplicities of experience and potential signifiers of meaning, each of which is fraught with various units of information and their accompanying emotional intensities. This means that the object world is necessarily constituted by the psychical apparatus in unique and novel ways that vary from person to person because of how our experiences are intrasubjectively organized, projected outwardly, and reassimilated based upon the interactional feedback loop that ensues during any act of information processing. Reality is therefore constructed and conforms to the lived experiential order we impose by our own psychologies.

Let us appeal to clinical fact. A depressed person does not see or perceive the natural world as does a non-depressed person. For the depressive, a piece of nature, let us say a lake surrounded by a forest, is not aesthetically pleasing or even neutral; it is colourless, amorphous, and unstimulating, lacking beauty and meaning. Life is dark and empty and, therefore, so is pristine nature.

Objects are structured through the mind's I and denuded of their independent status. Their identification, classification, and property attribution correspond to the processes that define and inhabit inner experience – that is, our internal objects. To be sure, objects of experience are subject to the ideas, affects, thoughts, and phantasies that define them through the various mental processes employed by each observer. In affectively charged situations, our constructions of reality are susceptible to all kinds of distortions with regard to observing and reporting events. Perhaps the absence of minds would not change natural objects in themselves, a debate we will leave to the realists, but they would surely not be conceived, nor would they be conceivable, without minds. Nothing could be discriminated or determined in a context that does not presuppose the existence of mental processes suitable for performing such cognitive tasks. For these reasons, any characterization of the real must necessarily be constructed as mind-dependent through the mediatory faculties that constitute psychic life.

For Freud (1926b), the ego is "modified by the external world" (SE 20:195). For process psychology, the ego also modifies the external world. In fact, the ego, by logical necessity, must modify external reality before it is reciprocally influenced and affected by the world around it. The ego is valuing and desirous: it is not merely a machine that records, measures, and calculates unadulterated events as it processes information; rather, it actively transforms and imbues objects with its ideational and emotional properties. Freud was content to adopt the scientism of his day, which privileged the observable actuality of the extant objective world. And we have every good reason to heed the reality principle. But we must not forget that the reality principle is conditioned on our original constitution as primary process mentation. Here archaic primacy infiltrates all constructions of reality.

For Freud (1930), the infant enters into a symbiotic unity with the mother upon birth: ego and otherness are one. Freud states: "an infant at the breast does not yet distinguish his ego from the external world as the source of the sensations flowing in upon him" (SE 21:66-7). Following this line of reasoning, the ego must differentiate itself from otherness and partition off an outside or external world of objects, the mother being only one such object, albeit the original and most important.[2] By way of our dialectical analysis, we have demonstrated that the unconscious ego is itself its original object within its own simple unity experienced as immediate sensuous corporeality. It has already modified itself before breaching the world of consciousness. Indeed, the object world is filtered through its own original template as the coming into being of determinate negation. Here Freud's conjectures that, when the infant experiences displeasure, an object is set over against the ego for the first time "in the form of something which exists 'outside'" (SE 21:67). This psychical act is prefigured by the differentiating and mediatory dynamics that bring the ego into being in the first place. Therefore, the presencing of an object that is set over against the ego is in fact a mental act of establishing difference through the negation of sameness. That which is determined to be external or outside is executed through these rudimentary movements of the dialectic.

It becomes important to address the question of breach. When does the ego of consciousness materialize and what becomes of the abyss? The breach is an extension of the unconscious ego's felt sensuousness, which is internally transposed and directionally reorganized when psychophysiological sensations arise upon entering the world of consciousness. There is a natural expansion of psychic complexity and intentional (teleological) force that emerges within the psychophysical correlates of sensual, affective, and embodied experience and that permeate the ego upon the concrete birth of the infant. At this stage in the ego's development, the exact mechanisms, developmental sequelae, and executions of cognition do not concern us (this is a subject we leave for cognitive science). For philosophical purposes, it is important to emphasize the second awakening of the apperceptive ego through another rupture: the ego now acquires for itself a supplemented perceptual and sensuous medium through consciousness proper.

There is, naturally, an organic progression to how the ego reorganizes its internal spacings and dialectical divisions when encountering the object world. And, naturally, conscious perception and sensuousness would have evolutionary forces informing the biologic substratum that allows consciousness to arise in the first place. Following this well accepted empirical given, would this not also extend to the unconscious dimensions of biological organizations? Clearly, the ego is not simply defined or caused by something outside its burgeoning internal activity (such as the familial, environmental, or cultural domains of otherness). Let us not forget that society is composed of a plurality of individual subjects and, hence, of particular egos. The ego's maturational path would naturally be informed by the bidirectional or bicameral interactional processes that define any organism. Within the epigenetic context of the ontogenesis of the self, the ego undergoes a steady expansion through incremental movements of self-elaboration proceeding from the inside world of its enclosed simple unity to the outside world of natural phenomena. The dialectic doubly divides or splits itself within these two realms, which are maintained by their symmetrical relations. Reality is enlarged in its scope, variety, and quality of experiential discoveries, which recommence through an expanse of internal spacings.

This second awakening is a *rebirth* of the ego's self-relation within an embodied context in spacetime. Here the spatiotemporal relations that influence the ego's capacities to process events commence with the novel experience of encountering something completely foreign to its current epistemology and organizational qualia. The ego is bewildered and bombarded by indiscernible flux as a cacophony of sense impressions overwhelm its stimulus barriers. But the incipient ego does not abandon its previous self-relation as felt self-certainty. It must, however, attempt to accommodate its situation and try to assimilate conscious sense-data within its previous self-organizing patternings. Here the ego finds itself once again as immediate sensuous being – but with the added robustness of sentient perceptual aliveness. Whereas the unconscious apperceptive ego aroused from its slumber finds itself as a sentient-desirous-affective pulsation, here the ego of consciousness further acquires a perceptual and sensuous – hence libidinal – capacity to process new sensations, sensory information, and external stimuli that impinge upon the subject's embodied faculties and sensory receptors. The sentience, affect, and desire that is originally established within the unconscious ego now gains in developmental capacity, richness, variation, and animation, which, of course, undergoes an organic maturational period mediated and nurtured by its environmental caregivers or attachment figures, which introduce the primacy of the social bond.

Because the ego is the developmental extension and elaboration of the abyss, it is conditioned through the dialectic of projective identification to incorporate its experiential world, which it engulfs and digests in its preliminary and rudimentary capacity to do so. Therefore, the abyss becomes the amplitude of a gradual yet vast ego expansion that maintains a dialectic between inner-outer, self-object, conscious-unconscious. Here the ego splits itself and maintains an internal and external relation to both its counterparts, one belonging to the domain and spacings of the abyss, the other belonging to conscious experience, developmental maturation, and personal identity. In other words, there is a doubling of the doubling due to the multiplicity and progressive mediations that transpire on myriad levels of information processing, whereby each micro-movement acquires a modicum of order within its own sublating process within countless processes that unfold exponentially.

Where does this leave us regarding the question of reality? All we can logically justify is that there is an internal rupture that punctuates the psyche's self-enclosed confinement, which propels it into another intervening realm of events that are already active and that impinge upon the organism's sentient receptive modes of organizing experience. Here reality is not differentiated as a dichotomy but as an expansion of a holistic process, where plurality must be mediated. It is only when determinate negation and splitting institutes a demarcation as difference that reality becomes polarized and categorized on different levels of information processing, where pockets of experiential organization are largely unconsciously forged. In fact, reality must be reconstituted from the limitedness of unconscious pre-reflectivity and catalogued through its new-found medium as conscious cognition. Here there must be a rudimentary process of deciphering what was indigenous to the ego's initial experiential attributes and properties (i.e., its intrinsic content) versus what new stimuli bring to its experiential patternings. Of course, a whole new world would open up to the nascent mind, bombarding it with a deluge of sensation it had never encountered before, hence reactively leading to a tendency to recoil in the face of an overwhelming sense of overstimulation and helplessness. This initial self-preservative reflex is mitigated by the mother's nurturing ministrations and physical comfort, which assuage the need to be comforted, protected, and cared for. This is the mind's initiation into the social bond, where the familial tie and, expressly, the special attachment to the mother is secured.

It is easy to imagine how the rich impressions and perceptual clarity of conscious life could overshadow the internality and self-ensconced reverberations of unconscious process. The ego's conception of reality would be expanded but would not be self-aware of this, as such: in fact, it is perfectly plausible that there would be no awareness whatsoever of how reality would be expanded or divided into dichotomous modalities, let alone of how an agentic ego becomes split into conscious and unconscious counterparts instantiated on a continuum of psychic continuities. It is the fact that the ego lacks recognition of itself as an observing agent at this stage in the emergence of consciousness that allows for a fundamental duality of self-modification, with dialectical symmetrical organizations operating on both unconscious and conscious levels. Here consciousness is the extension as sublation of unconscious process. By logical necessity, reality becomes *reconfigured* and *reconstituted* by mind.

Loewald (1951) points to two tensions in Freud's thinking about reality: one in which reality is seen as an external force, primarily symbolized by the father as an Oedipal hostile threat, and the other in which reality is seen as being symbiotic and internally derived from a primary narcissistic state of undifferentiated unity. One sees reality as harsh, fearful, and menacing, instituting a need for safety and defence, the other sees it as immature and solipsistic. Here Freud's thesis on primary narcissism deserves our attention.

In "On Narcissism: An Introduction" (1914), Freud tells us that, originally, the ego is a self-contained unity in which infant and mother, mouth and breast, are one in the same. There is as yet no objects to set over against the self for there really is nothing to mediate at this point. Ego development occurs when the experience of separateness is forced on the infant through frustration, excitability, or displeasure (such as that brought about by the absence or withdrawal of the breast). Here Freud says that "the development of the ego consists in a departure [*Entfernung*] from primary narcissism and gives rise to a vigorous attempt to recover that state" (*SE* 14:100). Freud believes that it is here that the mediatory, unifying, and synthetic powers of the ego take their initial shape. For Freud, the state in which the ego attempts to "recover" is found in "an ego ideal imposed from without" (*SE* 14:100), thus in a recovery of its self-value imported through identification with a cultural value, often transmitted through the symbolic (hence the father, but equally the mother). The primary self-valuation of infantile narcissism is replaced with the internalized ideality of parental valuation with which the ego identifies, wants to become or fulfil, and make its own. Here inner reality is transformed by external reality and transposed within the interiority of the ego's burgeoning development.

Loewald (1951, 10) summarizes Freud's position in the following way:

> In the primary narcissistic stage ... there is as yet no ego confronted with objects. It is the undifferentiated stage in which the infant and its world are still one, are only beginning to differentiate from one another, which means also that the differentiation of the psychic apparatus itself into its structural elements still is dormant.

Recall that Freud (1926a) stated later in his theorizing that the ego is a differentiated and modified agency that developmentally arises from the It, or, as we have shown, from the abyss. This would mean that differentiation, modification, and mediation would have already occurred on some minute level of psychic organization. When Freud and Loewald refer to objects, they mean the objective world of external reality. This does not mean, however, that the ego has not taken some rudimentary form or begun its mediatory operations, only that its *contents* have remained confined to inner experience and unconscious resonance states. In fact, there could be no mediation at all unless a priori processes, or what Loewald calls "structural elements," were not already active. Rather than being "dormant," they are in their initial stages of gestation, execution, and enactment prior to the birth of the human infant.

In *Civilization and Its Discontents* (1930), Freud continues his thought regarding the infantile mind as an undifferentiated unity:

> The ego detaches itself from the external world. Or, to put it more correctly, originally the ego includes everything, later it separates off an external world from itself. Our present ego-feeling is, therefore, only a shrunken residue of a much more inclusive – indeed, an all-embracing – feeling which corresponded to a more intimate bond between the ego and the world about it. (SE 21:68)

Freud emphases two important aspects of ego activity: symbiosis and separation. At first the ego includes "everything," only to partition off the external world from which it "detaches." Inner and outer are originally merged. External reality is *assigned*, hence a boundary is instituted by the ego between itself and the world. What Freud or Loewald do not address, however, is the question of breach.

In the first movement of the epigenesis of the ego, it encounters non-differentiation. Here we can observe a basic repetition of the original form of the dialectic that the incipient mind finds in its simple immediate unity as sentient desire: it merely *is*. This second awakening of the ego is the reiteration of its basic form, which it imposes on "everything." It is also here that it differentiates itself out from this generic universality and gives itself self-definition by demarcating otherness, that is, the manifold number of objects in the world. Here external reality is constituted by mind as demarcation. But, for Freud, this is not activated until the austerity of pain or displeasure is introduced: external reality forces itself upon the ego and obliges it to take notice of its own difference, individuality, and separateness. The two-way relation between inner and outer now forms a dialectical unit of its own, where divisions of inner and outer are instituted and maintained. Yet, under certain conditions, these boundaries can collapse, with the result that original form (symbiotic unity) is reinstated or recovered. Freud is fond of using the example of falling in love, where boundaries between ego and other melt away. We can also see this in the psychoneuroses and psychoses, where boundaries between ego and reality are not firmly established. This is also a normative feature of dissociation and the dissociability of the psyche in general. In its positive valence, this "all-embracing feeling" or "intimate bond" is what Freud refers to as "oceanic," a return to the undifferentiated peace of original being.

What is fascinating about Loewald (1978) is how he cogently argues for how the infant first encounters the unity of reality – equated primarily with the maternal object – and then must distinguish and differentiate distinct objects from its initial immersion within undifferentiated universality. More specifically, this discrimination is performed by the infantile ego with particular attention being paid to certain attributes that belong to the mother. It is here that language is distinguished as a discrete unit belonging to the properties of the mother. In other words, language – the mother's speech and sounds – are part of the universality of reality itself, only later to be segregated out as an independent aspect or particularity of the ego's original unity. This situates language as being ontologically present from the start of conscious life and not as just a developmental acquisition. We may even extend this argument to claim that the mother's sound transmissions, which occur when the foetus is in utero, is linguistic and part of the properties that define the presubject's experiential reality. Upon birth, the ego must separate itself from reality, and linguistic processes are only one aspect of its micro-distinctions, which are made among a whole host of other differentiated objects and part-objects that populate the plurality of the senses.

This argument can certainly be applied to the realm of embodiment in general: the self is within a world of dissimilar, sundry objects sharing simultaneous existence in spacetime as well as experiencing the peculiar dimensions and sensations of one's own body, which inhabit such spacings. Sensorium of sight and sound, whether this be the maternal imago and her voice or the non-verbal forms of touch, affective communication, and anaclitic interaction, must be dissected into differential units of signification and difference. This activity involves a partitioning-off through rudimentary semiotic categorization of the multiplicities and pluralities of experience that belong to the incipient ego, a simple unity that later augments in breadth and substance. Here the ego interposes multiple spacings into what it encounters as real, even if it is imagined or fantasized.

If we are justified in postulating an original undifferentiated unity, and I believe we are, then this transpires much earlier than the emergence of the conscious ego. It emerges and then is punctuated in that spacing within the abyss where rupture supersedes the simple immediate being of unconscious sentience. Here lies the nucleus of psychic reality: inner and outer form are the *constructions of negation*. Negation divides: it breaks up unity, it fractures semblance, only to be regathered and synthetically blended, and only then to have further divisions and demarcations spin on in dialectical circles of competing contextual complexities. However, this spinning on is maturational in scope and duration, with multiple complexities materializing, clashing, thriving, and becoming incorporated into the sublating ascendency of the dialectic. Here dialectics are operative within dialectics, the inner and outer each affecting the other, thereby forcing transmutations in their mutually co-extensive implicative structures. These intricate series of supple processes underlie the multiplicity of thought, a rumbling cloud resonating over the landscape of mind.

Peter Fonagy and Mary Target (2007) have recently explored the concept of psychic reality in relation to mentalization and attachment processes that transpire during early childhood. They argue that external reality is not simply an independent plurality the infant discovers; rather, such a discovery is made possible through other minds. Central to their argument is the fact that knowledge about the world is acquired through the subjectivities of others, most notably through primary attachment figures (paradigmatically the mother). Like Loewald, they also claim that reality itself is gradually distinguished into particularities, but they believe that the infant is first immersed into a non-differentiated unity where the ego assumes a naive isotrophy between the contents of its own mind and the rest of the world. As they specifically state: "At first the infant assumes that his knowledge is knowledge held by all, that what he knows is known by others and that what is known by others is accessible to him" (917). Of course, the experience of external reality is shaped by other subjectivities, or, more appropriately, through the identification with and internalization of others' subjective states of mind; but Fonagy and Target, following Marcia Cavell, assume that subjectivity cannot exist without intersubjectivity, "in which reality is defined as a relational matrix" (919). This ultimately presupposes a model of consciousness that predates unconscious process.

It is important to note that what Fonagy and Target are concerned with has to do with the infant's *epistemological* experience of knowledge of the external world and not specifically about reality per se, which is an ontological claim. But their theoretical position nevertheless imports metaphysical assumptions that experience and knowledge are contingent upon other minds, hence conscious minds. By extension, this assumes that psychic reality could not exist prior to conscious experience. This is where I respectfully disagree. What I believe they overlook is how unconscious genesis provides the prototype for subjectivity that is further enhanced by intersubjective relations that become so essential to the qualitative forces that structurally mould the architecture of internal life. Furthermore, if the infant first "assumes" that all his knowledge is transparent to all and that it and everyone else "knows" its knowledge, has not the infant already begun to make divisions of inner-outer/self-other by virtue of the fact that it has already determined it has knowledge shared by others? The minute we posit shared consciousness we have already, by definition, introduced a dialectic between self and world based on the notion that similarity, or, in this case, psychic equivalence, already presupposes the notion of separateness and distinction, hence negation. What I believe Fonagy and Target nicely capture, however, is how competing subjectivities become the central organizing forces that populate internal life based upon the internalization of other's states of mind, which lend knowledge and meaning – as well as disarray – to the world. Without question, personality structure is sculpted by other minds. In fact, the ubiquity of projective identification as communication, and the power differentials pertaining to how others attempt to force their minds on us, are formative in the normative processes that mould common (shared) beliefs, attitudes, and behavioural expectations as they are responsible for the pathognomonic features of illness and suffering.

For the generative psyche, reality is depicted as a series of infinite possibilities constructed by the interplay of dialectics, whereby each event or moment is merely a flash of activity that concretizes immediate experience, which is executed and mediated by mind as a systemic agency. There is no pretence that the world is a static object to be measured or observed in itself, for all events are process. All experience of reality is conditioned on the transmogrification of intercepting processes. The symbiotic nucleus of original undifferentiated being is the origin of psychic reality, where subjective universality makes both particularity and pluralism, as well as unification and inclusiveness, possible. It is the archetype for container-contained, individuality and collectivity, divisibility and wholeness – Plato's *chora*. Original being begins as unity and then breaks apart, dividing and multiplying, yet seeking to remain both united and divided. There is no unified unifier, no unmoved mover, no detached observer, only agentic activity as pure executed event.

Agency must have an agent, which we can properly say is a process system of dialectical elaborations brought together under the rubric of mind. Recall that agency, as we define it, is the capacity to invoke and institute determinate action. Here we can say that all elaborations of unconscious systemic modification must precede and spring forth from this symbiotic nucleus, which is the original instantiation of subjective universality. What this means is that all modifications of mind must necessarily participate in this basal psychic essence. What is further implied is that any particularity in content or form must be potentially connected to all other modified elements that constitute the plurality of psychic existence emanating from this singular essence. Through our subjective universality, we share the same monistic ontology. Therefore, at any given moment, we are never removed from all aspects of reality, which stand in relation to the interwoven yet differentiated web of signification. This is because we all participate in the same lacework and can potentially touch each other through our systemic ontic relations. This metaphysical character governs the solidarity of psychic life, which conditions the appearances that govern psychic phenomena. In other words, the ontological fabric of unconscious process constitutes the solidarity that underlies the matrices of mind.

All mental content is connected by the ontic thread of agentic reverberation that leaves somatic, affective, and semiotic distributions within the psyche. Mental content is event. To borrow Whitehead's terminology, it amounts to "occasions" for other events. Each occasion is a process of spontaneous generation in which a particular pattern of organization is derived from itself – from within its own interior constitution – and comes to attempt to unify its past within its present immediacy. But each schematic occasion has a character of its own that stands in relation to other events, each of which has its own unique structure, properties, modes of expression, and so forth. The universe of psychic process must privilege unitary activity and continuity, even though we may temporally highlight division, separation, duality, and disunity as discrete perspectives and moments of unfolding process. Here the ego is never ontologically distinct from the abyss for the abyss conditions all productions of psychic reality.

THE MIND'S I

The *I* is emergent, a developmental achievement. It does not exist at birth (in the sense that the sentient ego does) because, in order for there to be

"I-ness," there must also be otherness and, thus, a differentiated sense of self that stands in relation to other differentiated objects and subjects. In keeping with this point, contra the Kleinians, the superego does not exist at birth either. The superego is even more of a developmental achievement than is the I. The aggressive, persecutory, and punitive attributes that are ascribed to the superego are the forces of the negative that later become annexed by and incorporated into superego organization. The Kleinian insistence on the primacy of aggressivity should not be either equated with superego development or confused with a sublation of the ego at birth. It is important to retain the notion that superego organization is predicated on a sense of conscience, social order, justice, law, empathy, ideality, and moral sensibility, which is cultivated yet derives from our more innate elements of desire. This is what makes superego activity both a sublated and sublimated process without collapsing it into aggressive currents.

I wish to distinguish the I from the ego based on its personal and sublated levels of differentiated particularity and internal self-reference. This requires that the I posses a modicum of self-reflexivity in order to differentiate self from otherness as distinct and demarcated, a qualitative awareness that the formal ego lacks. The ego is valuing, but the I is self-valuing. The ego makes determinate judgments but lacks the sophistication of self-awareness that properly belongs to the I. This is why we say that the ego in its nascent form is pre-reflexive while the I is reflexive, although not necessarily reflective. Self-reflectivity depends upon the level of cultivation each personality achieves in relation to various competing parallel processes of psychic development. I-ness underscores the unique phenomenal element of lived subjectivity – of pure self-reference – a referent that derives from its original form of subjective universality.

The I is inherently self-valuing, marked by self-relatedness impregnated by the ontic influence of otherness. In other words, the I is mediated by the Other. But in order for us to value a certain content imposed on us by our cultural embeddedness, we must first appreciate the fact that we identify with ourselves as a uniquely embodied experiential being that has a conscious appreciation that it exists as a singular I possessing a singular identity that stands in relation to others. This identity is not ossified or rigidly defined as a solitary essence but, rather, is multifarious and composed of competing modes of self-reference and self-relatedness. Hence, self-identity is eclectic. It is only singular in the formal sense that self-experience is ontically privileged. This is why the I possesses an inherent sense of "mineness" that the ego in its nascent form does not.

What makes the mind's I so unique is the fact that, despite similarity or symmetry with others, the personal sense of lived experience has a feeling of ownership that cannot be compared to that of any other experiential being. Only the I knows its immediate experiential existence as a valuing agent juxtaposed to difference. The felt notion of *qualitative* self-certainty, mineness, ownership, and self-valuation differentiates the I from the ego, which, of course, is the maturational outgrowth of the incipient mind. The I possesses a personality that has the qualitative robustness to claim occupancy within one's embodiment, a psychic residence that demands the entitlement and dominion of pure proprietorship. In other words, the I owns itself. In this sense it is the sublation of ego. This distinction is more specified and nuanced than what we find in Freud's broad use of the term (*Ich*), which he used to stand for all activities of the ego. However, recall that Freud claimed that the I emerged from a primary state of narcissism, a self-enclosed solipsism that was both a universalized totality and a simple unity. Although Freud would place importance on the superego as a developmental achievement requiring self-reflection, we must acknowledge an intermediate, mesomaturational step and show how the ego ascribes the self-appreciating properties of I-ness that mark the qualitative notions of individuality, difference, separateness, and uniqueness that differentiate the mind's I from the formal agentic functions of the ego.

It can be argued that Freud's theoretical vision of the ego underwent more modifications than any other theoretical construct, experiencing important refinements through diligent attempts to work out problematics inherent in the ego's relation to the other competing psychical agencies that govern mental life. In my estimation, Freud's mature model of the mind is represented in three primary texts: *The Ego and the Id* (1923); *New Introductory Lectures on Psycho-Analysis* (1933); and the posthumously published uncompleted manuscript *An Outline of Psycho-Analysis* (1940). Here we can observe the overdetermined functions and processes at work in ego activity. For Freud, the ego is developmental (SE 14:77), both externalizing and internalizing, projective and incorporative. It is both information-emitting and information-processing, born/e from the abyss. In Freud's mature system, the ego can be characterized in the following fashions:

1. The ego is the heart of subjectivity and selfhood. As Freud says, "the ego is in its very essence a subject (*Subjekt*)" (SE 22:58). Elsewhere he states: "There is nothing of which we are more certain than the feeling of our self (*Selbst*), of our own ego (*Ich*)" (SE 21:65). Here Freud emphasizes the conscious elements of the ontology of the ego. The ego develops out of the unconscious It and becomes a conscious organization that mediates perception, motility, conscious thought, affect, and action (SE 20:195–6). However, as Freud reminds us, "the ego is also unconscious" (SE 19:23). In 1923, he believed that the ego "*starts out* ... from the system *Pcpt* [the perceptual apparatus], which is its nucleus, and *begins* by embracing the *Pcs* [preconscious system]" (SE 19:23, emphasis added). Note how Freud refers to points of origination when describing the coming into being of the ego. But he had stated in his earlier 1914 paper that the ego developed out of a narcissistic self-enclosed unity. In 1923, he situates this birth as having its "nucleus" in perception and preconscious functioning. But, by 1926, Freud amends his position to conclude that the ego is a "specially differentiated part of ... [and] organized portion of the It" (SE 20:97). Therefore, the ego is conditioned on unconscious processes and emerges from the unconsciously derived activities of differentiation and modification. Hence, the ego attains the acquired properties of freedom and executive agency that derive from its original primitive form.

2. The ego develops into an organized agency that must mediate between internal and external forces, those springing forth from the drives and impulses, and those that force their effects on the ego, which it is obliged to receive and mediate: "The ego is an organization. It is based on the maintenance of free intercourse and of the possibility of reciprocal influence between all its parts" (SE 20:98). Here Freud is referring to the tripartite functions of the soul (*Seele*). Notice he uses the term "free" (*freien*). Hence, both internal and external reality can present as autonomous forces the ego must register and to which it must respond.

3 The ego's tasks are multifaceted: it processes all the cognitive functions that belong to perceptual consciousness, information processing, motor- and goal-directed activities, affect regulation, and linguistic productions. It retrieves and bars memory. It censors, defends, finds compromises, reduces tensions, secures pleasure outlets, and "adapts" to symptoms. It is the conduit to unconscious life and resides in parallel realms of psychic spacing. It heeds external reality while attempting to fulfil the dialectic and vicissitudes of desire. It allows reason to surface, is pragmatically concerned with environmental forces that affect it, and maintains functional adaptation. It adjusts to the laws of secondary process thinking while subduing primary process mentation, despite the fact that it mediates and finds avenues for the fulfilment of pleasure. In short, the ego is the hub of the psyche.[7]

4 One motivational and functional aim the ego possesses is the act of synthetic mediation. This synthetic function is central to the dialectic. What distinguishes the ego from the It is its tendency towards synthesizing contents and unifying mental processes (SE 22:76). Freud further tells us that the ego "shows *traces of its origin* in its impulsion to bind together and unify, and this necessity to synthesize grows stronger in proportion as the strength of the ego increases" (SE 20:98, emphasis added). For the most part, Freud saw this synthetic function as an attempt to restore or reconcile tension or conflict generated among the competing forces that populate mental life and that pressure the ego for resolve. Here we see an underlying defensive purpose to ego activity, one aim of which is to control the passions (SE 22:76). Also note how Freud refers to a "trace" of the ego's "origin" (*Herkunft*), which he situates in the act of synthesizing. To be more accurate, the origin of ego activity bears its mark – hence its *semeion* – in the act of splitting.

5 For Freud, an ancillary albeit rudimentary aim of the ego is constituted through the act of splitting. In fact, this is more basic and primary in the ego, occurring long before synthetic functions monopolize psychic connections. Here it is important to underscore the logical priority of splitting as determinate negation. This is the initial act of the dialectic, while the attempt to unify is technically the third movement or consequence of the previous determinate events. The

second action is in the process of incorporation, which simultaneously subsumes otherness and unifies opposition within its active process of becoming. Freud recognized that the ego takes itself as an object. In this sense, it is "setting itself over against the rest. So the ego can be split; it splits itself during a number of its functions" (SE 22:58). Earlier Freud (1924a) commented on how the ego submits to "encroachments on its own unity ... by effecting a cleavage or division of itself" (SE 19:152–3). He specifically focused on cases of fetishism and psychosis, where a disavowal of external reality is employed, but he eventually attributed this process to the normative childhood ego whose attempts to detach from reality are simultaneously met with the obligation to acknowledge certain elements of the world around us. Splitting is operative in the defensive functions of inversion and turning the aim of a drive into its opposite form, as articulated in Freud's 1915 metapsychological paper entitled "Instincts and Their Vicissitudes." Ultimately, however, Freud (1940) highlights the inherently conflictual nature of splitting as a set of implicative dialectical relations: "two contrary and independent attitudes always arise and result in the situation of there being a splitting of the ego" (SE 23:204). The act of synthesis or integration is an attempt to unify opposition.

As we can see, Freud is the true founder of ego psychology, a direction of thought that was further taken up by Anna Freud and advanced by the American ego psychology movement. A concept advanced by this school of thought is the assumption, introduced by Hartmann (1939), that there is a "conflict-free sphere" or "autonomous" portions of the ego that are exempt from negativity and that allow the subject to function adaptively. From a pragmatic point of view, we can appreciate this functional attribute of human resilience; however, this is only the case on the phenomenological level. Formally, the ego is never free from conflict because it is part of the ontological fabric of the dialectic. During moments of autonomy that are seemingly devoid of conflict, the ego lives in a certain experiential realm, casting a certain shadow or appearance that defines its character at that time. It is merely a moment in the process of its own becoming, and, consequently, it does not reveal its whole truth. Structurally, conflict drives human experience and human relatedness. The ego must adapt to the constant bombardment of multiple conflicts. This is why Freud spoke of "self-preservation" as one task the ego must set for itself.

I wish to reiterate that the I becomes self-definitional while the ego technically does not. Here we may see an intermediate or mesostructural advance in the ego's epigenesis. At precisely where in the development of the ego this takes place, I cannot specifically say, for this would assume that all subjects' egos would mature in the same developmental sequence. However, we may speculate that, as soon as the child begins to recognize itself as a separate agent among other agents, the emergence of the I is in bloom. This of course requires a pittance of self-consciousness or self-reflexivity, albeit rudimentary and proportional to the more fully developed aspects of mentalization capacities that we see in later life. Here what is important is the phenomenology of the I as an experiential being qua being that maintains a primary relationship to itself as a self-referential and self valuing self identity.

The I must have a primary relationship to itself that it extends to other objects. That is, the I remains self-valuing and other-valuing in dialectical relation to other aspects of psychic reality. We must not forget that, when Freud talked about the motives and properties of a drive, he emphasized the inherent relatedness of the object aim. But there is always a dialectical tension between the need for self-definition, assertion, and individuality and the need for mutuality, inclusiveness, and communal participation in social life, a lesson we can appreciate from antiquity through to Hegel and Heidegger. The ego is the mediator and executor of those needs and mental functions; but the I is the experiential agent that mediates the awareness of them as such. Here we must acknowledge a cleavage or splitting between the I and the ego, the latter slipping back into the workings of the abyss, only to resurface again as I. In their duel modes of operating, the I can only maintain certain parameters of consciousness due to the limited capacity to process, hold, and retain information at any given time, which it must pass along to the ego, which formally mediates these multiple processes. Technically, the ego would be operating within spacings of the unconscious, yet be capable of breaching the abyss when the self-defining properties of the I dominate immediate mental awareness.

The I is a modified and differentiated part of the ego, but the ego is never separated from the I: it is the ego's sublation. What this means is that the I is necessarily and logically the intermediate movement of the ego's development into what Freud calls the superego, or over-I. This requires a formal ascendancy from consciousness to self-consciousness, or from the self-valuing of the I to the self-valuing of the other that the I desires, identifies with, and makes part of its internal host of self-objects. This is where the I becomes more appreciative and existentially self-aware of itself as a valuing being that identifies with the being and values of others that it finds within its social ontology, where one's parents or attachment figures become first and foremost the primary objects of this internalization process. This requires a further advance in the reflective function of self-consciousness, where self and other can never be ontologically separated: the I that is We and the We that is I.

REFLECTIONS ON O

Bion (1965, 1970) posits the notion of an absolutely unknowable truth that lies at the heart of every analytic session that is experienced by both patient and analyst as catastrophically frightening. This is what he calls "O" – intersubjective dread that threatens complete and utter deracination. While Bion situates O in the analytic process, we may generalize this epistemic position to the formal parameters inherent within the unconscious spacings of the abyss that resist presencing themselves and tarry in the negative functions of the dialectic. Epistemically, this unknown and unknowable truth is tantamount to the Kantian *Ding-an-sich*, the Fichtean *Anstoss*, the Lacanian *réel*, and the Gnostic *Bythos* (the ineffable Primal Ground) – put simply, the impossible. Speaking ontologically, what we do know is the presencing of negativity itself. There is no integrative function at work when the subject enters into O, only an omega and, hence, its end.

Bion's notion of O has a paranoiac quality that reverberates in the subject as the dread of immanent disintegration and death. From the standpoint of process psychology, O is structurally the negative element of the dialectic that informs the system itself. In fact, O is a symbol for the dialectic because, like Hegel's system, it is coherently circular and nonlinear, and one may enter the circle at any point, which inevitably stands in relation to the whole. O is also symbolic of nothingness – both a null and a self-enclosed eternity – the cosmos. Negation, conflict, death – these are structural constituents that dwell in and spring forth from the abyss, thereby giving life to mind. Unlike Bion's unknowable truth, for Hegel, mind is "not the life that shrinks from death and keeps itself untouched by devastation, but rather the life that endures it and maintains itself in it. It wins its truth only when, in utter dismemberment, it finds itself" (*PS* § 32). It is from negativity that psychic life is born and inhabits, and negativity is simultaneously responsible for the ascendancy of mind as well as for the dialectical regressions that inform the subject's subjective sense of suffering and all forms of psychopathology.

THE UNKNOWN, THOUGHT

Archaic primacy is the ontological backdrop against which human consciousness is predicated, and it makes its presence felt within each moment of subjective immediacy. As a general rule, archaic primacy belongs to the abyss, while immediational presence belongs to the ego. Immediational presence presupposes the presencing of the past within the present, and here we can justifiably say that all thought is predicated on a mode of thinking that precedes consciousness. The information processing capacity of immediational presence, which involves the ego that mediates and attempts to unify specific information in the immediate being of *is*ness, is processed by the unconscious ego, which is not aware of itself in that moment as an agent-for-itself. In other words, the ego is not in the mode of being-for-itself as a self-reflective self-consciousness; rather, it merely *is* and *acts*. If self-consciousness is suspended in that moment, it is because the unconscious ego is intentional (*intentus*). Here we may say that Brentano's thesis that consciousness is intentional is logically proven to be worthy of support only on the condition that consciousness is ontically prepared to process information because of its a priori substructure, which we logically equate with the ground (*Ungrund*) or prebeginning that we call the unconscious. Thus, intentionality of consciousness is only tenable if we necessarily postulate unconscious being. Thought begins underground.

How can one think the unthought? While Bion focuses on the unknowability of inner truth, Christopher Bollas (1987, 52) tells us that the unthought is known, albeit unmentalized, unrepresented, unformulated:

> The knowledge derived from the dialectic of the infant's true self and the subtle syllogisms of the maternal and paternal presence and care constitutes part of what will be later known but not

thought. This unthought known is not determined by abstract representations. It is established through countless meetings between the infant subject and his object world, sometimes in tranquillity, often in intense conflict. Through these meetings the infant's needs or wishes negotiate with the parental system and a compromise emerges. Ego structure records the basic laws which emerge from these meetings and its knowledge is part of the unthought known.

Bollas is describing the interpersonal world of the infant as being forged through intersubjective relations with its attachment figures, which become transposed onto unconscious structure. We may say that what is transposed are the multitudinous interactions that are sifted through the infant's intrapsychic affective processes, which are peculiar to it and are interpersonally negotiated within the parental triad. In other words, we are affected by these object relations even though we may not have deliberately thought about them. These early experiences leave their mark on our inner being to the degree that this unthought known "constitutes the core of one's being" (60).

Bollas emphasizes that what is internalized in the infant's ego is more about the processes that affect its inner world than about the objects themselves. In my interpretation of Bollas, the process of knowing is not confined to conscious thought but, rather, is affectively intuited or felt as a "sensation." Here there is an unconscious epistemology at play, which only later reveals itself as knowledge through some form of self-reflection, often mediated by the mother or, by extension, the analyst. Of course, this requires language and narration in order to represent the unrepresentable and to articulate the "inarticulate elements of psychic life" (Bollas 1987, 210).

It is important to note that when Bollas refers to the unthought known he relies on a model of consciousness to derive knowledge from a pre-symbolic experience that was encoded by the ego. In other words, conscious experience is a prerequisite to knowing, even if it is independent from thought. Although I do not dispute this claim, are we justified in going further? Are we justified in positing an unconscious mentation that thinks the unthought, an unknown that is thought? This would require positing an unconscious spacing that precedes experience, that prefigures the coming into being of agency. From Bollas's account, the "core of being" is derived from consciousness, the contents of which become deposited as unrepresentational form or dysformulated elements of experience.

What we have been preoccupied with all along is the presubjective organization of psychic life and the question, meaning, and truth of unconscious agency. The unthought known is necessarily preceded and mediated by relational involvement with the mother. But is this a sufficient condition for knowledge? Can there be thought and knowing prior to conscious experience? Following our dialectical analysis of the origins of psychic reality, the unconscious apperceptive ego already feels and intuits itself as an object, setting itself the developmental task of becoming a subject for itself. What Bollas refers to as the unthought is felt through self-sensation and previously known by unconscious mentation in order for it to be made conscious and articulate. Thus, what is unconsciously known is already preformulated and presymbolized, not simply unformulated. This means that unconscious agency *cognizes* itself as sentient experience. *It* thinks, although the contents of its cognition may remain unknown, hence ensconced in form.

The question of whether a sensation, intuition, or feeling should be equated with knowing and thought constitutes an area of considerable debate among philosophy, one we need not engage in this context. What is important to displace, however, is the rigid categories of thinking and thought that are said to properly belong to cognition, particularly rational consciousness. The non-representational experiences of form that resonate within our affective interior constitute a medium of knowing that must be processed and presymbolized as schemata by the unconscious ego or the conscious ego could not recognize its internal contents as having had any preexistence whatsoever, with the result that it could not be identified as being previously known. In other words, the unthought known would have to have been previously cognized in some crude capacity in order for the subject to recognize it as a piece of self-intuited knowledge. It cannot be felt or known as a preexistent unless there is some element of memorialization that has been somatically or affectively inscribed within unconscious semiotics. If it is not previously cognized, then it can never be known or recognized as an interiorized piece of self-knowledge because the subject would have had no self-referent or felt-prefamiliarity with itself (i.e., there would be no unknown that was previously thought). How often is it the case that, when we offer to patients interpretations that provide a new insight, it is accompanied with the self-affirmation – "Yes, you're right. I knew that."

Bollas clarifies how we may know an artefact of our interior – hence of our archaic primacy – that we do not consciously register or recollect. *It* makes itself known and makes its presence felt through the reverberation of our internalizations that no longer have a point of reference, that no longer demarcate a beginning. They are taken over as "mine" only in the moment of felt-familiarity with our past, with our interiorized intuition of self-experience. These artefacts of pre-experience with our interiority come to the fore in endless schemata, as we have shown, whether they are somatic, affective, perceptual, or conceptual representations that express and articulate themselves through conscious elucidations.

The more rudimentary – thus original – expressions of presubjective life are known through patternings or recapitualizations of original being. Marilyn Charles (2002, 23) refers to these recapitualizations as emotional patterns deriving from early "rhythms" of experience and "prosodies of affect." Patterns are building blocks of experience and are "primary unit[s] of meaning" (28). Patterns are impingements of otherness that become constituted and organized within unconscious structure. Like Bollas, Charles views affective knowing as one way of experiencing patterns. She emphasizes the basic movements of sensation, sentience, rhythmicity, and affect that comprise the earliest schemata of unconscious life that may become integrated into semiotic relations. This is based on a "language of the body … [A]spects of awareness that are so integral to our sense of self and world that they remain unnoticed" (Charles 2005, 491). They often appear as "autosensuous shapes" clamouring for proper metabolization within symbolic meaning relations articulated through gesture, narration, and metaphor.

Whether we discuss these early experiential-developmental encounters in terms of the dissociational processes that are operative during introjection or in terms of that which remain repressed, forgotten, unformulated, or inarticulate, the prosody of affective reverberations, the autosensuousness of sentience or bodily flux, and the rhythmicity of emotion, body comportment, and gesture are all prefigured and informed by the spacings of the abyss, which endeavour to institute some type of unifying organization on inner process. As we have argued, it is the imposition of schematic form that becomes the template – the archetype – through which all future elements of conscious experience will be filtered. Of course, consciousness fills in empty form, supplies content to inner life, and brings a flush, vigorous, and articulate quality to schemata. It is in these spacings of the ego and the abyss that meaning germinates and, like a dove, thought takes flight.

SPACINGS OF DEFENCE, DISSOCIATION, AND PHANTASY

Every vicissitude to which the instincts are liable has its origin in some ego activity.

A. Freud (1966 [1936], 44)

Anna Freud interprets her father correctly. In order for there to be any mediation of the drives, any alteration of original affect, desire, or competing conflicts between the inner world and external reality, the ego must be the mediatory agent that brings about transformation in content and form. The ego becomes the locus of agency, for drives are blind, amorphous, and directionless without ego intervention. The question now becomes: What constitutes defence? And when do defences first materialize? Does the institution of defence require conscious experience? Or does it transpire before the ego of consciousness appears? Put another way, are defensive processes already at play prior to the birth of the ego? We often consider defence as an unconscious process operative on multiple parallel levels of organization that is co-extensive with conscious experience, and this exists in tandem with unconscious phantasy. Sometimes phantasies are themselves defences against psychic pain and/or are in the service of protecting the ego from an unpleasant realization, an encroachment from a foreign body, or an unwanted imposition. In fact, the act of phantasizing is inherently wishful, whether this be in the service of pleasure or in the avoidance of pain. So how are defence and phantasy differentiated from one another if they are concurrent – perhaps even identical – in function? Is there a common pattern or form in which both defence and phantasy participate? These are important questions, and they rightfully lead us to distinguish the ego from the abyss.

Freud was preoccupied with the question of defence in his early psychoanalytic writings, and, despite his emphasis on repression as the fountainhead of the unconscious, he returned to his earlier views on defence in his mature theory. In the "Neuro-Psychoses of Defence"

(1894), Freud proffers the notion of defence (*Abwehr*) for the first time, differentiating it from Janet's view of dissociation as "an innate weakness of the capacity for psychical synthesis" and from the hypnoid "dreamlike states" that characterize Breuer's view of the splitting of consciousness (SE 3:46). Instead, Freud offers his competing thesis, which holds that psychical defence, in the form of splitting, is an "act of will." Thus, he uses the language of intentionality (*absichtlich*) and deliberateness (*willkürlich*) with regard to the ego. But Freud is also quick to offer this disclaimer: "By this I do not, of course, mean that the patient intends to bring about a splitting of consciousness. His intention is a different one; but, instead of attaining its aim, it produces a splitting of consciousness" (SE 3:46–7). Here Freud is underscoring the distinction – and, by definition, a different psychical operation – between conscious intentionality and unconscious motivation, the latter being the operative agency that institutes defence. What is even more remarkable is that Freud uses the language of contemporary theorists who favour a dissociative model of consciousness, but with the qualification that these enactments are unconsciously informed and executed.

Freud annexes the notion of intentionality because it nicely fits with the function and teleology of the unconscious ego's motivations: it is at once active, wishful, and protective. Moreover, the unconscious ego's agentic functions become the prototype of the conscious directionality of thought, hence the ground and impetus of intentional purpose. In this way, the ego remains inherently free, despite being partially determined by embodiment and culture due to its ontological thrownness. Freud's use of the terms "will" and "intentionality" may also reflect the German philosophies of the will that were popular during his time (e.g., those of Schopenhauer, Nietzsche, and Husserl [a fellow student who was also tutored by Brentano]) and that would surely have left an impression on his thinking. Freud was also a young man at this point, and this terminology was in keeping with the exclusive focus on consciousness rather than on the unconscious process he was attempting to elucidate.

What becomes interesting is how Freud first approaches the question and meaning of defence. He isolates the inception of defensive action due to "an occurrence of incompatibility" in a person's "*ideational life*, that is to say, until their ego was faced with an experience, an idea or a feeling which aroused such a distressing affect that the subject decided to forget about it because he had no confidence in his power to resolve the contradiction between the incompatible idea and his ego by means of thought-activity" (SE 3:47, emphasis in original). Notice that Freud says the subject *decides* to forget rather than merely being overwhelmed with trauma and hence unable to synthesize or resolve the incompatibility. Indeed, the institution of defence is itself an attempt at resolution through the determinate "intention of 'pushing the thing away,' of not thinking of it, of suppressing it" (SE 3:47). By introducing the notion of a deliberate or wilful intentionality to ego functioning, he assigns an inherent agentic purpose to psychical action, which differentiates it from dissociation, and here is his unique contribution. By introducing intentionality, he adds to the notion of psychic freedom by not merely making the mind a purely dissociative process enacted on a continuum through the splitting of consciousness, an underlying thesis that was promulgated by the theories of Janet, Charcot, and Morton Prince during Freud's time. At this point, we may define defence as the circuitous expression of unconscious motivation that takes a particular directionality based on an immediate assessment – hence a judgment – that is made in the dawn of anxiety.

For Freud, defence imports negation in the service of the positive significance of the negative: the act of denial keeps the synthetic process of mediation and understanding out of consciousness (despite the fact that denial is mediatory), and this is the most primordial mental operation of psychic survival. The ideational incompatibility is obviated, the affect is unacknowledged, the content and meaning become unformulated, and the representations remain underground. Rather than enjoy conscious experience and deliberation, they may undergo further unconscious elaboration, compromise, and symptomatic expression. Or they may peter out altogether. This remains the work of the abyss, for the ego is spared the immediate peril of processing the disruptive hegemony in the moment of lived time.

In this seminal essay on defence, and for the first time in his writings, Freud lays the groundwork for how unconscious agency separates the objectionable idea from the affect, which is "transformed" into somatic symptoms, obsessions, and psychotic ideas (delusions) through the process of "conversion" (SE 3:49). This is the locus of compromise formation, here used as a generic function or operation executed by unconscious agency. Freud acknowledges that defence is employed in the face of "traumatic experience," whereby the ego succeeds in freeing itself from the contradiction [with which it is confronted]; but instead, it has burdened itself with a mnemic symbol which finds a lodgement in consciousness, like a sort of parasite, either in the form of an unresolvable motor innervation or as a constantly recurring hallucinatory sensation, and which persists until a conversion in the opposite direction takes place. Consequently the memory trace of the repressed idea has, after all, not been dissolved; from now on, it forms the nucleus of a second psychical group. (SE 3:49)

Notice that Freud designates the "ego" as the subject that *frees* itself of the parallax – that space of contradiction or dialectical opposition in which no synthesis is possible, where there is a limit or check that is not surpassable – only to be mediated as a compromise through conversion, the psychic deposit of which is transformed into a "mnemic symbol," hence a *semiotic* that "burdens" the conscious mind. In fact, this conversive activity is an attempt at mediatory synthesis, but it is one achieved at a lower (unconscious) level, not a true sublation. What Freud designates as a "repressed" memory-trace is not accessible to immediate consciousness precisely because of the conversion and replacement by a "symbol" that stands for the original object (experience) of signification. It is here that this "repressed idea" forms the "nucleus" of reactionary unconscious life. What we can venture to say is that this nucleus is fuelled by unconscious phantasy systems at the hands of the agentic ego. Therefore, defence and phantasy emanate from the abyss as schematic productions.

In his 1894 paper, Freud makes several references to defence as the "effort of will," which he felt compelled to clarify in his 1896 paper entitled "Further Remarks on the Neuro-Psychoses of Defence." In that essay, he restates that "symptoms arise through the psychical mechanism of (unconscious) *defence*" (SE 3:162, emphasis in original). Of course, throughout his writings, Freud delineates many types of defence that undergo vicissitudes or transformations from their original form, whether through conversions, repetitions, condensations, transpositions, inversions, displacements, or whatever. What becomes important to address, however, is the question of essence. What is the essence of defence? Freud proclaims the "essence" (*Wesen*) of a drive (*Trieb*) to be its impetus, force, or thrust, hence its activity. But we have determined that a drive must have an agent and that agency is itself pure determinate activity. Therefore, defence must be a certain intentional stance mediated by the unconscious ego qua agency. In other words, there is a particularity to intentionality differentiated by purpose and form.

The unconscious ego becomes the logical locus of this original organization of agency, which must undergo modification via splitting, thus eventually accounting for the sophisticated processes belonging to the ego of consciousness, hence the sublation of the abyss. What does consciousness share with wish, phantasy, and defence? There is a directionality, an object, to intentionality (a focus), an aim (function), and a purpose (goal). In fact, directional intentionality is itself a spacing that commands agentic powers, such as the power to regulate, control, or authorize (*directus*, from *regere*, to guide). These are three components to Freud's 1915 theory on drives. What is missing in this early account is the "source."

Freud vacillates on this notion. In his original psychoanalytic papers he attributes the source of defence and symptomatology to "traumatic moments," while later he emphasizes constitutional factors and innate phantasy systems that are responses to forbidden or conflictual intra-psychic wishes derived from embodied urges. Here it becomes important to emphasize that a source of defence, like causality itself, is overdetermined and thus not reducible solely to its material parts or environmental contingencies. This would lead to a merelogical error as well as to the fallacy of misplaced concreteness. Instead, we should stay focused on the fact that the ego is executing a psychical act that "sets up a defence."

Freud talks about how the splitting of consciousness that takes place during defence is in the service of keeping affect and ideation "detached" from one another. This ideation, however, is not merely dissociative, where signification and thought are relegated to what is simply "unformulated," as Stern and Bromberg would tell us. Rather, for Freud, ideas are "weakened" yet held in dynamic reserve until a "fresh impression ... succeeds in breaking through the barrier erected by the will" (*SE* 3:50). This is the beginning of Freud's theory of a dynamic unconscious that thinks, feels, and actively converts mental phenomena either by producing associative links or by creating disjunctions: the former involves assigning a semiotic to unconscious experience, the latter involves instituting a protective function. Here I believe that Freud succeeds in accounting for both dissociation within consciousness and how the content of what becomes dissociated (i.e., affect, sense impressions, ideas) is organized within the abyss. This means that unconscious content has a life and a force of its own that is sustained within a dynamic underworld and creates unconscious pressure that becomes something with which the ego has to deal. What this ultimately means is that dissociation and repression are not incompatible processes or contrary psychoanalytic theoretical models that clash with one another or cancel each other out, as some contemporary theorists would have us believe; rather, they operate on stratified levels of psychic reality carried out and maintained by the dynamic agency that properly belongs to the unconscious ego.

If mind, by nature, is dialectical, and the dialectic is understood to operate on multiple levels that simultaneously transpire in response to the contingent relations that develop and envelop psychic life, then we can appreciate how sublation becomes relative to the contingencies the ego is compelled to mediate. It does so in multifarious ways, and this accounts for the plurality and multiplicity of human experience that further underscores difference. But this difference transpires within universality and simultaneity, which ultimately grounds the dialectic as a supraordinate governing totality. For some people, the ego will be attenuated and the sublation of their dialectics – that is, their personalities and lives – will be thwarted. In other words, they develop symptoms, experience neurotic misery, and are objectively and qualitatively unhappy. This also happens when traumas are introduced. In fact, one autonomous dialectical action from some other force independent of the individual subject (e.g., an environmental event, accident, tragedy) can impede that subject's sublative capacities. Although the conversion performed as an act of defence is mediatory and motivated to protect the subject from suffering, conversion can create its own form of suffering. Therefore, the dialectic is truncated, regresses, or lapses into a parallax. However, there is a greater synthetic principle to the psyche that governs the dialectic and that is responsible for why the valences of defence and conversion may also be in the service of forging a higher unity within mind and culture. This is why Freud eventually conceives of the notion of sublimation, in which desire is fulfilled through the higher developmental creations of mind. These creative forms of fulfilment of basal desire are brought about transformatively through the higher achievements of self-consciousness, which Hegel situates in education, art, political governance, ethics, religion, and reason, and to which Freud refers as *Logos* – the "scientific intellect."

If drive becomes the instantiation of unconscious desire, and defence becomes the instantiation of drive, then the greatest achievements of humanity are based on the vicissitudes of defence. Every great intellectual and creative act is a sublative manifestation of original form usually instituted by emotion, fear, avoidance, and/or mastery, or by the transmogrification of desire and its objects. Defence is not merely a reaction to danger but, rather, a creative process on the part of the generative psyche, which is looking for antidotes to discomfort, anxiety, and pain. It derives from the affective toll that encumbers the psyche by virtue of being a sentient entity that wants and craves fulfilment of its own choices, choices that are replete with competitive strivings from other self-states or antithetical dialectical forces enacted within the mind. And this is why anxiety is the great driving force behind human progress and *pathos*.

So where does phantasy figure in desire, drive, and defence? Phantasy is a specific derivation of desire – the object of a drive – the content of which is a wish, once again a specificity of desire with a certain aim or intentionality, namely, to become fulfilled. That is why conscious fantasy can be gratifying without a wish being gratified: it is both vessel and avenue, container and contained. *Phantasy* is a slave to raw emotions and urges derived from the pulsions, while *fantasy* is more subject to the will and is free to select how gratification may be obtained without imperiling the complex organization of personality. Indeed, conscious fantasy becomes containing for the fulfilment of phantasy (which, if actualized, would naturally jeopardize the integrity of the conscious ego) and, a fortiori, is a safeguard against the acting out of unconscious phantasy. In this sense, fantasy becomes play, play as free roaming, a wading into the possible pond through the experiential medium of imagination, an intimate engagement with the future as one conceives it to be. Indeed, fantasy is an engagement with the future as a trajectory of possibility: it involves leaving the past without the past leaving it. It needs the past – namely, previous experience – in order to remember what it desires and craves, and how it wishes to deviate from this original pulsation, attributable to the creative dexterity of desire. The ego materializes from the abyss only to generate its own determinate sense of self-organization while remaining embedded within an infinite realm of possibilities that are actualized or denied within the infinite spacings that encompass its horizons. Feral phantasy wants gratification and discharge, while fantasy is the tamer side of sublation: it seeks variety, novelty, and change as volitional experimentation. Some fantasy systems are quite deliberate, others are surreptitious and serendipitous. But fantasy is mostly passive, the silent dialogue the soul has with itself. And this is where we hear the echo of Freud's dictum: man is a wishing animal.

Defence and phantasy are the teleologic fate of a drive determined by unconscious intentionality subject to becoming more consciously expressed, realized, augmented, or altered – thus changed – by conscious will or determination. For example, patients are often very well aware of wanting to avoid talking about or directly dealing with certain conflicts in their lives, and they take deliberate action to institute protective manoeuvres to shelter them from discomfort or psychic pain. The same can be said for a system of fantasies we call the daydream, which is manufactured in imagination for the purpose of procuring pleasure. Here defence and phantasy are on a continuum of enactments, the realization of which are contingent upon the ego's awareness of them as such. But often the greater dynamics that fuel conversions, compromise formations, and lead to repetition compulsions are not governed by conscious volition. They are, however, directed by the impersonal agency that governs unconscious life. The teleological fate of pulsions and defence therefore achieves a completion that varies in content and form, hence allowing for a plurality of motives, aims, and differences, yet they are determinate rather than determined. In other words, the vicissitudes of psychic life are not predetermined end-states that are part of a fixed destiny innate within the organism; rather, they are subject to the intervening parameters that define freedom and will. This *freed will*, so to speak, is the sublation of agentic expression that has its origin and dawn in the abyss.

THE TRAJECTORY OF DYNAMIC PATTERN

As do most analysts, in my clinical work I listen for basic repetitive themes. A theme is represented in patterns – at once circuitous, sometimes simple yet often convoluted – echoing a motif with variegated content, affect, and relational properties. While patterns are variant in content (e.g., images, representations, ideation, fantasy, emotions, behaviour), they tend, for the most part, to be invariant in form; that is, they tend to appear as the recapitulation of dynamic thematic experience. This thematic pattern is unconsciously driven by the repetitive thrust of the dialectic channelled through the agentic purposeful action of the ego's mediating activity. We may say that the unconscious ego is attracted to and identifies with a core experience within the internality of its Self to such a degree that it is ontically compelled to repeat this trajectory of dynamic pattern. The source and degree to which such a basic pattern of repetition is informed are the result of the processes of overdetermination: constitutional or teleonomic pressures from the drives derived from our evolutionary biology, reiterations of defence and desire, developmental fixation, and so forth. Of course, repetitions may be enactments or re-enactments of various traumas – whether they are classically conditioned in the psyche (hence subjugated by the rotary motion of aimless duplication), or whether they are more teleologically guided in the service of achieving control, manipulation, mastery, and so on. Whatever the sources of overdetermination that are simultaneously operative within the abyss, they are the expression, as reconstitution and transformation, of archaic life communicated through multiple dynamic functions wed to context and contingency.

A formal yet impersonal aspect of the unconscious ego is the regeneration of repetitive desire based on a simple economy of rigid identification that is symbolized in the pattern or theme. Yet this symbolization is not only linguistically signified but also somatically and affectively fortified within a fluid process system we call mind. We have already elucidated this systemic complexity as a developmental unfolding of unconscious schemata. Here patternings are the regeneration of schemata and systems of schemata that have a particular rotary motion or concentric circularity peculiar to their specific self-organizations. Patterns may be circuitously expressed, enacted, or symbolically communicated through a theme, a symptom, an affect, a semiotic, and so forth. The schematic structure is architectonic yet malleable and shifting, and can bend or mutate itself based on internal impulsions and properties of wish, defence, desire, and the like. These somatic-affective-linguistic signifiers are themselves amalgamated within the dynamic repetition of pattern. This is the core of unconscious process as the universal repetition of *form*.

Form is empty and abstract in structure, yet it is continuous rotary activity as unconscious experience based on the organization of events ultimately springing forth from a desirous pulse. The actions of repetitive form are perpetually regenerated and constituted by the soul's pure activity. Here enters the basic aspect of agency for the repetition of empty form requires an object that it procures and makes part of its internal structure, which further coalesces within a broader thematic identification. This broader thematic identification becomes a self-organizing pattern, grouping, or spacing that can shift in content and contour as well as capture and hold onto objects through fixations of a particular internalized theme. Because schematic patterns have the ability to retain several levels of meaning and signification simultaneously, which is the formal house of overdetermination and multiple function, this process is ultimately an agentic one. Form is filled through our developmental life experiences, which become encoded and laid down in peculiar patterns modelled by the unique aspects of each subject's core personality.

Patterns are transmutational based on a creative alteration in the basic repetition of form. This alteration is itself a generative modification of thematic pattern brought about by the introduction of *intensities*, namely, quantitative and qualitative states of unconscious experience. This, indeed, may be the essence of freedom within the unconscious mind: namely, the capacity to introduce unconscious qualia. The question of whether the spontaneous introduction of qualia constitutes freedom is another matter; however, the novelty and creative latitude the unconscious ego possesses at this stage is what I wish to emphasize here. Each subject's core agency has the ability to mould patterns and to have determinate choice over the identification with, taking up, and regurgitation of objects. Of course, this choice gets realized on much higher levels of patterning in conscious life, with higher degrees of freedom; yet it has its source within the abyss. What we may posit is that each schematic organization may act in quasi-autonomous fashion, despite being indissolubly interconnected within the synthetic networks that unify mental operations. From this standpoint, mind is a monistic unifying order of disparate complexities brought under the harmony of holistic integrating dialectical forces.

Unconscious events pass into other events in their contentual intercourse and contextual intercessions, thus producing complex and competing after-effects with hybrid forms of manifestation, including clashes between oppositions that lead to conflicts and impasses. Here is where the potential for sublation may tarry in antinomies or fall into a parallax gap – a spacing of the abyss in which there is no discernable synthesis.[4] But transpositions and compromises are produced to relieve tensions and, therefore, point to the sublating features of the dialectic that *attempt* to integrate or adapt to such clashes as a functional way of ameliorating or resolving these dialectical complexifications. For example, dreams that attempt solutions through the viewer's dreamscape of altered consciousness, somatic symptoms that express underlying dilemmas in altered forms, affect that resists being integrated into conceptual awareness or expressed verbally, are all interplays of dialectical relations at various stages in their process as well as attempts at sublation.

The repetition of form as differential dynamic patterns of schematic emission has a trajectory that, in part, is causally teleonomic yet teleologically directed by the unconscious ego. In other words, this trajectory is impelled by the bodily drives yet taken over by agentic intentional mediation. The trajectory of repetitive form is a universal proclivity of mind that has the potential to encompass all temporal spacings within its directional activity. Put another way, the archaic past, presentational immediacy, and projective future coalesce within the extant processential moment. This triangulation, however, can be under a certain valence that has more dominance over the other two orders, spheres, or contexts of being. For example, when traumagenic features have more impact on the psyche and command more levels of intensity as they attach to endogenous or internalized events, they are more likely to be under the sway of archaic primacy. But these traumagenic dimensions are also triggered by momentary encounters with conscious experience in one's environment that involve the causal influences of immediational presence, which leads to institutions of defence, dissociation, fantasy, avoidance, or any number of intrapsychic events that evoke a state of non-realization that is only properly attainable as a future trajectory – hence the desire for a different state of affairs. This is what we usually attribute to the dynamics of a wish.

During the registration of sensory events, trauma can also split representations into discrete elements that coalesce in different schematic structures as atemporal fragments. If the psyche becomes largely formed though traumatic process, then the destructive principle is awakened, based on its identification with violence, death, and decay, to the point that mind is constantly drawn to negativity and swims in an effusive cesspool of *jouissance*. Here death, trauma, and conflict undergird the dialectic of desire. Eros and death are the same, just different manifestations of form. Yet it is in the manifestation of form that similarity is eclipsed by difference while remaining a universal. However, in order for schemata to persist within the abyss, they must be retained or preserved, hence remembered. This is why the abyss is inherently memorial.

MEMORIALIZATION AND TIME

When we think of memory, we may generally say that it is connected to the capacity to form representations, that is, to re-present or repeat previous encoded experience laid down as traces in mnemonic pathways within the night of the mind. In the fields of cognitive science and neuropsychoanalysis, memory is often divided into two broad categories, namely, explicit and implicit memory systems (Bohleber 2007; Eichenbaum et al. 1999; Pugh 2002), while specific activities of memory are further classified by their operations. In explicit memory, which may be generic and episodic, declarative, autobiographical, or narrative, accounts of remembrance depend on language and words to convey a meaningful sequence of past events that portray a decisive account or story, hence they have been mediated by perceptual and conceptual consciousness. In implicit memory, which is more procedural, non-declarative, and associative, it is posited that events are not explicitly encoded by the mind and are not retrievable, hence they are "unrecoverable as memories per se" (Blass and Carmeli 2007, 21). This may explain why many traumatized patients cannot have direct access to certain memories, especially when they were under dissociative strategies at the time of traumatic occurrences, yet they persist in memory centres inaccessible to conscious awareness and verbal articulation. Nevertheless, these events have left their mark – a semiotic, a "sensory signature," so to speak – which communicates through symptoms and suffering.

Although explicit declarative memory is narrative, drawing on images, percepts, and self-proclaimed indubitable thoughts of events that are said to have factually occurred in the past, we have already established that memory and recollection undergo transposition, metamorphosis, and translation, thereby drawing into question the epistemic verity of declarative memory. Furthermore, cognitive research tells us that we selectively extract and store key elements of our experiences, only then to reconstruct and recreate our experiences "rather than retrieve copies of them. Sometimes, in the process of reconstructing we add on feelings, beliefs, or even knowledge we obtained after the experience. In other words, we bias our memories of the past by attributing to them emotions or knowledge we acquired after the event" (Schacter 2001, 9). This process of recategorization of embodied memories (Leuzinger-Bohleber and Pfeifer 2002) is inherently part of the psyche's need to lend meaning, purpose, and rationale to historical experiences taken up by new modes of mediation. On the other hand, implicit procedural memory may be more mechanical, productive, and automated, such as the non-conscious pre-reflective operations that become habitually part of our behavioural repertory (e.g., driving a car, body gestures, facial expressions), but this does not necessarily mean that we have gained any explanatory power with regard to understanding the mechanics or processes responsible for this realm of memory, especially when it is foreclosed from conceptual narration. While neuroscience favours this dual classification of memory, this further generates debate about the role of the unconscious in these dual memory sectors.

When we consider the view from neuroscience, it becomes important to ask some fundamental questions: What exactly do we mean by memory? How can we classify, let alone substantiate, mental phenomena that are presumed to exist within the mind but that we do not remember occurring in the past? How do we distinguish between recollection and reconstruction, remembering and forgetting, representing and misrepresenting, re-calling (hence bringing back) and imagining or creating factitious events? Perhaps this is the same set of problematics psychoanalysis has when it posits that something pre-existent has been repressed or is unconscious, hence unrecollected, unrecognized, unrepresented. Or is it merely unrepresentable? In fact, this is the very issue at stake in contemporary controversies surrounding the question of the necessity of the concept of the unconscious in general. There are some contemporary analysts who subvert the notion of a dynamic unconscious altogether by favouring a dissociative model that privileges implicit memory structures as an alternative theory to unconscious process. For this group, the question of memory largely becomes a matter of separating that which is articulate from that which is inarticulate, that which is formulated (or formulable) from that which is not.

For classical psychoanalytic sensibility, the unconscious is implicit yet substantive, that is, it is real and has being or presence: *It* becomes symptomatic and declarative, hence is made actual through its phenomenal appearances. For some postmodern circles, the dissociative mind does not necessarily require unconscious structure to account for implicit memory: non-conscious or pre-reflective operations may be sufficiently explained as unformulated experience. But, as I have intimated, these accounts do not give an adequate account of agency, let alone explain the causal forces or operations that execute these mental acts to begin with. For it is not enough to say that psychic events are implicitly operative: one must also attempt to provide specific details as to how and why. More pointedly, how are implicit memory structures constituted and represented? Indeed, perhaps the whole question of memory hinges on the nature of representability.

When we refer to memory (from the Latin *memor*, mindful), we often associate its meaning with remembrance (which is a specific act of recall) or with recollection (which also refers to a particular recorded instance, whether deliberately or purposely willed or passively recollected). In these usages we think of memory as a conscious operation of cognition. What perhaps gets closer to a psychoanalytic theory of memory is the notion of commemoration – a symbol – of remembrance. This is why I prefer the term "memorialization" rather than "memory,"[5] because what the former term fundamentally emphasizes is not the notion of retrievability but, rather, the *preservative* element of retaining certain psychic events. Preservation is inherent to memory, whether we can retrieve mental data or not, and it is also a key motion in the process of sublation itself. Recall that the preservative element of the dialectic has a causal impetus we call archaic primacy, and it exerts its toll on all aspects of conscious life. The past is memorialized in the present and influences how we approach the future. Therefore, memorialization has a temporal function: it designates a time that is past but retained, something causally operative that, potentially, could be brought to presence, that is, that could make its effects expressed and known in the diachronic immediacy as well as the future.

What is further paradoxical is the fact that there is a certain ahistoricism to memorialization that materializes as the conscious counterpart of the inability to remember, despite the fact that what is preserved are historical events retained in schematic form. This leads Loewald (1976, 149) to say that "memory, in the broadest sense, is the activity by which, above all, some sort of order and organization and some sense of permanence, as well as movement and change, come into our world." The implication of this insight is that, without memory, there can be no time. Or, to be more precise, there can be no organized phenomenal lived-time that the psyche attempts to amalgamate into an interwoven context of meaningful experiential temporal events. Furthermore, memorialization constitutes a semiotic trace that impregnates itself within the varied schemata with distinctive properties that populate mental life. Thus, I believe that the term "memorialization" more accurately conveys the function of psychic retention that cognitive neuroscience highlights when it refers to implicit memory systems.

Our life experiences, including our suffering past, are enshrined as archaic primacy, which is summoned on various unconscious levels during immediational presence and, therefore, ontically informs the future trajectory of our aspirations, motivations, wishes, projections, and fantasy relations temporally executed within spacings of the abyss.

The past becomes memorialized within the various schematic systems that, in turn, leave specific memoric traces within unconscious organization, as well as through percepts and conceptual thought. Generally, we may say that what corresponds to implicit memory systems are somatic and affective representations, while explicit memory domains lie within perceptive and conceptual schemata, hence the domain of declarative and narrative, linguistic representation. Here the emphasis is on how the psyche retains, expresses, and re-presents its multi-contoured modes of memorialization through different pathways of presencing its interior spacings from within the abyss.

The spacings of the various schematic representations generated from the ego may be properly understood as a dynamic-systemic superordinate interweaving organization of agentically executed events through which schematic expression unfolds on multiple simultaneous levels. By way of example, consider how a visual percept in the present may trigger a specific memory from childhood, which sets off a chain of recollections in declarative memory that is further explored and elaborated upon in associational thought. This, in turn, simultaneously evokes affective states from the past that were hibernating or lying dormant; which, in turn, unearths visceral somatic reactions that represent a certain memorialization or meaning structure that had not been properly brought to light or consciously experienced as real. And when these interactional sequences of events occur, the past opens up and gives birth to new forms and transformations of schematic expression in terms of the reconstructions of certain events and the inevitable translations and constructions that follow. Of course, this triggers a trickle-effect, whereby new affective reverberations and emotional rumblings are awakened, which can either stimulate or thwart linkages between the past and the present. When associative linkages are favourable in integrating embodied affect and conceptual insight, new meaning structures emerge in the wake of what had up until now remained unformulated and unrealized.

The overdetermined simultaneity of schematic process institutes the most supple and subtle moves of thought. In fact, you can hardly detect they are happening at all: at once thought mediates sense impressions, such as visual percepts and sounds, which then echo through the affective topography of our inner representational worlds, which then opens up a whole lacework of signifiers and phantasy systems that the ego must mediate and to which it must assign meaning. When networks of signifiers are not blocked by defence, certain implicit memory structures may be dislodged and offered another avenue for representational expression through more explicit channels of information processing. When barred by the ego, signification may remain on the level of the somatic, affective, and pre-symbolic; tarry in repetitions; or become entrenched as reflexive procedural actions and behavioural patterns tied to the circular rotary of the drives that animate embodied desire.

Memorialization may be both concrete and metaphorical, hence inscribed on the visceral corporeality of our sentient nature as well as thought, and access to it is through the life of feeling. Feeling states resonate in the human being in trenchant and personally symbolic ways that give further value and meaning to being and *pathos*. It is here in the feeling soul that the metaphorical mind may find its most cherished and exalted ideals with which it deeply identifies as constituting the core of inner existence, that truly authentic aspect to personal identity – the *felt-I* within the abyss: "This is who *I* am, this is *me* – to the bone."

What is interesting to note is that the etymology of the word "memory" is derived from the Greek *martus*, meaning "to witness," adopted as *martyr* in late Latin and Indo-European languages, also becoming "to grieve" (*murnan*) in English, or, in the Germanic, "to mourn" (*mournen*). Therefore, the etymological significance of the words "memory" and "memorialization" involve the mindful remembrance of suffering. Suffering – our *pathos* – is something the mind does not forget, even when it wants to. It is not surprising that pronounced body and affective schemata that are so prevalent in traumatized patients still communicate their remembrances through symptomatic suffering, what Freud (1916–17) refers to as the "sense" of a symptom, by which he means that symptoms "serve a purpose" (*SE* 15: 239). They make sense.

TOWARDS PSYCHIC HOLISM

As I have repeatedly argued, the abyss is a vast psychic territory comprised of spacings and patternings of unconscious activity. The ego enacts itself within the abyss, but the abyss is not, properly speaking, an entity. It is more accurately described as a dispersal of unconscious subjectivity that can be modified, differentiated, and organized as well as alienated, dissociated, and disorganized, only to be (re)gathered up or split apart by an agentic force we equate with the impersonal process of the dialectic. Of course, this impersonal process is personally actualized within each embodied subject and animates the pulsional agent as a vital life force even when saturated with the negative forces that impel and sustain psychic existence.

Process psychology is committed to the notion that what fundamentally underlies the fabric of psychic reality is the dialectic, which is the vivacious force behind the process of mind. This naturally implies an appreciation for holism, what Jung would have equated with the pursuit of individuation, or Hegel with his quest for a grand synthesis embodied in the notion of the Absolute. But let us assume a more modest appreciation of holism grounded in the ongoing instantiation and actualization of human desire and its vicissitudes oriented towards cultivating, fulfilling, and sustaining higher developmental modes of being. This is the tenor of what Hegel had in mind when he envisioned *Geist* as a self-articulated complex totality of the coming into being of pure self-consciousness. I imagine mainstream psychoanalysis would like to remain on a more earthly plane when contemplating mind, but this does not mean that process psychology is not compatible with many great philosophical, religious, and spiritual traditions that have endeavoured to explain the riddle of being; secure meaning amidst contradiction, flux, paradox, and uncertainty; or reach a higher state of communion with what one may intuitively experience as a greater force underlying the nature of realty itself.

Dialectical psychoanalysis provides a supplemental complementarity to well established traditions that embrace holism. For example, the notion of the dialectic expressed within a unifying process may be said to exist in many forms in Western and Eastern philosophies alike, from Heraclitus' theory of unity within change to the Taoist doctrine of the Way as both a comprehensive dynamic structure of the universe and a path to harmonious co-existence with the world. There are various dialectical mystical and theosophic principles inherent in neo-Platonism, Gnosticism, and Medieval philosophies that posit one unitary world (*unus mundus*), as there are in the Eastern yin and yang (*Taijitu*), which symbolizes the mutually implicative duality of being.

The inherent diversity within unity that is symbolized by the mandala in Hinduism and Tibetan culture, as well as in the Confucian pursuit of an all-pervading unity (*Analects* IV, 15; XV, 2), further reflects a collective human need for universal inclusivity, belongingness, harmony, and reconciliation of opposites. From the pre-Socratic notion of *apeiron* – the boundless disarray that characterizes the multiplicity of nature – to the preoccupation with accommodating nature and mind, reason and science, self and society that characterizes modern philosophy, there is an inherent need to juxtapose and resolve opposition. The neo-Platonic emanationism that characterizes Plotinus' treatise on the One (*Enneads* VI) may also be said to permeate Ibn 'Arabī's emphasis on the "unity of being" (*wahdat al-wujūd*) characteristic of Sufism, a mystical theosophy that plays a vital role in many Islamic societies today. Of course, the dialectic between good and evil, nature and religion, God and man, is an ancient preoccupation upon which the whole edifice of Judea-Christianity is based.

Among the plurality of belief systems that differentiate people and cultures, it goes without saying that any interpretation of the ground, principle of the ultimate, or absolute structure of reality is ultimately a personally intimate enterprise that intersects the phenomenology of human desire and the metaphysical quandaries that we may properly relegate to the domain of wonder. These are the complex motivations of mind longing for various elements of being to be realized through the process of its own becoming.

Process psychology views human motivation as governed by a supraordinate overdetermined agentic system that cannot be logically reducible to its material substratum without jeopardizing psychic holism. When neuroscience wants to locate the source of motivational centres within the brain under the rubric of biologism, it does so at the expense of displacing the human being as a holistic existential agent. Not only does neuroscience commit the fallacy of simple location and make a merelogical attribution error when designating the locus of mind to the brain, but it also fails to adequately account for agency, assuming the agent is ultimately the cornucopia of neural structures that constitutes mental phenomena. What this means is that the motivational systems that are purported to undergird brain activity and to create human instinct, desire, and emotion are simply emergent properties of brain events, which makes them epiphenomena with no causal powers of their own.[6] In other words, if emerging brain events are said to be the quantitative (biologic) and qualitative (experiential) by-products of an executive self-organizing organ, then you automatically have a reductive paradigm that makes mind causally impotent and devoid of freedom.[7]

Understanding motivational complexity, as psychoanalysis shows, does not have to make biology a sufficient condition of mind, only a necessary condition of the pulsional lived-body. In other words, while our bodies are necessary, they are not sufficient to explain the complexifications and experiential patternings of mental life. In fact, when neuroscientists discuss the motivational centres of the brain, they use the language of desire. For example, motivational systems are said to seek, to want, to have expectations, and to elicit rewards. These desires are "activated" when stimulation levels are high and are "deactivated" when arousal is low; and they are said to be carried out through a superhighway of neural-fiber pathways. But, we may ask: How are these microsystems of specific desires activated? And by what are they activated, never mind by whom? How do you account for the agency that logically activates these motivation centres? If you appeal to mechanics or make agency an epiphenomenon, then the human being merely devolves into being a complex machine devoid of self-determinate generative agentic expression. If agency and human subjectivity are said to adhere to epiphenomenalism, then even the most sophisticated emergent properties of the brain that we attribute to a process system lack any causal determinism. Process psychology offers a theoretical structure that salvages agency from the bane of material reduction while at the same time offering neuroscience a complementary explanation that potentially enhances biologic theory by addressing the mind/body problem. Agency is at once embodied yet free due to determinate teleology and its ever-increasing self-derived capacities to actualize itself.

Mind is oriented towards holism in the sense that it seeks ever greater unification of its diverse internal spacings, felt-experiences, and subjective longings. Having its source and wellspring within the abyss, mind becomes more actualized through consciousness, where holistic integrations are actively pursued in the relational, intellectual, ethical, aesthetic, and spiritual life immersed within culture and socialization. As an aggregate of subjectivities that vies for expression, mind reflects a collectively shared objective: namely, to instantiate itself within society as the concrete embodiment of what it seeks and values. This is why all cultures have social structures, principles, mores, and rules for their peoples to observe, whether they reflect the most basic needs of human survival or a society's most exalted values, cherished convictions, and inherited ideals. As Freud articulated so well, human beings will always remain desirous and libidinal in their pursuit of pleasure and gratification, as well as in their avoidance of pain, and so we have erected social structures to ensure their attainment and continuance. We have communal infastructures that provide us with the basic necessities, such as water, clothing, food, shelter, commerce, and some degree of security based upon law and social order. We have educational systems and technologies that allow us to learn, work, and actualize our rational minds, which, in turn, allows for greater advancements, sublimations, and discoveries that afford further opportunities to secure enjoyment, entertainment, and meaning. We have cultural environs that honour aesthetics, whether this be the visual arts, architecture, literature, or music; and we have religious institutions and spiritual practices that attempt to lend unity to the aesthetic, ethical, and intelligible within the life of reason and feeling. These concrete universals are the incarnation of spirit, the *aufhebung* of mind.

The drive towards unification, synthesis, integration, and nexus inherent within the dialectic is evinced when we observe how these parallel activities of culture converge. Aesthetic expression conveys taste, emotive articulation, and intelligible meaning, and it institutes value and moral sensibility that has a rational structure. For example, that which is judged to be good is both beautiful and moral insofar as it transmits and symbolizes value. Ethics and religion, by extension, can be passionate and emotional (hence libidinal), intuitively felt, intelligently reasoned, and spiritually experienced. Of course, individuals will only partially succeed in assuaging and actualizing these diverse aspirations of mind, which involve intense existential labour, and some will remain stymied in the banality of lower pleasures, laziness, complacency, and/or indifference that has besieged nihilistic modernity rather than attempting to better themselves or care about others.

It takes a cultivated sensibility to pursue holism, a w(hole) that is never complete – itself a spacing, a lack in being, that which is symbolic of desire. In many ways, the hole or lacuna in being – namely, pervasive lack – is the foundation of freedom, itself unbounded, the antithetical inversion of which is to be simultaneously imprisoned by the confines of unboundedness that cannot be amended. Hence, lack cannot be gratified. Nor is it inherently gratifying: freedom and determinism are the same, only divided by phenomenal perspective. This is the parallax view of the dialectic. Mind is a unifying unifier that is never fully unified because it is condemned to perennially experience lack, the engine of the dialectic, the inveterate motility of the negative that infuses the very vital process of life. Despite the ever-presencing of lack, it is the pursuit of holism that is gratifying and meaningful to the cultivated mind. Such wholeness belongs to the greater shapes of self-consciousness, where contemplation, self-reflection, observation and critique, awareness and pondering converge into a heightened set of meaning structures seamlessly linked in relational harmony. And all these possible achievements of mind would not be possible if it were not for the *mysterium* that may be said to properly define unconscious existence.

In many ways the abyss is mysterious, indeed mysterial – enigmatic, strange, obscure. It is at once secret, in the sense associated with being initiated into a mystical (religious) order or guild (*mysterion*, from *myein*, to close [lips and eyes]). But we should not avoid an emphasis on the *mystique*, that which is earliest – *mu*, a groan (mute), hence silent negation riddled with pain: "I shut my mouth and close my eyes" (*mustēs* is *mūo*). We must not see – we must not speak – what the abyss metabolizes. *Es* must remain a secret – cryptic, buried, repressed, private. Perhaps, when the mystics speak of their communion or union with the transcendent, or achieve a state of heightened awareness and inner affective transformation that is beyond that which words can define, they are indeed immersed in the ineffability of the abyss that speaks to them in another language, that psychic spacing where intellectual apprehension is occluded. We may, perhaps not inappropriately, call this unconscious wisdom. What is of further etymological significance is that what we call the mystical is derived from *agein*, to *drive* or lead – to *act* or do, hence, to initiate (*ab initio*). Here the abyss becomes synonymous with agency. The intuitively derived truths, while being in communion with the transcendent, speak to the freedom of the soul, the beauty of spirit.

The pursuit of psychic holism involves ongoing efforts to unify various schemata in harmonious and meaningful ways, where mind, body, and soul co-exist, even if conflict sustains their orderings. This is not to say that strife, impasse, and disorder are not present among synthetic presences, for they are the complementarity of the dialectic. As Freud commonly observes, "Life is not easy!" (*SE* 22:78), even when we are happy. There are sublations within sublation, just as there are inevitable clashes, blockages, setbacks, slippages, and regressions punctuated by spacings of disharmony, tragedy, and psychic erosion. When the sublated mind achieves an enlightened sensibility that continues to provide structure and orientation to living, threads of unification, synthetic integration, and meaning are easier to attain and sustain. In the mind's transcendence over its more base instinctual urges, where Eros also desires to pursue good for its own sake, we see an even greater harmony between the aesthetic, the rational, and the ethical.

Both Freud and Hegel saw morality as a necessary developmental achievement of the psyche responsible for judging, curbing, transforming, and sublimating our more primitive constitutions in the service of our own survival, interpersonal adjustment, and social advancement, a process inherent in the progression of civilization. Although Freud was deeply engaged in the ethos of modern culture, particularly observing how social custom, law, aesthetics, and politics are based on the unconscious transmogrification of primitive mind, he declined to comment on just how one should lead a good life. Perhaps we find a kernel of such a prescription in his general reflection on mental health: the capacity to work, love, and play. Regardless of the recalcitrant debate surrounding what constitutes ethical identity (e.g., one's moral obligations, belief systems, duties, and justified actions), all ethical decisions are filtered through the subjective lens of our own personalities, developmental histories, unconscious conflicts, transference proclivities, and emotional dispositions. It is from this standpoint that we must necessarily engage our own internal processes when confronting the ethical. When we engage our moral agency, we have a tendency to suspend other considerations and give primacy to the inner experience that speaks to us as an emotional call we feel deep within our interior. Notwithstanding the sober grasp of reason, which may inform other ego capacities, we are often drawn to the emotionality of the ideal that, whether based in illusion or reality, captures us within the affective immediacy of our conscience or moral register, including the impulse to take moral action. We are always faced with a calculated risk when it comes to self-expression, for every subjective act communicates some form of self-valuation. We feel compelled to speak authentically even if we remain silent, even if we are self-conscious or ambivalent, thinking that such authenticity may negate the authenticity of the other. Even when we are afraid of confrontation or that the other will retaliate, we still pass our silent judgments.

Our superego visits us in both passivity and activity, that is, whether we disclose our personal views to another or whether we keep them in abeyance, mindful of our conscientiousness despite the fact that our silent mindfulness may betray our genuine moral principles. In either case, we are under the sway of internal judgments that guide our actions, which, in turn, lay down "definitive standards for [our] conduct" (SE 22:78). In this way, ethics obeys a logic of the interior based on emotional resonance states and affective truths that reverberate within our souls based on our primordial identifications with the parental agency or its surrogate, including all related derivatives.[8] Morality no longer remains an external presence: it becomes an internal presence based on internalized negation and absence, that is, the dialectic of prohibition and lack as desire for the ideal.[9] Ideality always remains something personal and private, sacred and secret, yet capable of transcending personal subjectivity within a collectively shared identification. But even when ideality is collectively united, it is never devoid of personal ownership or what we commonly refer to as "mine," for this is the affective invigoration that defines our unconscious soul, what Hegel refers to as the "law of the heart."

Ethics is not merely a set of prescribed precepts that inform a procedural code of conduct: it is an internalized law, both sacrosanct and taboo. Ethics is inner experience – the reverberation of inner truth – even if that truth is transient, dubious, dissolute. When we are attuned to our interior, we seek to express it outwardly in order to make it more real, to validate its presence, to vitalize our immediate self-certainty. But this does not come without consequences, especially when our ethical self-certainty is in response to others' who draw the truth of our inner experience into question: otherness vitiates personal subjectivity simply by being in a relationship of opposition. When our moral agency is challenged or feels threatened, we feel compelled to assert our interior as a matter of principle regardless of the cost, perhaps later justifying this as a heroic stand championing our ego ideal. Indeed, this compulsion may take the form of a defensive impulse to fulfil our wish to become our ideal ego through the act of self-assertion via negation of the other; hence, our ego ideal is validated and our ideal ego is advanced in the instance of self-posit. It is here that our identification with ideality breaches the ego's other sensibilities and the superego supersedes. This may lead to a clash of competing dialectics, subjects with different subjectivities, domestic and international; but, what I have in mind here is the universal propensity to consult one's own ideal interiority and to undertake a moral discourse with self and world. This is the domain of virtue theory, namely, what is good, what is right, what is best, what makes for desirable character, what the Greeks call human excellence.

Heidegger observes a basic triadic process that the human being has with the world, self, and others by virtue of its ontological facticity. This trinity is defined by an inseparable ontic web of interrelatedness the subject has with itself within social existence. We are thrown into a body and a world, in a particular place and in a particular time, without choice or consultation. This is our historicity, our fate, but not necessarily our destiny. We come to find that we inhabit and share with other people (our family, community) an embodied spacing that is disclosed and unconcealed to us as we developmentally mature as autonomous selves or subjects. Such individuation, however, is marked by the equiprimordiality of simultaneously being *in* an environment (*Umwelt*) and *with* others (*Mitwelt*) but, most important, with-oneself (*Eigenwelt*) as an authentic ethical self-relation the individual must struggle to self-actualize. For Heidegger, that authentic centre of self-relation is *care* disclosed through the call of conscience. In authentic self-relation, one is obliged to care for others just as the master came to recognize that the slave is a person like himself, with needs, feelings, aspirations, and anguish, a human being that deserves to be free. The call of conscience spawns empathy, compassion, and justice, which fortifies the social bond. The summons of care arguably makes the world lovable.

The crusade for wholeness necessarily adopts the ethical in the ego's integrative activity through the value of self-insight and virtuous action. In this way process psychology aspires towards eudaimonism, namely, ideality – what the ancients call the good life – contemplative, content, just. Notice that I say "aspire," for an ideal may never be fully achieved, only approached. And this always entails the endeavour to lead an ethical life, albeit imperfectly. For the enlightened soul, according to Plato, is the unification of the passions, reason, and morality actualized through leading a good life. However, as Freud reminds us, this necessarily produces a certain degree of *pathos*. For the Greeks, to be human is to suffer. From this standpoint, the pursuit of ideality becomes an infinite, poignant striving incessantly fraught with conflict.

Like the Platonists and the Idealists, I am of the opinion that we can approximate an ideal but that we can never attain it because ideality is an embodied (abstract) perfection, which I believe cannot be fully achieved. When we admire or strive for an ideal, it is because we identify with and covet it, and this is, a fortiori, because we lack it. Hence, absence is an important attribute because, with qualifications, we would not desire an ideal if we were already in possession of it; and even if we were, we would continue to desire it in order for it to be maintained. When I speak of ideality, I am generally referring to the greatest valued principles, such as wisdom, truth, justice, beauty, and other virtues. We can approximate these things, but, like others before me, I believe that we always fall short of attaining them in their most pristine forms because ideals are ultimately abstract formal concepts that can be known (in principle) as noncorporeal intelligibles but that cannot be tangibly procured. Yet, through particular concrete actions, we can nonetheless win some form of satisfaction or fulfilment in our pursuit of the ideal.

There is a certain ecstasy that comes from intellectual work, but perhaps this is more emotionally accentuated when we feel we have broached the ethical. When we embrace psychic holism as a moral enterprise, we must mollify the tension between the real and the ideal through some form of unitive conciliatory stance, which we often refer to as genuineness or authenticity. This is especially applicable when we feel compelled to live up to a professed self-ideal as a way of being. Of course, this way of being is always a process of becoming that is at once intimately distinctive and e/valuative by virtue of adopting an ongoing attitude of determinate reflective inquiry.[10] Put another way, mind continuously analyzes itself just as psychoanalysis continuously analyzes mind. Indeed, the analyst bequeaths value in every therapeutic moment as surely as he or she draws into question the legitimacy of the patient's valuation through the act of analysis itself. Here, like the dialectic, analytic engagement is a bid for creativity, freedom, and expressed individuality through volitional self-assertion and repose. It is in this spacing that we must surrender ourselves to faith and trust the process. In effect, through the analytic encounter, we are communicating to the other: "This is who I am, what I stand for, what you are obliged to recognize in me ... and I in you." Two subjects, two subjectivities – interfacing, clashing, championing, and reclaiming the covenant of similarity and difference – the evocative dance of discerning and defining value. In this sense, psychoanalysis is not only a moral venture but also an aesthetic gift to humanity. For what could be more beautiful than value?

ACKNOWLEDGMENTS

This book has been published with the help of a grant from the Canadian Federation for the Humanities and Social Sciences. I am deeply grateful for their generous support.

Throughout this work, I have produced, with permission, revised portions from various articles that have appeared in previous forms: "Dialectical Psychoanalysis: Toward Process Psychology," *Psychoanalysis and Contemporary Thought* 23, 3 (2000): 20–54; "Hegel on Projective Identification: Implications for Klein, Bion, and Beyond," *Psychoanalytic Review* 87, 6 (2000): 841–74; "Deciphering the 'Genesis Problem': On the Dialectical Origins of Psychic Reality," *The Psychoanalytic Review* 89, 6 (2002): 763–809; "Clarifications on *Trieb*: Freud's Theory of Motivation Reinstated," *Psychoanalytic Psychology* 21, 4 (2004): 673–7; "Process Psychology," in *Relational and Intersubjective Perspectives in Psychoanalysis: A Critique*, ed. J. Mills, 279–308 (Northvale, NJ: Aronson/Rowman and Littlefield, 2005); and "Reflections on the Death Drive," *Psychoanalytic Psychology* 23, 2 (2006): 373–82. I wish to thank the publishers for their courtesy.

I am truly fortunate to have three close friends who are scholars and practising psychoanalysts. Each has given me various degrees of inspiration and has influenced my intellectual development in numerous ways. In both informal conversation and in the formal evaluation of parts of my manuscript prior to submission for publication, Keith Haartman was an invaluable help in stimulating me to polish some key ideas. He has a gift of offering criticism that is advisory, corrective, and sensible. I am immensely thankful. I also wish to thank Stewart Sadowsky, whose expertise in phenomenological psychology has reinvigorated my appreciation of the lived body. I am very appreciative of the fact that he introduced me to many influential papers on the interface between psychoanalysis and philosophy written by the Belgium psychoanalyst Antoine Vergote (whom he has translated into English). I am equally grateful for many splendid hours of conversation with Gerald Gargiulo, who, despite our theoretical differences, is always a spirited source of creativity.

I am particularly indebted to my close personal friend, philosopher Janusz Polanowski, who, as a spiritual brother, is the moral exemplar of what I consider to be a decent human being. I have learned more about the meaning and nature of reality and the purpose of living through our relationship than any formal text in the history of philosophy could possibly provide. Finally, I wish to thank my existential friend and spiritual sister, Janneke van Linden, who reminds me that the sojourn of the authentic mystic is nothing other than the rational origin of an ever-deepening transcendence as our being unto death.

NOTES

INTRODUCTION

1 Jessica Benjamin (1988, 1992) is the only other applied Hegelian within psychoanalytic theory of whom I am aware; however, her work has exclusively focused on the *Phenomenology of Spirit*, and especially Hegel's treatment of intersubjectivity within the master-slave dialectic. My work centres on Hegel's mature system as outlined in his *Science of Logic* and the *Encyclopaedia of the Philosophical Sciences*, Vol. 3, *Philosophy of Spirit*. It should be noted that Benjamin's academic training was in sociology and not philosophy. Her account of Hegel's work is in fact very skewed and narrow in its application. She has been criticized, albeit respectfully, by Elliot Jurist, who, as a philosopher and psychologist, has pointed out that she misinterprets and misrepresents Hegel's project in the *Phenomenology*. In particular, she overemphasizes Hegel's notion of being-for-self as a desire for omnipotence at the expense of undermining the importance of being-for-another, when both are of reciprocal importance in Hegel's notion of the coming into being of self-consciousness (see Jurist 2000, 204–6). I should caution the reader not to equate our projects.

2 For those unfamiliar with the taxonomy of philosophy, it becomes important at this point to define what we mean by ontology, epistemology, and phenomenology in order to bring psychoanalytic thought within the context of philosophical discourse. Because these terms are tailored to signify particular meanings ascribed by a number of different philosophical traditions, systems, and individual philosophers, only a general understanding is needed to serve our purposes here.

"Ontology" is traditionally a branch of metaphysics dealing with "first principles," or the ground, scope, breadth, and limits to claims about absolute or ultimate propositions concerning the nature and structure of reality. "Metaphysics" is the name given to those of Aristotle's works that followed his book on physics, but it has generally taken on an all encompassing definition as well as having highly specified meaning for various philosophers. "Ontology" is more specifically concerned with the question, meaning, and essence of Being. While metaphysics is broadly concerned with the nature of the real, God, the universe and cosmology, causality, freedom and determinism, and the self – just to name a few, metaphysical claims are ultimately ontological statements about how things are, hence, about being qua being. In many ways, ontological arguments purport to explain the underlying conditions and fundamental assumptions of being and reality and, more specifically, human existence. Because psychoanalysis is arguably a general psychological theory of human motivation, cognition, and behaviour, it takes the human mind and all its manifestations as its general object of study, which, by definition, is an ontological endeavour.

"Epistemology" is concerned with the nature of knowledge and justification, which intimately engages the questions, criteria, and meaning of belief, truth, scepticism, and certainty. It is specifically concerned with the defining features, kinds, sources, conditions, and limits to knowledge and justification. Epistemological justification remains deeply entrenched in analysis and controversy over how we come to form judgments and defend them, our rationale, the probability and credibility of our conclusions, and the substantive validity about what we know and what eludes us. All disciplines, including psychoanalysis, must defend their fundamental epistemological assumptions about knowledge and reality as we can never escape the vexing question: How do you know?

Unlike the ancients' focus on being, "phenomenology" is a relatively modern philosophical concept now identified as a systematically developed movement within twentieth-century Continental philosophy, yet with no clear body of consensus among its diverse proponents. Generally, we may view phenomenology as the realm of appearance, disclosure, or that which shines forth or comes to presence. As such, it typically consists of a description and analysis of consciousness, but it may also be described as a methodological conception attributed to the study of essences, transcendental subjectivity, concrete existence, and/or a style of thinking and engaging the world. In this way, phenomenology deals with the realm of lived experience and our modes of awareness. As such, phenomenology privileges conscious subjectivity and experiential immediacy.

3 The perspicacious reader will discern that I have an affinity for Whitehead's system and that his philosophy has indelibly penetrated my thinking. I occasionally borrow some terms from Whitehead for their descriptive value, but this is not to imply the wholesale adoption of his metaphysical system within our process psychology.

4 The ontic, that which concerns beings (*Seiende*), and the ontological, that which concerns ways of being, are differentiated by virtue of their apophantical and hermeneutical referents. When I use the term "ontic," I am specifically referring to modes of relata and, in particular, to the microdynamics and nuances in which relational processes transpire.

5 Schelling's *System* offers an ontological account of mind that places the unconscious squarely within the centre of psychic life. Arguably offering the first coherent and systematic theory of the unconscious, he envisions mind as gen

erated from an unconscious will that conceives and produces. He tells us that mind "begins as unconscious and ends as conscious" where "unconscious activity operates ... through the conscious" (STI, 219). Nowhere do we encounter the ubiquity of the unconscious until von Hartmann and Freud.

Fichte declares that the *I* is entirely the result of its own activity – without prior ground. Hence, the activity of its self-positing is "unconditioned," that which is "*absolutely posited*, and *founded on itself*, [which] is the ground of *one particular* activity ... of the human mind, and thus of its pure character; the pure character of activity as such" (*W* § 1: I, 96).

7   *Pulsion* is the French word Vergote uses for *Trieb*, which grounds both the biological body-driven and vital processes of the human being with desirous need. In his translation of "The 'Death Drive': When Pulsional Desire Turns Deadly," Stewart Sadowsky defines the composite term "pulsional desire" (*desir pulsionnel*), the corollary to Freud's *Triebwunsch*, as "a structural unity that integrates a quasi-natural necessity with an open finality" (2009, 1n1). Although Lacan may be attributed to popularizing "the bastard term '*pulsion*'" (*E*, 300), it is Vergote who routinely and most originally uses this term in his writings. For an extended elaboration of this concept, see "Besoin, pulsion et inconscient originaire," in Vergote (1997, 79–89).

8   Here I am referring to the concept of teleonomy introduced by Monod and taken up by Vergote as a process of finality that lawfully organizes and regulates unconscious action devoid of intentionality. See Vergote (1998, 67–100).

9   This term was introduced by Whitehead (1925, 51, 58) in *Science and the Modern World*.

10 When I use the term "phantasy," I am specifically referring to psychic activity that is governed by unconscious processes; when I use the term "fantasy," I am denoting pre-conscious and conscious processes that are mediated by imagination.

PROLEGOMENA

1   Some readers may be concerned about my essentialism. For me, this is not a concern but, rather, an important element in providing a universal theory of mind. For me, following Hegel, essence is process, and this is never fixed or static but, instead, dialectically evolving and cultivating various architectonic forms. Hence, I am not a substance ontologist for whom things are uncompromisingly predetermined and unalterable – a position that we may attribute to the medievals, among others. However, I could loosely be viewed as adhering to Aristotle's notion that what makes something essential is necessary in order for it to exist. This is how I view the dialectic. Although there is a plurality of human expressions and personality organizations that populate the human species – what we may generally refer to as "human natures" (meaning, there is not just one human nature) – essence should be viewed within this context as

the dialectical universality that necessarily ties them together and that, furthermore, is the foundation from which plurality and variation derive in the first place.

2 See Freud's discussion, *SE* 19:24; 20:97; 22:75–6.
3 Hegel's conception of *Geist* is often interpreted to be a supraordinate spiritual force that animates nature and human experience unified by a cosmic process governed by universal logical operations of pure thought usually attributed to God. When I speak of spirit, I am referring to the individual and collective mind that is enacted through human subjectivity and that is both consciously and unconsciously informed, thereby generating the social structures we have come to call culture and civilization. Here spirit or mind should not be confused with a hypostatized entity, panpsychism, or a supernatural animating presence, which is neither necessary nor particularly desirable for psychoanalytic inquiry. In order to obviate potential confusion, here spirit, mind, and psyche should be viewed as synonymous constructs.
4 In his *Wissenschaftslehre* (*W* §§ 1–3), Fichte (1794) discerns these three fundamental principles or transcendental acts of the mind.
5 See Immanuel Kant (1781/1787), *Critique of Pure Reason*, second division: *Transcendental Dialectic*, bk. II, chaps. I–II. Kant is particularly interested in exposing logical inconsistencies and contradictions as paralogisms and antinomies of human reason, which are "wrongfully regarded as a science of pure reason" (*CPR*, A345/B403).
6 Donald Carveth (1994) is only one of many analysts who describe Hegel's dialectic as a process of thesis-antithesis-synthesis. Yet this is an endemic mistake that is even made by psychoanalysts who are academic philosophers. Most recently, Charles Hanly (2004, 284) makes this error when he declares: "According to Hegel ... an initial state generates its opposite. This opposing second state stands in contradiction to the first. The conflict produces a resolution in a higher synthesis that overcomes the contradiction." Here Hanly has immensely simplified the Hegelian dialectic by completely omitting how the process of opposition is generated in the first place, let alone explaining how "conflict" can resolve anything (not to mention how a synthesis is brought about).
7 For our purposes, we may view the striving for self-consciousness as a process of self-actualization that an individual or collective group can never fully achieve, only approximate through laborious dialectical progression. The striving for the fulfilment of an ideal can never completely be attained in actuality (although perhaps it can in theory) because this would mean that the human spirit would no longer need to surpass itself: the dialectic would be complete and thus would no longer desire and, hence, no longer create. We are always oriented towards higher modes of self-fulfilment, whether in action or fantasy. It is the striving, however, that forms a necessary aspect of any transcendental orientation or philosophy of living, and, like the pursuit of wisdom and contentment, it is a process of becoming.

- Cf. Petry (1978, 3:405nn).
- Compare to Freud (1923): "The ego is first and foremost a bodily ego" (SE 19:26).
- John Burbidge (1981, 7–21) provides a nice overview of this process.
- Freud (1895) is often misunderstood to be a reductive materialist, relying on his unofficial and immature views espoused in the *Project for a Scientific Psychology* (SE 1:295). Freud realized that he could never offer an adequate theory of mind solely from a neurophysiological account and, by 1900, had officially abandoned his earlier materialistic visions for a psychological corpus (See SE 4–5:536).

2 In the *Phenomenology*, Hegel tells us: "As Subject ... the True ... is the process of its own becoming, the circle that presupposes its end as its goal, having its end also as its beginning; and only by being worked out to its end, is it actual" (PS § 18). Later, he says, "The realized purpose, or the existent actuality, is movement and unfolded becoming ...; the self is like that immediacy and simplicity of the beginning because it is the result, that which has returned into itself" (PS § 22). In the *Science of Logic*, Hegel further extends the development of the Self to that of the Concept: "The Concept, when it has developed into a *concrete existence* that is itself free, is none other than the *I* or pure self-consciousness" (SL 583). Moreover, in the *Encyclopaedia Logic*, for Hegel, the Self and the Concept are pure becoming: "The Idea is essentially *process*" (EL § 215).

3 Some Hegel scholars would contest this claim (e.g., Harris 1993b); however, objective spirit is a higher stage than subjective spirit and thus would by definition sublate the individual to society, hence giving priority to the collective. Because collective *Geist* is an advanced stage in the development of the human race, it is presumed that all traces of psychopathology are dissolved in the cultivated modes of aesthetics, ethics, religion, and pure reason. From this perspective, there is no proper place for the irrational.

4 We seek wholeness in our thoughts and actions. Some are inclined to actively seek out transcending, spiritual, mystical, and/or deliberate integrative or unitive activities in order to elevate their human consciousness, as evinced by the myriad social practices and customs that span many diverse cultural anthropologies. And even in individuals who do not intentionally seek holism and transcendental actions, and who perhaps even dismiss them as pure myth, there still persists the *wish* for peace and contentment. For example, I once had a patient who was a vociferous atheist, having renounced every belief and every illusion, yet he could still concede that he harboured the wish for a heaven.

5 Psychoanalysis generally shies away from ontological commitments concerning freedom and, in some cases, displaces the notion altogether. Dialectical freedom points towards the power of determinate choice in the context of one's presentational immediacy by confronting contingencies, at once influenced by the archaic past and certain object relations within the environmental, political-cultural, and linguistic forces that form our social ontology. There are degrees of contextual freedom in the moment, in the nature of agency and choice, not as predetermined design but, rather, as determined by subjective forces that

are themselves teleologically driven. This ensures that not only does conscious agency influence contextual freedom but also that unconscious processes partially inform such conscious choices. What we may call *psychic determinism* (Brenner 1955) does not hold that conscious choices are already decided for us by an impersonal unconscious but, rather, that unconscious processes are teleologically constituted forms of liberty. In fact, unconscious teleology conditions – hence makes possible – conscious determinate choice. Therefore, unconscious teleology becomes the logical model for self-generative conscious freedom.

CHAPTER ONE

1. See *Timaeus*, 49a–b; 50d (Plato 1961d).
2. The following numerals indicate the logical importance and emphasis of the propositions under question. Decimals and their sequential ordering signify my commentary on such stated propositions.
3. Here I wish to appropriate Whitehead's term "actual occasions" to denote the fact that psychic events are indeed actual, hence real.
4. Notice I say "direct impositions." It is established that many indirect forces influence foetal development, including the crude introduction of sense data such as the physical invaginated sensation of being enveloped or confined in the womb and sound waves introduced in utero by the prenatal and perinatal environment, particularly through the mother's body. Foetal experience is further affected by the mother's emotional well-being, stress, and mental status as well as by teratogens of various forms. Upon the breach to birth, the perinatal milieu may prove to be the inauguration of consciousness proper.
5. Here Freud abandons his earlier commitment to psycho-physical parallelism endorsed in his 1891 monograph on aphasia. See translator's comments (*SE* 14:168n1, and Appendix B, 206–8).
6. Recall that "phantasy" is used to connote the unarticulated aspect of unconscious process, whereas "fantasy" is subject to the imagination, pre-conscious experience, and conscious self-reflection.
7. We encounter this routinely in the clinical situation when there is a disruption in the patient's free associations or when the patient suddenly develops a lapse in memory or experiences thought-blocking, which is revealed in the phrase: "I forgot what I was going to say."
8. See Lacan (1957).

CHAPTER TWO

1. The noun *Ich* stands in philosophic relation to German Idealism, particularly Fichte's (1993 [1794]) absolute self-positing self: *"The self exists for itself* [and] *begins by an absolute positing of its own existence"* (*W* § 1: I, 98, emphasis in original). Today it is almost exclusively a Freudian term.

Here unconscious phantasy appears to be operative as an unarticulated form of agentic enactment under the *telos* of negotiating some compromise in intrapsychic conflict.

For Freud (1940), the ultimate aim of Eros is to integrate differentiations of mind under the rubric of a synthetic unity, or, in his words, "to establish ever greater unities and to preserve them, thus – in short, to bind together" (*SE* 23:148–9). Notice here that Freud stresses the preservative aspect of unification.

In contrast to perspectivalism, which opposes absolute claims, I wish to argue for a psychoanalytic metaphysics that highlights the phenomenology of subjective experience and, at the same time, shows how subjectivity is ontologically conditioned on absolute, universal principles that inform the dialectic. This position, which I have called *processential realism* (Mills 2005b), underscores the notion that process dialectically conditions psychic reality, thus accounting for both first-person subjective experience and, at the same time, appreciating the universal ontological features of mind that provide the a priori structures necessary for subjectivity to emerge in the first place. Therefore, processential realism highlights the contexts and contingencies within the phenomenal lived encounter as distinct moments of the dialectic of becoming while acknowledging the whole process and dynamic teleological trajectory of pattern under consideration. This attempts to mitigate the subject-object polarity; yet, such distinctions become important, depending upon whether we wish to focus on ontological or phenomenological concerns. In this sense, the ontology of the dialectic makes the phenomenology of human experience possible – experience that, by its very nature, is highly contextualized and recalcitrant to reductive strategies. Although the dialectic is a generic process common to all human beings regardless of demographic or historical contingencies, the contextuality of lived experience gives rise to radical nominalistic expressions. It is in this way that subjectivity is grounded, emergent, and transforming experiential activity generated by the logical objectivity of the dialectic.

What becomes essential for processential realism is the appreciation of context and contingency within the dialectical unfolding of truth and reality in the overall process of becoming. And it is precisely in examining the subjective universality of the ontology of the dialectic that particular subjective experience is given phenomenal value. In other words, the subjective universality of the dialectic is the common patterning of human consciousness that informs our collective shared humanity, within which a world of infinitely distinct and value-laden experiences belonging to individual subjectivities contextually flourish as vibrant creative thrusts of personal expression. In this way, the individual and the community, particularity and contingency, are accounted for within universality, and each is ontologically united in the whole process of its burgeoning development.

5 Scepticism, like relativism, has been historically used to challenge realist claims to truth or to dispute universals, contending that we can never know what is

real, which is itself an absolute proposition. Yet, when you look at the sceptics' lifestyles (e.g., Pyro or Sextus Empiricus or Hume), they still ate, spoke, indulged their desires, and engaged in social customs. Their behaviour spoke differently than did their claim to radical doubt. Any concrete involvement and participation in a communal structure commits one to a realist position. Even though they claim they are creatures of habit, or they cannot help but respond to the demands of their body's needs for sustenance, or the contingencies of social interaction indigenous to custom, they still operated *as if* there *were* something real: even if such reality were appearance, it nevertheless was real by virtue of the fact that it appeared.

6 This position is in stark contrast to antisubjectivist perspectives popular among many forms of poststructuralism, postmodernism, and linguistic analytic philosophy (e.g., Cavell 1993). These approaches insist that the human subject is subverted by language, which structures and orders all experience. This position, like materialism, is essentially reductive. I am in agreement with Roger Frie (1997) that, while language is a necessary condition of human subjectivity, it is far from being a sufficient condition for capturing all aspects of lived experience. Sole linguistic accounts do not adequately explain how preverbal, extralinguistic, nonverbal, somatic, and unformulated unconscious affective experiences resonate within our intrapsychic lives. Furthermore, they assume a developmental reversal; namely, that language precedes thought and cognition rather than acknowledging bodily and preverbal forces, unconscious organizing principles, and unarticulated emotive processes that developmentally give rise to linguistic acquisition and expression. In effect, the linguistic claim boasts that meaning does not reside in the mind but, rather, in language itself. I find this position completely untenable: as mentioned earlier, *words don't think, only subjective agents do*. Despite the historicity of language within one's existing social ontology, the way language is acquired is potentially idiosyncratic and developmentally different for each child. Furthermore, words may be imbued with functional meaning that resists universal symbols and signifiers, hence ensuring the privatization of internally mediated signification.

7 Here, psychic reality is not to be solely equated with internal reality.

8 Recall that this is the term preferred by Antoine Vergote to emphasize the pulsations of urges emanating from the lived body.

9 To be fair to my relational colleagues, there have been some recent attempts to amend earlier views that the body is of less importance than human relatedness (see Aron and Anderson's [1998] *Relational Perspectives of the Body*). However, regardless of some relational authors' views on embodiment, the books that launched the relational movement – namely, Greenberg and Mitchell's (1983) *Object Relations in Psychoanalytic Theory*, Mitchell's (1988) *Relational Concepts in Psychoanalysis*, and Greenberg's (1991) *Oedipus and Beyond* – all position a relational theory by abnegating drive (hence embodiment). Consequently, I maintain that my critique of their work is still legitimate (see Mills 2005a).

We must acknowledge the multiple motivations and overdetermined processes operative within the drives, including economic and regulatory teleonomic functions as well as adaptation and defence under the influence of evolutionary currents. Objects are not only coveted for pleasure but also for the function and purpose they serve. And derived modes of relatedness, such as emotional connection and love, are based on early bonds and identifications with attachments figures.

In this relational age, the death drive appears to be a drowning man. Even many classical analysts have difficulty accepting this central postulate in Freud's theoretical corpus. From my account, these attitudes appear to be either based on unfamiliarity with what Freud actually said in his texts, are based on theoretical incompatibilities, or are the result of reactionary defences. It is incumbent on any critic to know exactly what he or she is criticizing, and that means delving into the nuances of what Freud truly had to say, not to mention what he implied or the logical inferences that may be deduced from it. Freud's seminal work on the primacy of death particularly highlights his ability to think as a philosophical scientist using the discipline of logical rigour wed to clinical observation. Recall that Freud had aspirations to become a philosopher before deciding on medicine, was tutored by Franz Brentano at university, and said to Fliess: "Through the detour of being a physician ... I most secretly nourish the hope of reaching my original goal, philosophy" (See Letter to Fliess, 1 January 1896 [Freud 1896b, 159]). Regardless of what opinion contemporary psychoanalysts have of Freud's conception of the death drive, for historical, clinical, and philosophical reasons it is worthwhile to engage Freud's thoughts on the matter. Here I am mainly interested in offering an exegetical reflection on Freud's introduction of the destructive principle to psychoanalytic theory; therefore, I do not address all the controversy, dissension, and detractors who have debunked his contributions largely on evolutionary grounds. If psychoanalysis is destined to prosper and advance, it must be open to revisiting the controversial ideas that gave it radical prominence to begin with.

2 Derived from Plautus, *Asinaria* II, iv, 88; see Freud (1930, 111).

3 The impetus, loci, and movement behind the force of the negative is the basis of Hegel's entire logic of the dialectic. Recall that this is exemplified in his treatise on the evolution of cognition, self-consciousness, and the ethical development of the human race in the *Phenomenology of Spirit* (Hegel 1807) and that it is ontologically grounded in his formal system, which is introduced in the *Science of Logic* (Hegel 1812).

4 I realize that many readers are not sympathetic to the death drive, but it is essential for understanding the interiorization of death as a metaphysical principle of negation and conflict that saturates the global universal structures of the dialectic. To dismiss death qua negation as an ontological structure would be to reject the dialectic, something I cannot theoretically justify. Here my views on death and desire are not a pure endorsement of Freud but, rather, a revisionist

perspective on the death drive within the context of the processential nature of the dialectic. Unlike other contemporary Freudians, who privilege libido or explain aggression within the context of desire and trauma, I argue that life and death, being and nothing, are ontologically the same.

15 Recall that Freud had lived through the savagery of the First World War, lost his daughter Sophie to influenza the same year he published *Beyond the Pleasure Principle*, and was in the early stages of cancer of the palate, which was formally diagnosed three years later, the same year he formally classified his dual drive theory.

16 It should be noted that, when describing mental functions, the language of energetics, homeostasis, and hydrolics has been replaced in contemporary discourse by equivalent metaphors that stress activity, experience, process, and action. Even physicists use the language of quantum mechanics, but they stress non-material reduction, highlight the energetic stratification of material interactions via systemic and holistic paradigms, and use the poetics of determinate possibilities when describing the emerging processes of cosmology.

17 It should be observed that Freud's original theory of neurosis is based on defensive, albeit adaptive, reactions to trauma. Here, in his mature theory, he cannot escape the resonance of his earlier position by privileging the role of traumatic interference on psychic organization introduced by the forces of external reality. In fact, the death drive is constituted in the immediacy of trauma, itself a defence against annihilation. Here Freud may be begging the question as to whether death is constitutive or reactionary, but it is nevertheless present in the genesis of the self-preservative drive towards life. Paradoxically, it is this defensive psychic order that is also inherently oriented towards destruction, whether this be internally or externally manifested. Proponents of an extrinsic trauma model may have no need to posit the primacy of a death drive when external intrusions give an adequate explanation. Freud, however, felt the theoretical need to explain the internal processes operative within unconscious mentation before incurring external trauma. Therefore, in my opinion, he attempts to logically prepare the psyche's response to trauma by accounting for a priori forces that govern the mind's primordial activity. Here Freud not only interiorizes death qua trauma but also privileges its sequence as an exogenous intrusive act that simultaneously arouses and institutes the psyche's aim towards self-destruction, albeit in routes it chooses through its own determinate teleology.

18 An Aristotelian interpretation can be supported by assigning death a final cause inherent in drive.

19 It is interesting to note that Whitehead's (1929) entire cosmology of process explains how each "actual entity" that comprises the universe is oriented towards seizing upon its inherent freedom to actualize its potential possibilities and actions, which are ultimately destined towards "perishing" into the next events that constitute an ongoing process. Hence, the *telos* of all living entities, or "occasions," is death. This is compatible with the beliefs of many contemporary theoretical physicists who postulate an inherent entropy to the cosmos.

Here we must stipulate that, while early life predisposes one to neurosis, it does not predetermine a hard and fast developmental sequence: personal maturation is radically moulded by context and contingency. Like Freud's concept of drive, which is mobile and transmutational, the notion of psychic adaptation requires a certain margin of freedom.

In evolutionary biology, as in history and in nature, sex and aggression are necessary conditions for organismic survival and self-preservation. Insofar as species could not continue without natural copulation, aggression be harnessed in order to ensure survival. In fact, the whole historical narrative of the human race may be viewed as a "slaughterbench" (Hegel 1833; RH 27) in order to advance human civilization, which still requires aggression to enforce law and order (Freud 1930).

This is primarily represented in his *New Introductory Lectures in Psycho-Analysis* (1932–33).

See my extensive critique of the relational school (Mills 2005a).

In Freud's *Gesammelte Werke*, vol. 14, the actual German words for the Latin "ego" and "id" are I (*Ich*) and It (*Es*), respectively (see GW 14:124).

From the standpoint of Whiteheadian process philosophy, an analysis of origin would indeed be interested in exploring the most fundamental building blocks of cosmic process, which would examine the material teleology of the natural world (in this instance, the psychophysical inception of biological life).

Here I use the term "apperception" to denote the pure experiential self-sense belonging to precognitive, pre-reflective unconscious thought.

Many Idealist perspectives posit the existence of pre-reflective, prelinguistic, or non-propositional self-consciousness. Sartre does this, as do contemporaries such as Manfred Frank (1991) and Dieter Henrich (1966). Such theories derive not only from modern philosophy but also, and ultimately, from a tradition that dates back to neo-Platonism and theosophic-mystical accounts of the soul. In this tradition, the father of German Idealism, J.G. Fichte, asserted that the prelinguistic subject originally generates and constitutes its own being; that is, the self freely posits or asserts itself absolutely. In his *Wissenschaftslehre* (1794), Fichte states: "*The self begins by an absolute positing of its own existence*" (W 99, emphasis in original). For Fichte, what ultimately characterizes the ground of human subjectivity is pure "activity as such." Before there is consciousness proper, thought lives underground as an "intellectual intuition" of itself – that is, as pre-reflective, non-representational self-consciousness. This original pre-reflective self-consciousness is in fact *unconscious*. Such unconscious self-consciousness is the pre familiarity the self has with itself before achieving conscious self-reflective awareness.

In the Idealist tradition, F.W.J. von Schelling made the unconscious the sine qua non of psychic life. Schelling's revision of Kant's and Fichte's transcendental idealism, together with his own philosophy of identity (*Identitätsphilosophie*) and philosophy of nature (*Naturphilosophie*), led to one of the first systematic conceptualizations of the unconscious. For Schelling (1811–15, 150), "all consciousness has what is unconscious as ground, and, just in coming to be conscious, this unconscious is posited as past by that which becomes conscious of itself." Freud (1923) echoes this sentiment: "The repressed [past] is the prototype of the unconscious ... We can come to know even the *Ucs.* only by making it conscious" (*SE* 19:15, 17). Schelling, like Freud, was deeply engaged with the problem of Beginning – that is, original ground (*Grund*). Recall that Hegel referred to this primordial ground as a "nocturnal mine" (*Schact*), what earlier, in the *Phenomenology* (1807), he labelled the realm of "*unconscious* Spirit" (*PS* 278, emphasis in original).

In all modern philosophies of the will, an unconscious ground – an *Ungrund* – precedes consciousness. The primacy of the *Ungrund* was first made sensible by the seventeenth-century philosopher, mystic, and theosophist Jacob Boehme, to whom Fichte, Schelling, and Hegel owe much. The *Abyss* (*Abgrund*), or *Ungrund*, is the "ground without a ground," a subject who "seeks," "longs," "lusts," and "finds." This conceptualization of unconscious activity bears comparison to a standard neo-Platonic idea: Proclus, Erigenia, and Plotinus conceived of the *Ungrund* as the *ens manifestativum sui*, "the being whose essence is to reveal itself" (see Koyré 1968; Mills 1996; von der Luft 1994; Walsh 1994; Weeks 1991).

28 Here I am referring to Aristotle's first two elements of determinism, namely, material and efficient causation.

29 For both Sartre and Lacan, consciousness itself takes the form of lack. While Lacan (1977) refers to a "lack of being" (*manque-à-être*) throughout his *Écrits*, Sartre (1943/1956) is more specific, telling us that "human reality ... exists first as lack ... In its coming into existence, human reality grasps itself as an incomplete being" (*BN* 89). For Sartre, human subjectivity is desirously compelled to fill the lack through projection of a future transcendence, hence a "being-for-itself."

CHAPTER THREE

1 When Klein republished her 1946 paper "Notes on Some Schizoid Mechanisms" in *Developments in Psycho-Analysis*, she added the term "projective identification" as a way of explaining the process of splitting in connection with projection and introjection (Klein et al. 1952, 300).

2 More recently, this concept has been given special attention in its relation to countertransference and empathy (see Mills 2004; Cashdan 1988; Ogden 1982; Tansey and Burke 1989). Generally, we may say that, within the context of therapy, the patient projects onto the analyst certain disavowed and repudiated internal contents that the analyst unconsciously identifies with, such as the behavioural fantasies, attributions, or personal qualities that are the objects of splitting, which the analyst then introjects as a function of his or her own ego, thus leading to conflicted inner states that the analyst must manage. If the analyst's countertransference reactions are too strong and/or remain unrecog-

nized as the internalized projected attributions of the patient, he or she may potentially act out such negative states within the therapeutic encounter, thus potentially leading to further internal disruptions in both parties and negatively affecting the intersubjective field. Seeing how such a process is dialectically informed may auger well for further advancements in theory and intervention. Hegel offers a cursory description of thought disorder and insanity; however, a critical discussion of his contributions is beyond the scope of this immediate project. For a more detailed analysis of Hegel's theory of abnormal psychology, see Berthold-Bond (1995) and Mills (2002).

For Hegel, phantasy developmentally and temporally precedes language or linguistic acquisition. In his discussion in the *Encyclopaedia*, §§ 456–7, phantasy occurs before symbolization and signification and "derives from what is furnished by intuition." It is not until § 458 that he introduces language proper. This account displaces the postmodern view that human subjectivity is subsumed by linguistic forces that define one's cultural ontology.

In his seminal essay, "The Pit and the Pyramid: Introduction to Hegel's Semiology," Derrida (1982, 77) traces the path that "leads from this night pit, silent as death and resonating with all the powers of the voice which holds it in reserve, to a pyramid ... there composing the stature and status of the sign ... That the pyramid becomes once again the pit that it always will have been – such is the enigma."

CHAPTER FOUR

1 This is a child's toy, which, today, would be referred to as an "Etch-a-Sketch" or something similar.
2 What the reader may observe is how Freud's technical language in his "Mystic Pad" paper is wed to the biologics of his earlier homeostatic model of economics. But we can also see that, clearly, by this time he has introduced his structural or process theory of psychic agencies and that the topography of psychic spacings have been expanded and subsumed within the economic, dynamic, and adaptive aspects of mental functioning.
3 It can be argued that waves of theoretical compatibility potentially exist between process psychology and the promising new discourse on biosemiotics; however, I wish to emphasize the primacy of the unconscious, which appropriates and executes biological and semiotic processes without reducing informational processing systems and communications networks to reductive frameworks. In my opinion, the language of unconscious mediation more broadly encompasses biosemiotics within a process paradigm of dialectical organizations that may find their expression in the most minute structural level of organic life (e.g., intercellular signalling) as well as in the higher forms of signification and communication that properly belong to animal behaviour and human linguistic patterns.

4 Refer to my extensive theoretical commentary on dissociation and my clinical treatment of a case of ritualistic trauma discussed in chapter 10 of *Treating Attachment Pathology* (Mills 2005).

5 Although distinctions can be made between affect (as sentient, psychophysiological manifestations of mental events) and emotions (as more qualitatively organized threads of experiential feeling), for the sake of parsimony, here I refer to each synonymously. In psychoanalysis, affects are generally seen as complex psychophysiological phenomena encompassing cognitive, physical, and qualitative subjective, experiential elements. Moore and Fine (1990) distinguish between affects, emotions, and feelings, although we are accustomed to view each as an interchangeable construct. *Feelings* refer to subjective experiential states that may or may not be accessible to consciousness, while *emotions* are viewed as outwardly observable manifestations of feelings. *Affects*, on the other hand, are broad and enveloping, comprising all qualitative and quantitative instantiations, from the most primordial to the most cognitively differentiated complex psychic state under the direction of both conscious and unconscious forces. In contrast, *moods* may be viewed as prolonged and enduring affect states dominated by unconscious phantasy. It can be argued that emotionality is imbued with affect and that they are one and the same. Emotion is the implosional interiorization of affect. That is, affect is as implosive as it is expressive. Emotionality is merely a return – a slippage – to its rumbling beginnings, which are externally directed albeit internally experienced.

6 This is in contradistinction to what Freud privileged: namely, that judgment denotes the process of thinking based on concept formation, a claim Cavell (2003) recently upholds following from contemporary analytic philosophy.

7 There is a logical and developmental necessity to conceive of internal sensuous experience as derived from somatic sources that organically and constitutionally stimulate desire as being-in-relation-to lack and drive, as both libidinous (hence sensual) and destructive activity, hence as interiorized conflict and negation, which prefigures our sense experience belonging to conscious qualia.

CHAPTER FIVE

1 For an extended discussion on this topic, see Mills (2002a, 137–9).
2 In fact, Freud (1940) unequivocally informs us that the "mother's importance, [is] unique, without parallel, established unalterably for a whole lifetime as the first and strongest love-object and as the prototype of all later love-relations – for both sexes" (SE 23:188).
3 Freud gives a very lucid description of the ego in its relation to the It and superego in Lecture 31, "The Dissection of the Psychical Personality," in *New Introductory Lectures* (SE 22:57–80).

Slavoj Žižek (2006, 4) makes the proper locus of his philosophy the parallax gap, where there is a fundamental displacement of difference that poses an "irreducible obstacle to dialectics" based on a pure shift of perspective that can lead to no higher synthesis.

Loewald (1976) prefers the term "memorial activity" as a linking process.

In philosophy of mind, epiphenomenalism is associated with brain-mind dependence. Much of empirical science would contend that any brain state can be causally explained by appealing to other physical states or structural processes. Philosophers typically qualify this explanation by saying that physical states cause mental events but that mental states do not have causal efficacy over anything, a point William James first made when he coined the term "epiphenomena" to account for phenomena that lacked causal determinism.

There have been minimal attempts to account for freedom within neuroscience and biosemiotics. One notable exception is the highly original and promising work of François Ansermet and Pierre Magistretti (2007, 13n3), who claim that the "neuronal apparatus" is actually based upon a biology of freedom that allows for plasticity or modification in how it encodes experience: "The concept of plasticity means that experience can be inscribed in the neuronal network. An event experienced at a given time is marked at the moment and can persist over time. The event leaves a trace, and simultaneously, time is embodied ... [T]he fact of plasticity thus involves a subject who actively participates in the process of his or her becoming." This nicely fits into the view held by process psychology. In principle, one can "conceptualize a psychic causality capable of shaping the organic" (7). However, there still remains the question of agency. Ansermet and Magistretti repeatedly situate the locus of agency within the "mechanisms of plasticity" (47), which they reduce to neuronal processes. Thus, they inadvertently collapse agency into biological structures without properly accounting for the agent directing these agentic functions. Here they commit the merelogical attribution error of assigning agency to a part or subsystem of the brain rather than addressing the human subject as a complex systemic hole. If agency is reduced to neuronal (and, specifically, synaptic) plasticity rather than being co-extensive with and directing neural modification, then mind becomes an epiphenomenon with no real causal powers of its own.

8 Unlike Klein, who views the origins of the superego as sadistic expression, Freud views the superego (*ÜberIch*) as a developmental achievement based upon the complex divisions and modifications the ego undergoes through maturation, differentiations that originally emanate from the epigenetic transformations of the It (*Es*). The superego is therefore a superior psychic construction based on ethical identifications with otherness, hence it is truly an agency that stands over the I (*Ich*) and unconscious impulse. Although Freud's views on the superego went through many theoretical modifications, his insistence on its later development out of primitive mind was due to his conviction that the

superego was originally conceived as an identification with a set of value ideals internalized and appropriated from parental authority or its cultural signifier. Here Freud wants to preserve the importance of the psychic function of ideality within the moral register we have come to call conscience.

9. Recall that, in the logic of the dialectic, negation is an act of every movement of thought, and it enters into opposition with any object of which we conceive. This is because oppositions are conjoined and are mutually implicative in all aspects of thinking and being, including unconscious phantasy. At the moment a certain object in thought is negated, it is also preserved within a new state of consciousness, as it is simultaneously surpassed into a higher plane of synthesis. An internal moral stance derived from identification with and internalization of the Other is based on a dialectical relation that necessarily requires the negation of a particular experience (e.g., a value, attitude, etc.) that stands in opposition to its complementary relation, which is incorporated as an implicit yearning for what is absent and, hence, endowed as an idealized object. Therefore, moral presence within the psyche is conditioned on certain prohibitions as well as on coveted value judgments that stand in relation to pursuing an ideal, a doubling effect of the dialectic of desire.

10. I say "e/valuative" to signify the double nature of valuation as both judgmental and affirmative.

BIBLIOGRAPHY

PRIMARY TEXTS

(listed in alphabetical order)

German Texts

Freud, Sigmund. 1968 [1940–52]. *Gesammelte Werke, Chronologisch Geordnet*, 18 vols. Ed. Anna Freud, Edward Bibring, Willi Hoffer, Ernst Kris, and Otto Isakower, in collaboration with Marie Bonaparte. London/Frankfurt am Main: Imago Publishing Co. Ltd.

Hegel, G.W.F. 1961. *Briefe von und an Hegel*, 4 vols. Ed. Johannes Hoffmeister and Rolf Flechsig. Hamburg: Felix Meiner.
- 1940. *Einleitung in die Geschichte der Philosophie*. Ed. J. Hoffmeister. Hamburg: Felix Meiner.
- 1988. *Einleitung zur Phänomenologie des Geistes*. Commentary by A. Graeser. Stuttgart: Reclam.
- 1830/1969. *Enzyklopädie der philosophischen Wissenschaften im Grundrisse*. Heidelberg: C.F. Winter. Ed. F. Nicolin and O. Pöggeler, 3rd ed. Hamburg: Felix Meiner.
- 1928. *Erste Druckschriften*. Ed. Georg Lasson. Leipzig: Felix Meiner.
- 1968ff. *Gesammelte Werke*. Ed. Rheinisch-Westfaelischen Akademie der Wissenschaften. Hamburg: Felix Meiner.
- 1820. *Grundlinien der Philosophie des Rechts*. Berlin. Reprinted in *Gesammelte Werke*, Bd 7.
  1978 *Hegel's Philosophy of Subjective Spirit* [*Hegel's Philosophie des subjektiven Geistes*]. Vol. 1: *Introductions*; Vol. 2: *Anthropology*; Vol. 3: *Phenomenology and Psychology*. Ed. M.J. Petry. Dordrecht, Holland: D. Reidel Publishing Company.
- 1982. *Naturphilosophie*, Bd 1, Die Vorlesung von 1919/20. Ed. M. Gies. Naples: Bibliopolis.

- 1970–71. *Nürnberger Schriften, Werke*, Bd 4. Ed. E. Moldenhauer and K.M. Michel. Frankfurt-am-Main: Suhrkamp Verlag.
- 1980. *Phänomenologie des Geiste*. Ed. W. Bonsiepen and R. Heede. Reprinted in *Gesammelte Werke*, Bd 9. Hamburg: Felix Meiner Verlag.
- 1927–40. *Sämtliche Werke: Jubiläumsausgabe*. Ed. H. Glockner. Stittgart: Fromann.
- 1923. *Schriften zur Politik und Rechtsphilosophie*, 2nd ed. Ed. G. Lasson. Leipzig: Felix Meiner.
- 1807. *System der Wissenschaft: Erster Teil, die Phänomenologie des Geistes*. Bamberg and Würzburg: Goebhardt.
- 1907. *Theologische Jugendschriften*. Ed. Herman Nohl. Tübingen: Mohr (reprinted 1968).
- 1986–94. *Vorlesungen über die Geschichte der Philosophie*. Ed. P. Garniron and W. Jaeschke. Hamburg: Felix Meiner.
- 1940. *Vorlesungen über die Geschichte der Philosophie, Einleitung*. Ed. J. Hoffmeister. Leipzig: Felix Meiner.
- 1983–85. *Vorlesungen über die Philosophie der Religion*, 3 Bde. Ed. W. Jaeschke. Hamburg: Felix Meiner.
- 1832–45. *Werke: Völlstandige Ausgabe durch ein Verein von Freunden der Verweigten*. Berlin: Duncker and Humbolt.
- 1978/1981. *Wissenschaft der Logik*, Bde 1 and 2. *Gesammelte Werke*, Bde 11 and 12, hrsg. v. Friedrich Hogemann und Walter Jaeschke. Hamburg: Felix Meiner.

English Translations

Freud, Sigmund. 1966–95 [1886–1940]. *The Standard Edition of the Complete Psychological Works of Sigmund Freud*, 24 vols. Trans. and gen. ed. James Strachey, in collaboration with Anna Freud, assisted by Alix Strachey and Alan Tyson. London: Hogarth Press.
- 1888. "Hysteria." In Freud 1966–95, 1:39–59.
- 1888. "Hystero-Epilepsy." In Freud 1966–95, 1:41–59.
- 1893. "Some Points for a Comparative Study of Organic and Hysterical Motor Paralyses." In Freud 1966–95, 1:160–72.
- 1895. *Project for a Scientific Psychology*. In Freud 1966–95, vol. 1.
- 1893–95. *Studies on Hysteria* (with Josef Breuer). In Freud 1966–95, vol. 2.
- 1894. "The Neuro-Psychoses of Defence." In Freud 1966–95, 3:43–61.
- 1896a. "Further Remarks on the Neuro-Psychoses of Defense." In Freud 1966–95, 3:159–85.
- 1896b. *The Complete Letters of Sigmund Freud to Wilhelm Fliess, 1887–1904*. Trans. and ed. J.M. Masson. Cambridge, MA: Harvard University Press, 1985.
- 1898. "The Psychical Mechanism of Forgetfulness." In Freud 1966–95, 3:287–97.

BIBLIOGRAPHY

- 1900. *The Interpretation of Dreams.* In Freud 1966–95, vols. 4–5.
- 1901. *The Psychopathology of Everyday Life.* In Freud 1966–95, vol. 6.
- 1905a. *Three Essays on the Theory of Sexuality.* In Freud 1966–95, vol. 7.
- 1905b. "Psychical (or Mental) Treatment." In Freud 1966–95, 7:283–304.
- 1909. *Analysis of a Phobia in a Five-Year-Old Boy.* In Freud 1966–95, vol. 10.
- 1911. "Formulations on the Two Principles of Mental Functioning." In Freud 1966–95, 12:213–26.
- 1912. "The Dynamics of Transference." In Freud 1966–95, 12:97–108.
- 1914a. *On the History of the Psycho-Analytic Movement.* In Freud 1966–95, vol. 14.
- 1914b. "On Narcissism: An Introduction." In Freud 1966–95, 14:67–104.
- 1915a. "Instincts and Their Vicissitudes." In Freud 1966–95, 14:109–40.
- 1915b. "Repression." In Freud 1966–95, 14:141–58.
- 1915c. "The Unconscious." In Freud 1966–95, 14:159–216.
- 1917 [1915]. "Mourning and Melancholia." In Freud 1966–95, 14:237–60.
- 1916–17. *Introductory Lectures on Psycho-Analysis.* In Freud 1966–95, vols. 15–16.
- 1918 [1914]. *From the History of an Infantile Neurosis.* In Freud 1966–95, vol. 17.
- 1919. "The 'Uncanny.'" In Freud 1966–95, 17:217–52.
- 1920. *Beyond the Pleasure Principle.* In Freud 1966–95, vol. 18.
- 1921. *Group Psychology and the Analysis of the Ego.* In Freud 1966–95, vol. 18.
- 1923. *The Ego and the Id.* In Freud 1966–95, vol. 19.
- 1924a [1923]. "Neurosis and Psychosis." In Freud 1966–95, 19:149–56.
- 1924b. "The Loss of Reality in Neurosis and Psychosis." In Freud 1966–95, 19:183–90.
- 1924c. "A Short Account of Psychoanalysis." In Freud 1966–95, 19:191–212.
- 1924d. "The Economic Problem of Masochism." In Freud 1966–95, 19:155–70.
- 1925a. "A Note upon the 'Mystic Writing-Pad.'" In Freud 1966–95, 19:226–32.
- 1925b. "Negation." In Freud 1966–95, 19:234–9.
- 1925c [1924]. "The Resistances to Psycho-Analysis." In Freud 1966–95, 19:212–22.
- 1925d. "An Autobiographical Study." In Freud 1966–95, 20:1–74.
- 1926a. *Inhibitions, Symptoms and Anxiety.* In Freud 1966–95, vol. 20.
- 1926b. "The Question of Lay Analysis." In Freud 1966–95, 20:179–258.
- 1927a. "Fetishism." In Freud 1966–95, 21:149–58.
- 1927b. *Future of an Illusion.* In Freud 1966–95, vol. 21.
- 1930. *Civilization and Its Discontents.* In Freud 1966–95, vol. 21.
- 1933a [1932]. *New Introductory Lectures on Psycho-Analysis.* In Freud 1966–95, vol. 22.
- 1933b [1932]. "'Why War?' Freud's Letter to Einstein." In Freud 1966–95, 22:197–218.
- 1940 [1938]. "Splitting of the Ego in the Process of Defence." In Freud 1966–95, 23:271–8.

Hegel, G.W.F. 1975. *Aesthetics*, 2 vols. Trans. T.M. Knox. Oxford: Clarendon Press.
- 1981. *The Berlin Phenomenology*. Ed. and trans. M.J. Petry. Dordrecht, Holland: D. Reidel Publishing Co.
- 1977 [1801]. *Difference between Fichte's and Schelling's System of Philosophy*. Trans. H.S. Harris and W. Cerf. Albany, NY: SUNY Press.
- 1948. *Early Theological Writings*. Trans. T.M. Knox with intro. and fragments trans. Richard Kroner. Chicago: Chicago University Press. (Reprinted Philadelphia: Philadelphia University Press, 1971).
- 1991 [1817/1827/1830]. *The Encyclopaedia Logic*. Vol. 1 of *Encyclopaedia of the Philosophical Sciences*. Trans. T.F. Geraets, W.A. Suchting, and H.S. Harris. Indianapolis: Hackett Publishing
- 1977 [1802–03]. *Faith and Knowledge*. Trans. Walter Cerf and H.S. Harris. Albany, NY: SUNY Press.
- 1975. *Hegel's Logic*. Trans. W. Wallace. London: Oxford University Press.
- 1985 [1833]. *Introduction to the Lectures on the History of Philosophy*. Trans. T.M. Knox and A.V. Miller. Oxford: Clarendon Press.
- 1988. *Introduction to the Philosophy of History*. Trans. L. Rauch. Indianapolis: Hackett.
- 1993 [1886]. *Introductory Lectures on Aesthetics*. Trans. Bernard Bosanquet, ed. Michael Inwood. London: Penguin Books.
- 1971. Jakob Böhme, in *Werke*, vol. 20: *Vorlesungen über die Geschichte der Philosophie* 3. Frankfurt/M: Suhrkamp.
- 1986. *The Jena System, 1804–5, Logic and Metaphysics*. Trans. and ed. John W. Burbidge and George di Giovanni. Kingston & Montreal: McGill-Queen's University Press.
- 1955 [1892]. *Lectures on the History of Philosophy*, 3 vols. Trans. E.S. Haldane ad F.H. Simson. London: Routledge and Kegan Paul.
- 1990. *Lectures on the History of Philosophy: The Lectures of 1825–1826*, vol. 3. Ed. Robert F. Brown, trans. R.F. Brown, J.M. Stewart, and H.S. Harris. Berkeley: University of California Press.
- 1962 [1895]. *Lectures on the Philosophy of Religion*. Trans. E.B. Speirs and J.B. Sanderson. London: Routledge and Kegan Paul.
- 1984. *The Letters*. Trans. Clark Butler and Christiane Seiler. Bloomington: Indiana University Press.
- 1956 [1857]. *The Philosophy of History*. Trans. J. Sibree. New York: Dover.
- 1977 [1807]. *Phenomenology of Spirit*. Trans. A.V. Miller. Oxford: Oxford University Press.
- 1971 [1817/1827/1830]. *Encyclopaedia of the Philosophical Sciences*. Vol. 3: *Philosophy of Mind*. Trans. William Wallace and A.V. Miller. Oxford: Clarendon Press.
- 1970 [1817/1827/1830]. *Encyclopaedia of the Philosophical Sciences*. Vol. 2: *Philosophy of Nature*. Trans. A.V. Miller. Oxford: Clarendon Press.

- 1967 [1821]. *Philosophy of Right*. Trans. T.M. Knox. Oxford: Oxford University Press.
- 1978 [1830]. *Philosophy of Spirit*. In *Hegel's Philosophy of Subjective Spirit*. Vol. 3: *Phenomenology and Psychology*. Trans. and Ed. M.J. Petry. Dordrecht, Holland: D. Reidel Publishing Company.
- 1900. *Reason in History*. Introduction to the *Lectures on the Philosophy of History*. Trans. J. Sibree. New York: Willey Book Co.
- 1969 [1812/1831]. *Science of Logic*. Trans. A.V. Miller. London: George Allen and Unwin Ltd.
- 1979. *System of Ethical Life and First Philosophy of Spirit*. Ed and trans. H.S. Harris and T.M. Knox. Albany, NY: SUNY Press.

WORKS CONSULTED

Adelman, Howard. 1990. "Of Human Bondage: Labor and Freedom in the *Phenomenology*." In *Hegel's Social and Political Thought*, ed. Donald Phillip Verene. Atlantic Highlands, NJ: Humanities Press, 1990.
Ameriks, Karl, and Sturma, Dieter, eds. 1995. *The Modern Subject*. Albany, NY: SUNY Press.
Ansermet, F., and P. Magistretti. 2007. *Biology of Freedom: Neural Plasticity, Experience, and the Unconscious*. New York: Other Press.
Archard, D. 1984. *Consciousness and the Unconscious*. LaSalle, IL: Open Court Publishing.
Aristotle. 1984. *Metaphysics*. Trans. W.D. Ross. *The Works of Aristotle*, 12 vols. Oxford: Oxford University Press.
- 1962. *Nichomachean Ethics*. Trans. Martin Ostwald. Englewood Cliffs, NJ: Prentice Hall.
Aron, L., and F.S. Anderson, eds. 1998. *Relational Perspectives on the Body*. Hillsdale, NJ: Analytic Press.
Beach, Edward Allen. 1984. *The Potencies of God(s): Schelling's Philosophy of Mythology*. Albany, NY: SUNY Press.
Beardsworth, Sara. 2004. *Julia Kristeva: Psychoanalysis and Modernity*. Albany, NY: SUNY Press.
Beebe, B., J. Jafee, and F. Lachmann. 1992. "A Dyadic Systems View of Communication." In *Relational Perspectives in Psychoanalysis*, ed. N. Skolnick and S. Warchaw, 61–82. Hillsdale, NJ: Analytic Press.
Beebe, B., and F. Lachmann. 2003. "The Relational Turn in Psychoanalysis: A Dyadic Systems View from Infant Research." *Contemporary Psychoanalysis* 39, 3: 379–409.
Beiser, F.C., ed. 1993. *The Cambridge Companion to Hegel*. New York: Cambridge University Press.
Benjamin, Jessica. 1988. *The Bonds of Love*. New York: Pantheon Books.

- 1992. "Recognition and Destruction: An Outline of Intersubjectivity." In *Relational Perspectives in Psychoanalysis*, ed. N. Skolnick and S. Warchaw, 43–60. Hillsdale, NJ: Analytic Press.
Bennett, M.R., and P.M.S. Hacker. 2003. *Philosophical Foundations of Neuroscience*. Oxford: Blackwell.
Berthhold-Bond, Daniel. 1995. *Hegel's Theory of Madness*. Albany, NY: SUNY Press.
Bettelheim, Bruno. 1982. *Freud and Man's Soul*. New York: Vintage Books.
Bion, W.R. 1954. "Notes on the Theory of Schizophrenia." *International Journal of Psycho-Analysis* 35: 113–18.
- 1957. "Differentiation of the Psychotic from the Non-Psychotic Personalities." In Spillius 1988, 61–78.
- 1959. "Attacks on Linking." In Spillius 1988, 87–101.
- 1962a. "A Theory of Thinking." In Spillius 1988, 178–86.
- 1962b. *Learning from Experience*. London: Heinemann.
Blass, Rachel B., and Zvi Carmeli. 2007. "The Case against Neuropsychoanalysis." *International Journal of Psychoanalysis* 88, 1: 19–40.
Boehme, Jacob. 1963–66. *Die Urschriften*. 2 vols. Ed. Werner Buddecke. Stuttgart: Frommanns Verlag.
- 1955–61 [1730]. *Sämtliche Schriften*. 11 vols. Ed. Will-Erich Peuckert and August Faust. Stuttgart: Frommanns Verlag.
- *Forty Questions*. In Boehme 1963–66, vol. 3.
- *The Human Genesis of Christ*. In Boehme 1963–66 [1620], vol. 4.
- *Of Divine Contemplation*. In Boehme 1963–66.
- *Mysterium Magnum*. In Boehme 1963–66.
- *Theosophia Revelata*. In Boehme 1963–66.
Bohleber, Werner. 2007. "Remembrance, Trauma, and Collective memory: The Battle for Memory in Psychoanalysis." *International Journal of Psychoanalysis* 88, 3: 329–52.
Bollas, Christopher. 1987. *The Shadow of the Object: Psychoanalysis of the Unthought Known*. New York: Columbia University Press.
Brenner. C. 1955. *An Elementary Textbook of Psychoanalysis*. New York: Doubleday-Anchor [rev. 1974].
Bromberg, Philip M. 1998. *Standing in the Spaces*. Hillsdale, NJ: Analytic Press.
Bucci, Wilma. 2003. "Varieties of Dissociative Experiences: A Multiple Code Account and a Discussion of Bromberg's Case of 'William.'" *Psychoanalytic Psychology* 20, 3: 542–57.
- 1997. *Psychoanalysis and Cognitive Science: A Multiple Code Theory*. New York: Guildford Press.
Buirski, Peter, and Pamela Haglund. 2001. *Making Sense Together: The Intersubjective Approach to Psychotherapy*. Northvale, NJ: Jason Aronson.
Burbidge, John. 1981. *On Hegel's Logic: Fragments of a Commentary*. Atlantic Highlands, NJ: Humanities Press.

- 1993. "Hegel's Conception of Logic." In *The Cambridge Companion to Hegel*, ed. F.C. Beiser, 86–101. New York: Cambridge University Press.
Carveth, D.L. 1994. "Selfobject and Intersubjective Theory: A Dialectical Critique. Part I: Monism, Dualism, Dialectic." *Canadian Journal of Psychoanalysis/Revue Canadienne de Psychanalse* 2, 2: 151–68.
Casey, E.S., and J.M. Woody. 1983. "Hegel, Heidegger, Lacan: The Dialectic of Desire." In *Interpreting Lacan*, ed. J.H. Smith and W. Kerrigan. New Haven: Yale University Press.
Cashdan, S. 1988. *Object Relations Therapy*. New York: Norton.
Cavell, M. 1993. *The Psychoanalytic Mind*. Cambridge, MA: Harvard University Press.
- 2003. "The Social Character of Thinking." *Journal of the American Psychoanalytic Association* 51, 3: 803–24.
Charles, Marilyn. 2002. *Patterns: Building Blocks of Experience*. Hillsdale, NJ: Analytic Press.
- 2005. "Patterns: Basic Units of Emotional Memory." *Psychoanalytic Inquiry* 25: 484–505.
Christensen, Darrel. 1968. "The Theory of Mental Derangement and the Role and Function of Subjectivity in Hegel." *The Personalist* 49: 433–53.
Collins, Ardis B., ed. 1995. *Hegel on the Modern World*. Albany, NY: SUNY Press.
Confucius. 1996. *The Analects*. Trans. A. Waley. Hertfordshire: Wordsworth.
Copleston, F. 1946. *A History of Philosophy*. Vol. 1: *Greece and Rome*. New York: Image Books.
Cullen, Bernard, ed. 1988. *Hegel Today*. Aldershot, UK: Gower Publishing.
Davidson, D. 1974. "On the Very Idea of a Conceptual Scheme." *Proceedings and Addresses of the American Philosophical Association* 47: 5–20.
De Waelhens, A., and W. Ver Eecke. 2001. *Phenomenology and Lacan on Schizophrenia after the Decade of the Brain*. Leuven: Leuven University Press.
Dennett, Daniel. 1991. *Consciousness Explained*. Boston: Little, Brown.
Derrida, Jacques. 1982 [1972]. "The Pit and the Pyramid: Introduction to Hegel's Semiology." In *Margins of Philosophy*. Trans. Alan Bass. Chicago: University of Chicago Press.
- 1998. *Resistances of Psychoanalysis*. Trans. P. Kamuf, P.A. Brault, and M. Naas. Stanford: Stanford University Press.
Desmond, William, ed. 1989. *Hegel and His Critics*. Albany, NY: SUNY Press.
D'Hondt, Jacques. 1998. *Hegel in His Time*. Trans. John Burbidge with Nelson Roland and Judith Levasseur. Peterborough, ON: Broadview Press.
DeVries, William A. 1988. *Hegel's Theory of Mental Activity*. Ithaca: Cornell University Press.
Eichenbaum, H.B., L.F. Cahill, M.A. Gluck, et al. 1999. "Learning and Memory: Systems Analysis." In *Fundamental Neuroscience*, ed. M.J. Zigmond, F.E. Bloom, S.C. Landis, J.L. Roberts, and L.R. Squire, 1455–86. San Diego: Academic Press.

Elder, Charles R. 1994. *The Grammar of the Unconscious.* University Park, PA: The Pennsylvania State University Press.
Elder, Crawford. 1980. *Appropriating Hegel.* Aberdeen: Aberdeen University Press.
Ellis, R. 1986. *An Ontology of Consciousness.* Dordrecht: Martinus Nijhoff Publishers.
Eriugena, Joannes Scotus. 1976. *Periphyseon: On the Division of Nature.* Trans. and ed. Myra Uhlfelder, summaries by Jean Potter. Indianapolis: Bobbs-Merrill.
Fairbairn, W.R.D. 1952. *Psychoanalytic Studies of the Personality.* London: Tavistock, Routledge and Kegan Paul.
Fichte, J.G. 1792. *Versuch einer Kritik aller Offenbarung.* Königsberg.
– 1845–46. *Johann Gottlieb Fichtes Sämtliche Werke,* 8 vols. Ed. I.H. Fichte. Berlin: Veit and Co.
– 1962. *Gesamtausgabe der Bayerischen Akademie der Wissenschaften.* Ed. R. Lauth and H. Gliwitzky. Stuttgart-Bad Cannstatt: Frommann-Holzboog.
– 1975. *Versuch einer neuen Darstellung der Wissenschaftslehre.* Ed. Peter Baumanns. Hamburg: Felix Meiner.
– *Neue Bearbeitung der Wissenschaftslehre,* Fichte 1845–46, vol. 2.
– *Wissenschaftslehre nova methodo-Halle,* Fichte 1845–46, vol. 4.
– *Wissenschaftslehre nova methodo-Krause,* Fichte 1845–46, vol. 7.
– *Versuch einer neuen Darstellung der Wissenschaftslehre,* Fichte 1845–46, vol. 14.
– 1988. *Early Philosophical Writings.* Trans. and ed. D. Breazeale. Ithaca: Cornell University Press.
– 1993 [1794]. *The Science of Knowledge.* Trans. and ed. P. Heath and J. Lachs. Cambridge: Cambridge University Press.
Findlay, John N. 1958. *Hegel: A Re-Examination.* London: G. Allen and Unwin.
– 1971. "Hegel's Use of Teleology." In *New Studies in Hegel's Philosophy,* ed. Warren E. Steinkraus. New York: Holt, Rinehart and Winston.
Flay, Joseph. 1984. *Hegel's Quest for Certainty.* Albany, NY: SUNY Press.
Fonagy, P., G. Gergely, E.L. Jurist, and M. Target. 2002. *Affect Regulation, Mentalization, and the Development of the Self.* New York: Other Press.
Fonagy, P., and M. Target. 2007. "Playing with Reality: IV. A Theory of External Reality Rooted in Intersubjectivity." *International Journal of Psychoanalysis* 88, 4: 917–37.
Forster, M. 1993. "Hegel's Dialectical Method." In *The Cambridge Companion to Hegel,* ed. F.C. Beiser, 130–70. Cambridge: Cambridge University Press.
Frank, George. 2003. "*Triebe* and Their Vicissitudes: Freud's Theory of Motivation Reconsidered." *Psychoanalytic Psychology* 20, 4: 691–7.
Frank, Manfred. 1989. *What Is Neo-Structuralism?* Trans. S. Wilke and R. Gray. Minneapolis: University of Minnesota Press.

Freud, Anna. 1966 [1936]. *The Writings of Anna Freud.* Vol. 2: *The Ego and the Mechanisms of Defense.* Madison: International Universities Press.

Frie, Roger. 1997. *Subjectivity and Intersubjectivity in Modern Philosophy and Psychoanalysis.* Lanham, MD: Rowman and Littlefield Publishers.

Frie, Roger, and Bruce Reis. 2001. "Understanding Intersubjectivity: Psychoanalytic Formulations and their Philosophical Underpinnings." *Contemporary Psychoanalysis* 37, 2: 297–327.

Forster, Michael N. 1993. "Hegel's Dialectical Method." In *The Cambridge Companion to Hegel,* ed. F.C. Beiser, 130–70. New York: Cambridge University Press.

– 1998. *Hegel's Idea of a Phenomenology of Spirit.* Chicago: University of Chicago Press.

Gadamer, Hans-Georg. 1971. *Hegel's Dialectic.* Trans. P. Christopher Smith. New Haven: Yale University Press (reprinted 1976).

Gardner, S. 1993. *Irrationality and the Philosophy of Psychoanalysis.* Cambridge: Cambridge University Press.

Gargiulo, Gerald J. 2004. *Psyche, Self, and Soul.* London: Whurr Publications.

– 2006. "Ontology and Metaphor: Reflections on the Unconscious and the 'I' in the Therapeutic Setting." *Psychoanalytic Psychology* 23, 3: 461–74.

Graham, D.W. 1999. "Heraclitus." In *Cambridge Dictionary of Philosophy,* ed. R. Audi, 376. Cambridge: Cambridge University Press.

Green, André. 1999. *The Work of the Negative.* Trans. Andrew Weller. London: Free Association Books.

Greenberg, Jay. 1991. *Oedipus and Beyond: A Clinical Theory.* Cambridge, MA: Harvard University Press.

Greenberg, Jay, and Steven Mitchell. 1983. *Object Relations in Psychoanalytic Theory.* Cambridge, MA: Harvard University Press.

Greene, Murray. 1972. *Hegel on the Soul: A Speculative Anthropology.* The Hague, Netherlands: Martinus Nijhoff.

Grotstein, James. 2002. *Who Is the Dreamer Who Dreams the Dream?* Hillsdale, NJ: Analytic Press.

Grünbaum, Adolf. 1984. *The Foundations of Psychoanalysis.* Berkeley: University of California Press.

Guntrip, Harry. 1969. *Schizoid Phenomena, Object-Relations, and the Self.* New York: International Universities Press.

– 1971. *Psychoanalytic Theory, Therapy, and the Self.* New York: Basic Books.

Haartman, Keith. 2006. "Attachment, Metaphor, and the Relationality of Meaning." In *Other Banalities: Melanie Klein Revisited,* ed. J. Mills, 188–216. London: Routledge.

Habermas, Jürgen. 1972. "The Interpretation of a Case." In *Knowledge and Human Interests.* London: Heinemann.

Hanly, Charles. 1992. *The Problem of Truth in Applied Psychoanalysis.* New York: Guilford Press.

- 2004. "The Third: A Brief Historical Analysis of an Idea." *Psychoanalytic Quarterly* 73, 1: 267–90.
Harris, Errol E. 1968 [1954]. *Nature, Mind, and Modern Science*. London: G. Allen and Unwin.
- 1971. "Hegel's Theory of Feeling." In *New Studies in Hegel's Philosophy*, ed. Warren E. Steinkraus. New York: Holt, Rinehart and Winston.
- 1983. *An Interpretation of Hegel's Logic*. Lanham: University Press of America.
- 1993a. *The Spirit of Hegel*. Atlantic Highlands, NJ: Humanities Press.
- 1993b. "Hegel's Anthropology," *Owl of Minerva* 25, 1: 5–14.
- 1998. "How Final Is Hegel's Rejection of Evolution?" In *Hegel and the Philosophy of Nature*, ed. Stephen Houlgate, 189–208. Albany, NY: SUNY Press.
Harris, H.S. 1977 [1801]. "Introduction to the *Difference* Essay." In *Difference between Fichte's and Schelling's Systems of Philosophy*, trans. H.S. Harris and W. Cerf, 1–75. Albany, NY: SUNY Press.
- 1977 [1802–03]. "Introduction." In *Faith and Knowledge*, trans. Walter Cerf and H.S. Harris. Albany, NY: SUNY Press.
- 1983. *Hegel's Development: Night Thoughts*. Oxford: Clarendon.
- 1995. *Hegel: Phenomenology and System*. Indianapolis: Hackett Publishing.
- 1996. "The Concept of Recognition in Hegel's Jena Manuscripts." In *Hegel's Dialectic of Desire and Recognition*, ed. John O'Neill. Albany, NY: SUNY Press.
- 1997. *Hegel's Ladder: A Commentary on Hegel's Phenomenology of Spirit*, 2 vols. Indianapolis: Hackett Publishing.
Hartmann, Heinz. 1958 [1939]. *Ego Psychology and the Problems of Adaptation*. New York: International Universities Press.
- 1964. *Essays on Ego Psychology*. New York: International Universities Press.
Heidegger, Martin. 1962 [1927]. *Being and Time*. Trans. J. Macquarrie and E. Robinson. San Francisco: Harper Collins.
Henrich, Dieter. 1971. "Hegels Theorie der Zufall." In *Hegel in Kontext*. Frankfurt: Suhrkamp.
- 1982. "Fichte's Original Insight." In *Contemporary German Philosophy*, vol. 1. Trans. D. Lachterman, ed. Darrell Christensen, 15–53. Pittsburgh: Penn State Press.
Herzog, Patricia M. 1988. "The Myth of Freud as Anti-Philosopher." In *Freud: Appraisals and Reappraisals*, 163–89. Hillsdale, NJ: Analytic Press.
Hibben, J.G. 1984. *Hegel's Logic: An Essay in Interpretation*. New York: Garland Publishing.
Hinshelwood, R.D. 1991. *A Dictionary of Kleinian Thought*, 2nd ed. Northvale, NJ: Jason Aronson.
Hoffman, I.Z. 1998. *Ritual and Spontaneity in the Psychoanalytic Process: A Dialectical-Constructivist View*. Hillsdale, NJ: Analytic Press.
Hölderlin, Friedrich. 1943. *Sämtliche Werke*, 7 vols. Ed. Friedrich Beissner and Adolf Beck. Stuttgart: Kohlhammer, Cotta. (Grosse Stuttgarter Holderlin-Ausgabe, vol. 7.)

Houlgate, Stephen. 1991. *Freedom, Truth and History: An Introduction to Hegel's Philosophy*. London: Routledge.
- 1995. "Necessity and Contingency in Hegel's *Science of Logic*." *Owl of Minerva* 27, 1: 37–49.
- 1998. *Hegel and the Philosophy of Nature*. Albany, NY: SUNY Press.

Howell, E.F. 2005. *The Dissociative Mind*. Hillsdale, NJ: Analytic Press.

Hvolbel, R.H. 1983. "Was Jakob Böhme a Paracelsian?" *Hermetic Journal* 19: 6–17.

Hylton, P. 1993. "Hegel and Analytic Philosophy." In *The Cambridge Companion to Hegel*, ed. F.C. Beiser, 445–86. Cambridge: Cambridge University Press.

Hyppolite, Jean. 1971. "Hegel's Phenomenology and Psychoanalysis." In *New Studies in Hegel's Philosophy*, ed. W.E. Steinkraus. New York: Holt, Rinehart and Winston.
- 1974. *Genesis and Structure of Hegel's Phenomenology of Spirit*. Trans. Samuel Cherniak and John Heckman. Evanston, IL: Northwestern University Press.

Iannuzzi, Victor P. 2006. "Is the Unconscious Necessary?" www.sectionfive.org.

Inwood, M.J. 1983. *Hegel*. London: Routledge and Kegan Paul.

Irenaeus of Lyons. 1965 [1857]. *Adversus Haereses*. 2 vols. Ed. W.W. Harvey. Ridgewood, NJ: N.p.

James, William. 1950 [1890]. *The Principles of Psychology*, 2 vols. New York: Dover.

Jonas, Hans. 1958. *The Gnostic Religion*. 2nd ed. Boston: Beacon Press.

Jones, Ernest. 1955. *The Life and Work of Sigmund Freud*. 3 vols. New York: Basic Books.

Jones, Rufus M. 1939. *The Flowering of Mysticism*. New York: Macmillian.

Joseph, B. 1989. *Psychic Equilibrium and Psychic Change*. London: Tavistock Routledge.

Jung, Carl G. 1989. "Letter to Rowland H., founder of Alcoholics Anonymous." From *The Wisdom of the Dream: Carl Gustav Jung*. A Border Television/Stephen Segallar Films Co-production.

Jurist, Elliot. 2002. *Beyond Hegel and Nietzsche: Philosophy, Culture, and Agency*. Cambridge, MA: MIT Press.

Kant, I. 1965 [1781/1787]. *Critique of Pure Reason*. Trans. N.K. Smith. New York: St Martin's Press.
- 1987 [1790]. *Critique of Judgement*. Trans. W.S. Pluhar. Indianapolis: Hackett Publishing.
- 1968. *Anthropologie in pragmatischer Hinsicht*. In *Kant's Werke*, bd. vii. Berlin: Walter de Gruyter.

Kelly, Sean. 1993. *Individuation and the Absolute: Hegel, Jung, and the Path toward Wholeness*. New York: Paulist Press.

Kernberg, Otto. 1975. *Borderline Conditions and Pathological Narcissism*. New York: Jason Aronson.

Kirk, G.S., J.E. Raven, and M. Schofield. 1957. *The Presocratic Philosophers*. Cambridge: Cambridge University Press.

Klein, Melanie. 1929. "Personification in the Play of Children." In Klein 1981, 199–209.
- 1930. "The Importance of Symbol Formation in the Development of the Ego." In Klein 1981, 219–32.
- 1932. *The Psycho-Analysis of Children*. London: Hogarth Press.
- 1946. "Notes on Some Schizoid Mechanisms." *International Journal of Psycho-Analysis* 27: 99–110. Also in Klein 1988, 1–24.
- 1952. "The Mutual Influences in the Development of the Ego and Id." In Klein 1988, 57–60.
- 1955. "On Identification." In Klein 1988, 141–75.
- 1957. "Envy and Gratitude." In Klein 1988, 176–235.
- 1958. "On the Development of Mental Functioning." In Klein 1988, 236–46.
- 1960. "On Mental Health." In Klein 1988, 268–74.
- 1963. "On the Sense of Loneliness." In Klein 1988, 300–13.
- 1981. *Love, Guilt and Reparation and Other Works, 1921–1945*. London: Hogarth Press.
- 1988. *Envy and Gratitude and Other Works, 1946–1963*. London: Virago Press.

Klein, M., P. Heinmann, S. Isaacs, and J. Riviere. 1952. *Developments in Psycho-Analysis*. London: Hogarth Press.

Klein, M., and J. Riviere, eds. 1964. *Love, Hate and Reparation*. New York: Norton.

Klemm, David E., and Günter Zöller, eds. 1997. *Figuring the Self*. Albany, NY: SUNY Press.

Kohut, Heinz. 1971. *The Analysis of the Self*. New York: International Universities Press.
- 1977. *The Restoration of the Self*. New York: International Universities Press.
- 1984. *How Does Analysis Cure?* Ed. A. Goldberg and P. Stepansky. Chicago: University of Chicago Press.

Kojève, Alexandre. 1980 [1969]. *Introduction to the Reading of Hegel: Lectures on the Phenomenology of Spirit*. Assembled by Raymond Queneau, Allan Bloom, ed., and James H. Nichols, Jr., trans. Ithaca: Cornell University Press.

Koyré, Alexander. 1968 [1929]. *La Philosophie de Jacob Boehme*. New York: Franklin.
- 1977. *Galileo Studies*. Brighton: Harvestor.

Kristeva, Julia. 1974. *Revolution in Poetic Language*. Trans. M. Waller. New York: Columbia University Press.
- 1986. "Woman's Time." In *The Kristeva Reader*, ed. Tori Moi. Oxford: Blackwell.

Lacan, Jacques. 1936 [1949]. "The Mirror Stage as Formative of the Function of the I." In Lacan 1977, 1–7.
- 1948. "Aggressivity in Psychoanalysis." In Lacan 1977, 8–29.
- 1953. "The Function and Field of Speech and Language in Psychoanalysis." In Lacan 1977, 30–113.

- 1953–54. "The See-Saw of Desire." In *The Seminar of Jacques Lacan. Book I: Freud's Papers on Technique, 1953–1954*. Trans. John Forrester, ed. Jacques-Alain Miller, 163–75. Cambridge: Cambridge University Press, 1988.
- 1954–55a. "The Dream of Irma's Injection (Conclusion)." In *The Seminar of Jacques Lacan. Book 2: The Ego in Freud's Theory and the Technique of Psychoanalysis, 1954–1955*. Trans. Sylvana Tomaselli, ed. Jacques-Alain Miller, 161–74. Cambridge: Cambridge University Press, 1988.
- 1954–55b. "A, m, a, S." In *The Seminar of Jacques Lacan. Book 2: The Ego in Freud's Theory and the Technique of Psychoanalysis, 1954–1955*. Trans. Sylvana Tomaselli, ed. Jacques-Alain Miller, 309–26. Cambridge: Cambridge University Press, 1988.
- 1955–56a. "Introduction to the Question of Psychoses." In *The Seminar of Jacques Lacan. Book 3: The Psychoses, 1955–1956*. Trans. Russell Grigg, ed. Jacques-Alain Miller, 1–58. New York: Norton, 1993.
- 1955–56b. "The Other and Psychoses." In *The Seminar of Jacques Lacan. Book 3: The Psychoses, 1955–1956*. Trans. Russell Grigg, ed. Jacques-Alain Miller, 29–43. New York: Norton, 1993.
- 1955–56c. "The Hysteric's Question." In *The Seminar of Jacques Lacan. Book 3: The Psychoses, 1955–1956*. Trans. Russell Grigg, ed. Jacques-Alain Miller, 161–72. New York: Norton, 1993.
- 1957. "The Agency of the Letter in the Unconscious or Reason since Freud." In Lacan 1977, 146–78.
- 1957–58. "On a Question Preliminary to Any Possible Treatment of Psychosis." In Lacan 1977, 179–225.
- 1958. "The Direction of the Treatment and the Principles of Its Power." In Lacan 1977, 226–80.
- 1959–60a. "*Das Ding*." In *The Seminar of Jacques Lacan. Book 7: The Ethics of Psychoanalysis, 1959–1960*. Trans. Dennis Porter, ed. Jacques-Alain Miller, 43–56. New York: Norton, 1992.
- 1959–60b. "The Death of God." In *The Seminar of Jacques Lacan. Book 7: The Ethics of Psychoanalysis, 1959–1960*. Trans. Dennis Porter, ed. Jacques-Alain Miller, 167–78. New York: Norton, 1992.
- 1960. "The Subversion of the Subject and the Dialectic of Desire in the Freudian Unconscious." In Lacan 1977, 292–325.
- 1964a. "Excommunication." In Lacan 1981, 1–16.
- 1964b. "Presence of the Analyst." In Lacan 1981, 123–35.
- 1964c. "Sexuality in the Defiles of the Signifier." In Lacan 1981, 149–60.
- 1964d. "The Subject and the Other: Alienation." In Lacan 1981, 203–15.
- 1964e. "Of the Subject Who Is Supposed to Know, Of the First Dyad, and Of the Good." In Lacan 1981, 230–43.
- 1966. *Écrits*. Paris: Éditions du Seuil.
- 1972–73. "On the Baroque." In *The Seminar of Jacques Lacan. Book 20: Encore, 1972–1973*. Trans. Bruce Fink, ed. Jacques-Alain Miller. New York: Norton, 1998.

- 1977. *Écrits: A Selection*. Trans. Alan Sheridan. New York: Norton.
- 1981 [1973–77]. *The Four Fundamental Concepts of Psycho-Analysis*. Trans. Alan Sheridan, ed. Jacques-Alain Miller. New York: Norton.

Lange, Wilhelm. 1909. *Hölderlin: Eine Pathographie*. Stuttgart: Enke.

Laplanche, Jean. 1970. *Life and Death in Psychoanalysis*. Baltimore: Johns Hopkins University Press.
- 2004. "The So-Called 'Death Drive:' A Sexual Drive." *British Journal of Psychotherapy* 20, 4: 455–71.

Lauer, Quentin. 1976. *A Reading of Hegel's Phenomenology of Spirit*. New York: Fordham University Press.

Lear, Jonathan. 1990. *Love and Its Place in Nature: A Philosophical Interpretation of Freudian Psychoanalysis*. New York: Noonday Press.
- 1998. *Open Minded: Working Out the Logic of the Soul*. Cambridge, MA: Harvard University Press.

Leibniz, G.W. 1981. *New Essays on Human Understanding*. Trans. and ed. Peter Remnant and Jonathan Bennett. Cambridge: Cambridge University Press.

Leuzinger-Bohleber, M., and R. Pfeifer. 2002. "Remembering a Depressive Primary Object: Memory in the Dialogue between Psychoanalysis and Cognitive Science." *International Journal of Psychoanalysis* 83, 13: 3–33.

Levin, J.D. 1992. *Theories of the Self*. Washington, DC: Hemisphere Publishing.

Levy, Donald. 1996. *Freud among the Philosophers*. New Haven: Yale University Press.

Lichtenberg, Joseph. 1989. *Psychoanalysis and Motivation*. Hillsdale, NJ: Analytic Press.

Loewald, Hans W. 1951. "Ego and Reality." In *The Essential Loewald: Collected Papers and Monographs*, 3–20. Hagerstown, MD: University Publishing Group, 2000.
- 1976. "Perspectives on Memory." In *The Essential Loewald: Collected Papers and Monographs*, 148–73. Hagerstown, MD: University Publishing Group, 2000.
- 1978. "Primary Process, Secondary Process, and Language." In *The Essential Loewald: Collected Papers and Monographs*, 1978–206. Hagerstown, MD: University Publishing Group, 2000.

Lucas, Hans-Christian. 1992. "The 'Sovereign Ingratitude' of Spirit Toward Nature." *Owl of Minerva* 23, 2: 131–50.

MacIntyre, Alasdair. 1958. *The Unconscious: A Conceptual Study*. New York/London: Humanities Press/Routledge.

MacVannei, John Angus. 1967. *Hegel's Doctrine of the Will*. New York: AMS Press.

Mahler, M.S., F. Pine, and A. Bergman. 1975. *The Psychological Birth of the Human Infant*. New York: Basic Books.

McTaggart, J. 1964. *A Commentary on Hegel's Logic*. New York: Russell and Russell.

Meissner, W.W. 2000. "The Self as Structural." *Psychoanalysis and Contemporary Thought* 23, 3: 373–416.
Merkel, Ingrid. 1988. "Aurora; or, the Rising Sun of Allegory: Hermetic Imagery in the Work of Jakob Böhme." In *Hermeticism and the Renaissance: Intellectual History and the Occult in early Modern Europe*, ed. I. Merkel and A.G. Debus, 302–10. Washington, DC: Folger Shakespeare Library.
Merrell, Floyd. 1997. *Peirce, Signs, and Meaning*. Toronto: University of Toronto Press.
Miles, T.R. 1994 [1966]. "The Unconscious." In *Philosophy and Psychoanalysis*, ed. Brian A. Ferrell, 17–26. New York: Macmillian. (Chapter 6 reprinted from *Eliminating the Unconscious*. Oxford: Pergamon Press, 1966.)
Mills, Jon. 1996. "Hegel on the Unconscious Abyss: Implications for Psychoanalysis." *The Owl of Minerva* 28, 1: 59–75.
– 2002a. *The Unconscious Abyss: Hegel's Anticipation of Psychoanalysis*. Albany, NY: SUNY Press.
– 2002b. "Five Dangers of Materialism." *Genetic, Social, and General Psychology Monographs* 128, 1: 5–27.
– 2005a. "A Critique of Relational Psychoanalysis." *Psychoanalytic Psychology* 22, 2: 155–88.
– 2005b. "Process Psychology." In *Relational and Intersubjective Perspectives in Psychoanalysis: A Critique*, ed. J. Mills, 279–308. Northvale, NJ: Aronson/Rowman and Littlefield.
– 2005c. *Treating Attachment Pathology*. Lantham, MD: Aronson/Rowman and Littlefield.
Mitchell, Stephen A. 1988. *Relational Concepts in Psychoanalysis: An Integration*. Cambridge, MA: Harvard University Press.
– 1992. "True Selves, False Serves, and the Ambiguity of Authenticity." In *Relational Perspectives in Psychoanalysis*, ed., N.J. Skolnick and S.C. Warshaw, 1–20. Hillsdale, NJ: Analytic Press.
Moggach, Douglas. 1999. "Reciprocity, Elicitation, Recognition: The Thematics of Intersubjectivity in the Early Fichte." *Dialogue: Canadian Philosophical Review* 38, 2: 271–96.
Moore, B.E., and B.D. Fine, eds. 1990. *Psychoanalytic Terms and Concepts*. New Haven: American Psychoanalytic Association/ Yale University Press.
Mure, G.R.G. 1940. *Introduction to Hegel*. Oxford: Clarendon.
Naso, R.C. 2007. "In the 'I's of the Beholder: Dissociation and Multiplicity in Contemporary Psychoanalytic Thought." *Psychoanalytic Psychology* 24, 1: 97–112.
Neuhouser, Frederick. 1986. "Deducing Desire and Recogntion in the *Phenomenology of Spirit*." *Journal of the History of Philosophy* 24, 2: 243–64.
– 1990. *Fichte's Theory of Subjectivity*. Cambridge: Cambridge University Press.
Newirth, Joseph. 2003. *Beyond Emotion and Cognition: The Generative Unconscious*. New York: Other Press.

Nicolin, F. 1960. "Hegels Arbeiten zur Theorie des subjektiven Geistes." In *Erkenntnis und Verantwortung: Festschrift für Theodor Litt*, ed. J. Derbolav and F. Nicolin, 356-74. Düsseldorf: N.p.
- 1961. "Ein Hegelsches Fragment zur Philosophie des Geistes." *Hegel-Studien* 1: 9-15.

Noy, P. 1977. "Metapsychology as a Multimodal System." *International Review of Psychoanalysis* 4: 1-12.

O'Connell, David O., ed. 1996. *G.W.F. Hegel*. New York: Twayne Publishers.

Ogden, Thomas. 1982. *Projective Identification and Psychotherapeutic Technique*. New York: Jason Aronson.
- 1986. *The Matrix of the Mind*. Northvale, NJ: Jason Aronson.
- 1989. *The Primitive Edge of Experience*. Northvale, NJ: Jason Aronson.
- 1994. *Subjects of Analysis*. Northvale, NJ: Jason Aronson.

Olson, Alan M. 1992. *Hegel and the Spirit: Philosophy as Pneumatology*. Princeton: Princeton University Press.

O'Neill, John, ed. 1996. *Hegel's Dialectic of Desire and Recognition*. Albany, NY: SUNY Press.

Orange, Donna M. 1995. *Emotional Understanding*. New York: Guilford Press.

Orange, Donna M., George Atwood, and Robert D. Stolorow. 1997. *Working Intersubjectively: Contextualism in Psychoanalytic Practice*. Hillsdale, NJ: Analytic Press.

Peirce, Charles Sanders. 1931-35. *Collected Papers of Charles Sanders Peirce, 1931-1935*, Vols. 1-6. Ed. C. Hartshorne and P. Weiss. Cambridge, MA: Harvard University Press.

Petry, M.J. ed. 1978. *Hegel's Philosophy of Subjective Spirit*. Vol. 3: *Phenomenology and Psychology*. Dordrecht, Holland: D. Reidel Publishing.

Peuckert, Will-Erich. 1924. *Das Leben Jakob Böhmes*. Jena: E. Dieterichs.

Pinkard, Terry. 1988. *Hegel's Dialectic*. Philadelphia: Temple University Press.
- 1994. *Hegel's Phenomenology: The Sociality of Reason*. Cambridge: Cambridge University Press.

Pippin, Robert B. 1989. *Hegel's Idealism: The Satisfactions of Self-Consciousness*. Cambridge: Cambridge University Press.

Pizer, Stuart. 2006. "'Neither Fish nor Flesh': Commentary on Jon Mills (2005)." *Psychoanalytic Psychology* 23, 1: 193-6.

Plato. 1961a. *Gorgias*. In *The Collected Dialogues of Plato*. Ed. Edith Hamilton and Huntington Cairns. Princeton: Princeton University Press (hereafter *Collected Dialogues*).
- 1961b. *Phaedrus*. In *Collected Dialogues*.
- 1961c. *Republic*. In *Collected Dialogues*.
- 1961d. *Timaeus*. In *Collected Dialogues*.
- 1961e. *Laws*. In *Collected Dialogues*.

Plotinus. 1966. *Enneads*. In *Greek and Roman Philosophy after Aristotle*. Ed. J.L Saunders. New York: Free Press.

Pugh, G. 2002. "Freud's 'Problem': Cognitive Neuroscience and Psychoanalysis Working Together on Memory." *International Journal of Psychoanalysis* 83, 6: 1375–94.

Rangell, Leo. 1977. "Into the Second Psychoanalytic Century: One Psychoanalysis or Many? The Unitary Theory of Leo Rangell, M.D." *Journal of Clinical Psychoanalysis* 6: 451–612.

– 2000. "Psychoanalysis at the Millennium: A Unitary Theory." *Psychoanalytic Psychology* 17, 3: 451–66.

Rauch, Leo, and David Sherman. 1999. *Hegel's Phenomenology of Self-Consciousness: Text and Commentary*. Albany, NY: SUNY Press.

Rapaport, David. 1960. *The Structure of Psychoanalytic Theory: A Systematizing Attempt*. Psychological Issues, monograph 6, vol. 2. New York: International Universities Press.

Redding, Paul. 1996. *Hegel's Hermeneutics*. Ithaca: Cornell University Press.

Reisner, Steven. 1992. "Eros Reclaimed: Recovering Freud's Relational Theory." In *Relational Perspectives in Psychoanalysis*, ed. N.J. Skolnick and S.C. Warshaw, 281–312. Hillsdale, NJ: Analytic Press.

Ricoeur, Paul. 1970. *Freud and Philosophy*. New Haven: Yale University Press.

Robinson, D.N. 1982. *Toward a Science of Human Nature*. New York: Columbia University Press.

Rockmore, Tom. 1996. *On Hegel's Epistemology and Contemporary Philosophy*. Atlantic Highlands, NJ: Humanities Press.

– 1997. *Cognition: An Introduction to Hegel's Phenomenology of Spirit*. Berkeley: University of California Press.

Rosenkranz, Karl. 1844. *G.W.F. Hegels Leben*. Berlin: Duncker und Humbolt Verlag (reprint, Darmstadt: Wissenschaftliche Buchgesellschaft, 1977).

Rudolph, Kurt. 1977. *Gnosis: The Nature and History of Gnosticism*. San Francisco: Harper and Row.

Russon, John. 1997. *The Self and Its Body in Hegel's* Phenomenology of Spirit. Toronto: University of Toronto Press.

Sallis, John. 1987. *Spacings of Reason and Imagination: In Texts of Kant, Fichte, Hegel*. Chicago: University of Chicago Press.

Sartre, J.-P. 1943 [1956]. *Being and Nothingness*. Trans. H.E. Barnes. New York: Washington Square Press.

Sarup, Madan. 1992. *Jacques Lacan*. Toronto: University of Toronto Press.

Schacter, D.L. 2001. *The Seven Sins of Memory: How the Mind Forgets and Remembers*. Boston, MA: Houghton Mifflin.

Schelling, F.W.J. 1856–61. *Sämtliche Werke*, 14 vols. Ed. K.F.A. Schelling. Stuttgart and Augsburg: Cotta.

– 1967 [1811–1815]. *Ages of the World*. A fragment from writings left in manuscript. Trans. Frederick de Wolfe Bolman. New York: AMS Press.

– 1978 [1800]. *System des transzendentalen Idealismus*. Trans. Peter Heath. *System of Transcendental Idealism*. Charlottesville: University Press of Virginia.

- 1994. *On the History of Modern Philosophy*, Munich lectures of 1833–34. Trans. Andrew Bowie. Cambridge: Cambridge University Press.
- 1997. *Die Weltalter*. Trans. Judith Norman. In Slavoj Žižek and F.W.J. Von Schelling, *The Abyss of Freedom/Ages of the World*. Ann Arbor: University of Michigan Press.

Searle, John. 1992. *The Rediscovery of Mind*. Cambridge, MA: MIT Press.

Segal, Hanna. 1957. "Notes on Symbol Formation." *International Journal of Psycho-Analysis* 38: 391–97.
- 1964. "Phantasy and Other Mental Processes." *International Journal of Psycho-Analysis* 45: 191–4.

Siegel, D.J. 1999. *The Developing Mind*. New York: Guilford.

Simpson, Peter. 1998. *Hegel's Transcendental Induction*. Albany, NY: SUNY Press.

Smith, R. 1999. "Dialectic." In *Cambridge Dictionary of Philosophy*, ed. Robert Audi, 232–3. Cambridge: Cambridge University Press.

Snow, Dale. 1989. "The Role of the Unconscious in Schelling's System of Transcendental Idealism." *Idealistic Studies* 19, 3: 231–50.

Solomon, Robert C. 1972. "Hegel's Concept of *Geist*." In *Hegel: A Collection of Critical Essays*, ed. A. MacIntyre, 125–49. Garden City, NY: Anchor Doubleday.
- 1981. *Introducing the German Idealists*. Indianapolis: Hackett.
- 1983. *In the Spirit of Hegel*. New York: Oxford University Press.

Spillius, E.B., ed. 1988. *Melanie Klein Today: Developments in Theory and Practice*. Vol. 1: *Mainly Theory*. London: Routledge.

Stepelevich, Lawrence S., and David Lamb, eds. 1983. *Hegel's Philosophy of Action*. Atlantic Highlands, NJ: Humanities Press.

Stern, Daniel. 1985. *The Interpersonal World of the Infant*. New York: Basic Books.

Stern, Donnel B. 1997. *Unformulated Experience: From Dissociation to Imagination in Psychoanalysis*. Hillsdale, NJ: Analytic Press.

Stierlin, Helm. 1972. "Lyrical Creativity and Schizophrenic Psychosis as Reflected in Friedrich Hölderlin's Fate." In *Friedrich Hölderlin: An Early Modern*, ed. Emery E. George. Ann Arbor: University of Michigan Press.

Stolorow, Robert D. 2001. Foreword to P. Buirski and P. Haglund, *Making Sense Together: The Intersubjective Approach to Psychotherapy*, xi–xiii. Northvale, NJ: Jason Aronson.

Stolorow, Robert, George Atwood, and Donna Orange. 2002. *Worlds of Experience*. New York: Basic Books.

Stolorow, Robert, and George Atwood. 1992. *Contexts of Being: The Intersubjective Foundations of Psychological Life*. Hillsdale, NJ: Analytic Press.

Stolorow, Robert, B. Brandchaft, and George Atwood. 1987. *Psychoanalytic Treatment: An Intersubjective Approach*. Hillsdale, NJ: Analytic Press.

Stolorow, Robert, Donna Orange, and George Atwood. 2001. "World Horizons: A Post-Cartesian Alternative to the Freudian Unconscious." *Contemporary Psychoanalysis* 37, 1: 43–61.

Sulloway, Frank. 1979. *Freud: Biologist of the Mind*. Cambridge, MA: Harvard University Press.
Tansey, Michael J., and Walter F. Burke. 1989. *Understanding Countertransference: From Projective Identification to Empathy*. Hillsdale, NJ: Analytic Press.
Taylor, C. 1995 [1975]. *Hegel*. Cambridge: Cambridge University Press.
Ver Eecke, Wilfred. 1971. "Myth and Reality in Psychoanalysis." *Proceedings of the American Catholic Philosophical Association* 45: 158–66.
– 1983. "Hegel as Lacan's Source for Necessity in Psychoanalytic Theory." In *Interpreting Lacan*, ed. J.H. Smith and W. Kerrigan. New Haven: Yale University Press.
– 2006. *Denial, Negation and the Force of the Negative: Freud, Hegel, Spitz and Sophocles*. Albany, NY: SUNY Press.
Vergote, Antoine. 1997. *La psychanalyse à l'épreuve de la sublimation*. Paris: Cerf.
– 1998. "Finality in Psychology." Trans. S. Sadowsky. Paris: Cerf. ("Finalité en Psychologie In La fin et le temps," *Revue d'éthique et Théologie morale, Le Supplément 207*.)
– 2009/1982. "The 'Death Drive': When Pulsional Desire Turns Deadly." Trans. by S. Sadowsky. Unpublished translation of "Pulsion de mort et destins mortifères de la pulsion." *Psychanalyse à l'Université* T.7 # 28: 561–82.
Verene, Donald Phillip. 1985. *Hegel's Recollection: A Study of Images in the Phenomenology of Spirit*. Albany, NY: SUNY Press.
von der Luft, Eric. 1994. "Comment." In *History and System: Hegel's Philosophy of History*, ed. Robert L. Perkins. Albany, NY: SUNY Press.
von Hartmann, Eduard. 1931 [1868]. *Philosophy of the Unconscious*. Trans. W.C. Coupland. New York: Harcourt, Brace and Company.
Walsh, David. 1994. "The Historical Dialectic of Spirit: Jacob Boehme's Influence on Hegel." In *History and System: Hegel's Philosophy of History*, ed., Robert L. Perkins. Albany, NY: SUNY Press.
Wartenberg, T.E. 1993. "Hegel's Idealism: The Logic of Conceptuality." In *The Cambridge Companion to Hegel*, ed. F.C. Beider, 102–29. New York: Cambridge University Press.
Webster, R. 1995. *Why Freud was Wrong*. New York: Basic Books.
Weeks, Andrew. 1991. *Boehme: An Intellectual Biography of the Seventeenth-Century Philosopher and Mystic*. Albany, NY: SUNY Press.
Whitehead, Alfred North. 1925. *Science and the Modern World*. New York: Free Press.
– 1929. *Process and Reality*. Corrected Edition. Ed. D.R. Griffin and D.W. Sherburne. New York: Fice Press, 1929/78
Winnicott, W.D. 1958. *W.D. Winnicott, Collected Papers*. London: Tavistock.
– 1960. "Ego Distortion in Terms of the True and False Self." In Winnicott 1965, 140–52.
– 1965. *The Maturational Processes and the Facilitating Environment*. London: Hogarth Press.
– 1971. *Playing and Reality*. London: Tavistock.

Wittgenstein, Ludwig. 1958 [1933–34]. *The Blue and Brown Books.* Oxford: Blackwell. (First dictated in 1933–34.)
- 1966. "Conversations on Freud." In *Lectures and Conversations on Aesthetics, Psychology and Religious Belief,* ed. C. Barrett. Berkeley: University of California Press.

Wollheim, Richard. 1971. *Sigmund Freud.* New York: Cambridge University Press.

Wood, Allen W. 1990. *Hegel's Ethical Thought.* Cambridge: Cambridge University Press.

Zeddies, Timothy J. 2000. "Within, Outside, and in Between: The Relational Unconscious." *Psychoanalytic Psychology* 17, 3: 467–87.

Žižek, Slavoj. 1993. *Tarrying with the Negative.* Durham: Duke University Press.
- 1997. *The Abyss of Freedom.* In *The Abyss of Freedom/Ages of the World,* ed. Slavoj Žižek and F.W.J. Von Schelling, 1–104. Ann Arbor: University of Michigan Press.
- 2006. *The Parallax View.* Cambridge, MA: MIT Press.

Zöller, Günter. 1995. "Original Duplicity: The Ideal and the Real in Fichte's Transcendental Theory of the Subject." In *The Modern Subject: Conceptions of the Self in Classical German Philosophy,* ed. Karl Ameriks and Dieter Sturma, 115–30. Albany, NY: SUNY Press.
- 1997. "An Eye for an I: Fichte's Transcendental Experiment." In *Figuring the Self: Subject, Absolute, and Others in Classical German Philosophy,* ed. D.E. Klemm and G. Zöller, 73–98. Albany, NY: SUNY Press.

SUBJECT INDEX

Absolute, the: displacement of, 52, 57–8; knowing/knowledge, 52, 58, 249, 264n7
abyss: as ego, 142, 206–58; as integral to Hegel's system, 45; intelligence of, 162–4; as *mysterium*, 71, 253; as resisting sublation, 15–16, 19, 29, 52–4; as *Schacht*, 45, 163, 271n27; spacings of, 61–88; as *Ungrund*, 62, 148, 271n27. *See also* unconscious
additions, the. *See Zusätze*
affect, definition of, 274n5
agency, definition of, 83–8, 134–6, 268n6; unconscious, 9–10, 13, 15, 17, 66, 124–7, 139, 142, 181, 191, 198–202, 209–11, 220–3, 229–31, 237, 242, 253–4, 267n2, 275n7
alpha function, 155, 158
Anstoss, 93, 228
anthropology, Hegel's, 45–7
anxiety, 117–19, 189–90, 239
Apeiron, 250
appearance, as essence, 23
apperception, 10, 26–7, 70, 130–4, 136–9, 149, 158, 181
archaic primacy, principle of, 24, 54–6, 87, 194, 198, 210–12, 243, 246
art/aesthetics, 120, 252, 254
attachment, and meaning, 187
attacks on linking, 153–9
attention, process of, 160–4

Aufhebung, aufheben, Aufgehoben. *See* dialectic
axioms, of process psychology, 23–31

Becoming, process of, 17, 23–4, 37, 55, 57, 265n12
beginnings. *See* origins
Begriff, 47, 162
Being: gaps in, 72–88; as nothingness, 20, 31, 111, 133–4, 178, 228
body/embodiment, 10–13, 112; as biological reduction, 12; as corporeal, corporeality, 45–7, 143; as ego, 112, 143
bythos, 228

causality. *See* determinism
chora, 61, 220
circularity, of Hegel's system, 57
cognition. *See* mind; psychic reality
concept: as conception/conceiving, 57–8. *See also Begriff*
Confucianism, 250
consciousness, 47–9; awakening of, 212–13; on continuum, 214; as externalization of unconscious, 39, 70, 206–58; mirror theory of, 207–8. *See also* ego
construction/constructivism, 9, 184–5, 208–11, 218
context(ualism), 13, 57

contingency, ubiquitous nature of, 57–8
corporeal(ity). *See* body

death: drive (*Todestrieb*), 109–19, 269n11; as forces of the negative, 129; as primordial principle, 129, 269n14. *See also* negation
defense/mechanisms, 105–9, 123, 171, 198–203, 233–40
denial, 151. *See also* negation; repression
desire: as being-in-relation-to-lack, 9, 10, 13, 20, 26, 30, 69, 272n29, 274n7; as death, 30, 109–19, 134, 269n11; definition of, 272n29; dialectic of, 29
destruction. *See* death, drive; negation
determinism (causality), 10–11, 12, 14, 57, 133–6, 162, 178, 275nn6–7
dialectic(al): amendments to Hegel, 25–6, 37, 51–8; as *Aufhebung*, 39–41, 98; definition of, 24–6, 34–8; as essence, 40; Fichte's, 35; Freud's, 96–9; Hegel's, 35–44; Hoffman's, 41–2; Kant's, 35; logic of, 195, 276n9; as mediation, 25, 42–4; as negation/negativity, 29–31, 228; Ogden's, 41–2; ontology of, 24–6; and parallax gap, 242; as projective identification, 145–7; as regression, 29, 52–4; of unconscious experience, 95–9
Ding-an-sich (thing-in-itself), 93, 228
dissociation, 76–86, 141, 193, 234; definition of, 78–81; theoretical problematics of, 77, 79–83, 245–6
dreams, interpretation of: navel, 173–4
drive (*Trieb*): death, 109–19; definition of, 105–9; as ego, 140; transmogrification of, 119–27. *See also* desire
dualism: Bromberg's, 83–4; misattribution to Freud, 98; Plato's, 97

ego (*Ich*), 89–95, 263n1; and the abyss, 206–58; development, 16–17, 224–7; as foetal activity, 138, 266n4; in Freud's theory of development, 223–8; as illusory, 82; as mind's I, 211, 221–8; psychology, 226; and reality, 208–21; as rupture, 136–44, 213; as second awakening, 16, 207, 213, 217; as unifying principle, 202, 210, 220, 253, 267n3
embodiment. *See* body
emotions. *See* affect
epiphenomenalism, 275n6
epistemology, 5–6, 71, 84, 103, 121, 184, 261n2
Eros, 95, 109, 117, 126
essence, 40, 219, 263n1, 265n12; as appearance, 23, 71; doctrine of, 23
ethics/ethical, 95, 120, 252, 254–8
evolution, 114, 269n11, 271n21

fantasy. *See* phantasy
feeling. *See* affect
foetal life, 8, 138, 174–5, 218, 266n4
forgetting. *See* memory; repression
freedom, 15, 18, 24, 27, 109, 134–6, 177, 224, 240, 242, 253, 256, 265n15, 275n7; and biology, 109, 271n20, 275n7; essence of, 242; and future, 24. *See also* determinism

genesis problem, 7, 60, 62, 89–144
genetic fallacy, 271n20
Gnosticism, 61, 228, 250
God, 38, 57, 250
ground, original, 66, 88, 99, 100–1, 228, 271n27. *See also* principle of sufficient reason

heart, law of the, 255
Hinduism, 250
holism, 4, 13, 18–20, 28–9, 247–58

'I,' the (*Ich*), 221–8. *See also* ego
Id (*Es*), 89–95
idealism, 101, 209, 271n27;
    psychoanalytic, 208–12
identity, 25
ideographs, 154, 168–9, 181–3, 191
imagination, 164–5, 168–70
immediational presence, principle of, 24, 54–6, 184
inhibition. *See* repression
instincts. *See* drive; unconscious
intelligence, 162–4
intentionality, 134–6, 234–40. *See also* teleology; teleonomy
intuition, 160, 166

knowledge/knowing. *See* epistemology

lack. *See* desire
language/linguistic determinism, 9, 13, 16, 70, 76–7, 177, 180, 273n4. *See also* semiotics
libido. *See* drive; unconscious
logic, of dialectic, 35, 57, 42–4

materialism, 10–12, 60, 62, 127, 188
memory/memorialization, 168, 172, 179, 183–4, 204, 231, 244–9; etymology of, 246, 248; and neuroscience, 244–6
merelogical fallacy, 12, 251
mind: definition of, 13, 26–8, 38–9; Hegel's philosophy of, 44–50; as material reduction, 127, 188; mind/body problem, 9–10, 12, 205, 207, 251; mind's I, 211, 221–8; and neuroscience, 244–6, 250, 275n7; as projective identification, 145–70; schematic structure of, 26; as teleology, 24; as unifying unifier, 86, 220

mirror thesis of consciousness, 207–8
misplaced concreteness, fallacy of, 10–11
monism, 98, 125
moral/morality. *See* ethics
mysticism, 253

negation/negativity: forces of the negative, 29–30, 129, 171, 178; positive significance of, 13, 19, 29–31, 67, 129, 235, 249; and sublation, 19, 269n13
Neo Platonism, 250, 271n27
neuroscience, 10–13, 60, 62, 249–51, 275nn6–7

O, in Bion, reflections on, 228–9
objectivity. *See* subjectivity
oceanic feeling, 217
ontic, definition of, 25, 262n4
ontology; definition of, 5–6, 261n2; ontological propositions, 64–71
origins, 127–34, 139–44, 178; of the abyss, 136–44, 219–20; as birth of psyche, 139; as original ground, 99, 209; as trace, 171–205, 225, 236, 244

parallax, 159, 211, 236, 242, 253
patterns, trajectory of dynamic, 23, 240–4
petite perceptions, 61
phantasy, 157, 165–70, 188, 205, 233–40, 263n10
phenomenology: definition of, 5–6, 47, 261n2; in Hegel, 47–9
phylogenetic, 111–12
pleasure principle, 117, 156, 180
postmodernism, 13, 16, 102, 177, 245–6, 273n4
poststructualism, 76, 101, 176–7
presentation (*Vorstellung*), 159, 164–70

principle of sufficient reason, 8, 88, 100
process, 23–4; dialectics, 24–6; primacy of, 23–4; processential realism, 267n4. *See also* becoming
projective identification, 18, 145–70, 180; as process of mind, 145–70; as trajectory of dynamic pattern, 18
projective teleology, 24, 54, 56
psyche, definition of, 91–5, 139
psychic determinism. *See* determinism
psychic holism, 13, 18, 28–9, 214, 249–58, 265n14
psychic reality, 10, 15, 25, 99–105, 210–14, 218, 220. *See also* reality
psychology, Hegel's, 49–50, 159–70
pulsions, 119, 140, 189, 263n7, 268n8

rationality (as pure reason), 57
realism/anti-realism debate, 101, 208–10
reality, 99–105, 208–10, 214, 261n2; constituted by mind, 16, 208–13, 215; definition of, 218; processential, 104, 267n4; psychic, 10, 15, 25, 99–105, 210–13; psychic conception of, 10, 15, 209
religion, religious, 252–3. *See also* God
repetition: of dynamic pattern/form, 240–4
repetition compulsion, 113
representation, 123, 183–8, 246
repression, 171, 186, 233

schema/schemata: affective, 14–15, 87, 195, 204, 232; as building blocks of psychic reality, 14, 26, 202; as communities/colonization, 14, 27, 199–204; and defensive cores, 198–203; definition of, 26–8, 188–9, 195–205; emergence of, 200–5; as form, 14, 87, 188, 204, 241; as microagency, 15, 27, 197; as phantasy systems, 263n10; and semiotics, 14–15, 27, 171–205; structure of, 26–8, 188–205
science/empiricism, limits of, 11, 100
self, the, 89–93, 130; knowledge, 103; multiplicity of, 83–8; self/ego-states, 83–6; unifying unifier, 86, 220
self-certainty, 137–9
semiotics, 13–16, 171–205, 210, 236; biosemiotics, 273n3; in Kristeva, 178–9; in Lacan, 177–8; in Peirce, 177–9
sense-certainty, 136–40
sign, sign-making, signification, 2, 8, 161, 166–8, 171–205
simple location, fallacy of, 11–12, 251, 263n9
skepticism, 267n5
soul, the (*Seele*): and the ego, 136–44; epigenesis of, 127–34, 136–44; Freud on the, 6, 93, 105–6, 224, 270n16; as sentience, 131–2, 137
spacetime, 213
spacings: of the abyss, 9, 23–31, 61–88; of defense and phantasy, 233–40
speculative philosophy, 161
spirit/*Geist*: definition of, 18, 38, 264n3. *See also* mind
spiritual, 250–2
splitting: of consciousness, 149; as defense, 147–52; of the ego, 148; as negation, 149; as normative, 145–7, 169
subject/subjectivity: emergence of, 136–44, 188–205; inception of, 7, 100; unconscious, epigenesis of, 136–44
subject-object dichotomy, 24, 102, 267n4
subjective universality, 13, 24, 104, 220–1, 267n4
sublation: definition of, 29–31. *See also* dialectic
sublimation, 121, 238

superego (*ÜberIch*), 89–95, 275n8
symbiosis, union, fusion, 212, 217
symbolic, the, 166, 170, 176–8, 207
Symposium, The, 123
system, Hegel's, amendments to, 25–6, 37, 51–8

Taoism, 250
teleology, 6, 19, 23–4, 57, 116, 124, 134–6, 141, 200, 212, 240, 270n17
teleonomy, 23, 132, 134–6, 141, 172, 200, 269n10
temporal mediacy, 54–6
thought, thinking: in Bion, 152–9; in Freud, 156–8; in Hegel, 159–70; unconscious, 136–44. *See also* epistemology
Timaeus, The, 61
time/temporarily, 61, 178, 235, 244–9
trauma: and dissociation, 234–40, 248; Freud's theory of, 173, 234–41, 270n17
truth, 255

unconscious: agency, 9–10, 13, 15, 17, 66, 124–7, 139, 142, 181, 191, 198–202, 209–11, 220–3, 229–31, 237, 242, 253–4, 267n2, 275n7; as alien, 93, 142; apperception, 10, 26–7, 70, 130–4, 136–9, 149, 158, 181; definitions of, 64–76; dialectical structure of, 50–1; ego, 10, 13, 127–34, 148; epigenesis of, 136–44; as experiential units of organization, 86–8; forms of, 62–71, 196; as generative, 7, 209; as house of being, 59, 66; intelligence, 162–4; intensities, 26, 87, 196, 204, 242; as intro-reflection, 150, 161; ontological propositions, 64–71; as original ground, 66, 88, 99, 100–1, 228, 271n27; pre-reflective/non-propositional, 17, 150, 158; as process, 23–4, 64; qualia, 26, 87–8, 196, 204, 242; as real, 9, 64; as rupture, 10, 132–4, 137–40, 194, 214; schemata (*See* schema); self-consciousness, 132, 161; semiotics, 14, 69, 169–205; spacings, 65, 73; as spacings, 9, 23–31, 61–88; teleology (*See* agency and teleology); treatise of, 3; valence, 26, 87, 196, 204. *See also* abyss
unformulated experience, 76–86
Ungrund. *See* abyss
universals/universality, 48–9, 166; concrete, 159
unthought known, the, 229–33
Unus mundus, 250

will, philosophies of, 139, 234, 271n27

Zusätze, discussion of, xiii

AUTHOR INDEX

Alexander, Samuel, 6
Anderson, Francis S., 268n9
Ansermet, F., 275n7
Aristotle, 12, 34, 57, 97, 270n18, 272n28
Aron, Lewis, 268n9
Atwood, George, 78–9, 122

Beardsworth, Sara, 179
Beebe, Beatrice, 207
Beiser, F.C., 39
Benjamin, Jessica, 261n1
Bennett, M.R., 12
Berthhold-Bond, Daniel, 53, 273n3
Bettelheim, Bruno, 91, 94
Bion, Wilfred, 139, 145, 152–9, 176, 181–2, 228
Blass, Rachel, 244
Boehme, Jacob, 62, 148
Bollas, Christopher, 80, 229–31
Brenner, Charles, 265n15
Brentano, Franz, 229, 234, 269n11
Bromberg, Philip, 76–86
Bucci, Wilma, 188
Burbidge, John, 36, 39, 265n10
Burke, Walter, 272n2

Carmeli, Zvi, 244
Carveth, Donald, 264n6
Casdan, Sheldon, 272n2

Cavell, Marcia, 219, 268n6, 274n6
Chalybäus, Heinrich M., 39
Charcot, J. M., 185, 234
Charles, Marilyn, 232–3
Confucius, 250
Copleston, F., 35
Cullen, B, 57

Davidson, Donald, 103
Deleuze, Gilles, 82
Dennett, Daniel, 12
Derrida, Jacques, 61, 82, 174, 273n5
Desmond, W., 57

Eichenbaum, H.B., 244
Elder, Charles, 63
Erigena, Joannes Scotus, 271n27

Fichte, J.G., 35, 40, 42, 62, 93, 263n6, 266n1, 271n27
Findlay, John, 57
Fine, B.D., 274n5
Fliess, W., 112, 269n11
Fonagy, Peter, 207, 219
Forster, M., 39
Foucault, M., 82
Frank, George, 106, 108
Frank, Manfred, 271n27
Freud, Anna, 226, 233
Frie, Roger, 268n6

AUTHOR INDEX

Gargiulo, Gerald, 6, 77
Gergely, G., 207
Graham, D.W., 35
Greenberg, Jay, 121
Groddeck, Georg, 89
Grotstein, James, 80

Haartman, Keith, 187
Hacker, P.M.S., 12
Hanly, Charles, 52, 264n6
Harris, Errol E., 57
Harris, H.S., 265n13
Hartmann, Heinz, 226
Hartshorne, Charles, 6
Heidegger, Martin, 109, 256
Henrich, Dieter, 271n27
Heraclitus, 35–6, 250
Hibben, J.G., 39
Hinshelwood, Bob, 13, 153
Hoffman, Irwin, 41–2
Howell, Elizabeth, 85
Hume, David, 267n5
Husserl, E., 234
Hylton, P., 36

Iannuzzi, Victor, 11

James, William, 275n6
Janet, P., 185, 234
Joseph, Betty, 37
Jung, Carl G., 6, 125
Jurist, Elliot, 207, 261n1

Kant, I., 35, 40–1, 61, 93, 101, 271n27
Kirk, G.S., 35
Klein, Melanie, 117–19, 126, 130, 139, 145–52, 175, 275n8
Kohut, Heinz, 130, 204
Koyré, Alexander, 271n27
Kristeva, Julia, 37, 178–9

Lacan, Jacques, 75–6, 82, 177–8, 272n29

Lachmann, Frank, 207
Laplanche, Jean, 77
Leibniz, G., 61
Loewald, Hans, 215–18, 246
Leuzinger-Bohleber, M., 245

MacIntyre, Alasdair, 63
Magistretti, P., 275n7
Marx, K., 35, 42
McTaggart, J., 39
Meissner, W.W., 93
Merrell, Floyd, 178
Miles, T.R., 63
Miller, A.V., xiii
Mills, Jon, 4, 38, 45, 53, 98, 148, 267n4, 271n27, 272n2, 273n3, 274n4, 274n1
Mindell, Arnold, 6
Mitchell, Stephen, 107, 120–1
Moore, B.E., 274n5

Naso, Ronald C., 81
Newrith, Joseph, 7
Nietzsche, F., 89, 234

Ogden, Thomas, 41–2
Orange, Donna, 78–9, 122

Peirce, C.S., 177–8
Petry, M. J., xiii, 265n8
Pfeifer, R., 245
Pinkard, Terry, 57
Pippin, Robert B., 57
Pizer, Stuart, 107
Plato, 34, 61–2, 97, 123
Plautus, 269n12
Plotinus, 250, 271n27
Prince, Morton, 185, 234
Proclus, 271n27
Pugh, G., 244
Pyro, 267n5

Raven, J.E., 35
Reisner, S., 124

AUTHOR INDEX

Sadowsky, Stewart, 263n7
Sartre, Jean-Paul, 272n29
Schacter, D.L., 245
Schelling, F.W.J., 42, 58, 62, 262n5, 271n27
Schiller, 39
Schofield, M., 35
Schopenhauer, A., 234
Searle, John, 12
Sextus Empiricus, 267n5
Siegel, Daniel, 10
Smith, R., 34
Socrates, 34
Solomon, Robert C., 39
Spillius, E.B., 155
Spinoza, 58
Stern, Daniel, 100
Stern, Donnel, 76–86
Stolorow, Robert, 78–9, 121–2
Sulloway, Frank, 114

Tansey, Michael, 272n2
Target, Mary, 207, 219
Taylor, Charles, 57

Vergote, Antoine, 134, 263n7, 268n8
von der Luft, Eric, 271n27
von Hartmann, Eduard, 96

Walsh, David, 271n27
Webster, R., 114
Weeks, Andrew, 271n27
Whitehead, Alfred North, 35–6, 96, 221, 262n3, 263n9, 266n3, 270n19, 271n25
Wittgenstein, Ludwig, 63

Zeddies, Timothy J., 78
Žižek, Slavoj, 275n4
Zeno, 34